Evolutionary Psychology

Series editors
Todd K. Shackelford
Viviana A. Weekes-Shackelford

For further volumes:
http://www.springer.com/series/10583

Todd K. Shackelford • Ranald D. Hansen
Editors

The Evolution of Violence

Foreword by Steven Pinker

Springer

Editors
Todd K. Shackelford
Department of Psychology
Oakland University
Rochester, MI, USA

Ranald D. Hansen
Department of Psychology
Oakland University
Rochester, MI, USA

ISBN 978-1-4614-9313-6 ISBN 978-1-4614-9314-3 (eBook)
DOI 10.1007/978-1-4614-9314-3
Springer New York Heidelberg Dordrecht London

Library of Congress Control Number: 2013953283

Printed on acid-free paper

Springer is part of Springer Science+Business Media (www.springer.com)

Foreword

In the century and a half of politically motivated opposition to Darwinism, no issue has energized the evolution-phobic as much as violence. It has always been easy to interpret Darwin's "struggle for survival" as a *violent* struggle, and Darwin himself wrote that "from the war of nature … the most exalted object which we are capable of conceiving, namely, the production of the higher animals, directly follows." The movement called "social Darwinism" that emerged in Darwin's time was interpreted as justifying violent struggle as the engine of civilizational progress, and 1960s-era ethology, such as Konrad Lorenz's *On Aggression* and Lionel Tiger and Robin Fox's *Men in Groups,* were interpreted as positing a primal thirst for aggression in men that had to be periodically slaked. Napoleon Chagnon's famous studies of the Yanomamö, which showed that aggressive men had more wives and offspring, reinforced the idea that natural selection implies selection for violence. Small wonder, that peace-loving progressives have often railed against the application of evolution to human affairs. It would seem to imply that aggression is inevitable, so attempts to reduce war, rape, and domestic violence are futile—or even undesirable, since violence is necessary to produce "the most exalted object which we are capable of conceiving."

But this construction of the link between evolution and aggression, however prevalent among academics and pundits, gets almost every aspect of the history and science backwards. Darwin himself was what we would today call a progressive, not only abhorring the violent coercion that he saw around him but also explaining how societies, over time, increase their levels of harmony: "As man advances in civilization, and small tribes are united into larger communities, the simplest reason would tell each individual that he ought to extend his social instincts and sympathies to all the members of the same nation, though personally unknown to him. This point being once reached, there is only an artificial barrier to prevent his sympathies extending to the men of all nations and races". As for so-called Social Darwinism, it was the brainchild of Herbert Spencer, and not Darwin, and in any case Spencer was a laissez-faire libertarian who had no sympathy for imperial conquest or other violent adventures. The glorification of violent struggle as an impeller of human progress was far more popular among romantic poets and revolutionary activists for much of the nineteenth and twentieth centuries than it ever has been among scientists.

Indeed, the very logic of natural selection militates against an indiscriminate instinct for aggression, a lust for blood, a death instinct, or a hydraulic pressure for violence that must be periodically discharged. Any tendency toward violence must have evolved in a world in which every other member of the species was evolving the same tendency. Any move toward harming a fellow human instantly gives the target an overriding goal of harming you before you harm him, and even if you prevail by killing him, you will have given his kin the goal of killing you in revenge. Initiating serious aggression in a symmetrical standoff is something a Darwinian creature must consider very, very carefully and motives for violence are apt to be complex and regulated by many countervailing mechanisms. These mechanisms include a panoply of switches and knobs that allow violence to be inhibited and controlled. Not only does an evolutionary analysis of violence fail to imply that high rates of war and violence are inevitable; it shows precisely how they can be reduced.

And reduced they have been. It was a classic evolutionary study of violence—Martin Daly and Margo Wilson's 1988 book *Homicide*—that alerted me to a pair of astonishing facts: the foraging societies in which we evolved were far more dangerous than today's state societies, and within those societies, rates of homicide have plunged over the centuries by a factor of thirty or more. These phenomena eventually led me to write a book on historical declines of violence and their evolutionary psychological roots, *The Better Angels of Our Nature*. In it I proposed that evolution gave us a number of distinct motives for violence, including rage, predation, exploitation, revenge, and dominance—and also a number of motives that can inhibit violence, including self-control, empathy, reason, and social and moral norms. None of them are homeostatic urges, like hunger or the need to sleep; all are responsive to inputs from the social and physical environment. Whether violence actually breaks out depends on which subsystems have the upper hand, a balance that can change with historical changes in societies.

While writing the book I was struck by how indispensable evolutionary insight was to the attempt to the understanding of violence and its prevention. Not only would it have been crippling for me to consider changing rates of violence without an appreciation of the roots of violence and nonviolence in human nature, but also, far more than its own practitioners may realize, evolutionary thinking has taken hold of an increasing number of criminologists, historians, and international relations scholars. In particular, I was inspired and edified by the work of many of the contributors to this volume, and wish I had the time and space to incorporate the work of the others. This collection represents the scientific and intellectual richness of the contemporary understanding of violence from an evolutionary perspective, and amply demonstrates why an understanding of the biological roots of violence (and nonviolence) is indispensable to our species' attempt to reduce it.

Steven Pinker
Department of Psychology
Harvard University

Preface

In April 2012, we invited dozens of scholars from around the USA to join us at Oakland University in Rochester, Michigan for a day-long interdisciplinary conference on "The Evolution of Violence." This conference followed a visit and lecture the day before by Steven Pinker on his recent book, *The Better Angels of Our Nature.* We invited as panelists some of the leading violence scholars from many different disciplines, including psychology, criminology, biology, anthropology, archeology, law, philosophy, and medicine. Each of these scholars had conducted and published significant and substantial work addressing violence from an evolutionary perspective. This volume showcases the groundbreaking empirical and theoretical work from several of these panelists and other distinguished conference guests.

Steve Pinker provides a thoughtful Foreward to the volume, setting the stage for the remaining chapters. Next, evolutionary psychologists David Buss and Joshua Duntley summarize some of their own and others research on intimate partner violence, guided by an evolutionary psychological perspective. A key contribution of this work is that there may be functional design in the atrocities men inflict on their intimate partners, to control women's sexual behavior. In the next chapter, anthropologist Lawrence Keeley updates his classic book, *War Before Civilization* and provides insightful commentary on the changing state of the field of anthropology, which now includes thoughtful analyses of our warring evolutionary past, despite persistent efforts by others to maintain the fiction of the "noble, peaceful savage". Literary scholar Joe Carroll presents an overview of the new field called "Darwinian literary analysis", which he helped to create. In a stunningly original contribution, Carroll applies an evolutionary lens to violence in literatures of the past and present, showcasing the value of Darwin's insights for securing a richer appreciation of core themes and characters in literature.

Legal scholar David Herring shines a brilliant evolutionary light on the law, with special consideration of child welfare laws. Herring is among a vanguard of lawyers at the forefront of a new field of legal scholarship, "Darwinian legal analysis." Next, archeologist Steven LeBlanc trains a keen eye on what the archeological record tells us about our ancestral history of war, updating the groundbreaking analysis from his book, *Constant Battles*. In short, the archeological record clearly indicates that human history has been a series of constant battles. We are a warring species, and the bones tell the tale in no uncertain terms. Evolutionary psychologists Carlos Navarrete and Melissa McDonald offer a clear and powerful summary of the value of applying Darwin's theory of sexual selection to the psychology of intergroup conflict, including violence and war. For a number of years, criminologist Kevin Beaver et al. have led the application of evolutionary principles to crime, and more recently they have been among just a handful of daring scholars attempting an integration of evolutionary psychology with behavioral genetics and criminology. The results of these efforts—as this chapter showcases—have pushed each of these fields into new intellectual territory and opened doors to exciting new interdisciplinary work.

Sibling conflict is ubiquitous among humans and extraordinarily common across many species. This conflict sometimes takes a deadly turn, with one sibling killing another. Evolutionary psychologists Catherine Salmon and Jessica Hehman offer a thoughtful evolutionary psychological analysis of this conflict and, in the process, provide a clear and compelling summary of historical and recent empirical and theoretical work in this interdisciplinary field. In the next chapter, David Bjorklund and Patricia Hawley make a strong case for the heuristic value of an evolutionary developmental perspective, especially as this perspective can shed light on the causes and consequences of human violence. Social psychologists Robin Vallacher and Christopher Brooks, in turn, make an equally compelling case for the empirical and theoretical harvest that might be won by careful integration of evolutionary psychology with dynamical systems theory. In the closing chapter, psychologists Catherine Cross and Anne Campbell provide a masterful summary of recent work—including some of their own brilliant contributions—addressing violence and aggression in women.

The Evolution of Violence showcases the intense intellectual value of an interdisciplinary approach to human psychology and behavior. Guided by Darwin's insights, the contributions to this volume provide a staggeringly compelling case for an evolutionary analysis of violence.

Rochester, MI, USA — Todd K. Shackelford

Rochester, MI, USA — Ranald D. Hansen

Contents

Contributors

Kevin M. Beaver College of Criminology and Criminal Justice, Florida State University, Tallahassee, FL, USA

David F. Bjorklund Department of Psychology, Florida Atlantic University, Boca Raton, FL, USA

Christopher Brooks Department of Psychology, Florida Atlantic University, Boca Raton, FL, USA

David M. Buss Department of Psychology, University of Texas, Austin, TX, USA

Anne C. Campbell Department of Psychology, Durham University Science Site, Durham, UK

Joseph Carroll Department of English, University of Missouri–St. Louis, St. Louis, MO, USA

Eric J. Connolly College of Criminology and Criminal Justice, Florida State University, Tallahassee, FL, USA

Catharine P. Cross School of Psychology & Neuroscience, University of St Andrews, St Andrews, UK

Joshua D. Duntley The Richard Stockton College, Galloway, NJ, USA

Patricia H. Hawley Educational Psychology & Leadership College of Education, Texas Tech University, Lubbock, TX, USA

Jessica A. Hehman Department of Psychology, University of Redlands, Redlands, CA, USA

David J. Herring School of Law University of New Mexico Albuquerque, NM, USA

Lawrence H. Keeley Department of Anthropology, University Of Illinois at Chicago, IL, USA

Steven A. LeBlanc Peabody Museum, Harvard University, Cambridge, MA, USA

Melissa M. McDonald School of Psychology, Interdisciplinary Center, Herzliya, Israel

Carlos David Navarrete Department of Psychology, Michigan State University, MI, USA

Joseph L. Nedelec College of Criminology and Criminal Justice, Florida State University, Tallahassee, FL, USA

Catherine A. Salmon Department of Psychology, University of Redlands, Redlands, CA, USA

Joseph A. Schwartz College of Criminology and Criminal Justice, Florida State University, Tallahassee, FL, USA

Robin R. Vallacher Department of Psychology, Florida Atlantic University, Boca Raton, FL, USA

Chapter 1
Intimate Partner Violence in Evolutionary Perspective

David M. Buss and Joshua D. Duntley

Humans possess a range of tactics to influence other humans to obtain reproductively relevant resources (Buss et al. 1987). Within intimate relationships, these include benefit-bestowing tactics, such as pleasure induction, monetary reward, and reciprocity (Buss 1992). They also include exploitative tactics by which people extort resources through deception, manipulation, coercion, intimidation, or violence (Buss and Duntley 2008). Specific cost-inflicting tactics in intimate relationships include yelling, making demeaning comments, emotional or psychological abuse, threats of monetary withdrawal, threats of desertion, threats of bodily harm, threats of sexual violence, rape, nonsexual physical violence, threats of murder, and actual murder (Buss 1992; Frieze 2005).

Humans, unlike our closest primate relative the chimpanzee, form long-term intimate mateships that last years or decades. From an evolutionary perspective, long-term mating offers a number of benefits to both women and men (Buss 2012). Benefits women can accrue include: (1) physical protection for themselves against aggressive men; (2) physical protection of their children; (3) a recurrent supply of provisions, including food and resource-rich habitats, which in traditional societies increase the odds of their children's survival (Hill and Hurtado 1996); and (4) help with the socialization, training, and influence of their children, which historically translated into fitness-relevant benefits ranging from increased survival to better mating prospects.

Men, from an evolutionary perspective, also benefit greatly from committing to a long-term mating strategy in at least the following ways: (1) increasing their ability to attract a desirable mate; (2) increasing their paternity certainty by prolonged proximity and sexual access; (3) increasing the survival of their children; (4) increasing the reproductive success of their children through paternal investment; and

---

D. M. Buss (✉)
Department of Psychology, University of Texas, Austin, TX 78712, USA
e-mail: dbuss@austin.utexas.edu

J. D. Duntley
The Richard Stockton College, 101 Vera King Farris Drive, Galloway, NJ 08205, USA
e-mail: joshua.duntley@stockton.edu

T. K. Shackelford, R. D. Hansen (eds.), *The Evolution of Violence*,
Evolutionary Psychology, DOI 10.1007/978-1-4614-9314-3_1,

(5) increasing status and coalitional allies through their wife's extended kin (Buss 2012; Buss and Schmitt 1993). In short, our species is marked by a transition to long-term mating with biparental care, which could not have evolved if the fitness benefits did not outweigh the fitness costs for both men and women.

In order to reap the benefits inherent in long-term mateships, people must engage in actions that ensure that the potential benefits of long-term committed mating are indeed received. Without ensuring access to those benefits, the costs of long-term mating (e.g., in time devoted to courtship; in forgone mating opportunities) would have precluded the evolution of long-term mating to begin with. Indeed, the heavy costs of long-term committed mating may explain why it is so rare. Monogamy characterizes only 3–5% of mammalian species (Kleiman 1977).

Given the tremendous benefits both sexes reap from long-term mateships, it may seem counterintuitive or bizarre that violence sometimes pervades intimate relationships. Each year, more than half a million women in the USA report to law enforcement violent attacks by current or former romantic partners (Peters et al. 2002). Annually, rates of violent victimization of women range from 14 to 16%. Lifetime prevalence of women being battered by an intimate or an ex-intimate is estimated to be roughly 27% in Canada and 30% in the USA, and some studies put the figure as high as 34% (Frieze et al. 1980; McHugh and Frieze 2006). Rates of marital rape, one of several forms of intimate violence, are also disturbingly high (Russell 1982). A recent review estimated that between 10% and 14% of all married women had experienced rape at the hands of their intimate partner (Martin et al. 2007). Other reviews that include cross-cultural data estimate the marital rape rate to range even higher, from 10 to 26% (Kaighobadi et al. 2009). These statistics do not include psychological and emotional abuse, which is likely to be even more common. Many men clearly attempt to exert reproductive control over their intimate partners, often through violent means. Why are the rates of intimate partner violence so high?

To answer this puzzling question, we first introduce sexual conflict theory as a broad framework for understanding conflicts that occur between men and women in the mating arena. Then, we outline an evolutionary perspective on intimate partner violence. We then turn to key adaptive problems women and men face in intimate mateships, and present extant evidence bearing on the hypothesis that different forms of violence are evolved tactics used for solving these problems. Discussion focuses on the context dependence of intimate partner violence, psychological processes by which violence may attain its effectiveness, and coevolved defenses in victims. We highlight the utility of an evolutionary psychological lens for providing both heuristic value and novel insights into intimate partner violence.

The Evolution of Sexual Conflict in Mating

Throughout much of the history of thinking about the psychology of intimate couples, the dominant assumption has been that harmony is, or should be, the norm, and that major deviations from harmony reflect dysfunctional relationships. Entire research programs and therapeutic offerings are devoted to fixing “dysfunctional” intimate relationships. Interestingly, the field of evolutionary biology long held the same assumptions for species that formed long-term mateships. Mating was assumed to be fundamentally a cooperative harmonious endeavor, in which a male and female paired up for the mutual goal of bearing and rearing offspring (Parker 1979).

Within evolutionary biology, a sea change in thinking occurred with the development of sexual conflict theory, which forecasts predictable forms of conflict in the mating arena (Parker 1979, 2006). Although a full explication of the theory is beyond the scope of this article, the core of the theory has profound bearing on intimate partner violence. In a nutshell, sexual conflict occurs whenever “there is a conflict between the evolutionary interests of individuals of the two sexes” (Parker 2006, p. 235). When there exist different fitness optima for men and women in a particular domain, evolution by selection will tend to fashion adaptations in each sex to influence or manipulate the other to be closer to its own optimum. These refer to conflicts between individual males and individual females. Notions of “males as a group” in conflict with “females as a group” are logically incoherent from an evolutionary perspective (Buss 1996). Although men often strive to control and monopolize women’s sexuality, men are in competition primarily with other men and women with other women (Daly and Wilson 1992).

Sexual conflicts caused by recurrent differences between women and men in fitness optima set into motion coevolutionary arms races between the sexes, analogous to arms races that occur between predators and prey. Selection favors offenses in one sex to influence the other to be close to its optimum. Coevolved selection pressure, in turn, favors victim defenses in the other sex to counteract offenses that maneuver it away from its own optimum. These coevolved defenses, in turn, favor the evolution of coevolved offenses in the other that circumvent, nullify, or mitigate those defenses. Sexual conflict, in short, can produce perpetual coevolutionary arms races, unless natural constraints limit further coevolution.

In the mating domain, one useful scheme for partitioning sexual conflict is a temporal one—conflict before mating has taken place, conflict during the course of a mateship, and conflict in the aftermath of a breakup (Buss, under review). Sexual conflict, for example, can occur on the “mating market” over whether or not sexual intercourse will occur or in the amount of time and investment required before sexual intercourse will occur. *Deception* and *sexual persistence* are two common tactics men use in the “battleground” of pre-mating sexual conflict (Buss 1989a; Haselton et al. 2005). Deflecting sexual attention, imposing longer time delays, and requiring additional signals of commitment are common tactics women use in the “battleground” of pre-mating sexual conflict. Sexual conflict also occurs after a mateship has formed. “Battlegrounds” include frequency of sexual intercourse, expenditures of pooled economic resources, effort devoted to one set of kin versus the other, amount of parental investment each allocates, and mating effort diverted to others outside the primary mateship. Even after a couple breaks up, sexual conflict-can continue (Duntley and Buss in press). A former mate, for example, might persist in unwanted sexual advances or attempt to reestablish the mateship. Stalking is a common phenomenon—some studies estimate that as many as 49 % of individuals have been stalked (Bjorklund et al. 2010), although lower estimates are given by studies that use stricter legal definitions of criminal stalking (Tjaden and Theonnes 1998). Stalking by former intimate partners appears to be a sexual conflict tactic used by the jilted partner either to interfere with a former partner's attempts to re-mate with someone else or to regain some form of access to the reproductively relevant resources of the former mate, or both (Duntley and Buss in press).

The key point is that sexual conflict theory provides a powerful framework for understanding that regions of conflict are common and predictable. Rather than being seen as dysfunctional, sexual conflict is expected, recurrent, and widespread in the initiation, duration, and aftermath of mating relationships. This perspective, of course, does not imply that sexual conflict and the cost-inflicting tactics used by men and women in these "battlegrounds" should be condoned or excused. On the contrary, this evolutionary perspective highlights the domains of danger most urgently in need of potential intervention and amelioration.

Human mating and sexual reproduction, of course, are also partly a cooperative venture, and sexual conflict must be understood within this context (Cronin 2006). It becomes especially cooperative when it is characterized by strict monogamy, with no likelihood of infidelity or defection, no children by former mates, and no kin in proximity for differential resource allocation (Alexander 1979; Daly and Wilson 1988). Whenever there is deviation from strict monogamy, some likelihood of infidelity, some prospect of relationship dissolution, extant children by former mates, and kin in proximity, however, the "battlegrounds" for sexual conflict,become multiple and pervasive.

An Evolutionary Perspective on Intimate Partner Violence

Daly and Wilson (1996, 1998)have been at the forefront in examining intimate partner control and violence through the lens of evolutionary psychology. According to their position, males have evolved adaptations summarized by the phrase "male sexual proprietariness," particularly in response to adaptive problems of a woman's sexual infidelity or losing her to a rival. Male sexual proprietariness is not proposed to be invariantly expressed in men's behavior. Rather, it becomes activated by various cues indicating that the man is confronting the relevant adaptive problems: "any variable that has been a statistical predictor of variations in the risk of loss of reproductive and productive control of his wife" (Wilson and Daly 1998, p. 201). Moreover, there are costs to husbands of using violence, such as potential retribution from the wife's kin or loss of the mating relationship itself, which provide contextual variables that can inhibit men's use of violence to control their wives.

The functions of intimate partner violence center on limiting female autonomy and retaining control over her sexual and nonsexual resources: "The link between male sexual proprietariness and violent inclinations has presumably been selected for because violence and threat work to deter sexual rivals and limit female autonomy" (Wilson and Daly 1996). From an evolutionary perspective, warding off mate poachers and limiting a woman's potential sexual contact with other men historically would have increased a man's paternity probability, which would have translated into increased reproductive success.

Evolved functional violence toward mates is hypothesized to be context dependent. One context is the cost–benefit calculus linked with alternative means of solving each of the relevant adaptive problems. Tactics to solve the diversion of mating resources to others outside the mateship range widely from vigilance to violence (Buss 1988; Buss and Shackelford 1997; Daly et al. 1982; de Miguel and Buss in press; Goetz et al. 2008; Shackelford et al. 2005). Many, probably most, problems of resource diversion are solved through nonviolent means. Continuous resource provisioning by a man, for example, can increase the likelihood that his wife will remain sexually faithful (Buss 2000). Providing sexual inducements, a tactic of mate retention used in intimate relationships, can sometimes ensure the ongoing commitment of a partner. Coercive strategies, such as threats of defection, threats of violence, and aggression, are hypothesized to be merely components of the diverse tactical arsenal that men have evolved or exapted to maintain access to a partner's reproductively relevant resources. These coercive tactics, of course, are also used to obtain resources from non-intimate others (Buss and Duntley 2006).

The key point is that most social adaptive problems can be solved with an array of tactics, only some of which involve violence. In order to examine the circumstances in which violence is used in intimate relationships, we must outline in greater specificity the adaptive problems toward which violence is often directed. In principle, adaptive problems within intimate relationships center on (1) the loss of access to key resources inherent in the intimate relationship, (2) threatening events that increase the likelihood of the loss of those resources, or (3) a failure of the mate to confer those benefits.

Adaptive Problems Toward Which Partner Violence is Directed

We now turn to the multiple adaptive problems faced during the course of mateships and in the aftermath of breakups. These provide higher-resolution conceptual lenses for predicting the specific circumstances conducive to intimate partner violence. In this article, we focus primarily on violence perpetrated by men, since men, more than women, are more likely to use extreme forms of violence, such as sexual coercion, sexual assault, choking, strangling, and other forms of severe assault (Archer 2002; Tanha et al. 2010). Nonetheless, many studies, including meta-analyses of multiple studies, reveal that women also perpetrate violence toward partners, including pushing, shoving, scratching, kicking, biting, and punching (Archer 2002; Carney et al. 2007; Tanha et al. 2010). Hence, a comprehensive theory of partner violence must include women-initiated and bidirectional partner violence (Frieze 2005).

Mate Poachers. Mate poaching turns out to be a surprisingly common mating strategy (Schmitt and Buss 2001; Schmitt et al. 2004). In American samples, for example, 93 % of men and 86 % of women reported having attempted to lure someone out of an existing relationship for a long-term mateship (Schmitt and Buss 2001). Similarly, 87 % of men and 75 % of women report having attempted to poach for short-term mating goals. Although rates of reported mate poaching vary from culture to culture, the vast majority of individuals have experienced mate poaching—as a mate poacher, as the recipient of mate poaching attempts, or as the "victim" whose mate someone attempted to lure for a short-term liaison or a long-term mateship (Schmitt et al. 2004). Mate poachers pose an adaptive problem. They threaten to usurp the mating resources previously accessed by another. This may help explain how "love triangles" are especially vulnerable to extreme forms of violence, including murder (Shackelford et al. 2003).

As predicted by evolutionary psychological hypotheses, men are particularly threatened by potential mate poachers who have superior job prospects, financial resources, and physical strength (Buss et al. 2000). Women are particularly threatened by potential rivals who surpass them on facial or bodily attractiveness. These gender differences in levels of distress about rivals have been documented, to a limited extent, across cultures—in Korea, the Netherlands, and the USA (Buss et al. 2000).

When violence is used, it is often directed at the mate poacher rather than at the mate (Wilson and Daly 1998). Nonetheless, men sometimes direct violence toward their intimate partners when faced with the threat of mate poachers. Battered women, compared with non-battered women, endorse the following items much more frequently about their intimate partner: "He is jealous and doesn't want you to talk to other men"; "He tries to limit your contact with family and friends"; and "He insists on knowing who are you with and where you are at all times" (Wilson and Daly 1996, p. 3). In short, men who use violence often do so to deter their partners from consorting with other men or to limit their opportunities for contact with potential mate poachers.

Sexual infidelity. Another recurrent problem that afflicts long-term mateships is sexual infidelity (Buss 2000; Daly et al. 1982; Symons 1979). From an evolutionary perspective, sexual infidelity by a woman puts her primary mate at risk of investing in another man's genetic children. The cuckolded man risks channeling his valuable resources into a child in the mistaken belief that the child is his own. The loss is compounded by a rival's gain, since the cuckolded partner's resources can be diverted to supporting the child of the interloper, thereby contributing to the fitness of the rival. Although women do not suffer from "maternity uncertainty," since women always have a 100 % certain genetic relationship with their children due to internal female fertilization, women too can suffer costs from their partner's infidelity. At a minimum, time and energy spent in sexual congress with another woman is time and energy not devoted to the original woman and her children. Since men tend to channel resources to women with whom they have sex, a man's sexual infidelity can inflict resource loss on his long-term mate. Finally, if either the man or the woman becomes emotionally involved with an affair partner, which occurs with perhaps 70 % of women and 35 % of men (Glass and Wright 1985, 1992), either sex risks the defection of the partner to an intrasexual rival.

Men use an array of tactics in an attempt to solve the problem of a partner's sexual infidelity, and violence is one tactic in that array. Indeed, the detection or suspicion of infidelity is one of the key predictors of intimate partner violence (Daly et al. 1982). In one study, battered women were interviewed and then divided into two groups (Shields and Hanneke 1983). One group had been both raped and beaten by their husbands. The second group had been beaten, but not raped. These two groups were then compared to a control group of non-victimized women. The women were asked whether they had "ever had sex" with a man other than their husband while living with their husband. Ten percent of the non-victimized women reported having had an affair; 23% of the battered women reported having an affair; and 47% of women who were both battered and raped reported committing adultery.

These findings, if taken at face value, suggest that female sexual infidelity may dramatically increase a woman's risk of being battered. Causality, of course, cannot be determined from this study. It is possible, for example, that men who batter or who batter and rape their wives drive them into the arms of other men. Furthermore, even if female sexual infidelity is identified as part of the causal chain leading to male partner violence, this in no way justifies or excuses what are clearly abhorrent, repugnant, and illegal actions by the husbands. Nonetheless, these findings support the evolutionary hypothesis that sexual infidelity, which from an evolutionary perspective jeopardizes a man's paternity certainty and risks the allocation of resources to a rival's child, is a key adaptive problem for which intimate partner physical abuse has evolved, or been co-opted from already existing adaptations, as one potential solution.

Sexual coercion or partner rape appears to be another consequence of men's perceptions or suspicions of a mate's sexual infidelity (Goetz et al. 2008; Russell 1982). One study found that risk of a woman being unfaithful was linked with their male partner's sexual assault of her (Camilleri 2004). Another study found that men's perceptions of partner infidelity were linked with increased risk of using sexual coercion (Goetz and Shackelford 2006). Similar findings have been documented for convicted partner rapists (Camilleri and Quinsey 2009).

One hypothesis advanced to explain these findings is that men have evolved adaptations to combat sperm competition, and that partner sexual coercion is one violent manifestation of sperm competition adaptations (see Goetz et al. 2008 for a review of the arguments and evidence). Another hypothesis is that partner sexual coercion is motivated by the drive to dominate, control, or exert power over women (Brownmiller 1975). Goetz and colleagues (2008) suggest that these hypotheses are not incompatible. Men's drive to control and dominate their female partners may have evolved, in part, to solve the adaptive problem of sperm competition. A third hypothesis is that the apparent causal link between partner infidelity and partner rape is a nonadaptive by-product of some other evolved mechanisms, as yet unspecified. Future research is needed to adjudicate among these competing hypotheses. Sexual infidelity, in short, appears to be a key statistical predictor of multiple forms of intimate partner violence, ranging from verbal abuse to battering to sexual assault.

Pregnancy with another man's child—suspicions of genetic cuckoldry. Sexual infidelity by a woman can sometimes lead to pregnancy. From the perspective of the investing long-term man, this could be disastrous in the currency of relative reproductive success. If carried to term, the man risks investing in the offspring of an intrasexual rival. To compound this cost, he loses the parental investment of his mate, since it would be diverted to the rival's child instead of his own.

We present pregnancy with another man's child as a separate, although clearly closely related, adaptive problem to that of the woman's sexual infidelity. It is distinct because the hypothesized function of violence differs in the two cases. In the case of infidelity or infidelity threat, violence is presumably directed at deterring infidelity or deterring future episodes of infidelity. When a woman becomes pregnant with another man's child, in contrast, the hypothesized function of violence is to terminate the pregnancy, thus eliminating the incipient offspring of an intrasexual rival and freeing up the partner's parental resources (Friedman and Shackelford 1999).

The hypothesis that a man who suspects or believes his intimate partner is pregnant with another man's child will be more likely to inflict violence on her remains just that—a hypothesis. However, there is some supporting evidence for it. Burch and Gallup (2004)found that the frequency of violent acts toward pregnant mates was roughly double that directed toward partners who were not pregnant. Furthermore, they found that sexual jealousy is more likely to characterize men who committed violence on their pregnant partners, providing circumstantial evidence consistent with the hypothesized function. A more direct test compared violent and nonviolent couples, and found that women abused while pregnant were in fact more likely to be carrying the child of a man other than her current mate (Martin et al. 2004; Taillieu and Brownbridge 2010).

Clearly, further empirical work is needed to test the hypothesis that violence contingent on suspicions of nonpaternity, mediated by the psychological mechanism of sexual jealousy, functions to eliminate the offspring of rivals. One prediction, for example, would be that the specific form of violence would be designed to produce the highest probability of aborting the fetus, such as blows to the woman's abdomen. Interestingly, a study in Nicaragua found that half of a sample of pregnant women who were abused had suffered from blows directed at their abdomen (Valladares et al. 2005). Competing "by-product" hypotheses need to be tested as well; perhaps the increase in violence is an incidental by-product of greater psychological and economic stress brought on by an untimely or unwanted pregnancy, rather than by suspicions of cuckoldry per se. The key point is that an evolutionary lens has heuristic value for predicting the circumstances in which intimate partner violence is likely, and even the particular forms it is likely to take.

Resource infidelity. Long-term mating typically involves the pooling of resources. In hunter–gatherer societies, these resources might include meat or honey secured by the man and gathered food provided by the woman. Mated couples also tend to pool their labor, as when both contribute to constructing a shelter or providing protection for their children. In modern societies, mated couples often pool their finances. Either party, however, can use pooled resources for their own goals at the expense of their partner's goals. Either might divert resources to their own genetic relatives preferentially over the genetic relatives of their partner. Either might use resources to secure additional mating opportunities, as when a husband buys dinners or jewelry for another woman or when a woman expends pooled resources to make herself more sexually attractive to other men.

A concrete example of resource infidelity occurs when an Ache hunter sends a prime piece of meat to his mistress, prior to bringing the main cache of meat back to his wife and family (Hill and Hurtado 1996). Men, in short, can divert resources away from their mate's children and toward extra-pair mating effort. Because opportunities for resource infidelity are ubiquitous, it is not surprising that mating conflict over money is so common (Buss 2003). To our knowledge, resource infidelity per se has not been examined as a circumstance conducive to intimate partner violence. Because resource infidelity is a predictable form of couple conflict, however, an evolutionary lens points to this circumstance as a potential predictor of mating violence.

Resource scarcity. A well-established universal component of women's evolved mate preferences centers on a man's ability and willingness to provide resources (Buss 1989b). Failure to provide such resources during the course of a mateship violates women's initial desires and can consequently lead to marital dissatisfaction and marital conflict. Men who cannot provide resources for the goal of mate retention may be inclined to use cost-inflicting tactics for mate retention (Wilson and Daly 1993). Empirical evidence consistent with this hypothesis comes from studies that find that poverty, or lack of economic resources, is linked with an increase in intimate partner violence—links have been documented in the USA (Flynn and Graham 2010)as well as in Turkey (Balci and Ayranci 2005).

These findings have typically been interpreted as mediated through "stress" (Flynn and Graham 2010). Economic deficits, along with other factors such as alcohol and drug abuse, have been assumed to produce psychological stress, which in turn increases violence toward mates. An evolutionary psychological lens provides a more nuanced understanding, although one that is not incompatible with the "stress" hypothesis. It suggests that male-linked failures to provide the economic resources inherent in women's initial mate selection criteria are the underlying circumstances that trigger sexual conflict within the couple, and hence intimate partner violence. In contrast, resource scarcity caused by a woman's failure to provide economic resources, according to this view, should be less likely to lead to violence. This sex-differentiated prediction, not generated by the more domain-general "stress" hypothesis, remains to be tested.

Mate value discrepancies. Assortative mating is the nonrandom coupling of individuals based on similarity on one or more characteristics. One of the strongest domains of mating assortment is for overall mate value (Buss and Barnes 1986). Although mate value has a technical definition in the evolutionary psychological literature (Symons 1987), at a rough approximation it can be described as an individual's overall level of consensually assessed desirability on the mating market (Buss 2003). Although individuals tend to assort on mate value, with the "8s" mating with other "8s" and the "5s" mating with other "5s," discrepancies sometimes arise.

One source of discrepancies occurs through errors of selection. An individual may have successfully deceived a prospective mate about their resource-holding potential or prior number of sex partners, for example, prior to mating (Haselton et al. 2005). The consequence is that the deceiver is lower in mate value than initially perceived. A second source of discrepancies occurs when a hidden cost does not come to light until after the mateship has been formed. A man might turn out to have children by a former mate. A woman might turn out to be secretly in love with her first romantic partner. Either sex might turn out to have a sexually transmitted disease, extended kin who siphon off resources, or personality dispositions such as emotional instability or aggressiveness that inflict a heavy "relationship load" (Buss 2006). Another source of discrepancies occurs when individuals mate while young, prior to establishing an accurate assessment of their own mate value. A teenage girl, for example, may get taken out of the mating market by an older man before she is able to accurately evaluate her level of desirability on the mating market.

In addition, mate value discrepancies can arise over the temporal course of a mateship. A man or a woman's career can skyrocket, creating a discrepancy between partners where none previously existed. A permanent injury or serious disease can lower the mate value of one party, opening up a discrepancy where none existed. Because overall mate value has many components, most of which change over time, the odds are low that an initially matched couple will remain perfectly matched in their mate value trajectories over a span of years.

We predict that mate value discrepancies will be one link in the causal chain leading to intimate partner violence, especially when the female emerges as higher in mate value. This prediction is based on the activation of several psychological circuits. First, the higher mate value individual is more likely to be sexually unfaithful (Buss 2000; Buss and Shackelford 1997b). Second, the higher mate value individual is more likely to give cues to relationship defection. Third, if the man is lower in mate value, he will have greater difficulty providing resources to the woman that were inherent in her initial mate selection, which also increases the odds of infidelity or outright defection. All of these variables are hypothesized to be linked to an increased probability of violence toward the mate. Indeed, there is some evidence that those lower in mate value show more controlling and aggressive behavior toward their partners (Graham-Kevan and Archer 2009).

Mate violence can serve at least two related functions in the context of mate value discrepancies. First, it can function to deter a mate from the temptation to stray or defect, as discussed above (Wilson and Daly 1993). Second, it can reduce the women's perceptions of the magnitude of the mate value discrepancy. There is some evidence that self-esteem tracks a person's self-perceptions of mate value (Kirkpatrick and Ellis 2001). Being abused verbally, psychologically, physically, or sexually typically lowers an individual's self-esteem (McHugh and Frieze 2006; Russell 1982). The abused woman might come to feel that she is unattractive and undesirable, and may even be convinced that her abuser is the only potential mate who would have her. As abhorrent as this idea is, mating violence may serve the functions of infidelity deterrence and mate retention by damaging a women's self-esteem, resulting in a reduction in what she might otherwise perceive as a mate value discrepancy.

Stepchildren. Stepchildren pose multiple adaptive problems for intimate relationships (Daly and Wilson 1988, 1998). From the perspective of the stepparent, a stepchild typically is viewed as a cost, not a benefit, of the mating relationship. Resources from the stepparent get channeled toward the offspring of same-sex rivals. The mate's parental resources also get channeled toward the offspring of same-sex rivals. Furthermore, the presence of a stepchild may delay reproduction. Breastfeeding tends to produce anovulatory cycles (Perez et al. 1971), so a woman who breastfeeds a man's stepchild has reduced odds of becoming newly pregnant. Even if she is not breastfeeding, the woman may be reluctant to have another child while she has a young child heavily dependent on her. Delayed reproduction adds another cost to the presence of stepchildren. Finally, if and when reproduction does occur, those progeny will be half-siblings rather than full siblings with the stepchildren. The decreased genetic relatedness among children residing in the same household can create additional conflicts of interest among them. Children of differing genetic relatedness to the two parents can also create conflict, since one partner might be prone to withhold resources from the stepchild in favor of their own genetic progeny.

These propensities may explain why stepparents typically invest fewer resources in stepchildren than in genetically related children in currencies such as dollars for college education (Anderson et al. 1999). They may also explain why physical abuse of stepchildren is between 40 and 100 times higher than physical abuse of children residing with both genetic parents (Daly and Wilson 1988, 2008). In addition, they help to explain why being a stepchild is the single largest risk factor for the killing of infants and young children, far exceeding other variables such as poverty and socioeconomic status (Daly and Wilson 1988, 2008).

The genetic parent also faces adaptive problems as a consequence of partnering with someone other than the genetic father or mother of the child. A woman, for example, can be torn between two goals that may be inherently in conflict. One is securing investment for her child. The second is securing a long-term committed mateship. If a woman's child is perceived as interfering with her new mateship, she may be inclined to withhold resources from the child or even side with the new mate in inflicting costs on her child, in order to solidify the mateship. In extreme cases, such as Diane Downs or Susan Smith, the mother may attempt to kill her own children in order to clear the way for a new mateship (Buss 2000).

These extreme cases, of course, do not imply that there are adaptations specifically designed to kill stepchildren. Stepchildren are rarely killed. Most stepparents invest at least some resources in their stepchildren. Such investment, from an evolutionary perspective, is typically considered to be "mating effort" rather than "parental effort" (Daly and Wilson 1988, 1998; Rohwer et al. 1999). That is, the proper function of this form of investment is to secure access to a mate's resources, and not to increase the fitness of the stepchild. Child killing or even mild forms of abuse may not reflect adaptations for inflicting costs, but rather, as Daly and Wilson suggest, failures to engage the normal mechanisms of parental love. Although we do not suggest that women have adaptations to murder their own children in these circumstances, it is not inconceivable that they have adaptations to inflict costs on, or withdraw resources from, their own children in order to solidify an incipient mateship. Regardless of which specific adaptations or by-products of adaptations explain violence toward stepchildren, the occurrence of such violence is clearly explicable from an evolutionary understanding of the "conflicts of interest" inherent in intimate relationships that involve the presence of stepchildren (Daly and Wilson 1988).

Terminating the mateship. Roughly half of all marriages in America end in divorce. Mateship dissolution typically comes with a large loss of the partner's reproductively relevant resources. For some, it carries with it a total loss of those resources. Consequently, when the net benefits of keeping a partner outweigh the net benefits of alternative options, we expect adaptations designed to prevent a partner from defecting.

A partner's defection carries with it not merely the direct loss of the partner's resources; it can also inflict damage to the social reputation and consequent mate value of the person who is "dumped." Empirical evidence suggests that the discovery that someone was dumped by their previous partner has a negative impact on people's desire to pursue a romantic relationship with them (Stanik et al. 2010). Consequently, defection by an intimate partner could potentially jeopardize access to future mates, compounding the costs associated with the loss of the current mate.

Solutions to the adaptive problem of defection, like solutions to many of the adaptive problems we have been discussing, range from elevated vigilance to the escalation of violence (Buss 1988; Buss and Shackelford 1997a). Indeed, those who are jettisoned from long-term romantic relationships employ a variety of coping strategies, including physical threats, stalking, and violence (Perilloux and Buss 2008). Unfortunately, these violent tactics sometimes work. Some battered women remain in violent relationships. Some return to them even after they have sought help at a shelter. In a study of 100 women at a shelter for battered women, 27 returned to their partner after he promised that he would change and refrain from violence (Gayford 1975). An additional 17 returned as a direct result of threats of further violence if she did not return. Another 14 returned because they had no alternative places to go, and 13 returned because of their children. Eight returned because they said they were still in love with the man or felt sorry for him. In short, the majority of battered women ended up returning to live with their abuser.

Intimate partner violence, of course, does not always succeed in getting a partner to remain in a relationship. It can backfire on the abuser, as some women find avenues for escaping from a violent mate. Violence may represent a last-ditch desperate tactic to keep a mate who has already decided to leave, suggesting a hierarchical deployment of tactics of mate retention (Daly and Wilson 1988; Shackelford et al. 2005). Nonetheless, based on existing evidence, we cannot discount the possibility that in some contexts, violence functions to prevent a partner from leaving, giving the abuser some level of temporary or long-term access to the partner's reproductively valuable resources.

Mate reacquisition and preventing a former partner from remating. As we have seen, violence and the threat of violence can prevent a partner from leaving a mateship, or encourage a woman who has temporarily left to return to that relationship. There may be no sharp dividing line between the adaptive problems of *preventing* a partner from terminating a mateship and *reacquiring* a mate who has decided to terminate; the two adaptive problems clearly overlap. We separate them here not because they are totally distinct, but rather because one specialized tactic seems especially prevalent among men after their partner has left the relationship—stalking (Duntley and Buss in press).

Stalking encompasses a range of repeated behaviors, including inundating the victim with letters, phone calls, emails, text messages, repeated visits, verbal insults, and persistent following (Duntley and Buss in press). Many stalkers spy on their victims (75 %), make explicit threats (45 %), vandalize property (30 %), and sometimes threaten to kill them or their pets (10 %) (Buss 2000). Stalkers sometimes assault their ex-partners physically and sexually, and they are known to become especially violent when the ex-partner becomes romantically involved with someone new.

Some instances of stalking are clearly pathological, in addition to being bizarre, criminal, and morally repugnant. Nonetheless, we cannot discount the hypothesis that stalking, like some forms of violence prior to relationship termination, may be a desperate measure designed to get someone back into a relationship or restore a love that was lost. Women are far more often victims of stalking than men are (Tjaden and Thoennes 1998). Younger women are more often victims of stalking than older women are. A full 87 % of stalking victims are under the age of 40, and the majority are between the ages of 18 and 29 (Buss 2000). Like victims of spousal battering, victims of stalking tend to be disproportionately young and hence high in fertility.

Studies estimate that between 30 % and 58 % of stalkers' motivation came from not accepting the end of a romantic relationship, and attempting to resume it (Duntley and Buss in press). Stalkers who are former mates tend to be lower in mate value compared to the partner who jilted them. Furthermore, although most stalkers do not succeed in permanently reacquiring a former mate, roughly a third of stalking victims end up giving in to some of the demands of their stalkers, and some men gain at least temporary sexual access to their victims (Buss and Duntley 2010). Stalking also sometimes succeeds in interfering with the victim's attempts to establish new romantic relationships. As abhorrent as it may be, stalking sometimes functions to fend off intrasexual competitors and regain partial access to a former intimate partner's reproductively relevant resources.

Discussion

We have proposed that an evolutionary psychological lens provides heuristic value in illuminating the causes and underlying psychology of intimate partner violence. Sexual conflict theory suggests that mating relationships, far from being univocally harmonious, are predicted to be rife with conflict. This theoretical lens has heuristic value in guiding researchers to problems of mating for which intimate partner violence may have evolved, or been co-opted, as adaptive solutions. These include adaptive problems such as mate poachers, sexual infidelity, partner pregnancy by intrasexual rivals, resource infidelity, resource scarcity, mate value discrepancies, stepchildren, relationship termination, and mate reacquisition. Where available, we have presented evidence bearing on the hypothesis that intimate partner violence is often directed toward solving these adaptive problems. In this discussion, we highlight several key issues—the context dependency of violence, possible psychological mechanisms involved in achieving its functional ends, whether mating violence stems from adaptations for violence or is a nonadaptive by-product of other mechanisms, and practical implications for reducing mating-related violence.

The Context Dependence of Intimate Partner Violence

Mating violence does not represent some sort of pent-up "instinct" that must get expressed regardless of context. Rather, an evolutionary psychological perspective suggests that violence will be selectively deployed in ways highly contingent on personal, relationship, social, economic, and cultural conditions. Men who have economic resources, for example, are less likely to resort to cost-inflicting tactics to retain a mate. Some personality variables, such as a slow life history strategy and high levels of empathy, make men less inclined to resort to violence (Tanha et al. 2010). Biological sex influences intimate partner violence, with men generally being more prone to committing sexual assault and severe forms of physical abuse (Tanha et al. 2010).

The proximity of close kin and other "bodyguards," to take another example, seems to deter men from wife battering, at least in some cultures (Figueredo et al. 1998). Close male kin may also deter sexual assault (McKibbin et al. 2011). Relationships characterized by a mate value discrepancy are hypothesized to be more violence prone than those more assortatively matched. Moreover, cultural contexts, legal sanctions, police enforcement of those sanctions, and other societal circumstances influence the cost–benefit calculations of potential perpetrators of mating violence (Pinker in press). This list of context dependencies, of course, is not exhaustive. Many more remain to be discovered. The key point is that an evolutionary psychological lens provides guidance in identifying the features of personal, social, relationship, economic, ecological, and cultural contexts that influence an individual's proclivity to inflict violence on a mate.

Violent Perpetrator Psychology: The Costs of Aggressive Tactics

Identifying the underlying psychological mechanisms that both motivate intimate partner violence and mediate the effectiveness of violence on the victim's behavior has only just begun. Sexual jealousy is an excellent candidate for one such psychological mechanism (Buss 2000; Daly et al. 1982), although this broad label subsumes many functional design features of perpetrator psychology—specific cues to infidelity, sensitivity to the contexts noted previously, such as mate value discrepancies and the presence of viable mate poachers.

Violence is often a costly strategy to implement. The aggressor risks retaliation from the mate, the mate's kin, or the mate's opposite-sex friends (Bleske and Buss 2001). Aggressors can suffer damage to their social reputation. Being known as a "wife beater" can also lower a man's perceived mate value in the eyes of other women and their kin (Burkett and Kirkpatrick 2006). Furthermore, enacting a cost-inflicting strategy also carries with it the risk of losing the mate entirely. Consequently, we expect potential perpetrators to be highly sensitive to the potential costs they might incur from adopting cost-inflicting tactics. Perceived costs might deter a violent tactic entirely. Alternatively, perpetrators might seek ways to minimize the costs. They might damage a mate in ways that are not obviously visible to the partner's kin or other bodyguards. And they might issue threats of more severe violence to deter the mate from seeking social aid. Most of these aspects of perpetrator psychology remain somewhat or entirely unexplored. An evolutionary lens can guide future researchers to examine these heretofore hidden components of perpetrator psychology.

The Psychology of Victims of Intimate Partner Violence

Even less well explored are the psychological mechanisms of the victims of violence. Some are obviously related to individual survival. Threats of violence and death threats attain effectiveness because victims have adaptations designed to keep themselves alive (Campbell 1999; Cross and Campbell 2011; Duntley 2005). Women may give in to a mate's sexual coercion, in order to avoid the physical damage threatened if she does not accede. Indeed, sheer survival in the form of self-defense is likely to be a key adaptive function of women's aggression toward their intimate partners.

Adaptations to protect children compose another class. Women may comply with the violent threats of a mate in order to prevent harm to their children. Children by a former mate are especially at risk (Daly and Wilson 1988), so child-protection adaptations may be especially activated when the current mate is not the genetic parent. Women's violence toward their intimate partners may sometimes serve the function of protecting their children, either directly or preemptively.

A promising set of victims' adaptations are those involved in calculating welfare trade-off ratios (WTRs; Tooby et al. 2008). A WTR is hypothesized to be a psychological regulatory variable that reflects the ratio of the value placed on oneself and one's own interests relative to the value placed on the interests of someone else. Displays of anger have been hypothesized to alter WTRs in victims. Anger and behavioral manifestations of anger in aggressive acts signal to the relationship partner that not enough value is being placed on the aggressor relative to that of the victim. If successful in its hypothesized function, the victim alters this internal regulatory variable, and grants higher value to the aggressor. The victim may subjugate her own needs to those of her partner, relinquish personal access to previously pooled resources, or sever social alliances that the violent partner perceives as siphoning off resources properly belonging to him. The victim may allocate more time and attention to the partner, even at the expense of others such as her children. Moreover, the victim may accede to sexual overtures even when they are unwanted, untimely, or impose costs.

From a coevolutionary perspective, victims of aggression are unlikely to be passive recipients of violence. Evolutionarily recurrent costs to victims establish selection pressure for the evolution of defenses to prevent one from becoming a victim and to minimize the costs when aggression proves unavoidable. Violence perpetrated by women on their intimate partners may be one coevolved defense. An evolutionary lens provides a roadmap for violence researchers to explore the underlying psychological terrain of victims of violence. Hypothesized internal regulatory variables and their component design features may be critical for understanding how perpetrator aggression attains its functionality. Analysis of coevolved defenses in victims will pave a critical path for the goal of eliminating intimate violence and for minimizing its costs when it does occur.

Summary and Practical Implications

Contrary to ideals of romantic harmony, sexual conflict is predicted to be common and pervasive and to occur in identifiable regions or "battlegrounds" in intimate relationships. The battlegrounds of sexual conflict center on reproductively relevant resources inherent in committed long-term mating and the allocations of those resources. Men and women use a range of tactics to secure access to resources in regions in which resources can be diverted due to the conflicting interests of the partners. Tactics range from benefit-bestowing to cost-inflicting. Cost-inflicting tactics span the gamut, ranging from mild forms of verbal derogation to severe forms of sexual and physical assault. An evolutionary perspective suggests that many cost-inflicting tactics in intimate relationship will be targeted toward solving specific adaptive problems, although perpetrators obviously need not be consciously aware of these adaptive problems nor of their underlying evolutionary logic. Adaptive problems toward which violent tactics are targeted include the presence of mate poachers, potential or actual sexual infidelity, mate pregnancy by a rival, resource infidelity, resource deprivation, mate value discrepancies, the presence of stepchildren (who pose multiple adaptive problems), the threat of relationship termination, and mate reacquisition after termination.

Although there is evidence consistent with a few of these evolution-based hypotheses, many remain untested. The hard hand of empirical evidence may eventually strongly support some, partially support others, and refute some entirely. Even with those that receive support, much conceptual and empirical work remains to be done. The precise psychological mechanisms by which intimate partner violence attains its effectiveness, for example, remain largely unexamined. Do subtle forms of psychological abuse, for example, actually undermine a victim's self-perceived mate value? Coevolved adaptations in victims of violence also remain largely unexamined. Do victims placate their intimate partners with declarations of love in order to buy additional time so that they can secure help from kin, friends, or back-up mates (Duntley and Buss in prep.)? Finally, the coevolved offences of perpetrators of intimate partner violence designed to circumvent victim defenses also have barely been explored. Does stalking, for example, function to sever a woman's external relationships, undermining her defense of protection from a back-up mate?

An evolutionary perspective on intimate partner violence, in many respects, complements rather than competes with other theoretical perspectives (see Frieze 2005, and Shorey et al. 2008 for analyses of other theoretical perspectives). For example, it is complementary to perspectives that emphasize situational determinants, such as threats to relationships and self-defense (Wilkinson and Hamerschlag 2005). An evolutionary perspective views these situations as recurrent adaptive problems, and raises the possibility that violence may have evolved as a context-dependent solution to those problems. A functional perspective complements some feminist theories of intimate partner violence—both concur that control over women's sexuality and reproduction is a central motive of men's coercive behavior (Buss and Schmitt in press). By offering a functional analysis of historically recurrent adaptive problems, an evolutionary perspective can augment rather than necessarily displace other theoretical perspectives.

Our coevolutionary theory of intimate partner violence clearly offers just a preliminary roadmap and makes no pretence to completeness. Nonetheless, as a novel theoretical perspective, we suggest that it can guide researchers toward predictable regions of sexual conflict. It can identify adaptive problems or subtleties of adaptive problems that may have been previously missed. It can identify possible functionality in domains previously viewed as dysfunctional or pathological, and potentially, it can offer new avenues for intervention in order to reduce the insidious and destructive phenomena of intimate partner violence.

Acknowledgement The authors thank Laith Al-Shawaf, Jaime Confer, Dan Conroy-Beam, Judy Easton, Aaron Goetz, Cari Goetz, David Lewis, Vibeke Ottesen, and Carin Perilloux for insightful comments on a previous draft of this article. This chapter is based on Buss and Duntley (2011), with permission.

References

Alexander, R. D. (1979). *Darwinism and human affairs*. Seattle: University of Washington Press.

Archer, J. (2002). Sex differences in physically aggressive acts between heterosexual partners: A meta-analytic review. *Aggression and Violent Behavior*, *7*, 313–351.

Arnqvist, G., & Rowe, L. (2005). *Sexual conflict*. Princeton: Princeton University Press.

Balci, Y. G., & Ayranci, U. (2005). Physical violence against women: Evaluation of women assaulted by spouses. *Journal of Clinical Forensic Medicine*, *12*, 258–263.

Bjorklund, K., Hakkanen-Nyholm, H., Sheridan, L,. & Roberts, K. (2010). The prevalence of stalking among Finnish university students. *Journal of Interpersonal Violence, 25*, 684–698.
Bleske, A. L., & Buss, D. M. (2001). Opposite sex friendship: Sex differences and similarities in initiation, selection, and dissolution. *Personality and Social Psychology Bulletin, 27*, 1310–1323.
Brownmiller, S. (1975). *Against our will.* New York: Bantam Books.
Burch, R. L., & Gallup, G. G., Jr. (2004). Pregnancy as a stimulus for domestic violence. *Journal of Family Violence, 19*, 243–247.
Burkett, B. N., & Kirkpatrick, L. A. (2006). *What are deal breakers in a mate: Characteristics that are intolerable in a potential mate.* Paper presented at the Annual Meeting of the Human Behavior and Evolution Society, Philadelphia, PA, June 10, 2006.
Buss, D. M. (1988). From vigilance to violence: Tactics of mate retention in American undergraduates. *Ethology and Sociobiology, 9*, 291–317.
Buss, D. M. (1989a). Conflict between the sexes: Strategic interference and the evocation of anger and upset. *Journal of Personality and Social Psychology, 56*, 735–747.
Buss, D. M. (1989b). Sex differences in human mate preferences: Evolutionary hypotheses tested in 37 cultures. *Behavioral and Brain Sciences, 12*, 1–49.
Buss, D. M. (1992). Manipulation in close relationships: The five factor model of personality in interactional context. *Journal of Personality, 60*, 477–499.
Buss, D. M. (2000). *The dangerous passion.* New York: The Free Press.
Buss, D. M. (2005). The murderer next door: Why the mind is designed to kill. New York: The Free Press.
Buss, D. M. (2006). The evolutionary genetics of personality: Does mutation load signal relationship load? *Behavioral and Brain Sciences, 29*, 409.
Buss, D. M. (2012). *Evolutionary psychology: The new science of the mind* (4th ed.). Needham Heights: Allyn & Bacon.
Buss, D. M. (under review). *Sexual conflict theory: An evolutionary perspective on the 'battle of the sexes.'* Department of Psychology, University of Texas, Austin, Texas.
Buss, D. M. & Barnes, M. L. (1986). Preferences in human mate selection. *Journal of Personality & Social Psychology, 50*, 559–570.
Buss, D. M., & Duntley, J. D. (2008). Adaptations for exploitation. *Group Dynamics: Theory, Research, and Practice, 12*, 53–62.
Buss, D. M., & Duntley, J. D. (2010, June). *The evolution of stalking.* Paper presented at the Annual Meeting of the Human Behavior and Evolution Society, Eugene, OR, U.S.A.
Buss, D.M. & Duntley, J.D. (2011).The evolution of intimate partner violence. *Aggression and Violent* Behavior, 16, 411–419
Buss, D. M., & Schmitt, D. P. (in press). Evolutionary psychology and feminism. *Sex Roles.*
Buss, D. M., & Shackelford, T. K. (1997a). From vigilance to violence: Mate retention tactics in married couples. *Journal of Personality and Social Psychology, 72*, 346–361.
Buss, D. M., & Shackelford, T. K. (1997b). Susceptibility to infidelity in the first year of marriage. *Journal of Research in Personality, 31*, 193–221.
Buss, D. M., Gomes, M., Higgins, D. S. & Lauterbach, K. (1987). Tactics of manipulation. *Journal of Personality & Social Psychology, 52*(6), 1219–1229.
Buss, D. M., Shackelford, T. K., Choe, J., Buunk, B. P., & Dijkstra, P. (2000). Distress about mating rivals. *Personal Relationships, 7*, 235–243.
Campbell, A. (1999). Staying alive: Evolution, culture and women's intra-sexual aggression. *Behavioural and Brain Sciences, 22*, 203–252.
Camilleri, J. (2004). *Investigating sexual coercion in romantic relationships: A test of the cuckoldry risk hypothesis.* Unpublished master's thesis, University of Saskatchewan, Saskatoon, Saskatchewan, Canada.
Camilleri, J. A. & Quinsey, V. L. (2009). Testing the cuckoldry risk hypothesis of partner sexual coercion in community and forensic samples. *Evolutionary Psychology, 7*, 164–178.
Carney, M., Buttell, F., & Dutton, D. (2007). Women who perpetuate intimate partner violence: A review of the literature with recommendations for treatment. *Aggression and Violent Behavior, 12*, 108–115.

Cronin, H. (2006). The battle of the sexes revisited. In A. Grafen, Alan & M. Ridley (Eds.), *Richard Dawkins: how a scientist changed the way we think* (pp. 14–26). Oxford: Oxford University Press.
Cross, C. P., & Campbell, A. (2011). Women's aggression. *Aggression and Violent Behavior, 16,* 390–398..
Daly, M. & Wilson, M. (1988). *Homicide*. New York: Aldine de Gruyter.
Daly, M., & Wilson, M. (1998). *The truth about Cinderella*. London: Weidenfeld & Nicolson.
Daly, M., & Wilson, M. (2008). Is the "Cinderella Effect" controversial?: A case study of evolution-minded research and critiques thereof. In C. Crawford & D. Krebs (Eds.), *Foundations of evolutionary psychology* (pp. 383–400). New York: Erlbaum.
Daly, M., Wilson, M. I., & Weghorst, S. J. (1982). Male sexual jealousy. *Ethology & Sociobiology, 3,* 11–27.
de Miguel, A., & Buss, D. M. (in press). Mate retention tactics in Spain: Personality, sex differences, and relationship status. *Journal of Personality*.
de Waal, F. (1982). *Chimpanzee politics: Sex and power among apes*. Baltimore: The Johns Hopkins University Press.
Duntley, J. D. (2005). Adaptations to dangers from other humans. In D. M. Buss (Ed.), *The handbook of evolutionary psychology* (pp. 224–249). Hoboken, NJ: Wiley.
Duntley, J. D., & Buss, D. M. (2010). The evolution of stalking. *Sex Roles*.
Duntley, J. D., & Buss, D. M. (In prep.). *Backup mates*. Manuscript in preparation, Department of Criminal Justice and Psychology, The Richard Stockton College.
Figueredo, A. J., Corral-Verdugo, V., Frías-Armenta, M., Bachar, K., Goldman-Pach, J., McNeill, P. L., Valiente-Ots, M., & Villavicencio-Carillo, P. (1998). La influencia de la familia consanguínea de la mujer en la ocurrencia de violencia intramarital: Una comparación de muestras piloto de Madrid y Hermosillo. *Enseñanza e Investigación en Psicología, 3*(2), 103–117.
Flynn, A., & Graham, K. (2010). "Why did it happen?" A review and conceptual framework for research on perpetrators' and victims' explanations for intimate partner violence. *Aggression and Violent Behavior, 15,* 239–251.
Friedman, B. X., & Shackelford, T. K. (1999, June). *Re-allocation of mating effort as a result of pregnancy*. Paper presented at the annual meeting of the Human Behavior and Evolution Society, Salt Lake City, UT.
Frieze, I. H. (2005). Hurting the one you love: Violence in relationships. Pacific Grove: Thomson.
Frieze, I. H., Knoble, J., Washburn, C., & Zomnir, G. (1080). *Types of battered women*. Paper presented at the Association for Women in Psychology. Santa Monica, CA.
Gayford, J. J. (1975). Wife battering: A preliminary survey of 100 cases. *British Medical Journal, 1,* 194–197.
Glass, S. P, & Wright, T. L. (1985). Sex differences in the type of extramarital involvement and marital dissatisfaction. *Sex Roles, 12,* 1101–1119.
Glass, D. P., & Wright, T. L. (1992). Justifications for extramarital relationships: the association between attitudes, behaviors, and gender. *Journal of Sex Research, 29,* 361–387.
Goetz, A. T., & Shackelford, T. K (2006). Sexual coercion and forced in-pair copulation as sperm competition tactics in humans. *Human Nature, 17,* 265–282.
Goetz, A. T., Shackelford, T. K., & Camilleri, J. A. (2008). Proximate and ultimate explanations are required for a comprehensive understanding of partner rape. *Aggression and Violent Behavior, 13,* 119–123.
Goetz, A. T., Shackelford, T. K., Starratt, V. G., & McKibbin, W. F. (2008). Intimate partner violence. In J. D. Duntley & T. K. Shackelford (Eds.), *Evolutionary forensic psychiatry* (pp. 65–78). New York: Oxford University Press.
Graham-Kevan, N., & Archer, J. (2009). Control tactics and partner violence in heterosexual relationships. *Evolution and Human Behavior, 30,* 445–452.
Haselton, M. G., Buss, D. M., Oubaid, V., Angleitner, A. (2005). Sex, lies, and strategic interference: The psychology of deception between the sexes. *Personality and Social Psychology Bulletin, 31,* 3–23.

Hill, K., & Hurtado, A. M. (1996). *Ache life history: The ecology and demography of a foraging people*. New York: Aldine De Gruyter.
Kaighobadi, F., Shackelford, T. K., & Goetz, A. T. (2009). From mate retention to murder: Evolutionary psychological perspectives on men's partner-directed violence. *Review of General Psychology, 13*, 327–334.
Kirkpatrick, L., & Ellis, B. J. (2001). An evolutionary-psychological approach to self-esteem: Multiple domains and multiple functions. In M. Clark & G. Fletcher (Eds.), *The Blackwell Handbook in Social Psychology, Vol. 2: Interpersonal Processes* (pp. 411–436). Oxford: Blackwell Publishers.
Kleiman, D. G. (1977) Monogamy in mammals. *The Quarterly Review of Biology, 52*, 39–68.
Martin, S. L., Harris-Brit, A., Li, Y., Moracco, K. E., Kupper, L. L., & Campbell, J. C. (2004). Changes in intimate partner violence during pregnancy. *Journal of Family Violence, 19*, 201–210.
Martin, E. K., Taft, C. T., & Resick, P. A. (2007). A review of marital rape. *Aggression and Violent Behavior, 12*, 329–347.
McKibbin, W. F., Shackelford, T. K., Miner, E. J., Bates, V. M., & Liddle, J. R. (2011). Individual differences in women's rape avoidance behaviors. *Archives of Sexual Behavior, 40*, 343–349.
Parker, G. A. (1979). Sexual selection and sexual conflict. In M. S. Blum & A. N. Blum (Eds.), *Sexual selection and reproductive competition among insects* (pp. 123–166). London: Academic Press.
Parker, G. A. (2006). Sexual selection over mating and fertilization: An overview. *Philosophical Transactions of the Royal Society, B, 361*, 235–259.
Perez, A., Vela, P., Potter, R., & Masnick, G. S. (1971). Timing and sequence of resuming ovulation and menstruation after childbirth. *Population Studies, 25*, 491–503.
Perilloux, C. & Buss, D. M. (2008). Breaking up romantic relationships: Costs experienced and coping strategies deployed. *Evolutionary Psychology, 6*, 164–181.
Peters, J., Shackelford, T.K, & Buss, D.M. (2002). Understanding domestic violence against women: Using evolutionary psychology to extend the feminist functional analysis. *Violence and Victims, 17*, 255–264.
Pinker, S. (in press). *Better angels*. New York: Norton.
Rohwer, S., Herron, J. C., & Daly, M. (1999). Stepparental behavior as mating effort in birds and other animals. *Evolution and Human Behavior, 20*, 367–390.
Russell, D. (1982). *Rape in marriage*. New York: Macmillon.
Schaik, C. P. V., & Dunbar, R. I. M. (1990). The evolution of monogamy in large primates. *Behaviour, 115*, 30–62.
Schmitt, D. P., & Buss, D. M. (2001). Human mate poaching: Tactics and temptations for infiltrating existing mateships. *Journal of Personality and Social Psychology, 80*, 894–917.
Schmitt, D. P., Alcalay, L., Allik, J., Angleiter, A., Ault, L., Austers, I., et al. (2004). Patterns and universals of mate poaching across 53 nations: The effects of sex, culture, and personality on romantically attracting another person's partner. *Journal of Personality and Social Psychology, 86*, 560–584.
Shackelford, T. K., Buss, D. M., & Weeks-Shackelford, V. (2003). Wife-killings committed in the context of a lovers triangle. *Journal of Basic and Applied Social Psychology, 25*, 137–143.
Shackelford, T. K., Goetz, A. T., Buss, D. M., Euler, H. A., & Hoier, S. (2005). When we hurt the ones we love: Predicting violence against women from men's mate retention tactics. *Personal Relationships, 12*, 447–463.
Shields, N. M., & Hanneke, C. R. (1983). Battered wives reactions to marital rape. In D. Finkelhor, R. J. Gelles, G. T. Hotaling, & M. A. Straus (Eds.), *The dark side of families* (pp. 131–148). Beverly Hills: Sage.
Shorey, R. C., Cornelius, T. L., & Bell, K. M. (2008). A critical review of theoretical frameworks for dating violence: Comparing the dating and marital fields. *Aggression and Violent Behavior, 13*, 185–194.
Smuts, B. B. (1985). *Sex and friendship among baboons*. New York: Aldine.
Stanik, C., Kurzban, R., & Ellsworth, P. (2010). Rejection hurts: The effect of being dumped on subsequent mating efforts. *Evolutionary Psychology, 8*, 682–694.

Symons, D. (1979). *The evolution of human sexuality*. New York: Oxford University Press.
Symons, D. (1987). If we're all Darwinians, what's the fuss about. In C. Crawford, D. Krebs, & M. Smith (Eds.), *Sociobiology and psychology* (pp. 121–145). Hillsdale: Erlbaum.
Taillieu, T. L., & Brownridge, D. A. (2010). Violence against pregnant women: Prevalence, patterns, risk factors, theories, and directions for future research. *Aggression and Violent Behavior*, *15*, 14–35.
Tanha, M., Beck, C. J. A., Figueredo, A. J., & Raghavan, C. (2010). Sex differences in intimate partner violence and the use of coercive control as a motivational factor for intimate partner violence. *Journal of Interpersonal Violence*, *25*, 1836–1854.
Tjaden, P., & Thoennes, N. (1998). *Stalking in America: Findings from the national violence against women survey*. Washington, DC: U.S. Department of Justice, National Institute.
Tooby, J., Cosmides, L., Sell, A., Lieberman, D., & Sznycer, D. (2008). Internal regulatory variables and the design of human motivation: A computational and evolutionary approach. In Andrew J. Elliot (Ed.) *Handbook of approach and avoidance motivation (pp.* 251–271). Mahwah: Erlbaum.
Valladares, E., Peña, R., Persson, L. A., & Högberg, U., (2005). Violence against pregnant women: prevalence and characteristics. A population-based study in Nicaragua. *BJOG: An International Journal of Obstetrics & Gynaecology*, *112*, 1243–1248.
Wilkinson, D. L., & Hamerschlag, S. J. (2005). Situational determinants in intimate partner violence. *Aggression and Violent Behavior*, *10*, 333–361.
Wilson, M. I., & Daly, M. (1992). The man who mistook his wife for a chattel. In J. Barkow, L. Cosmides, & J. Tooby (Eds), *The adapted mind* (pp. 289–326). New York: Oxford University Press.
Wilson, M. I., & Daly, M. (1993). An evolutionary perspective on male sexual proprietariness and violence against wives. *Violence and Victims*, *8*, 271–294.
Wilson, M. I., & Daly, M. (1996). Male sexual proprietariness and violence against wives. *Current Directions in Psychological Science*, *5*, 2–7.
Wilson, M. I., & Daly, M. (1998). Lethal and nonlethal violence against wives and the evolutionary psychology of male sexual proprietariness. In R. E. Dobash & R. P. Dobash (Eds.), *Rethinking violence against women* (pp. 199–230). Thousand Oaks: Sage.
Wrangham, R. & Peterson, D. (1996). *Demonic Males*. Boston: Houghton Mifflin.

Chapter 2
War Before Civilization—15 Years On

Lawrence H. Keeley

Introduction

For the past 20 years, in my study of warfare, I have received many surprises. When I began my book (Keeley 1996)on recent tribal and ancient prehistoric war, I expected to find that, while warfare had existed in the deep human past, it had increased in deadliness and destructiveness with time and social evolution. Instead, what I found astounded me; I rechecked, and added as much as possible to my data. I found that the warfare of non-states was more deadly, as destructive and, frankly, as despicable as that conducted by any ancient or modern state. One particular comparison that epitomizes this fact is to consider the war deaths incurred at the 4-day Battle of Gettysburg and by the people of Central California between 500 B.C. and 500 A.D. (the "Middle Horizon" or Emeryville Focus). The Union and Rebel armies fighting at Gettysburg both incurred less than 4 % killed, slightly more for the losers than the winners. More than 5 % of Middle Horizon Native Californian buried human skeletons have stone projectile points embedded in their bones (as Milner 1999)argues from U.S. Indian Wars data, usually only one in three striking arrows becomes bone-embedded). These figures imply that, for a 1,000 years, the lives and deaths of the ancient Californians were at least as violent as the bloody four days at Gettysburg, if not more so. I found that war was hell, whether it was fought with wooden spears or with cannons.

When it was published, I thought my book would annoy everybody. Other than a few anthropologists whom I either ridiculed or found rather obvious mistakes in their analyses, the reception was instead surprisingly positive. This positive response was especially true of archaeologists. Archaeologists, like most scholars, tend to be intellectually parochial. For example, we argue vehemently over the timing and distribution of certain stone tool types or pottery styles; whether the spectacular mounds and other remains at Cahokia (IL) were produced by a state or

L. H. Keeley (✉)
Department of Anthropology, University Of Illinois at Chicago, IL, USA
e-mail: lpkeeley@aol.com

T. K. Shackelford, R. D. Hansen (eds.), *The Evolution of Violence*,
Evolutionary Psychology, DOI 10.1007/978-1-4614-9314-3_2,

some less complex sociopolitical organization; whether the Natufians (c. 14,000 to 11, 000 years ago) of the southwestern Near East were cultivators or gatherers of plants; etc. However, if you convince archaeologists that other social scientists are speaking nonsense because the latter (also parochial) have paid little attention, if any, to archaeological data, and that archaeology can address a major social science issue, then stand back! Archaeologists will reconsider and look for relevant data, concentrate our ingenuity, and use every one of our considerable technical resources to address such questions.

The Archaeology of War

Prehistoric and ancient warfare has become a major concern of archaeologists worldwide (we are a small but a widespread academic field and English has become our *lingua franca*). Many regional surveys of the archaeological evidence for warfare have been published recently or are in preparation (e.g., Arkush and Stanish 2005). This evidence comes in several forms. The most unequivocal are human remains bearing weapons traumas: cut marks from swords or scalping knives, bones (especially skulls) broken by axes or maces but, most commonly, projectile points embedded in bone. As noted above, it seems that only one in three or four arrowheads striking a body become embedded in bone (Milner 1999; Keeley 1996).

Fortifications are often obvious because they involve major human modifications of the earth. However, these only occur where and after their builders store considerable quantities of food and, therefore, settle for most of the year, if not permanently, in the location (i.e., groups become "sedentary"). Why expend the extraordinary efforts necessary to fortify a place or a nearby refuge that a group will occupy for only a few weeks and contains nothing of value? Certain features of enclosures are unequivocally defensive. These features include "defended" gates, especially the forms called "baffled," V-cross-sectioned ditches deeper than a meter, and bastions projecting from an enclosure wall (Keeley et al. 2007). An enclosure with many or, better, all of these features was built to defend humans from other humans.

Weapons of war are commonly also used in hunting–fishing. Thus, distinguishing prehistoric hunting weapons from war weapons is not always easy, but it can be done. War weapons often have features that distinguish them from hunting weapons. For example, the arrowheads of war arrows sometimes have a different hafted portion from those used in hunting/fishing such that they more easily slip off the arrow shaft when extracted from a wound. This is so the arrowhead remains in the wound to cause infection and further tissue damage. Killing a prey animal days after it is wounded is useless; killing or permanently debilitating an enemy weeks or months later is, alas, desirable. When weapon heads are common but hunting (judging from food remains) is rare, the arrow/spear heads found were most probably used in war (Keeley 1997). Also, weapons that could have been used for hunting have been found clustered along and in front of clear fortifications, strongly implying that they were also used in warfare. Certain weapons have little or no use in everyday life but are commonly used for war: maces, swords, broad-bladed axes, halberds, etc. When certain projectile point types are found almost exclusively with human remains or embedded in human bones, they are not "mortuary points" but are almost certainly weapons of war (e.g., Keeley 1974, 1996).

The most obvious and seemingly clear evidences of prehistoric and ancient warfare are iconographic. These consist of paintings and other representations of groups or weapon-wielding men facing another group of armed men. Such representations of combat are known from the late hunter-gatherers (Mesolithic) and early farmers (Neolithic) of Europe, the late prehistoric period (both hunter-gatherers and farmer-herders) of Southern Africa, and the late prehistoric (hunter-gatherers) of Australia. But these representations must be interpreted cautiously. In a few historical examples, it seems that depictions of warfare became less common rather than more common during prolonged periods of intense warfare as, for example, in Classical Greece during the Peloponnesian Wars (Keeley 2001).Nevertheless, depictions of combat, however uncommon or mythological, can have no meaning to either their creators or their audiences if they are not already familiar with war.

Why and When War?

For the past 15 years, archaeologists' renewed interest in warfare has led them to ask what environmental, demographic, and social conditions encourage widespread and vicious warfare and characterize the most violent times and places. The hypotheses, some of which are long-standing proposals, can be encapsulated as: (1) "Hard Times"; (2) political centralization and control; (3) rape and recruitment; (4) slaves and taxes; (5) trade disputes; and (6) frontiers.

Among archaeologists, the most popular hypotheses for periods of intensified warfare involve "hard times" created by droughts, environmental changes both terrestrial and aquatic, and demographic growth by humans or their livestock—in short, more mouths to feed on static or declining resources. This hypothesis (which was first stated, but only in demographic terms, by Malthus, 1798, 1999) is popular with archaeologists because it is testable and observable archaeologically, is rational and realistic, and, most important, has a great deal of evidential support in a number of times and places. Climatic and environmental changes are evident in preserved pollen, geological sedimentary and soil chemistry, fauna, and certain features on human remains caused by dietary deficiencies. The clearest, most thorough and most general exposition of this explanation is provided by Steven LeBlanc (2003) in his book, *Constant Battles*. He argues that it is theoretically improbable and, in reality, impossible for human populations to be in a long-term balance with the resources necessary to sustain them—that there were no "ecologically balanced" Edens. In fact, human populations often are adversely affected by immediate or obviously impending shortfalls of necessary resources, especially food and water. Such crises provoke rational human groups to war over what resources are available, since the alternatives were usually as ghastly as war.

Many examples support the "hard times" hypothesis. Some prehistoric examples mentioned several years ago include the American Southwest during the thirteenth century, the late prehistoric north central Plains and Middle Missouri, the Late Palaeolithic Nubia, and proto-historic southeast Africa (Keeley 1996; LeBlanc 2003). These examples have been bolstered, and several more have been exposed, by recent archaeological research. Two recent examples are documented by Arkush (2011), who found that drought and environmental change played an important role in impelling a period of increased warfare in the prehistoric Andes, as did Lambert (1997) on the prehistoric Santa Barbara coast of California. However, the climate and environment are always changing (a point made in LeBlanc's arguments against past humans being able to live in "ecological balance" and, at least on a short-term basis, a fact to which any farmer or pastoralist can attest). The changeability of the climate means that it is, therefore, always possible to find some environmental change that correlates with some sociocultural change, including increased warfare. What is necessary is to link by logic, timing, and relevant data a particular environmental change to a particular social change. In many of the instances or references mentioned above, this has been done. For example, in the very periods that environmental deterioration (from the point of view of then contemporary human ecology) and increased warfare were especially evident on the prehistoric Southern California coast and in Egyptian Nubia 12,000 B.C., evidence of dietary deficiencies was especially common on human bones. Whether the evidence is weak or strong, I predict that claims by archaeologists of "hard times"-driven warfare will increase and encompass more regions and periods.

One cause of increased warfare that anthropologists have found reasonable and supported by some evidence is political consolidation, especially the emergence and expansion of states. Regarding the emergence of states, the principal anthropological proponent of the essential role of warfare in this process has been, for almost 50 years, Robert Carneiro (for his latest exposition, see Carneiro 2003). This hypothesis argues that chiefdoms and chiefs do not usually voluntarily yield their autonomy but must be forced to do so by warfare. Haas (2001)has expanded this concept to the formation of chiefdoms from tribes. One corollary of these ideas is that warfare should be more ferocious during periods of sociopolitical consolidation—tribes into chiefdoms and smaller, less organized societies into states. A popular but less logical presumption would be that warfare did not and has not occurred except in the emergence of and between competing states. This more tenuous supposition is contrary to ethnological and archaeological fact. Of course, the role of warfare in the creation of empires (i.e., collections of previously independent chiefdoms and states subject to centralized hegemony) in Europe and Asia is well documented and well known.[1] Arkush (2011)argues that in fact the collapse of the prehistoric large

[1] Ironically, the philosopher Hobbes has been accused of advocating this state-formation hypothesis and of being an apologist for the violent expansion of European empires (Ferguson and Whitehead 1992). When, in fact, he argued (contrary to much prehistoric and historic data that we now possess) that states were created by covenants or agreements and that strong, centralized states that resulted from these covenants were the rational antidote to the violent anarchy of non-states or dissolved states.

state or empire of Tiwanaku in the Andes at least "set the stage" for a bellicose period of warring chiefdoms; and that the later Inka state began in relatively peaceful circumstances, even if its imperial expansion did involve warfare or the threat of warfare. Her work reminded me of the collapse of the Western Roman Empire and the contemporary Han Empire and their aftermaths of smaller "Warring States." In any case, like historians, archaeologists have seen periods of more intense warfare occurring during periods of both political consolidation and dissolution.

It is clear from history and ethnology that, unlike people organized into bands or tribes, countless chiefdoms and states have gone to war not for mere territory or nubile women, but to increase the numbers of commoners who can become slaves or producers of tribute and taxes. Without written records or ethnohistorical observations, it is difficult, if not impossible, for archaeologists to distinguish slaves from members of the lowest class (Junkers 1998) or to determine whether an item (especially a foodstuff) was acquired by trade or taxation/tribute. When we find large settlements whose residents could not have been supported by the food resources available in their immediate vicinity, we can reasonably infer that those resources were extracted from other, smaller nearby communities under the control of the elites of the larger settlement. However, for many other items, whether "wealth" for elites (e.g., quetzal feathers, bronze tools or weapons, gold, and fine pottery) or essential to the daily life of commoners (e.g., staple foods and stone for cutting or grinding), archaeologists tend to interpret these as procured by trade. Much more thought and research are required regarding the archaeology of slavery, tribute, and taxes.

It will surprise some that a large number of violent conflicts arise from trade. Many think that trade obviates warfare and that warfare prevents trade. History is replete with instances of trade imbalances and disputes leading to warfare and trade taking place between active enemies; many similar cases are known from ethnography (Keeley 1996). These have included, depending on the relevant technologies and geography, the sources of such normally traded materials as salt, hard stone for tools, metals (or their ores), preservative spices, and, most recently, fossil fuels. The "trade raid" connection has not received much attention from archaeologists studying ancient warfare or has been subsumed as a corollary of "hard times" (for example, trade is hardly mentioned in LeBlanc's 2003 book; see Golitko 2010 about this neglect). Golitko (2010) found that during the settlement of a region of northeast Belgium by the first farmers (c. 5200 B.C.), two important aspects of trade were related to warfare. While obtaining some of their axe material from sources from the areas occupied by indigenous hunter-gatherers, the farmers were fortifying their frontier villages against the former (see also Golitko and Keeley 2007). At the same time, trade in pottery, flint, and some other items between the farmers' villages became more structured and more common, probably to maintain military alliances between themselves and against the hostile foragers.

One common context for warfare is frontiers, whether persistent or moving (Keeley 1996; especially see Anthony's work 1990 and 2007). The topic of frontiers, especially moving frontiers of settlement (i.e., colonization), was widely neglected or dismissed by Western archaeologists between the early 1960s and the late 1980s.

When hypotheses attributing cultural changes to major population movements were disallowed or ignored, any warfare associated with such movements was similarly ignored (unless it arose from the expansion of European hegemony). Even many non-Western archaeologists outside the influence of the Western archaeological bias against prehistoric migrations, nationalists in other parts of the world, were inclined to see the present-day inhabitants of their countries as autochthonous. Both the inexorable archaeological record and the revival of anthropological interest in warfare (Wiessner 1998; Kelly 2000)have changed the intellectual climate such that the violence of non-Western and prehistoric frontiers is now considered a legitimate subject of archaeological study (Golitko and Keeley 2007; Arkush 2011). For example, Anthony (2007) finds that the expansion and, in most affected regions, the colonization of Indo-European speakers from their central Eurasian homeland were certainly accompanied and, therefore, aided by, the use of domesticated horses, wheeled vehicles, and, relevant here, the war chariot. In any case, many archaeologists have begun to consider the warfare that they document on frontiers.

The major problem with most historical and archaeological explanations of major events and processes is that many plausible "causes" seem to happen at the same time. This contemporaneity of plausible causes is the source of many scholarly disagreements and, because of the statistical indeterminacy of our dates, a real problem for archaeologists. By definition, a cause should precede its effect, yet even in modern human affairs, causes and effects are so closely linked chronologically that we usually have great difficulty sorting one from the other. It seems that many of these "causes" are closely linked as parts of chains of efficient causes or even "feeding" one another as parts of feedback loops. It is common to find that periods of intensive warfare are also periods of political consolidation or dissolution, environmental change, moving frontiers of colonization or conquest, increasing population density, human nutritional deficiencies, and so on. At the moment, the best we can do is to investigate all of these possibilities and to propose multivariate explanations using the variables that best fit particular instances. Certainly, at the moment, one size does not fit all. However, note that genetic explanations do not figure in any of those proposed by archaeologists or historians.

The more biogenetic explanations of war emphasize the inferred genetic traits that promote human (especially male) aggressiveness and the evolutionary strategies that seem to impel male violence against competing males and capture/rape of fertile females. Many of the chapters in this volume promote this interpretation and adduce data from modern industrial societies to support it. This interpretation is more popular among nonanthropologist social scientists who do not study directly the remarkable varieties of human behavior that have been displayed over the globe and over great reaches of time, or the incredible plasticity of human behavior in the recent or distant human past. Both myself (Keeley 1996)and LeBlanc (2003)have argued against such propositions based on our broad anthropological surveys of warfare worldwide and into the depths of the human past. Our dismissal of genetic or "selection" arguments for warfare is based also on our personal research and the research of colleagues in our respective research foci—the American Southwest and prehistoric Europe. For my area of expertise, there is evidence that both the Late

Mesolithic hunter-gatherers and the invading farmers who replaced them in some areas were equally war torn (Keeley 1997; Golitko and Keeley 2007; Golitko 2010). LeBlanc and I both have noted, indeed emphasized, for example, that in the archaeological sequences of our respective regions, there have been very bellicose periods with settlements fortified and/or moved to more defensible locations, high proportions of human remains showing weapons traumas or "disrespectful" treatment of some (enemy?) dead, and great abundances of weapons yet no increases in hunting. Yet, there have also been periods in our respective foci when such evidences of warfare were less common. We both argue that for situations in which the more bellicose were the ancestors or descendants of much more peaceful people, it is difficult to see how genetics could play a role. Unless, of course, violent rapacious (males) were deleterious mutants whose genes were removed by selection before they could have many descendants or died before they reproduced, unlike the less violent and rapacious. Because the genetic "evolutionary" explanations of warfare are so contrary to archaeological data, archaeologists, by and large, ignore them.

Anthropologically, such "genetically selective" propositions imply that the capture of and impregnation of nubile women should be both the universal goal and the usual result of warfare. Indeed, the capture of women, especial young women, is a common but not universal feature of warfare among the non-state societies known to ethnography and has been documented among several prehistoric people (Keeley 1996). However, ethnology, history and archaeology document many instances in which nubile women were not kidnapped, either because they were killed along with everyone else or because they were left alive with all survivors (Keeley 1996).[2] It seems that the capture of primarily young women of breeding age is only common among societies organized as tribes or petty chiefdoms. Bands tend to take no captives of any sex or age, or, only on occasion, young women with girl and boy children. States commonly have taken everyone captive because they could become slaves or tax payers. Considering ethnological and archaeological facts, whatever the role of human genetics in inducing some individuals (in any social group of

[2] Any anthropologist interested in warfare and violence is questioned about Chagnon's description of the Yanamomo/i. The basic question should be and is: what are the facts, as far as we can know or reasonably infer them? Those are that the Yanomano frequently resorted to deadly violence, including warfare, as did neighboring "tribal" groups. Instead, Chagnon's critics seem to have been driven to the functional equivalent of idiocy by his sociobiological interpretations (which, as noted above, I do not find compelling) rather than the facts he recorded regarding Yanamomo life and society in the 1950s, 1960s, and 1970s. The critics have ignored or illogically (see below) dismissed many other observers, both anthropologists and laypeople (including a kidnapped Brazilian girl who lived with them for several years), who have clearly described the common resort to violence and warfare by the Yanomomi and its effects, or documented the same behaviors among many other neighboring non-Yanomomo "tribal" groups in the Amazon and Orinoco Basins. These critics have also resorted almost entirely to a logically and scientifically invalid form of argument—*ad hominem*—against not just Chagnon but any other ethnographers whose observations parallel his. The only reasonable conclusions about the traditional life of the Yanomamo are that they were a violent people, often kidnapped young women (Early and Peters 1990) and used nondeadly forms of physical violence (chest-pounding and club fights) as their principal method to prevent wars.

whatever size) to violence and rape, genetic selection for warfare and rape is a poor explanation for the actual occurrences of the collective violence of war.

One feature that makes war so terrible is not the human vice of violent aggression but the human virtue of courage. There would be no war if humans were cowards. They would be afraid to resort to violence because it might be returned and if attacked would run or acquiesce. Instead, humans refuse to "go gently into that good night"—they fight back. Furthermore, in both their aggression and their resistance to it, they will try to inflict injury for injury, death for death, horror for horror—in short, intensify and literally double the awfulness of war. It seems that among the humans known to anthropology, peace is more desirable to everyone everywhere than violence or war, including rape [both in the modern legal sense and the ancient meaning "theft of women" (e.g., "Rape of the Sabine Women"; Keeley 1996). Therefore, should not there be some human genetic-based preference for courage in the face of all adversities and for maintaining peace?

Conclusions

In the past 20 years, there has been a resurgence of archaeological interest in prehistoric and ancient warfare. Whether warfare is seen as a cause or an effect of certain features of and changes in the archaeological, ethnohistorical, or ancient historical record, it is back "in play." This change was the result of a number of archaeologists working in Europe and the New World who were confronted by the warfare obvious in archaeological records in their areas of research. They then all argued in the most widely read and stringently refereed publication venues, citing unequivocal evidence and using clear logic, that prehistoric and ethnohistoric warfare did occur and needs attention (i.e., Vencl, Milner, Haas, Keeley, Cahen, LeBlanc, and Guillane, among others). Of course, much of the subsequent work has focused on the contentious and difficult but, therefore, academically attractive question of cause. However, this major change in archaeological attention has entailed an increased proportion of the ever-pitiful research monies given to archaeologists and publications in our major journals and books. One area that is still neglected by archaeologists (but not by Otterbein (2004) or Kelly (2000), although both are socio-cultural anthropologists) are the rare periods of relative peace—meaning periods during which evidences of both war and homicide were rare. Archaeologically, the three best-known examples are the Middle Woodland (Hopewell-Adena) of the eastern Midwest, the Natufian and Pre-Pottery Neolithic A of the Levantine Near East, and the early Jomon of Japan; but there are others less well known (Milner 1999; Goring-Morris 2009; Habu 2004). If archaeologists recently have shown limited interest in peace, they have at least now recognized that prehistoric war is not an oxymoron. While we vehemently disagree about the causes of war and when it began, all of those "pioneers" mentioned above agree that ancient and prehistoric warfare did exist and that it is a topic that we can and should investigate, and, as far as I know, are gratified by the attention given this subject by a new generation of scholars.

References

Anthony, D. W. (1990). Migration in archeology: The baby and the bathwater. *American Anthropologist, 92*, 895–914.
Anthony, D. W. (2008). *The Horse, the wheel, and language: How Bronze-Age riders from the Eurasian steppes shaped the modern world.* Princeton: Princeton University Press.
Arkush, E. (2011). *Hillforts of the ancient Andes: Colla warfare, society, and landscape.* Gainesville: University Press of Florida.
Arkush, E., & Stanish, C. (2005). Interpreting conflict in the ancient Andes: Implications for the archaeology of warfare. *Current Anthropology, 46*, 3–28.
Carneiro, R. L. (2003). *Evolutionism in cultural anthropology: A critical history.* Boulder, CO: Westview Press.
Early, J. D., & Peters, J. F. (1990). *The population dynamics of the Mucajai Yanomama.* New York: Academic Press.
Ferguson, R. B., & Whitehead, N. L. (1992). The violent edge of empire. In R. B. Ferguson & N. L. Whitehead (Eds.), *War in the tribal zone: Expanding states and indigenous warfare* (pp. 1–30). Santa Fe, NM: School of American Research Press.
Golitko, M. (2010). *Warfare and alliance building during the Belgian early Neolithic, late sixth Millennium BC.* Unpublished doctoral dissertation, Department of Anthropology, University of Illinois, Chicago.
Golitko, M., & Keeley, L. H. (2007). Beating ploughshares back into swords: Warfare in the *Linearbandkeramik. Antiquity, 81*, 332–342.
Goring-Morris, A. N. (2009). Two Kebaran occupations near Nahal Soreq, and the reconstruction of group ranges in the Early Epipalaeolithic of the Israeli littoral. *Eurasian Prehistory, 6*, 75–93.
Haas, J. (2001). *From leaders to rulers.* New York: Kluwer.
Habu, J. (2004). *Ancient Jomon of Japan.* New York: Cambridge University Press.
Junkers, L. (1999). *Raiding, trading, and feasting: The political economy of Philippine chiefdoms.* Honolulu: University of Hawaii Press.
Keeley, L. H. (1974). Technique and methodology in microwear studies: A critical review. *World Archaeology, 5*, 323–336.
Keeley, L. H. (1996). *War Before Civilization.* New York: Oxford University Press.
Keeley, L. H. (2001). Giving war a chance. In G. E. Rice & S. A. LeBlanc (Eds.), *Deadly landscapes: Case studies in prehistoric Southwestern warfare* (pp. 332–342). Salt Lake City: University of Utah Press.
Keeley, L. H., Fontana, M., & Quick, R. (2007). Baffles and bastions: The universal features of fortifications. *Journal of Archaeological Research, 15*, 55–95.
Kelly, R. L. (2000). Elements of a behavioral ecological paradigm for the study of prehistoric hunter-gatherers. In M. B. Schiffer (Ed.), *Social theory in archaeology* (pp. 63–78). Salt Lake City: University of Utah Press.
Lambert, P. M. (2007). The osteological evidence for indigenous warfare in North America. In R. J. Chacon & R. Mendoza (Eds.), *North American indigenous warfare and ritualized violence* (pp. 202–221). Tucson: University of Arizona Press.
LeBlanc, S. A., & Register, K. E. (2003). *Constant battles: The myth of the peaceful, noble savage.* New York: St. Martin's Press.
Malthus, T. R. (1999). *An essay on the principle of population.* New York: Oxford University Press (originally published 1798).
Milner, G. R. (1999). Warfare in prehistoric and early historic eastern North America. *Journal of Archaeological Research*, 7, 105–151.
Otterbein, K. F. (2004). *How war began.* College Station: Texas A & M University Press.
Weissner, P. (1998). Indoctrinability and the evolution of socially defined kinship. In F. Salter & I. Eibl-Eibesfeldt (Eds.), *Warfare, ideology and indoctrinability* (pp. 133–150). New York: Berghahn Books.

Chapter 3
Violence in Literature: An Evolutionary Perspective

Joseph Carroll

> Murder gives us an X-ray of the inner core of human nature. It lays bare the things that matter most to humans everywhere—the necessities of survival, the attainment of status, the defense of honor, the acquisition of desirable partners, the loyalty of our lovers, the bonding of our allies, the vanquishing of our enemies, the protection of our children, and the successes of the carriers of our genetic cargo. These are the things that we humans and our astonishingly victorious ancestors have always been willing to kill and die for. (Buss *The Murderer Next Door: Why the Mind is Designed to Kill*, 2005, p. 244)

Core Motives, Culture, and the Adaptive Function of the Arts

Violence is pervasive in literature because literary authors and their readers want to get at the inner core of human nature. All human interests are set in conflict with the interests of others. Even among the closest kin, fitness interests partially overlap and partially conflict. Between parents and children, siblings, spouses, coalitional partners, and members of one's own tribe, shared fitness interests prompting love or friendship clash with individual interests prompting suspicion, envy, resentment, anger, and sometimes hatred. Violence is the flash point at which the tensions aroused by conflicting interests reach critical mass. In literature as in life, violence reveals the underlying structure of human motives and passions.

This chapter first describes the way core motives interact with imaginative cultural constructs, explains the crucial importance of point of view in creating literary meaning, and then examines specific instances of violence in literature.

The basic motives identified by Buss fit together into the larger logic of human life history (Kenrick 2011; Muehlenbein and Flinn 2011). That larger logic is governed by inclusive fitness, differential parental investment, and the dynamics of social interaction: dominance, reciprocation, cooperative group effort, and competi-

J. Carroll (✉)
Department of English, University of Missouri–St. Louis, St. Louis, MO 63121, USA
e-mail: jcarroll@umsl.edu

T. K. Shackelford, R. D. Hansen (eds.), *The Evolution of Violence*,
Evolutionary Psychology, DOI 10.1007/978-1-4614-9314-3_3,

tion between groups (Boehm 1999; Kurzban and Neuberg 2005). Relative to body size, humans have uniquely large brains, and they display extended cultural phenotypes vastly more complex than those of any other species. Those human peculiarities have not cancelled the constraining force of evolved primate dispositions, but they have altered the ways those dispositions manifest themselves in human behavior and human experience (Buss 1997). A comprehensively adequate account of human evolution will thus necessarily include a theory of "gene–culture coevolution" (Carroll 2008c, pp. 318–326; Cochran and Harpending 2009; Hill 2007; Lumsden and Wilson 1981; Richerson and Boyd 2005). Regrettably, ideas about gene–culture coevolution are still in a rudimentary stage of development. Kim Hill gets this problem into sharp focus:

> Given the recent convergence of evolutionary psychology and human behavioral ecology–sociobiology, one might expect that the next generation of researchers will rapidly untangle all the major mysteries of human behavior and cognition. Unfortunately, I do not think that this will happen quickly. The main reason is that no branch of the evolutionary social sciences has an adequate understanding of human culture. Culture is a product of evolved cognitive mechanisms, but its existence may significantly alter behavioral patterns from those normally expected (from non-cultural organisms), and its emergence has probably uniquely shaped evolved human cognition and emotion. (Hill 2007, p. 351)

Some nonhuman animals make tools, share information, and learn behaviors from observing each other. Because of their expanded neocortex, humans have been able to develop these capabilities in three ways either unique to human culture or exceptionally developed in human culture: (a) they produce art (Brown 1991; Dissanayake 2000; Dutton 2009); (b) they retain and develop social, mechanical, and intellectual innovations, adding new innovations to old (Richerson and Boyd 2005; Sterelny 2003; Tomasello et al. 2005); and (c) they extrapolate general ideas (Baumeister et al. 2011; Chiappe and MacDonald 2005; Geary 2005; Hawkins 2004). Through cumulative innovation, humans have transformed techniques into technology, tribes into civilizations, discoveries into progressive sciences, and artistic novelties into aesthetic traditions. By extrapolating general ideas, they have produced theology, philosophy, history, the sciences, and theories about the arts. Animals of other species produce emotionally expressive vocalizations and engage in play. Humans alone produce oral narratives and visual artifacts designed to depict objects and actions, evoke subjective sensations, and delineate through symbols the salient features of their experience.

Distinguishing human culture from the transmission of information among nonhuman animals, Hill observes that only humans use signals to communicate and enforce social "norms." In Hill's conception, human culture embodies "the morality of a social group," that is, "rules of behavior" that are communicated through "rituals (religious practices) and ethnic markers" (p. 353). This formulation rightly identifies culture as an adaptively significant form of behavior, but it leaves out much of what counts as culture. The Ten Commandments and other such regulative codes are part of culture but not the whole of culture. Imaginative constructs like pictures, songs, and stories sometimes contain moral lessons, but they appeal also to impulses of cognitive play, emotional responsiveness, and aesthetic pleasure (Boyd

2009; Dissanayake 2000; Roth 2007). Works of fiction situate individual characters in relation to both the particular cultural norms and the primal passions that form the core features of human nature (Boyd 2009; Carroll 2011; McEwan 2005). Epics, novels, stories, plays, and poems sometimes affirm specific cultural norms but also sometimes resist those norms.

The largest purpose of the representational arts is to evoke and depict the qualities of experience. The arts influence behavior not only by transmitting culturally specific codes of conduct but also by influencing the way people perceive the world and their own experience in the world. Some such wider conception of the arts has entered into many arguments that the arts are adaptively functional (Boyd 2005, 2009; Carroll 2008c, pp. 349–368, 2011, pp. 20–29, 2012a; Carroll et al. 2012, pp. 81–92; Dissanayake 2000; Gottschall 2012; Salmon and Symons 2004; Scalise Sugiyama 2005; Tooby and Cosmides 2001; Wilson 1998, Chap. 10).

The Interplay of Perspectives in Literature

Fictional stories create virtual worlds and enable people to explore possible forms of experience. Authors of stories and plays typically have exceptional insight into the sources of human behavior and the qualities of experience. Usually, readers are invited to share vicariously in the experience of characters and to respond emotionally to the characters. Since imagined worlds bear the impress of the minds that created them, readers are also invited to share in an author's feeling and judgment about the events of a story. To read a fictional story is, thus, to engage in an emotionally responsive simulation of a social interaction (Mar and Oatley 2008).

All experience ultimately takes place in individual minds. As Tooby and Cosmides observe, "what mostly remains, once you have removed from the human world everything internal to individuals, is the air between them" (Tooby and Cosmides 1992, p. 47). There is, consequently, only one possible location for "meaning" and "effect" in a story: the perspectives of authors, characters, and readers. Characters have impressions about one another; authors have impressions about characters; and readers have impressions about both characters and authors. Authors anticipate the responses of readers. Even if readers reject an author's values and beliefs, they register what authors intend them to feel and think. Good interpretive criticism tries to get at the interaction among all these perspectives.

In the interaction between author and reader, the author gets the first word, but the reader gets the last. The author fabricates a situation—characters, setting, and interlaced events (plot)—and conveys his or her own attitude toward that fabricated situation. An interpretive critic working at the highest level evaluates as accurately as possible what the author means readers to understand but also situates the author's intended meaning within the critic's own theoretical framework.

Critics use explanatory ideas from other disciplines to provide conceptual content for interpretive commentaries on literary works. The most commonly used explanatory ideas derive from various forms of psychology, social theory, and philosophy.

Most academic literary critics at the present time adopt a theoretical framework cobbled together from Freudian psychoanalysis, Marxist social theory, feminist gender theory, and deconstructive epistemology (Boyd 2006; Boyd et al. 2010, introduction; Carroll 1995, 2004, 2010, 2011, 2012c, in press; Culler 2011; Menand 2005). This standard amalgam has various labels: "poststructuralism," "new historicism," "cultural materialism," "Foucauldian cultural critique," or, most simply, "Theory." Despite differences in labels and differing points of emphasis, all versions of "Theory" share one crucial characteristic: they all presuppose the blank slate model of the human mind. They all suppose that human nature is an empty vessel into which culture pours all particular content. Evolutionary literary critics reject the blank slate model and use findings from the evolutionary social sciences to replace the obsolete forms of psychology, sociology, and epistemology that make up poststructuralism.

Three Examples from Literature

Violence in literature has no inherent valence or significance. Violence can be heroic, triumphant, cruel, vicious, or futile and ineffectual. The value attached to any particular instance of violence derives from occasions and circumstances, the motives of characters, the author's attitude toward the depicted characters, the author's general outlook on life, and the responses of readers.

A previous essay by this author offered a survey of violence in world literature (Carroll 2012b). This current chapter takes a different tack: giving a close comparative look at violence in just three works: two versions of the "Little Red Riding Hood" story and Shakespeare's play *King Lear*. The two versions of "Little Red Riding Hood" are those of the brothers Grimm and of Angela Carter, a contemporary writer. These three works have been chosen to illustrate the proposition that the significance of violence in any given work depends on the interactions between core human concerns, specific cultural values, individual differences in authorial vision, and relations between the minds of authors and readers in response to characters.

The Grimms' version of "Little Red Riding Hood," though polished by literate adult tellers of tales, emerged from the folk psychology of a largely illiterate peasant population (Crick 2009; Dundes 1989a). It captures the imagination of children and invites them to identify with its protagonist. Angela Carter's retelling of the story is aimed at adults and invites its readers to share the ideological standpoint of its author. Both versions of the fairy tale are short, and both involve a limited range of motives for violence.

King Lear offers a full spectrum of violence—parents against children and children against parents, siblings against each other, suicide (violence against the self), violence to assert and resist domination within a social group, and violence between social groups. Since *King Lear* is a play, it has no overt declarations by a narrator, but it does have an implied author whose own perspective on the depicted events can be inferred from the relations among characters and the responses of readers. We can make reasonable suppositions about the impact the author intends to have on his audience. Shakespeare appeals to an audience that shares with him basic values centered on family bonds and social obligations. Like the brothers Grimm, and unlike Carter, Shakespeare invites readers to participate empathically in the experience of the depicted characters.

The action of *King Lear* is fast and violent, but the play is also reflective and meditative. The characters are occupied not just with attaining goals such as sex and power but also with understanding the meaning of life. In *Sex, Murder, and the Meaning of Life* (2011), Douglas Kenrick suggests that "the meaning of life" can be found in meditative attention to the core concerns of human nature and the rhythms of human life history. Shakespeare suggests something very similar. In folk traditions, this kind of moral vision is often characterized as a form of "wisdom."

Violence in Grimms' "Little Red Riding Hood"

"Little Red Riding Hood" is a particular version of a common folk tale motif: a protagonist swallowed by a predator but then rescued (Bolte and Polívka 1963; Dundes 1989a; Sugiyama 2004). In Europe and the Anglophone world, the most familiar version of this story is that produced by the brothers Grimm in their 1812 collection. (Their title is more properly translated "Little Red Cap," but "Little Red Riding Hood" is the title by which the story is universally recognized.) In the Grimms' version, Little Red Riding Hood's mother tells her to take cake and wine to a sick grandmother, who lives in the woods, and warns her not to stray from the path. On the way, the girl meets a wolf, who encourages her to dally, picking flowers. The wolf precedes her to the grandmother's house, swallows the grandmother whole, dons the grandmother's clothes, and climbs into the grandmother's bed. When the girl arrives, she engages in a dialogue with the wolf:

> Oh, grandmother, what big ears you have!
> All the better to hear you with.
> Oh, grandmother, what big eyes you have!
> All the better to see you with.
> Oh, grandmother, what big hands you have!
> All the better to grab you with!
> Oh, grandmother, what a horribly big mouth you have!
> All the better to eat you with!
> The wolf had scarcely finished speaking when he jumped from the bed with a single leap and ate up poor Little Red Cap. (Grimm and Grimm 1998–2011)

The wolf falls asleep. A hunter passes by, cuts open the wolf's belly, and frees the two people. The girl puts stones in the wolf's belly. When he wakes and tries to run away, he falls down dead.

To understand the significance of violence in fairy tales, we have to understand how they affect children's imagination—how symbolic meaning works in them and how they affect children emotionally. Efforts to understand how fairy tales work have proceeded through three main historical phases: mythic, Freudian, and evolutionary. The Grimm brothers and many of their successors envisioned fairy tales as demotic versions of myths such as the ancient Germanic myths or solar or lunar myths (Bettelheim 2010; Dundes 1989a; Grimm and Grimm 2012). For the past half century or so, symbolic interpretations of the Grimms' fairy tales have been dominated by Freudian readings, supplemented in recent decades by feminist commentaries emphasizing gendered power relations (Dundes 1989b; Zipes 1993). Specifically evolutionary theories about imaginative processes are still under construction but have already made important advances over previous efforts.

Evolutionary literary scholars typically reject Freudian developmental psychology and in its place use evolutionary concepts of childhood development (Boyd 2009; Carroll 2008a; Scalise Sugiyama 2001). The evolutionary critic Scalise Sugiyama argues that oral and written narratives, even fairy tales, function chiefly by transmitting practical information on such adaptively important matters as resource acquisition, predator avoidance, and social interaction. Literature and its oral antecedents are, she proposes, "an information acquisition strategy" (Sugiyama 2006, p. 319). "Little Red Riding Hood," she explains, "packs a double emotional wallop by combining our evolved fear of being harmed by animals with our evolved fear of being harmed by strangers" (Sugiyama 2004, p. 123). So far as it goes, that explanation is clearly correct. Invoking adaptive concerns grounded in forager conditions and in evolutionary developmental psychology offers a valuable corrective to claims that the story reflects lingering "oedipal attachments" (Bettelheim 2010, p. 171) or that it is "a parable of rape" (Brownmiller 1975, p. 310). However, the story does more than teach children to distinguish wolves from grandmothers and convey practical lessons about avoiding strangers. A purely didactic interpretation cannot account for departures from strict realism, and such departures are, of course, a defining feature of fairy tales. More importantly, a didactic interpretation fails to explain how the story provides emotional and imaginative satisfaction for children.

The most influential Freudian theorist of fairy tales, Bruno Bettelheim, is wrong to affirm that "the oedipus complex is the crucial problem of childhood" (2010, p. 38). He is right, though, to affirm that fairy tales have psycho-symbolic meanings and that they influence emotional development:

> For a story truly to hold the child's attention, it must entertain him and arouse his curiosity. But to enrich his life, it must stimulate his imagination; help him to develop his intellect and to clarify his emotions; be attuned to his anxieties and aspirations; give full recognition to his difficulties, while at the same time suggesting solutions to the problems which perturb him. (Bettelheim 2010, p. 5)

Many thinkers who are not Freudians have recognized that fairy tales are the richest literature of early childhood. (Tatar [2012] offers a compendium of statements by writers about how fairy tales affect childhood development.)Stories that merely conveyed information or taught lessons in an overt, didactic way would have little interest for children and would have little impact on their emotional development.

"Little Red Riding Hood" seems aimed at a very young child, a child young enough to envision someone being swallowed whole by a wolf. For a child, between, say, the ages of 2 and 7, the greatest source of fear, apart from the immediate fear of death, would be separation from kin. "Little Red Riding Hood" climaxes emotionally in the revelation, step by step, that the grandmother is the wolf. Detailing the parts of the wolf makes Little Red Riding Hood, and child readers who identify with her, linger in slow motion, with a sensation of strangeness and horror, at the blended images. Superimposing the image of a wolf over the expected image of the grandmother creates emotional and cognitive dissonance for the child. That kind of confusion, the inability to distinguish loving kin from predatory strangers, is bad in itself. Behind that confusion, there might be a hint of a still greater fear, the fear that the adults on whom one relies can turn vicious and predatory.

The child's terror, climaxing in being swallowed, is followed by the relief of escape, and then emotional tension is defused by the comic denouement. Simply killing the wolf would have eliminated the danger. Playing a joke on him by placing stones in his belly enhances the relief and satisfaction produced by his death, changing him from a figure of terror into a comic butt. By placing stones where she was herself trapped, the girl replaces the image of herself, helpless and terrified, with the insensate mass of the stones. She acts out symbolically a transformation from being a terrified and helpless victim to an active agent of revenge and justice. The story as a whole, thus, enacts an emotional process through which the child, as reader or listener, achieves mastery over the fear elicited by the wolf in grandmother's clothing. At the end of the story, the grandmother is restored to her rightful place; the menacing stranger is replaced by a beneficent stranger; and the terror produced by the wolf is transformed into comedy, self-assertion, and ethical triumph.

The story elicits fear in a child and then relieves that fear, returning the child to emotional equilibrium. It might be that such forms of vicarious emotional play are a kind of practice that builds emotional resilience when a child is faced with actual danger. The story also subliminally enacts a crucial phase in social development. By depicting a shift from the menacing stranger to the beneficent stranger, the story simulates the emotional process in which a child eventually replaces a fear of all strangers with a willingness to engage in social interactions outside the immediate family.

At the end of the Grimms' version of the story, Little Red Riding Hood draws a moral: "As long as I live, I will never leave the path and run off into the woods by myself if mother tells me not to." Scalise Sugiyama supplements this purely didactic conclusion with specific practical lessons: avoid wolves and be careful of strangers. However, if the story were only didactic in purpose, then the tale could have ended with Little Red Riding Hood's death—a more effective way to scare children into caution. And indeed, the first literary version of the tale, Perrault's version written for the court of Louis XIV, ends with the death of the child (Perrault 2009). In the Grimms' version that has become canonical, the emotional lesson is that dangers can be overcome, that enemies can be defeated and rendered harmless, and that the wider social world holds promise of beneficent interactions.

Violence in Angela Carter's "The Werewolf"

Angela Carter started publishing in the 1960s and died in 1992. Writing in 1995, Salman Rushdie observes that "she has become the contemporary writer most studied at British universities" (Rushdie 1997, p. xiv). Rushdie defends her against the charge of "political correctness" (Rushdie 1997, p. xiv), but it is quite certain that no politically incorrect writer could be the centerpiece of contemporary literary education in Britain. Suffice it to say that she is highly attuned to contemporary ideological attitudes in academic literary study in the Anglophone world.

In contrast to the story told by the brothers Grimm, Angela Carter's version of the Little Red Riding Hood story, "The Werewolf," does not invite simple emotional involvement in the trials and tribulations of the protagonist. Instead, Carter invites readers to share in her own ironic contempt for her characters: brutish medieval people who believe in witches and a psychopathic little girl who exploits their superstitions.

The Carter story is very short, 826 words. It consists of three parts. The first part is an introduction in which Carter describes life in an impoverished medieval village—"harsh, brief, poor lives" (1995, p. 210). The second part is the main narrative sequence. Little Red Riding Hood goes to visit her grandmother, meets a wolf, cuts off its paw, finds her grandmother ill in bed, missing a hand, discovers that the wolf's paw has turned into the missing hand, and calls out to the villagers, declaring that her grandmother is a witch. The villagers stone the old woman to death. The third part is a single sentence, the last sentence in the story. "Now the child lived in her grandmother's house; she prospered" (p. 211).

It is not until that last sentence that readers are let in on the secret that the main narrative sequence has been a false story, a lie. There never was a wolf. The main body of the narrative about the wolf and the grandmother, we are to understand, was the story Little Red Riding Hood told the villagers. The final sentence is enough to identify the main story as a lie because Carter has already indicated, in the introductory section of the story, that witches, in this story, do not exist:

> At midnight especially on Walpurgisnacht, the Devil holds picnics in the graveyards and invites the witches; then they dig up fresh corpses, and eat them. Anyone will tell you that.
>
> Wreaths of garlic on the doors keep out the vampires. A blue-eyed child born feet first on the night of St John's Eve will have second sight. When they discover a witch—some old woman whose cheeses ripen when her neighbors' do not, another old woman whose black cat, oh, sinister! Follows her about all the time, they strip the crone, search her for marks, for the supernumerary nipple her familiar sucks. They soon find it. Then they stone her to death. (p. 210)

This introductory passage establishes a division between the villagers' beliefs and the author's beliefs. Carter gives big nudges and winks to clue readers in to her beliefs. She sneers at the triviality of the villagers' reasons for believing in witches—cheeses ripening, a black cat—and underscores her scorn with the sarcastic phrase "oh, sinister!" In the main body of the narrative, the seemingly magical events—the wolf's paw turning into an old woman's hand and the grandmother missing a hand—create a moment of cognitive dissonance. The last sentence resolves the dissonance. The aim of the story is to make us feel that we share with the author a special insight into the true story behind the fabrication foisted off on the villagers.

The resolution in the final sentence of the story would be satisfying chiefly for readers who are primed to participate, consciously or not, in a specific ideological construct: the idea that social interactions involve three main kinds of persons: manipulative oppressors, innocent victims, and shrewd intellectuals who see into the manipulations. That construct is characteristic of the poststructuralist mindset that has dominated the humanities for the past three decades. Michel Foucault, the most prominent and influential poststructuralist theorist, offers representative formulations. Foucault asserts that "power is always exercised at the expense of the people" (1977, p. 211). "The intellectual's role," he explains, is to engage in "a struggle against power, a struggle aimed at revealing and undermining power where it is most invisible and insidious" (p. 207, 208).

It is in the nature of fairy tales to suggest archetypal, mythic conditions. Their characters and situations seem to embody universal psychological truths about human experience (Bettelheim 2010, p. 26, 58; Grimm and Grimm 2009). Carter's story has the same effect, but only for readers who have internalized the Foucauldian mindset—a world reduced to three possible perspectives: the perspective of evil oppressors; the perspective of a deluded and exploited populace; and the perspective of intellectuals who are morally and intellectually superior to the world they observe.

In the folk versions of the story, the threat of violence against Little Red Riding Hood is frightening, and the violence done to the wolf, at the end, offers the satisfaction of dispatching a devious enemy. That kind of emotional response is simple, basic, and universal. In the Carter story, Little Red Riding Hood experiences no fear. The tone of the scene in which she cuts off the wolf's paw is flip, comic.

> The child had a scabbby coat of sheepskin to keep out the cold, she knew the forest too well to fear it but she must always be on her guard. When she heard that freezing howl of a wolf, she dropped her gifts, seized her knife, and turned on the beast.
>
> It was a huge one, with red eyes and running, grizzled chops; any but a mountaineer's child would have died of fright at the sight of it. It went for her throat, as wolves do, but she made a great swipe at it with her father's knife and slashed off its right forepaw.
>
> The wolf let out a gulp, almost a sob, when it saw what had happened to it; wolves are less brave than they seem. (pp. 210–211)

The violence against the wolf is cartoonish, inviting only laughter. The main violence in the story, in Carter's version, is the violence done to the grandmother:

> They know the wart on the hand at once for a witch's nipple; they drove the old woman, in her shift as she was, out into the snow with sticks, beating her old carcass as far as the edge of the forest, and pelted her with stones until she fell dead. (p. 211)

This scene does not invite readers to share vicariously in the grandmother's terror. It invites readers to feel indignation at injustice and wanton cruelty. If readers accept the role Carter tacitly assigns to them, then they can feel intellectually superior to the populace and morally superior to both the populace and the psychopathic child protagonist. They do not share the perspective of any character. Instead, they form a community of feeling with the author and with other readers.

In its full flowering, a poststructuralist way of thinking implies a utopian worldview in which violence is merely a product of moral and intellectual failure (Carroll et al. 2012, pp. 160–161). In the world of the classic fairy tales, in contrast, violence is a natural outcome of ineradicable conflicts. No form of violence is more basic or more common, across the whole animal kingdom, than the conflict between predators and prey.

Violence in King Lear

Like Carter's "Werewolf," Shakespeare's *King Lear* reworks an old tale; and like Carter, Shakespeare creates a circle of privileged understanding between himself and his audience—an understanding greater than that of any character in the play. Unlike Carter, though, Shakespeare does not stand apart from his characters. He feels with them and is, thus, able to evoke their inner lives—their inmost thoughts and emotions. No one character is able to take in the full scope of meaning in the story, but some characters are in close touch with the values that Shakespeare expects to share with his audience. Those values tie in closely with what Buss calls the core features of human nature, especially the bonds of family.

King Lear has many characters and a fast-moving, complicated plot. Before further interpretive comment, it would be helpful to identify the main characters, describe the setting, and give a summary of the action.

The Main Characters

King Lear's family and associates

Goneril, Lear's oldest daughter, married to the Duke of Albany
Regan, Lear's second daughter, married to the Duke of Cornwall
Cordelia, Lear's youngest daughter, married to the King of France
The Earl of Kent, a loyal retainer
The Fool, Lear's court jester
Oswald, Goneril's servant, killed by Edgar

The Earl of Gloucester's family

Edgar, product of a lawful union, Gloucester's legitimate son and heir,
Edmund, an illegitimate son, sought in marriage, ultimately, by both Goneril and Regan

The Historical Setting

Historical period is notoriously vague in *King Lear*. The source story is set in a pre-Christian era. Except for one glancing reference to God in the singular, Shakespeare's characters refer only to pagan deities. However, the ranks, titles, military accoutrements, and matters of daily life depicted or mentioned in the play are more appropriate to the sixteenth century than to a barbarous British antiquity. By blurring historical period while simultaneously invoking multitudinous images of nature, animals, and the human body, Shakespeare directs attention away from any culturally specific setting and directs it instead toward human universals—toward physical sensations (especially pain), basic motives, basic emotions, intimate family relationships, and elementary principles of social organization. (On the animal imagery, see Bradley 2007, pp. 244–245; Holloway 1961, pp. 80–84; Knight 1949, pp. 205–211; Spurgeon 1930, p. 342.)

A Summary of the Action

Despite moments of humor and tenderness, the dominant emotions in *King Lear* are rage, resentment, vindictiveness, fear, jealousy, hatred, outrage, anguish, remorse, and grief. Betrayal and cruelty dominate the action, which centers on the disintegration of two families, those of King Lear and the Earl of Gloucester. By the end of the play, Lear and all three of his adult daughters are dead. One daughter poisons the other and then commits suicide. Gloucester and one of his sons is dead, one brother having sought the life of the other and then been killed by the other. Along the way, other lives are swallowed up in this vortex of family violence. The play concludes in a battle and its aftermath. In the final scene, the stage is littered with corpses, including those of Gloucester's second son and all the members of Lear's family.

At the beginning of the story, Lear is more than 80 years old and becoming mentally infirm, liable to fits of reckless and impulsive behavior. He proposes to divide his kingdom into three parts, giving one part to each of his adult daughters, Goneril, Regan, and Cordelia. He plans to retire and live with Cordelia, his youngest and most beloved. In a freak of fancy, he subjects the three daughters to a love test. Each is to outvie the others in declaring their love for him. The two oldest daughters, Goneril and Regan, flatter him shamelessly, declaring they love him more than life itself. Cordelia says only that she loves him in the measure and quality appropriate to their filial relationship. Lear foolishly believes the older daughters, or at least enjoys their flattery, and he flies into senile rage over Cordelia's "plainness" of speech. He disinherits her and declares he will alternate between living with his two older daughters, transferring to them all his power and wealth but stipulating that he will keep a hundred knights as retainers, his "train." The Earl of Kent, a loyal and honest follower, tries to intervene and prevent the folly. Lear banishes him. The King of France elects to marry Cordelia without a dowry, and they leave for France.

While this main plot is being set in motion, the subplot also gets started. Edmund, the bastard son of Gloucester, tricks his father into believing that the legitimate son, Edgar, wishes to murder Gloucester so as to acquire his title and property before the old man dies a natural death. Gloucester puts out a writ on Edgar's life, who escapes by disguising himself as a mad beggar. Gloucester says he will make Edmund his heir.

Lear begins his sojourn with Goneril, who quickly strips him of power, treats him contemptuously, and demands that he reduce the number of his followers. Enraged, Lear invokes the gods to curse Goneril with sterility and leaves to go live with Regan. To announce his arrival at Regan's, he sends Kent, who has disguised himself and become one of Lear's followers. To avoid receiving Lear, Regan and Cornwall leave their home and go to visit the Earl of Gloucester. Lear follows them there. Before Lear arrives, Kent, in disguise, meets Goneril's servant Oswald and attacks him. Cornwall has Kent put in the stocks, an outrage against Lear's dignity.

When Lear and his two eldest daughters are together at Gloucester's, the daughters join together in stripping him of the rest of his followers. They mock and humiliate him. Again enraged, and beginning to lose his wits, Lear runs out into the heath in the midst of a violent thunderstorm, accompanied only by his court jester and the disguised Kent. They come across Gloucester's son Edgar, disguised as a mad beggar. Lear, by now fully deranged, has a long dialogue with the mad beggar.

Cornwall, Regan, and Goneril have shut their gates and have issued a declaration that anyone giving aid to Lear will be executed. Gloucester nonetheless secretly leads Lear to shelter. He also confides in his illegitimate son Edmund that he has received a secret message that Cordelia is returning to England with an army to rescue her father. Edmund turns the letter over to Cornwall, who gouges out Gloucester's eyes. When one of Cornwall's servants tries to stop Cornwall from gouging out Gloucester's second eye, the servant and Cornwall fight with swords. The servant is killed but wounds Cornwall, who later dies from the wound. Gloucester, blinded, is set free. His legitimate son Edgar, disguised as the beggar, leads him toward Dover, where Cordelia's army is landing. Gloucester now knows that Edmund has betrayed him and also that Edgar had been falsely accused. Overcome with despair and remorse, he attempts to commit suicide but is prevented by Edgar. Later, after Edgar reveals his identity, Gloucester dies, shattered physically and emotionally.

Goneril's husband Albany is mild-tempered and morally sensitive. He severely disapproves of the way Goneril has persecuted her father. He nonetheless gathers an army to defend England from Cordelia's army. Both Goneril and Regan (now a widow) are sexually attracted to Edmund. Goneril sends a letter to Edmund suggesting that he should murder Albany, thus making her a widow, and then marry her. Oswald, Goneril's servant, is carrying the letter when he comes across Gloucester, wandering on the heath, and tries to kill him to gain favor with Goneril and Regan. Edgar kills Oswald instead, finds Goneril's letter, and gives it to Albany, as proof of Goneril's treachery.

Cordelia and Lear lose the battle. Edmund secretly orders a soldier to murder them in prison. Goneril, jealous of Regan and determined to prevent her from marrying Edmund, poisons her. Edgar appears, challenges Edmund to single combat, and mortally wounds him. Albany produces Goneril's letter revealing her plot against his life. When confronted, she stabs herself to death. Edmund, before dying, discloses his command to have Lear and Cordelia executed. The soldier has already hanged Cordelia and has in turn been killed by Lear. Lear dies in grief over Cordelia's body.

Action Movies, Tragedy, and the Adaptive Function of Literature

To narrow down the way violence works specifically in *King Lear,* we can compare it to the way violence works in action movies. In action movies, as in "Little Red Riding Hood," the audience is expected to identify with the protagonist and to experience vicariously the pleasure of triumphant self-assertion. The victims of violence are reduced to the status of automatons, little more than animated targets. In *King Lear,* the audience is invited to see into the inner lives even of antagonists, and empathy for the protagonists involves more suffering than pleasure. Violence gives expression to emotional stress, and the consequences of violence, practical and emotional, are carried through to their necessary conclusions.

Action movies typically induce a contraction in sympathy. Tragedies like *King Lear*, in contrast, typically induce an expansion in compassionate understanding. When Lear is cast out into the storm, deprived of all social standing and power, he recognizes the plight of "Poor naked wretches" who have no protection from the elements (Shakespeare 1997, 3.4.28). Gloucester, after he is blinded, takes comfort in the thought that his misfortune will benefit a mad beggar. Edgar, betrayed and hunted, describes himself as a man whom sorrow has made "pregnant to good pity" (4.6.219). These statements are made by Shakespeare's characters; they are not his own direct pronouncements. Nonetheless, we can say with confidence that the ethos of the play—Shakespeare's own ethos—includes a sense of universal human compassion.

Action movies are like pornography. They are fantasies designed to simulate pleasurable sensations (Ellis and Symons 1990; Pinker 1997; Salmon 2003). Tragedy does not simulate pleasurable sensations. It does exactly the opposite. Why do audiences willingly endure simulations of painful experience? To answer that question, one must almost necessarily invoke the idea that literature and its oral antecedents serve an adaptive function: they help humans organize motives and emotions and, thus, direct behavior in adaptively functional ways (Boyd 2005; Carroll 2008b, pp. 119–128, 2008c, pp. 349–368, 2012a; Dissanayake 2000; Dutton 2009; Salmon and Symons 2004; Tooby and Cosmides 2001). In lay terms, literature and its oral antecedents help provide a sense of meaning and purpose to behavior. Humans have a unique need for meaning and purpose because their behavior, unlike behavior in animals of other species, involves flexible choice among competing alternative scenarios. All human action takes place within imaginative structures that include past and future, locating present action in relation to an awareness of a continuously developing individual identity (McAdams 2008, 2011). That sense of identity includes internal conflicts and concerns, relations to other people (both living and dead), relations to nature, and relations to whatever spiritual forces people might imagine to exist. Tragedy puts the heaviest possible pressure on the human need to find meaning and purpose in life.

Normative Universals and the Responses of Readers

King Lear contains a great deal of violence and cruelty, but it does not invite its audience to participate vicariously in the enjoyment of sheer malevolence. Some readers with a sadistic streak might thrill with pleasure when Cornwall sneers at Gloucester's eye, "Out, vile jelly,/Where is thy lustre now?" (3.7.82–83). However, such readers would be responding in an emotional key out of harmony with the larger emotional orchestration of the play. When Cornwall's servant takes up a sword to defend Gloucester, and is killed, there is no voice in the scene to honor his heroism. Cornwall dismisses him with the utmost contempt. "Throw this slave/Upon the dunghill" (3.7.95–96). A reader who is attuned to the larger emotional orchestration in the play will nonetheless stand apart from Cornwall, registering the values of courage and decency that correspond to the sympathies activated in the play as a whole.

In anticipating emotional responses to the action of his play, Shakespeare could confidently depend on dispositions that are so basic a part of human nature that they appear in all known cultures (Brown 1991). For forms of value that have universal, cross-cultural force, we can use the term "normative" universals. Normative universals include horror at the murder of kinsfolk, respect for family obligations, and appreciation for honesty in social relations.

When Goneril and Regan persecute their father and then seek his death, they violate moral dispositions deeply rooted in human nature. When Goneril poisons Regan out of jealousy, most readers can only be appalled at the quality of mind she reveals—the coldness of heart, the murderous viciousness of the sibling rivalry, and the absence of any moral component in her estimate of what makes a man desirable. Her willingness to poison a sister is concordant with her passion for a man willing to murder his brother. Though highly articulate, Goneril seems scarcely human. Gloucester and Albany are right to characterize her as a savage beast. In contrast, when Cordelia and Kent remain loyal to Lear despite his senile rages, and when Edgar remains loyal to his father despite his father's attempt to have him executed, Shakespeare can anticipate that most of his audience will resonate to their motives.

Edmund, Goneril, Regan, and Cornwall speak hypocritically, using honorable words to characterize morally depraved behavior. The use of honorable words reveals their awareness that their actions violate public norms. Indeed, they remark, toward the end of the play, that their rule has excited widespread public unrest. The public that dislikes both depravity and hypocrisy includes not only their contemporaries but also most readers over the past four centuries. By definition, true normative universals transcend variations in culturally specific systems of value. Shakespeare could not have anticipated the cultural changes that would take place over a period of four centuries. Nonetheless, because he appeals to normative universals, for modern readers, his anticipations of audience response continue to operate as he intended.

The normative universals that make readers disgusted with the antagonists have, of course, a converse effect in responses to Cordelia, Kent, Edgar, and the Fool. Those characters remain "true" in both social commitment and manner of speech—loyal to the people they love and honest in their dealings with others. Shakespeare can depend on his audience to respond with admiration to those qualities.

The Largest Frame of Meaning in *King Lear*

No character in *King Lear* takes in the whole tragic vision Shakespeare shares with his implied audience. Two factors limit the scope of understanding in the characters: the action is too broad and complex for any one character to be involved in all of it; and many characters adopt religious or metaphysical ideas out of keeping with Shakespeare's naturalistic perspective. Like those characters, many of Shakespeare's critics, even among the most astute, have sought consolation through metaphysical or religious ideas that are not in accord with the action of the play. By providing a thematic framework adequate to the whole scope of the play, an evolutionary perspective can help us approximate more closely to Shakespeare's own encompassing vision of human life.

From an evolutionary perspective, life is a mechanical and blindly developing process. More organisms are born in any generation than can survive and reproduce; organisms vary in the traits conducing to survival and reproduction; the organisms that possess more favorable variations reproduce at a higher rate and also transmit their more favorable characteristics to their offspring. This simple causal sequence entails no cosmic purpose for the evolution of life. Nor does it entail a divine source for human motives and values. From an evolutionary perspective, if we wish to justify ethical values, we can look for justification only within a purely human context.

At one time or another, Lear, Kent, Edgar, Albany, and Gloucester all affirm that human lives are governed by divine justice. For instance, on hearing that Cornwall has died from the wound given him by his servant, Albany declares, "This shows you are above,/You justicers, that these our nether crimes/So speedily can venge!" (4.2.79–81). All such proclamations generalize beyond the facts of the play. The antagonists unleash violence that rebounds lethally against themselves, but that same violence takes the lives of Cordelia, Lear, Gloucester, Cornwall's servant, and probably the Fool (he disappears after the third act). Kent, too, is so shattered that he anticipates death. Among the major characters, only Albany and Edgar remain standing. A naturalistic view of human social relations can easily enough make sense of these outcomes. A providential worldview cannot. Shakespeare understands the human need to project human values into the cosmic frame of things, but he evidently does not himself require that basis for moral judgment.

Since the end of the eighteenth century, few readers have tried to defend the idea that rewards and punishments correspond to merits and faults. Modern readers have, though, softened the painfulness of *King Lear* by emphasizing themes of redemption—Christian or quasi-Christian ideas that take two forms: either the idea that through suffering characters achieve a sublime vision of a transcendent spiritual order, or the idea that a character like Cordelia gives evidence of that spiritual order (Bradley 2007; Dowden 1918; Knight 1949). (For critical commentaries on such readings, see Everett 1960; Foakes 2004, pp. 45–54; Vickers 1993, Chap. 7.)Shakespeare himself is more tough-minded than that. Gloucester is talked out of committing suicide but dies from stress and shock. Lear has a reconciliation with Cordelia, acknowledges that he has been foolish and unjust, and asks for forgiveness. He nonetheless dies in torment. Regan has no moment of moral transformation. She pursues a course of lust and viciousness and then is poisoned. Goneril defies all moral judgment—"the laws are mine" (5.3.156) and then stabs herself. Kent, crushed by the death of Cordelia and Lear, is unable to bear life longer. Edmund, as he is dying, concurs with Edgar's delusional belief in poetic justice. He tries unsuccessfully to save Lear and Cordelia from the executioner, but few readers would argue that this one moral impulse gives evidence of a transcendent spiritual order. Despite having proclaimed a faith in divine justice, Edgar and Albany find little reason to rejoice in the final scene. They are humbled and subdued amid the destruction.

True tragedy does not absolve the grief produced by destructive human impulses; but neither is it nihilistic. Nihilism renders human concerns trivial and insignificant. Tragedy makes us feel their weight and significance.

Human Life History and Moral Judgment

Though appealing to no higher spiritual order, Shakespeare tacitly affirms an ethos of domestic and social order grounded in a sane understanding of systemic relations in human life history. The central theme of the play is announced in Cordelia's first speech to Lear, refusing his demand for flattery:

> I love your majesty
> According to my bond, no more nor less....
> You have begot me, bred me, loved me: I
> Return those duties back as are right fit,
> Obey you, love you, and most honour you.
> Why have my sisters husbands, if they say
> They love you all? Haply, when I shall wed,
> That lord whose hand must take my plight shall carry
> Half my love with him, half my care and duty. (1.1.92–102)

Had Cordelia thought a little further ahead, she might have added that once she had children, she would have to further subdivide her love, leaving a third, or perhaps less than a third, for Lear. She could also have added something about her engagement with the wider social world. Though her statement is schematic and incomplete, Kent is right to praise it for justness of thought. Cordelia, here, enunciates the central principle that is violated in the play: due proportions in the phases and offices of life: the balance in attention and concern distributed among parents and children, marital partners, and the larger community (Holloway 1961, pp. 94–95).

Cordelia is not of course an evolutionist; nor is Shakespeare. They are both intuitive folk psychologists. Even so, the wisdom of their moral sense depends on their intuitive insight into human life history. The significance of the violence in *King Lear* depends on normative values rooted in human life history. The destructive violence inflicted by the protagonists takes its evil cast from the breaking of family bonds integral with the logic of human reproduction. The defensive violence of the protagonists takes its moral coloring from a commitment to family bonds and the extension of those bonds to a wider social network.

Though four centuries old, and set within systems of belief and social organization long obsolete, *King Lear* can still speak to modern audiences. In becoming modern, humans have not escaped from human life history. Their passions and their moral judgments are still rooted in the reproductive cycle. The meaning they give to violence now, as always, can be traced back to the core concerns of human life.

Conclusion

"Little Red Riding Hood" and *King Lear* are both classics. They have had enduring appeal and have crossed many boundaries of language and culture. Classic works of literature typically penetrate below the surface of conventional beliefs and evoke passions embedded in ancient, evolved features of human nature. Violence is not absolutely indispensable for evoking those passions, but a great many works that we identify as classics do in fact contain lethal violence (Carroll 2012b). Conflict is inherent in life and in human nature. Violence pushes conflict to its extreme and, thus, reveals the underlying forces that govern our lives. We read great literature chiefly because we feel a compelling need to understand our own experience and the experience of others.

Carter's "Werewolf" is not yet a classic. Only time can make that distinction. One can speculate, though, about how well the story will wear over time. I think it unlikely that Carter will endure, even in the small way that classic short stories have endured—stories like those of Poe, Maupassant, or Hans Christian Andersen. Carter's story does not transport us to the state of mind of medieval people. The characters in her story are thrust off into an alien distance, condemned and despised for their lack of modern enlightenment. We are thus restricted, while reading Carter, to her own mind, and that mind is too self-regarding and self-congratulating to take us deep into our shared humanity. Works that endure typically do not restrict their imaginative scope to contemporary ideological constructs nor aim chiefly at flattering the vanity of their audience.

Because humans have evolved as social animals, great literature almost necessarily appeals to normative universals grounded in positive social relationships. Since those relationships always involve conflict, and the ultimate forms of conflict involve violence, violence can serve as a touchstone for evaluating literature. Plays and stories that have most fully satisfied the imaginative needs of most readers register the tensions that sometimes erupt into violence, but they also encompass those tensions within a generous understanding of human nature, including the bonds of family and friendship.

King Lear moves one step beyond those core features of human nature and takes in also our need to make sense of the world. Though Shakespeare does not share the belief in divine justice to which some of his characters appeal, his scope, like theirs, takes in the whole of nature. For those of us who are atheists or agnostics, Shakespeare's naturalistic worldview has a special value. In *King Lear,* he gives evidence that one can accept the vast bleak indifference of the cosmos and still feel the force and necessity of intimate human connections.

References

Baumeister, R. F., Masicampo, E. J., & Vohs, K. D. (2011). Do conscious thoughts cause behavior? *Annual review of psychology*, *62*, 331–361. doi: 10.1146/annurev.psych.093008.131126

Bettelheim, B. (2010). *The uses of enchantment: The meaning and importance of fairy tales*. New York: Vintage.

Boehm, C. (1999). *Hierarchy in the forest: The evolution of egalitarian behavior*. Cambridge, MA: Harvard University Press.

Bolte, J., & Polivka, J. (1963). *Anmerkungen zu den Kinder- und Hausmarchen der Brüder Grimm* (2. unveranderte Aufl. ed.). Hildesheim: G. Olms.

Boyd, B. (2005). Evolutionary theories of art. In J. Gottschall & D. S. Wilson (Eds.), *The literary animal: Evolution and the nature of narrative* (pp. 147–176). Evanston, IL: Northwestern University Press.
Boyd, B. (2006). Getting it all wrong: Bioculture critiques cultural critique. *American Scholar*, *75*(4), 18–30.
Boyd, B. (2009). *On the origin of stories: Evolution, cognition, and fiction.* Cambridge, MA: Harvard University Press.
Boyd, B., Carroll, J., & Gottschall, J. (Eds.). (2010). *Evolution, literature, and film: A reader.* New York: Columbia University Press.
Bradley, A. C. (2007). *Shakespearean tragedy: Lectures on Hamlet, Othello, King Lear, Macbeth* (4th ed.). Basingstoke England: Palgrave Macmillan.
Brown, D. E. (1991). *Human universals.* Philadelphia: Temple University Press.
Brownmiller, S. (1975). *Against our will: Men, women, and rape.* New York: Fawcett Columbine.
Buss, A. (1997). Evolutionary perspectives on personality traits. In R. Hogan, J. A. Johnson, & S. Briggs (Eds.), *Handbook of personality Psychology* (pp. 346–366). San Diego: Academic.
Buss, D. M. (2005). *The murderer next door: Why the mind is designed to kill.* New York: Penguin.
Carroll, J. (1995). *Evolution and literary theory.* Columbia: University of Missouri Press.
Carroll, J. (2004). *Literary Darwinism: Evolution, human nature, and literature.* New York: Routledge.
Carroll, J. (2008a). The cuckoo's history: Human nature in wuthering heights. *Philosophy and Literature*, *32*(2), 241–257.
Carroll, J. (2008b). An evolutionary paradigm for literary study. *Style*, *42*(2–3), 103–135.
Carroll, J. (2008c). Rejoinder to the responses. *Style*, *42*(2–3), 308–411.
Carroll, J. (2010). Three scenarios for literary Darwinism. *New Literary History*, *41*(1), 53–67.
Carroll, J. (2011). *Reading human nature: Literary Darwinism in theory and practice.* Albany: State University of New York Press.
Carroll, J. (2012a). The adaptive function of the arts: Alternative evolutionary hypotheses. In C. Gansel & D. Vanderbeke (Eds.), *Telling stories: Literature and evolution* (pp. 50–63). Berlin: De Gruyter.
Carroll, J. (2012b). The extremes of conflict in literature: Violence, homicide, and war. In T. K. Shackelford & V. Weekes-Shackelford (Eds.), *The oxford handbook of evolutionary perspectives on violence, homicide, and war* (pp. 413–434). Oxford: Oxford University Press.
Carroll, J. (2012c). The truth about fiction: Biological reality and imaginary lives. *Style*, *46*(2), 129–160.
Carroll, J. (in press). *Correcting for The Corrections: A Darwinian critique of a Foucauldian Novel.* Style.
Carroll, J., Gottschall, J., Johnson, J. A., & Kruger, D. (2012). *Graphing Jane Austen: The evolutionary basis of literary meaning.* New York: Palgrave Macmillan.
Carter, A. (1995). The werewolf. In *Burning your boats: The collected short stories/Angela Carter* (pp. 210–211). New York: Penguin.
Chiappe, D., & MacDonald, K. (2005). The evolution of domain-general mechanisms in intelligence and learning. *Journal of General Psychology*, *132*(1), 5–40.
Cochran, G., & Harpending, H. (2009). *The 10,000 year explosion: How civilization accelerated human evolution.* New York: Basic Books.
Crick, J. (2009). Introduction. In J. Crick (Ed.), *Selected tales [of the brothers Grimm]* (pp. xiii–xlii). Oxford: Oxford University Press.
Culler, J. D. (2011). *Literary theory: A very short introduction* (2nd ed.). Oxford: Oxford University Press.
Dissanayake, E. (2000). *Art and intimacy: How the arts began.* Seattle: University of Washington Press.
Dowden, E. (1918). *Shakspere: A critical study of his mind and art* (3rd ed.). New York: Harper.
Dundes, A. (1989a). Interpreting "Little Red Riding Hood" psychoanalytically. In A. Dundes (Ed.), *Little red riding hood: A casebook* (pp. 192–236). Madison: University of Wisconsin Press.
Dundes, A. (1989b). *Little Red Riding Hood: A casebook.* Madison: University of Wisconsin Press.

Dutton, D. (2009). *The art instinct: Beauty, pleasure, and human evolution*. New York: Bloomsbury Press.
Ellis, B. J., & Symons, D. (1990). Sex differences in sexual fantasy: An evolutionary psychological approach. *The Journal of Sex Research, 27*(4), 527–555.
Everett, B. (1960). The New *King Lear*. *Critical Quarterly, 2*(4), 325–339.
Foakes, R. A. (2004). *Hamlet versus Lear: Cultural politics and Shakespeare's Art*. Cambridge, UK: Cambridge University Press.
Foucault, M. (1977). *Language, counter-memory, practice: Selected essays and interviews* (D. F. Bouchard & S. Simon, Trans.). Ithaca, NY: Cornell University Press.
Geary, D. C. (2005). *The origin of mind: Evolution of brain, cognition, and general intelligence*. Washington, DC: American Psychological Association.
Gottschall, J. (2012). *The storytelling animal: How stories make us human*. Boston: Houghton Mifflin Harcourt.
Grimm, J., & Grimm, W. (1998–2011). Little Red Cap (D. L. Ashliman, Trans.). In D. L. Ashliman (Ed.), The Grimm Brothers' children and household tales (Grimms' fairy tales). http://www.pitt.edu/~dash/grimmtales.html.
Grimm, J., & Grimm, W. (2009). Preface to the second edition of *Grimms' Fairy Tales* (1819). In J. Crick (Ed.), *Selected tales* (pp. 3–10). Oxford: Oxford University Press.
Grimm, J., & Grimm, W. (2012). Preface to volume 2 of the first edition of the children's stories and household tales (1812) (M. Tatar, Trans.). In M. Tatar (Ed.), *The annotated brothers Grimm* (bicentennial ed., pp. 442–462). New York: Norton.
Hawkins, J., with Sandra Blakeslee. (2004). *On intelligence*. New York: Times Books.
Hill, K. (2007). Evolutionary biology, cognitive adaptations, and human culture. In S. W. Gangestad & J. A. Simpson (Eds.), *The evolution of mind: Fundamental questions and controversies* (pp. 348–356). New York: Guilford.
Holloway, J. (1961). *The story of the night: studies in Shakespeare's major tragedies*. London,: Routledge & Kegan Paul.
Kenrick, D. T. (2011). *Sex, murder, and the meaning of life: A psychologist investigates how evolution, cognition, and complexity are revolutionizing our view of human nature*. New York: Basic Books.
Knight, G. W. (1949). *The wheel of fire: Interpretations of Shakespearian tragedy with three new essays* (4th ed.). London: Methuen.
Kurzban, R., & Neuberg, S. (2005). Managing ingroup and outgroup relationships. In D. M. Buss (Ed.), *The handbook of evolutionary psychology* (pp. 653–675). Hoboken, NJ: Wiley.
Lumsden, C. J., & Wilson, E. O. (1981). *Genes, mind, and culture: The coevolutionary process*. Cambridge, MA: Harvard University Press.
Mar, R. A., & Oatley, K. (2008). The function of fiction is the abstraction and simulation of social experience. *Perspectives on Psychological Science, 3*(3), 173–192.
McAdams, D. P. (2008). Personal narratives and the life story. In O. P. John, R. W. Robins, & L. A. Pervin (Eds.), *Handbook of personality: theory and research* (3rd ed., pp. 242–262). New York: Guilford.
McAdams, D. P. (2011). Life narratives. In K. L. Fingerman, C. A. Berg, J. Smith, & T. C. Antonucci (Eds.), *Handbook of life-span development* (pp. 509–610). New York: Springer.
McEwan, I. (2005). Literature, science, and human nature. In J. Gottschall & D. S. Wilson (Eds.), *The literary animal: Evolution and the nature of narrative* (pp. 5–19). Evanston, IL: Northwestern University Press.
Menand, L. (2005). Dangers within and without. In R. G. Feal (Ed.), *Profession 2005* (pp. 10–17). New York: Modern Language Association of America.
Muehlenbein, M. P., & Flinn, M. V. (2011). Patterns and processes of human life history evolution. In T. Flatt & A. Heyland (Eds.), *Mechanisms of life history evolution: The genetics and physiology of life history traits and trade-offs* (pp. 153–168). Oxford: Oxford University Press.
Perrault, C. (2009). *The complete fairy tales* (C. J. Betts, Trans.). Oxford: Oxford University Press.
Pinker, S. (1997). *How the mind works*. New York: Norton.

Richerson, P. J., & Boyd, R. (2005). *Not by genes alone: How culture transformed human evolution*. Chicago: University of Chicago Press.
Roth, I. (Ed.). (2007). *Imaginative minds*. Oxford: Oxford University Press.
Rushdie, S. (1997). Introduction. *Burning your boats: The collected short stories/Angela Carter* (pp. ix–xiv). New York: Penguin.
Salmon, C. (2003). *Warrior lovers: Erotic fiction, evolution and female sexuality*. New Haven, CT: Yale University Press.
Salmon, C., & Symons, D. (2004). Slash fiction and human mating psychology. *Journal of Sex Research, 41*(1), 94–100.
Scalise Sugiyama, M. (2001). New science, old myth: An evolutionary critique of the Oedipal paradigm. *Mosaic, 34*(1), 121–136.
Scalise Sugiyama, M. (2005). Reverse-engineering narrative: Evidence of special design. In J. Gottschall & D. S. Wilson (Eds.), *The literary animal: Evolution and the nature of narrative* (pp. 177–196). Evanston, IL: Northwestern University Press.
Shakespeare, W. (1997). *King Lear*. London: Arden Shakespeare.
Spurgeon, C. (1930). *Leading motives in the imagery of Shakespeare's tragedies*. London: Oxford university press.
Sterelny, K. (2003). *Thought in a hostile world: The evolution of human cognition*. Malden, MA: Blackwell.
Sugiyama, M. S. (2004). Predation, narration, and adaptation: "Little Red Riding Hood" revisited. *Interdisciplinary Literary Studies, 5*(2), 110–129.
Sugiyama, M. S. (2006). Lions and tigers and bears: Predators as a folklore universal. In H.-E. Friedrich, F. Jannidis, U. Klein, K. Mellmann, S. Metzger, & M. Willems (Eds.), *Anthropology and Social history: Heuristics in the Study of Literature* (pp. 319–331). Paderborn, Germany: Mentis.
Tatar, M. (2012). The magic of fairy tales. In M. Tatar (Ed.), *The annotated brothers Grimm* (bicentennial ed., pp. 463–481). New York: Norton.
Tomasello, M., Carpenter, M., Call, J., Behne, T., & Moll, H. (2005). Understanding and sharing intentions: The origins of cultural cognition. *Behavioral and Brain Sciences, 28*(5), 675–691.
Tooby, J., & Cosmides, L. (1992). The psychological foundations of culture. In J. H. Barkow, L. Cosmides, & J. Tooby (Eds.), *The adapted mind: Evolutionary psychology and the generation of culture*. (pp. 19–136). New York: Oxford University Press.
Tooby, J., & Cosmides, L. (2001). Does beauty build adapted minds? Toward an evolutionary theory of aesthetics, fiction and the arts. *Substance: A Review of Theory and Literary Criticism, 30*(1/2), 6–27.
Vickers, B. (1993). *Appropriating Shakespeare: contemporary critical quarrels*. New Haven: Yale University Press.
Wilson, E. O. (1998). *Consilience: The unity of knowledge*. New York: Knopf.
Zipes, J. (1993). *The trials & tribulations of little red riding hood* (2nd ed.). New York: Routledge.

Chapter 4
Evolutionary Perspectives on Child Welfare Law

David J. Herring

Introduction

Children confront a risk of harm at the hands of their adult caretakers. The potential harm could manifest in three primary forms of violence: physical abuse; neglect or emotional abuse that threatens serious physical harm; and sexual abuse.

Public child welfare systems and child welfare laws are designed to address the risk of violence faced by children. Although preventive approaches exist, the primary legal approach is reactive. The law presumes that a child's adult caretakers are at least minimally adequate parents. Thus, child welfare laws allow the state to intervene to protect children only after there is reason to believe that a particular child has suffered some form of harm and is likely to suffer additional harm.[1] In addition, once a child is victimized, public child welfare systems seek to secure the child's well-being. The system must construct the child's living situation in a way that protects the child from further violence and produces acceptable outcomes in terms of the child's development. Each of these two facets of the child welfare endeavor places a premium on the assessment and prediction of human behavior.

This chapter describes how evolutionary theory and behavioral biology research provide insights that are useful in examining, critiquing, and reconstructing child welfare laws, policies, and practices. Together, these concepts and the related research have produced knowledge of behavioral tendencies. Several of these tendencies have direct implications for the prediction of violence against children and for the effort to secure child well-being.

This chapter provides two primary examples that illustrate the usefulness of evolutionary theory and research in this area. Each example provides a description of a particular child welfare problem confronted in the field and of the current systemic

[1] *See generally* Santosky v. Kramer, 455 U.S. 745 (1982); Smith v. Organization of Foster Families, 431 U.S. 816 (1977).

D. J. Herring (✉)
School of Law University of New Mexico Albuquerque, NM 87131, USA
e-mail: herring@law.unm.edu

T. K. Shackelford, R. D. Hansen (eds.), *The Evolution of Violence*, Evolutionary Psychology, DOI 10.1007/978-1-4614-9314-3_4,

approach to the problem. This chapter then explains the relevant evolutionary concepts and behavioral research, discusses the relevant empirical research, and delineates the implications for child welfare law, policy, and practice. Finally, this chapter explores additional areas worthy of inquiry based on the relevant evolutionary concepts and emerging research.

Risk Assessment: The Prediction of Violence Against Children

Public child welfare agencies have adopted various risk assessment tools to predict the risk of child maltreatment in a particular family situation. These tools usually take the form of a checklist that an agency worker can complete in investigating alleged maltreatment. There are two basic types of checklists. The first includes items that practitioners deem relevant based on their experiences in the field and that often call for subjective assessments (e.g., whether past incidents of abuse were "isolated" or "intermittent"). These consensus-based checklists are not supported by rigorous empirical studies (Austin et al. 2005; Baird and Wagner 2000). The second type includes items that researchers have found to be correlated with future child maltreatment (e.g., whether there was a prior injury to a child from abuse or neglect). Most child welfare officials and scholars consider these actuarial-based checklists to be superior (Austin et al. 2005; Gambrill and Shlonsky 2000). However, the development of these checklists has proven difficult and expensive (Knoke and Trocme 2005; Rycus and Hughes 2003).

Those attempting to develop research-based risk assessment tools face at least one major difficulty—they lack a conceptual framework that allows them to identify factors that are worthy of examination (Knoke and Trocme 2005). Much of the current research is conducted based on the fortuity of a data element being included in an administrative data set constructed for administrative purposes or in a longitudinal study data set built on an unfocused or incoherent theory of potential risk factors. The result is a broad, largely unguided search for correlations within a massive jumble of complex data. To date, this process has resulted in weak risk assessment tools that fail to predict maltreatment accurately (Knoke and Trocme 2005). Evolutionary theory and behavioral research have the potential to address this difficulty and contribute to the construction of valid and reliable risk assessment tools.

Example #1—Children Living with Unrelated Adults

Evolutionary theory indicates that a child residing with a genetically unrelated adult faces an increased likelihood of child maltreatment. This situation is common for children in our society (Pew Research Center 2011), and a significant portion of children who enter the child welfare system reside with an unrelated adult such as a stepparent, a term that includes a genetic mother's boyfriend. Child welfare laws do not have specific provisions that address the situation of a child living with an unrelated adult. Child welfare agency policies and risk assessment tools fail to fully consider this situation. Although caseworkers often record data on each member of a child's household, their use of such data is largely unclear. In practice, judges tend to focus on the genetic parent or parents without much attention to other adults unless there are indications of domestic violence within the household. Moreover, although agency caseworkers may recognize the risk posed by an unrelated adult, they lack formal administrative or legal channels to address this potential risk.

The relevant evolutionary concepts begin with the widely accepted premise that there is selection for altruism toward offspring (Hamilton 1964). An individual who possesses this trait reaps reproductive benefits as long as the reproductive costs incurred in assisting the offspring are less than the reproductive benefits realized through the offspring (Hamilton 1964). For this calculation, reproductive costs include the reduction in parental resources available to invest in other offspring, including current and future offspring. Reproductive benefits consist of the reproductive success of the recipient of parental solicitude, discounted by the degree of relatedness. The degree of relatedness between parent and offspring is 50 %, meaning that there is a 50 % probability that the offspring and parent share a specific gene (Hamilton 1964). Thus, the reproductive benefits must be more than twice the reproductive costs for a trait of parental solicitude to be favored by natural selection. Because this condition was fulfilled in evolutionary environments, offspring altruism has evolved in humans (Trivers 1985).

A logical corollary to these concepts is that an individual gains nothing in terms of reproductive benefits by exhibiting altruism toward children who are not his or her genetic offspring. A reproductive cost incurred for the benefit of a child who is not genetically related to the altruist would constitute a net loss in terms of the altruist's reproductive success. Thus, a behavioral tendency for altruism toward all children has not evolved in humans (Jones 1997).

This distinction between genetic offspring and other children underlies an aspect of discriminative parental solicitude, one which predicts that an individual will invest much less in genetically unrelated children than in genetic offspring. Although an individual may invest in an unrelated child to achieve future reproductive benefits through the child's genetic parent (i.e., potential or current mate), it is likely that this investment will be less than that made in one's genetic child (Daly and Wilson 1998). This general prediction leads to several more specific predictions. For example, in his pathbreaking work concerning evolutionary analysis in law, Owen Jones addresses infanticide, discussing the predictions of discriminative parental solicitude theory. He notes that evolved behavioral predispositions may contribute to an unrelated adult causing the death of an infant, stating that

> An infant that must rely on the resources of an unrelated adult is somewhat more likely to die of neglect or to be killed by that adult, simply because, on average, the infant will not evoke the same solicitousness as would an offspring. Since *not* caring for infants is the default (or initial) evolved predisposition (in the absence of relatedness cues), the adult will on average be less tolerant, less willing to provide, and less protective than would the infant's own parents. (Jones 1997 at 1177)

Thus, evolutionary theory predicts that, at the extreme margins of adult caretaking behavior (i.e., infanticide), we will find that the percentage of unrelated adult caretakers who engage in violence is greater than the percentage of genetic parents who engage in violence.

Martin Daly and Margo Wilson had previously used this theoretical framework to formulate and test the hypothesis that the risk of maltreatment is higher within families that include a stepparent, with stepparent defined as "the coresiding partner of a (presumed) genetic parent, regardless of marital status" (Daly and Wilson 1988). Their research confirmed the hypothesis. In studies of fatal beatings of small children (newborn to 2 years), data from Canada revealed that the rate of child homicide for stepfathers was more than 120-fold greater than the rate for putative genetic fathers (Daly and Wilson 2001). Data from the USA indicated that newborn children up to 2 years of age face about a 100 times greater risk of being killed by a stepparent (Wilson et al. 1980). In terms of nonfatal abuse, they found that stepparents physically and sexually abuse children at a much higher rate than genetic parents (Daly and Wilson 1985; Wilson et al. 1980). Their research also indicated that rates of physical abuse by stepmothers and stepfathers are roughly equivalent, with rates for both far in excess of those for genetic parent households (Daly and Wilson 1981).

Subsequent studies support these findings. One study examined all fatal beatings in Missouri from 1992 through 1999 in which a child less than 5 years of age died as the result of injuries inflicted by a parent or caregiver. The researchers found that a child living in a household with an unrelated adult faced a 50 times greater risk of death than a child living only with a genetic parent (Schnitzer and Ewigman 2005).

Another study used a national database of criminal homicides maintained by the United States Federal Bureau of Investigation to examine homicides of children less than 5 years of age by parents or stepparents. Even though this database included only stepparents who were legally married to a genetic parent, the rate of child homicide for stepfathers was approximately 8 times greater than for genetic fathers. The rate for stepmothers was almost 3 times greater than that for genetic mothers (Weekes-Shackelford and Shackelford 2004).

A noteworthy study examined the characteristics of child maltreatment perpetrators in 126 fatality cases and compared them to a matched set of child maltreatment perpetrators in nonfatal cases. The researchers found that being a genetically unrelated caregiver is the strongest predictor of fatal child maltreatment. Perpetrators who were genetically unrelated to the child victim were almost 17 times more likely to commit a fatal assault compared to genetic parents (Yampolskaya et al. 2009).

Researchers have also examined the method used by the parent to kill the child. Stepfathers tend to beat and bludgeon the child victim, whereas genetic fathers tend to use relatively quick and painless methods, often followed by suicide (Daly and Wilson 1994; Weekes-Shackelford and Shackelford 2004). This difference may indicate that stepfathers have a higher level of animosity and resentment toward the child victims than genetic fathers. Another study indicated that this difference in method was even more pronounced for stepmothers in comparison to genetic mothers and that stepchildren were even more at risk if their stepparent had genetic offspring in the household (Harris et al. 2007).

One study examined unintentional fatalities of preschool-aged children in Australia, finding the risk of fatal injury was 2–15 times greater for stepchildren than for children from intact genetic families. The risk was greatest for drowning deaths, a type of unintentional death that may indicate a failure of a parent to supervise the child. The risk for children from single genetic parent households was not higher than that for intact genetic families, indicating that the factor that increases the risk of unintentional child fatality is the addition of an unrelated adult (Tooley et al. 2006).

Subsequent studies also support Daly and Wilson's findings related to nonfatal abuse. In one study of fatal abuse, the researchers' findings indicated that children killed by stepparents are more frequently subject to repeated abuse and neglect prior to their death than children killed by their genetic parents. Thus, the rate of maltreatment was higher in households that included an unrelated adult (Harris et al. 2007).

Several studies have examined nonfatal abuse directly. One study of male perpetrators of physical abuse in Bogota, Colombia found that stepfather status was associated with abuse (Klevens 2000). Another study examined all cases of child maltreatment in the Netherlands in 2005, finding that stepparent families evidenced elevated risks for child maltreatment (van IJzendoorn et al. 2009). Researchers in Brazil have studied whether the presence of a stepfather constituted a risk factor for physical abuse of children as reported by their mothers. Children with stepfathers had almost 3 times the risk for abuse as children in two genetic parent households (Alexandre et al. 2010). Interestingly, the mothers in many cases indicated that they were the abuser, not the stepfather. The researchers concluded that "Brazilian mothers professed to abuse their own children at substantially higher rates when their male partners were stepfathers to the focal child as compared to genetic fathers" (p. 959). These studies indicate that children face a heightened risk of violence in households that include stepparents.

This conclusion is further supported by studies that indicate discrimination against stepchildren that falls short of physical abuse. Several studies reveal that stepchildren in the USA receive less support than genetic children for higher education, regular medical care, and food, and that both parents and children express the view that stepparents' level of parental investment is lower than that of genetic parents (Case and Paxson 2001; Case et al. 2000; Zvoch 1999). Stepparents appear to manifest lower parental emotional investment, higher parental resentment, and higher parental jealousy, indicating the presence of stepparental antagonism (O'Connor and Boag 2010; Anderson et al. 1999).

In summary, research findings support the hypothesis that children living in households with unrelated adults face a higher risk of maltreatment. Although many genetically unrelated adults provide at least adequate care and invest heavily in the well-being of the children with whom they reside, the risk of violence is higher for children in stepparent households. Thus, one would reasonably be more concerned for children living with an unrelated adult than children living solely with a genetic parent or parents.

Child welfare law, policy, and practice is, in large part, a matter of prediction. For example, in determining whether a child can safely remain in a particular family home or must be removed to foster care, a caseworker, his or her supervisors, and eventually a judge must predict behavior within the family home. This is the essence of risk assessment, and the findings on the risk presented by stepparent care can contribute in this area.

Owen Jones has provided a long list of specific possibilities for the use of this new knowledge, noting that the implications extend throughout the child welfare process (Jones 1997). To begin, child welfare system personnel could train mandatory child abuse reporters to record the presence of an unrelated adult in the child's household. Child welfare intake workers could incorporate this information into their decision-making process, with households that include an unrelated adult more likely to be investigated further when all else is equal. During an investigation, caseworkers could use an actuarial risk assessment tool that properly scores the risk presented by an unrelated adult. Relatedly, child welfare agency administrators could work to develop and implement such a risk assessment tool, training caseworkers on how to score research-based risk factors (Yampolskaya 2009).

To be more concrete, caseworkers could consider the presence of an unrelated adult in making placement decisions for a specific child. In the early stages of a case, caseworkers are often called on to make relatively swift decisions on whether a child should remain in his or her current home or be placed in another home. In cases in which the presence of an unrelated adult presents a significant risk of harm to the child, a caseworker could request that the unrelated adult move out of the house. If the family refuses, the caseworker could offer the family in-home services that would allow the agency to monitor the home and the child so as to reduce the risk of harm to an acceptable level. If the family refuses such services, then the caseworker could seek a court order mandating such services or could seek court approval to place the child in a foster home.

If such a case proceeded to court, the judge could consider this risk factor in making decisions on the four essential legal issues. First, the judge must decide if the child welfare agency has made reasonable efforts to prevent removal of the child from the family home.[2] Thus, the judge could require the agency to work with the genetic parent to remove the unrelated adult rather than the child. Or the judge could mandate that the agency provide services that allow caseworkers to adequately monitor the household.

Second, if the judge finds that the agency has made reasonable efforts, he or she must determine whether removal of the child is warranted in light of the risks (Yampolskaya 2009). As the research indicates, the presence of an unrelated adult is relevant to this assessment.

Third, if placement is warranted, the judge must determine visitation. The judge may consider the presence of an unrelated adult in determining where visits should take place (e.g., the family home and the child welfare office), who should be allowed to participate (e.g., all members of the household or genetic relatives only), and whether the visits should be supervised by a third party (e.g., a neighbor or a child welfare agency worker).

[2] *See* Adoption Assistance and Child Welfare Act of 1980, Pub. L. 96–272.

Fourth, the judge must determine the services the agency will be required to provide to the family to achieve family reunification. The judge may want to consider services designed to educate genetic parents and nongenetic caretakers about the psychological dynamics and risks associated with an unrelated adult caring for a child. The judge may also want to order the agency to work carefully toward reunification and to monitor the situation closely (Yampolskaya 2009).

It is important to make clear that the research findings do not mandate these legal, policy, and practice measures. The research merely provides knowledge to lawmakers and policymakers for their consideration. It does not provide the answer as to what should be done with this knowledge. For example, policymakers may decide that the consideration of stepparent status as a risk factor stigmatizes that status to an unacceptable degree in a society such as ours in which stepparenthood has become prevalent. They may decide that the avoidance of some child maltreatment is not worth the cost of such stigmatization. This is a legitimate choice, but the important thing is that policymakers make this choice with a fuller realization of the potential consequences (Jones 1997).

The research to date also has implications for future research in this area. For example, researchers have tended to conduct bimodal comparisons between all genetic fathers and all other fathers (i.e., stepfathers). This latter group potentially includes many different types of "stepfathers" who warrant separate examination, such as stepfathers married to the child's genetic mother, mother's live-in boyfriend, adoptive fathers, foster fathers, not to mention more distant kin such as grandfathers and uncles (Herring 2009a). Well-designed studies may help reveal specific father-types that present relatively high risks of child maltreatment.

In addition, researchers could attempt to address broader questions that differentiate stepparent family situations. For example, researchers could address whether the risk of maltreatment is elevated in families with two nongenetic parents, such as adoptive parent families and foster parent families. Researchers could also examine gay and lesbian parent families (Adler-Baeder 2006).

Regardless of how the research in this area proceeds, the potential contribution of evolutionary theory to the construction of actuarial-based risk assessment tools extends beyond the relatively well-researched area of unrelated adult caretakers. One area of developing research illustrates this point.

This illustration of evolutionary theory's potential to contribute in the area of risk assessment draws on the concepts of sexual selection and parental investment. Women select men as sexual partners based on numerous factors. Evolutionary theory posits that one factor relevant to a woman's selection of a long-term mate is her conscious assessment of a man's likely level of investment in children (Sugiyama 2005; Anderson et al. 1999). From this conceptual perspective, a man's parental investment is, in part, a form of mating effort (Van Schaik and Paul 1997). One could predict that as long as this aspect of mating effort yields positive results in terms of a man's relationship with a woman, it will evoke sustained paternal investment and better treatment of children. One could also predict that if the relationship is troubled or uncertain, it will yield worse treatment of children, including higher rates of maltreatment (Herring 2009a).

Research supports these hypotheses. Men in a relationship with the mother of their children report higher levels of parental investment than men who are not (Apicella and Marlowe 2004; Anderson et al. 1999). Observations of parent/child interactions indicate that there is a relationship between marital satisfaction and a man's treatment of, and engagement with, children (Hofferth and Anderson 2003; Geary 2000). Children of married parents consistently receive higher levels of male parental investment than children of unmarried parents (Hofferth and Anderson 2003).

The research also indicates that men's assessment of their mates' fidelity, a possible cue to both paternity and to the quality of the relationship, predicts male parental investment (Apicella and Marlowe 2004). One study examined the relationship between men's paternity confidence and their investment in children (Anderson et al. 2007). The researchers found that low confidence in paternity reduces paternal investment on two of three measures—the time men spend with a child in a group and involvement with the child's educational progress. They concluded that the results suggest that "paternity confidence plays an important role in influencing men's relationships with the women who bear their children and with the children themselves" (Anderson et al. 2007 at 9).

Based on these findings, a team of researchers hypothesized that the risk of a man's physical abuse of children will be heightened by cues of nonpaternity (Alexandre et al. 2011). The researchers used a man's failure to cohabitate with the mother of his putative child at the time of conception as a cue of paternity uncertainty and an indicator of relationship quality. Based on interviews with mothers in Brazil, the researchers found that failure of parents to live together at conception quadrupled the risk of child physical abuse by fathers who subsequently coresided with the mother and child (Alexandre et al. 2011).

In another study, the researchers used a different measure of relationship quality—intimate partner violence during pregnancy—to determine if there was a link to subsequent child maltreatment by a man (Chan et al. 2012). Conducting a longitudinal follow-up study of Chinese women who had experienced intimate partner violence during pregnancy, the researchers found that such violence predicted subsequent physical abuse of children but not subsequent neglect of children. The odds of subsequent abuse were about twice as high as those for non-abused women (Chan et al. 2012).

In addressing the risk posed to children from poor relationships between a child's mother and her partner, legal scholars, lawmakers, and policymakers have focused primarily on the occurrence of domestic violence (*see, e.g.*, Weithorn 2001). Studies indicate that children face a heightened risk of maltreatment in households where domestic violence occurs (Lee et al. 2004; Rumm et al. 2000; Appel and Holden 1998). There is also support for the proposition that children are harmed by witnessing violence between their mother and her partner (Weithorn 2001). Thus, the legal and policy focus on this risk factor appears appropriate.

However, evolutionary theory and behavioral research indicate that this focus is too narrow. Any situation that indicates poor relationship quality between a mother and her male partner may present a heightened risk of child maltreatment. Thus, it may be useful for lawmakers and policymakers to consider relationship quality as a factor in risk assessment. More research needs to be done in this area concerning indicators of paternity uncertainty and poor relationship quality, but such research could lead to the further development of actuarial-based risk assessment tools and the related legal and policy protocols.

Foster Care Placement Decisions: The Prediction of Parental Investment

State laws authorize public child welfare agencies, working under court supervision, to remove a child from parental custody if the child faces a substantial risk of maltreatment. Once public officials decide to remove a child from a family, they must place the child in another home, most often a foster care home. Caseworkers must often make a placement decision in chaotic, emergency situations. Both caseworkers and judges face severe constraints of time and resources. In addition, child welfare agencies and the courts have largely failed to develop specific criteria or guidelines in this area. Caseworkers and judges are often left to exercise wide, unguided discretion in making placement decisions. Working in this context, caseworkers often simply look for any open bed that they can find for a child. Moreover, although the courts review the caseworker's decision to remove a child from parental custody, they usually fail to review the caseworker's decision to place a child in a particular foster home (Herring 2003).

Within such a decision-making environment, caseworkers and judges need research-based criteria that are straightforward and easy to use in a time-constrained and complex setting. Aspects of evolutionary theory and behavioral research could support the development of such criteria—criteria that are based on more than intuition and the pressure of limited resources.

Example #2: Placement of Children with Kin Foster Parents

Child welfare laws now strongly favor the placement of children with foster parents who are kin. The 2008 Fostering Connections to Success and Increasing Adoptions Act requires states to identify, locate, and notify relatives in a timely manner when a child is removed from parental custody.[3] The notice must explain the opportunity for the relative to serve as the child's foster parent and the support available to them. The law gives states discretion to define "relative" to include distant genetic kin and even individuals who simply have an established relationship with the child, but

[3] Fostering Connections to Success and Increasing Adoptions Act of 2008, Pub. L. 110–351.

no genetic relationship. The law also allows states to waive non-safety foster care licensing standards for relatives on a case-by-case basis, thus eliminating potential barriers to kinship placement. In addition, the law gives states the option to use federal funds to provide financial assistance to kin foster parents who commit to serving as a child's permanent legal guardian (Grandfamilies State Law and Policy Resource Center 2012). Commentators have encouraged attorneys and judges to ensure that the child welfare agency has exercised due diligence to identify and notify all relatives, including both paternal and maternal relatives (Wentz and Beck 2012). As a result of this legal and policy support for kin placements, these types of placements have become prevalent, especially in large urban areas (Herring et al. 2009b).

In enacting the 2008 law and previous laws that encourage kin foster placements, Congress has failed to explain clearly the basis for its kin placement preference, a preference that is a break from past practice. Kin placements had been perceived as risky because they returned a child to an extended family within which maltreatment had occurred. The new preference for kin foster parents, thus, indicates a change in view concerning the risks and benefits of such placements, with many child welfare officials and lawmakers perceiving significant benefits arising from the familiarity and continuity offered by kin. The preference for kin also provides a placement decision rule that is relatively easy for resource-poor child welfare agencies and workers to apply (Herring 2012).

Child welfare researchers have been examining this preference by comparing kinship placements to non-kin placements. To date, this research has not been guided by any coherent theoretical approach or framework (Herring 2012). Researchers are now beginning to draw on evolutionary theory to fill this void (Perry et al. 2012; Zinn 2010; Herring et al. 2009b; Testa 2005). This theoretical perspective has the potential to raise novel questions and produce knowledge that would support more sophisticated foster care placement policies, possibly alleviating concerns about, and improving practice related to, kinship foster care placements.

For example, evolutionary concepts support the formulation of two testable hypotheses concerning kinship foster care placements (Herring 2008). The first is that, on average, children are likely to experience better treatment and outcomes in kinship foster care than in non-kin foster care. The concepts of degree of relatedness and inclusive fitness give rise to this hypothesis. These concepts begin with the premise that an individual benefits both from his or her own reproductive success and from the reproductive success of his or her genetic kin through the passing of shared genes to future generations (Hamilton 1964). Because of the indirect benefits realized from the reproductive success of kin, a mutation for kinship altruism will spread if the reproductive costs incurred by the altruist (C) are less than the reproductive benefits realized by the recipient (B) discounted by the degree of relatedness (i.e., the probability that they share specific genes) (r): $C < Br$. This condition often existed within the ancestral evolutionary environment, favoring kinship altruism (Hamilton 1964; Trivers 1985). The conceptual result is that one would reasonably expect individuals to favor close kin, especially in areas that impact reproductive success (e.g., provision of food and child care) (Hamilton 1964). As to child care specifically, one would reasonably expect higher levels of investment from close kin in comparison to more distant kin, and certainly in comparison to non-kin.

Empirical research provides support for the first hypothesis. An early comprehensive review found that despite the fact that kinship foster homes received less support and monitoring, they produced outcomes similar to those produced by non-kin foster homes (Cuddeback 2004). In addition, several studies indicate that kinship placements are more stable, with stability an important indicator of positive outcomes (Cuddeback 2004; Chamberlain et al. 2006). Subsequent studies have confirmed this finding. For example, researchers expressly drawing on evolutionary concepts found that genetic kin placements are more stable than both nongenetic kin placements[4] and non-kin placements (Perry et al. 2012).

Several researchers have begun to examine specific child well-being outcomes and levels of parental investment related to different types of foster homes. One study using a national longitudinal data set found that children placed in kinship care exhibited a higher level of mental health and well-being than children placed in non-kin care (Rubin et al. 2008). Another study using the same national data set compared parenting provided by grandmothers to that provided by non-kin foster parents, finding that grandmothers had better parenting scores (Dolan et al. 2009).

The second hypothesis that arises from evolutionary concepts is that children in kinship foster care are likely to experience, on average, better treatment and outcomes when placed with some types of kin rather than others. Two additional concepts give rise to this hypothesis. The first is the concept of paternity uncertainty and the laterality effect (Herring 2008). There is a difference in certainty of genetic relationship to a child for men versus women. Women can be virtually certain that the child they care for is their genetic child, whereas men cannot be so certain (Buss 2008). Thus, the patrilineal line is less certain and one would expect, on average, the parental investment of matrilineal kin to be higher than that of patrilineal kin (Buss 2008; Gaulin et al. 1997). For example, one could expect behavioral tendencies that yield, on average, a higher level of investment in grandchildren by maternal grandmothers than by paternal grandmothers.

The second relevant evolutionary concept is a sex effect (Herring 2008). Because women, on average, have a greater genetic stake in their children than do men, women have evolved a tendency to invest more in their children and men have evolved a tendency to invest more in mating effort and less in childcare (Buss 2008; Gaulin et al. 1997). This difference also impacts behavior toward other kin. For example, as women age and their fertility decreases, investing in close kin enhances their net inclusive fitness, whereas older men can pursue additional mating (Huber and Breedlove 2007). The conceptual result is that women tend to invest more in kin than men. For example, one could expect a maternal grandmother to invest more in her grandchild than would a maternal grandfather.

Research on grandparent investment supports the hypothesis concerning different types of kin placements. One line of grandparent investment studies examines

[4] In the child welfare field, the definition of kin includes individuals who have a prior relationship with a child, but who are not genetically related to the child.

population registries in terms of child nutrition and mortality (Ragsdale 2004; Jamison et al. 2002; Voland and Beise 2002; Sear et al. 2000). A study using a registry from a village in central Japan is representative. The researchers studied the effects of grandparental presence on the probability of a child's death, finding that a child was 35 % less likely to die if his or her maternal grandmother was present in the household. The presence of the paternal grandmother and both types of grandfather increased the likelihood of child death (Jamison et al. 2002).

Two comprehensive reviews of these population studies have been completed. Sear and Mace (2008) reviewed 45 studies and concluded that maternal grandmothers have consistent beneficial effects in terms of child survival, whereas paternal grandmothers have a more variable effect—sometimes beneficial, sometimes harmful. Grandfathers do not appear to affect child survival (Sear and Mace 2008). In response to Sear and Mace's work, Strassman and Garrard (2011)completed a meta-analysis of 17 core studies, concluding that both maternal grandparents have beneficial effects, whereas both paternal grandparents have negative effects (Strassman and Garrard 2011).

The debate and research in this area continues. However, the research to date indicates that maternal grandmothers have a positive effect. There may be no positive effects from other grandparents, with the possibility of negative effects for some grandparents.[5]

Another line of studies asks subjects to characterize the level of investment made by their grandparents. The early studies used young adults, with respondents indicating that maternal grandmothers invested the most, followed by maternal grandfathers and paternal grandmothers. Paternal grandfathers invested the least (Euler and Weitzel 1996). Subsequent studies have replicated these results, which remain robust when controlling numerous variables such as physical distance between grandparent and grandchild residence (Pollet et al. 2007; Laham et al. 2005). Two studies of note have used extensive data sets to generate similar findings (Danielsbacka et al. 2011; Pollet et al. 2009). Researchers have also found laterality effects and sex effects when examining investment by aunts and uncles and by cousins (Jeon and Buss 2007; McBurney et al. 2002; Gaulin et al. 1997).

In the child welfare context, researchers have begun to examine different types of kin foster placements. An early study in this area examined whether there were different levels of parental commitment exhibited by different types of foster parents (Testa 2005). The only differences were by degree of relatedness between foster parent and foster child. For example, as to intent to raise a child to adulthood, grandparents and aunts and uncles (second-degree kin) were more likely than more distant relatives, who were more likely than nonrelatives, to raise the foster child to adulthood (Testa 2005). These findings support an inquiry concerning distinctions among genetic kin rather than a simple bimodal inquiry comparing all genetic kin to all nongenetic kin (Herring 2008).

[5] It should be noted that this research fails to identify the mechanism for these grandparent effects. Contemporary longitudinal studies of different grandparent/grandchild relationships may help address this gap in knowledge.

One researcher has pursued this line of inquiry. Using cluster analysis, Zinn (2010) has identified four distinct types of kin placement. The degree and type of kinship relationship between the foster parent and child is one of two primary indicators of caregiver competence.[6] The first study that compares the four kinship placement types has found differences in terms of the timing and type of placement outcome (e.g., disruption, return to original family, or adoption) (Zinn 2012).

This line of research begins a worthwhile inquiry, but evolutionary concepts suggest that finer distinctions among kin-types may exist. This possibility raises the potential for additional fruitful research in this area.

In the meantime, the conceptual and empirical work to date has produced knowledge that has implications for child welfare law and policy. First, this work appears to support the current trend to use kin as foster parents. More controversially, this work may support the current situation in which child welfare agencies provide less service to kinship foster families. In an environment of severely limited time and resources, it may offer a justification for the kind of difficult choices that policymakers may have to consider.

The research may support distinctions between close kin and relatively distant kin in making placement decisions. It may also support distinctions among second-degree kin. For example, all else being equal, child welfare agencies and the courts may be warranted in favoring placements with maternal grandmothers over placements with paternal grandmothers. More generally, these actors may rationally prefer matrilineal relatives over patrilineal relatives.

Researchers must conduct more studies that compare different types of kin foster parents before child welfare officials implement such placement policies, because the research to date does not yet provide robust support for these placement policies (Herring et al. 2009b). The current research may, however, support the less radical policy of using kinship type to determine the level of support services. For example, all else equal, child welfare agencies and the courts are likely warranted in considering the provision of higher levels of monitoring and support services to a paternal grandmother foster parent than to a maternal grandmother foster parent. Placements with paternal relatives would not be precluded, but the agencies and the courts could respond to such placements with higher levels of support and scrutiny. Such an approach may help achieve an optimal allocation of severely limited service resources.

In the meantime, research in this area must continue. For example, researchers could use the large longitudinal data set from the National Survey of Child and Adolescent Well-being (NSCAW) to compare placements with maternal grandmothers to those with paternal grandmothers. This data set would allow for a comparison of numerous parental investment and child outcome measures (*see, e.g.*, Dolan et al. 2009). Findings from such an analysis may justify a primary data collection project designed to test a series of hypotheses derived from evolutionary theory concerning kinship care.

[6] The other primary indicator is number and age of non-foster children in the home.

Leading figures in the field of evolutionary psychology and the field of social work support further inquiry in this specific area. Evolutionary scholars Martin Daly and Gretchen Perry have advocated for the consideration of kinship in child welfare research and policy (Daly and Perry 2011). Moreover, social work researchers Richard Barth and Mary Hodorowicz have asserted a similar position in relation to foster care and adoptive placements (Barth and Hodorowicz 2011). These contributions add intellectual energy and depth to the inquiry. Together, they identify the opportunity for rich interdisciplinary research that has significant implications for child welfare law, policy, and practice.

The potential contribution of evolutionary theory and behavioral research in this area is not limited to the consideration of kinship types. One line of inquiry illustrates this point. An essential component of kinship altruism is an ability to recognize kin. A behavioral tendency to perceive certain signals as indicators of kinship serves this function. These kinship cues often operate at an unconscious level, and because these cognitive mechanisms are fallible, an individual may unconsciously and erroneously perceive another as kin (Park et al. 2008).

One category of kinship cues relies on phenotypic resemblance. These cues include resemblance of facial features, shared attitudes, and similar body odor (Park et al. 2008; Burnstein 2005). According to evolutionary theory, such cues may evoke favorable treatment whether or not the individuals are genetic kin (Park et al. 2008). In addition, in light of paternity uncertainty these cues are likely to affect patrilineal relationships more than matrilineal relationships because kin with uncertain genetic links are more likely to depend on external signals of kinship (Park et al. 2008; Platek et al. 2002, 2003, 2004).

Researchers have tested the predictions related to these kinship cues. Several researchers have conducted studies that use arrays of photographs of children's faces, with one photograph being a morph of a child's face with the subject's face. The researchers have consistently found that adults favor a child with a face that has been morphed with their own facial features (Platek et al. 2002, 2003, 2004; DeBruine 2004). Some studies indicate that this behavioral tendency is stronger for men (Alvergne et al. 2007, 2010; Platek et al. 2002, 2003, 2004). For example, studies have found that men place much more emphasis on perceived resemblance between self and child than women in considering the adoption of an unrelated child (Volk and Quinsey 2002, 2007). Additional studies have found that men's actual resemblance to their putative children as assessed by objective observers is positively correlated with men's level of parental investment (Alvergne et al. 2009, 2010; Prokop et al. 2010).

This type of research has implications for foster care placement policy and practice. The recent work suggests that objective third parties can assess foster parent/child facial resemblance so as to predict levels of parental investment (Alvergne et al. 2010). This raises the possibility that child welfare agency caseworkers could consider and assess facial resemblance in placing children with a particular set of foster parents, especially in regard to the foster father.

Of course, the consideration of facial resemblance would not necessarily be determinative. However, if a caseworker places a child in a setting with little parental/

child resemblance, the caseworker would be on notice that the placement may present a risk of relatively low parental investment. In such a situation, it may be appropriate for the caseworker to consider enhanced support and monitoring services.

This research may also have implications for federal law that precludes the consideration of race in making placement decisions.[7] Race certainly has implications for facial resemblance, with different-race placements possibly increasing the risk of low parental investment. A legal mandate to ignore this factor when deciding where to place a child may expose the child to an increased risk of harm. Conversely, the consideration of race in making placement decisions may enhance child well-being. (It should be noted that the benefits of considering race extend beyond the reduction in the risk of harm theorized here, and include, for example, enhanced guidance from adult caretakers who have personal knowledge and direct experience with the social and cultural effects of the child's race. Common specific examples in the field include the capacity for black foster parents to provide a black child with guidance on hair care and on the likelihood of racial profiling by police. This capacity for enhanced parental guidance provides benefits to the child, allowing him or her to more effectively navigate a society in which race matters.) Thus, this type of behavioral research may support not only the development of policy and practice, but also law reform in this area (Herring 2007).

Conclusion

The two primary examples included in this chapter illustrate the potential for evolutionary theory and behavioral research to produce knowledge relevant to child welfare law, policy, and practice. This knowledge may contribute to the construction of research-based risk assessment tools by identifying conditions or situations that increase the risk of violence and other forms of maltreatment towards children. The research in this area may also contribute to the delineation of criteria for foster care placement decisions by identifying factors that predict the level of parental investment. In addition, the knowledge concerning conditions, situations, and factors that present a relatively high risk of maltreatment and/or low parental investment may guide child welfare caseworkers and agencies, along with judges, in making decisions concerning the appropriate type and level of support and monitoring services. This would assist actors in the child welfare system in their attempts to wisely allocate severely limited resources.

There is great potential for additional useful research in this area. New developments in evolutionary theory and behavioral research may have implications for child welfare. One example is provided by the research related to the possible downstream effects of the X-chromosome. This research suggests that paternal grandmothers may have evolved a behavioral tendency to favor granddaughters at the expense of grandsons (Fox et al. 2011; Johow et al. 2011). Further research in

[7] The Multiethnic Placement Act, Pub. L. 103–382, sect. 551.

this area could have implications for kin foster care placement policy and practice because, on average, placing boys with paternal grandmothers may increase the risk of harm and the likelihood of low parental investment. This line of inquiry calls for interdisciplinary research, with researchers from the fields of evolutionary science, law, and social work collaborating to produce knowledge that is relevant to child welfare law, policy, and practice.

This area of research presents a rich opportunity for researchers from several fields to learn about one another's issues and approaches to address the phenomenon of violence. Evolutionary theory and behavioral biology research can serve as the coalescing force for initiatives that may yield significant benefits in the field.

References

Adler-Baeder, F. (2006). What do we know about the physical abuse of stepchildren? A review of the literature. *Journal of Divorce & Remarriage, 44*, 67–81.

Alexandre, G. C., Nadanovsky, P., Moraes, C. L., & Reichenheim, M. (2010). The presence of a stepfather and child physical abuse, as reported by a sample of Brazilian mothers in Rio de Janeiro. *Child Abuse & Neglect, 34*, 959–966.

Alexandre, G. C., Nadansky, P., Wilson, M., Daly, M., Moraes, C. L., & Reichenheim, M. (2011). Cues of paternal uncertainty and father to child physical abuse as reported by mothers in Rio de Janeiro, Brazil. *Child Abuse & Neglect, 35*, 567–573.

Alvergne, A., Faurie, C., & Raymond, M. (2007). Differential facial resemblance of young children to their parents: who do children look like more? *Evolution and Human Behavior, 28*, 135–144.

Alvergne, A., Faurie, C., & Raymond, M. (2009). Father-offspring resemblance predicts paternal investment in humans. *Animal Behaviour, 78*, 61–69.

Alvergne, A., Faurie, C., & Raymond, M. (2010). Are parents' perceptions of offspring facial resemblance consistent with actual resemblance? Effects on parental investment. *Evolution and Human Behavior, 31*, 7–15.

Anderson, K. G., Kaplan, H., & Lancaster, J. B. (1999). Paternal care by genetic fathers and stepfathers I: Reports from Albuquerque men. *Evolution and Human Behavior, 20*, 405–431.

Anderson, K. G., Kaplan, H., & Lancaster, J. B. (2007). Confidence of paternity, divorce, and investment in children by Albuquerque men. *Evolution and Human Behavior, 28*, 1–10.

Apicella, C. L., & Marlowe, F. W. (2004). Perceived mate fidelity and paternal resemblance predict men's investment in children. *Evolution and Human Behavior, 25*, 371–378.

Appel, A. E., & Holden, G. W. (1998). The co-occurrence of spouse and physical child abuse: A review and appraisal. *Journal of Family Psychology, 12*, 578–599.

Austin, M. J., D'Andrade, A., Lemon, K., Benton, A., Chow, B., & Reyes, C. (2005). Risk and safety assessment in child welfare: Instrument comparisons. Bay area social services consortium evidence for practice series. www.bassc.net. Accessed Sept 2012.

Baird, C., & Wagner, D. (2000). The relative validity for actuarial- and consensus-based risk assessment systems. *Children and Youth Services Review, 22*, 839–871.

Barth, R., & Hodorowicz, M. (2011). Foster and adopted children who die from filicide: What can we learn and what can we do? *Adoption Quarterly, 14*, 85–106.

Burnstein, E. (2005). Altruism and genetic relatedness. In D. M. Buss (Ed.), *The handbook of evolutionary psychology* (pp. 528–551). Hoboken, NJ: John Wiley & Sons, Inc.

Buss, D. (2008). *Evolutionary psychology: the new science of the mind*. Pearson/Allyn and Bacon, Boston, MA.

Case, A., & Paxson, C. (2001). Mothers and others: Who invests in children's health? *Journal of Health Economics*, *20*, 301–328.

Case, A., Lin, I. F., & McLanahan, S. (2000). How hungry is the selfish gene? *Economic Journal*, *110*, 781–804.

Chamberlain, P., Price, J. M., Reid, J. B., Landsverk, J., Fisher, P. A., & Stoolmiller, M. (2006). Who disrupts from placement in foster and kinship care? *Child Abuse and Neglect*, *30*, 409–424.

Chan, K. L., Brownridge, D. A., Fong, D. Y. T., Tiwari, A., Leung, W. C., & Ho, P. C. (2012). Violence against pregnant women can increase the risk of child abuse: A longitudinal study. *Child Abuse & Neglect*, *36*, 275–284.

Cuddeback, G. S. (2004). Kinship family foster care: A methodological and substantive synthesis of research. *Children & Youth Services Review*, *26*, 623–639.

Daly, M., & Perry, G. (2011). Has the child welfare profession discovered nepotistic biases? *Human Nature*, *22*, 350–369.

Daly, M., & Wilson, M. (1981). Abuse and neglect of children in evolutionary perspective. In R. D. Alexander & D. W. Tinkle (Eds.), *Natural selection and social behavior*. New York: Chiron.

Daly, M., & Wilson, M. (1985). Child abuse and other risks of not living with both parents. *Ethology & Sociaobiology*, *6*, 197–210.

Daly, M., & Wilson, M. (1988). *Homicide*. Hawthorne, NY: Aldine de Gruyter.

Daly, M., & Wilson, M. (1994). Some different attributes of lethal assaults on small children by stepfathers versus genetic fathers. *Ethology and Sociobiology*, *15*, 207–217.

Daly, M., & Wilson, M. (1998). *The truth about Cinderella*. London: Weidenfeld & Nicolson.

Daly, M., & Wilson, M. (2001). An assessment of some proposed exceptions to the phenomenon of nepotistic discrimination against stepchildren. *Annales Zoologici Fennici*, *38*, 287–296.

Danielsbacka, M., Tanskanen, A. O., Jokela, M., & Rotkirch, A. (2011). Grandparental child care in Europe: Evidence of preferential investment in more certain kin. *Evolutionary Psychology*, *9*, 3–24.

DeBruine, L. M. (2004). Resemblance to self increases the appeal of child faces to both men and women. *Evolution and Human Behavior*, *25*, 142–54.

Dolan, M. M., Casanueva, C., Smith, K. R., & Bradley, R. H. (2009). Parenting and the home environment provided by grandmothers of children in the child welfare system. *Children & Youth Services Review*, *31*, 784–796.

Euler, H. A., & Weitzel, B. (1996). Discriminative grandparental solicitude as reproductive strategy. *Human Nature*, *7*, 39–59.

Fox, M., Johow, J., & Knapp, L. A. (2011). The selfish grandma gene: the roles of the X-chromosome and paternity uncertainty in the evolution of grandmothering behavior and longevity. *International Journal of Evolutionary Biology*, *2011*, 1–9.

Gambrill, E., & Shlonsky, A. (2000). Risk assessment in context. *Children and Youth Services Review*, *22*, 813–837.

Gaulin, S. J. C., McBurney, D. H., & Brakeman-Wartell, S. L. (1997). Matrilateral biases in the investment of aunts and uncles: a consequence and measure of paternity uncertainty. *Human Nature*, *8*, 139–151.

Geary, D. C. (2000). Evolution and proximate expression of human paternal investment. *Psychological Bulletin*, *126*, 55–77.

Grandfamilies State Law and Policy Resource Center. (2012). Judges' roles in implementing fostering connections: Relative caregiver provisions. *Child Law Practice*, *31*, 88–93.

Hamilton, W. D. (1964). The genetical evolution of social behavior. I, II. *Journal of Theoretical Biology*, *7*, 1–52.

Harris, G. T., Hilton, N. Z., Rice, M. E., & Eke, A. W. (2007). Children killed by genetic parents versus stepparents. *Evolution and Human Behavior*, *28*, 85–95.

Herring, D. J. (2003). Child placement decisions: The relevance of facial resemblance and biological relationships. *Jurimetrics*, *43*, 387–414.

Herring, D. J. (2007). The mulitethnic placement act: Threat to foster child safety and well-being. *University of Michigan Journal of Law Reform*, *41*, 89–120.

Herring, D. J. (2008). Kinship foster care: Implications of behavioral biology research. *Buffalo Law Review*, *56*, 495–556.
Herring, D. J. (2009a). Fathers and child maltreatment: A research agenda based on evolutionary theory and behavioral biology research. *Children and Youth Services Review*, *31*, 935–945.
Herring, D. J. (2012). Evolutionary theory and behavioural biology research: Implications for law. In S. C. Roberts (Ed.), *Applied Evolutionary Psychology*. Oxford: Oxford University Press.
Herring, D. J., Shook, J. J., Goodkind, S., & Kim, K. H. (2009b). Evolutionary theory and kinship foster care: An initial test of two hypotheses. *Capital University Law Review*, *38*, 291–318.
Hofferth, S. L., & Anderson, K. G. (2003). Are all dads equal? Biology versus marriage as a basis for paternal investment. *Journal of Family and Marriage*, *65*, 213–232.
Huber, B. R., & Breedlove, W. L. (2007). Evolutionary theory, kinship, and childbirth in cross-cultural perspective. *Cross-Cultural Research*, *41*, 196–219.
Jamison, C. S., Cornell, L. L., Jamison, P. L., Nakazato, H. (2002). Are all grandmothers equal? A review and a preliminary test of the "grandmother hypothesis" in Tokugawa, Japan. *American Journal of Physical Anthropology*, *119*, 67–76.
Jeon, J., & Buss, D. M. (2007). Altruism towards cousins. *Proceedings of the Royal Society B*, *274*, 1181–1187.
Johow, J., Fox, M., Knapp, L. A., & Voland, E. (2011). The presence of a paternal grandmother lengthens interbirth interval following the birth of a granddaughter in Krummhorn (18th and 19th centuries). *Evolution and Human Behavior*, *32*, 315–325.
Jones, O. D. (1997). Evolutionary analysis in law: An introduction and application to child abuse. *North Carolina Law Review*, *75*, 1117–1242.
Klevens, J., Bayon, M. C., & Sierra, M. (2000). Risk factors and context of men who physically abuse in Bogota, Colombia. *Child Abuse & Neglect*, 24, 323–332.
Knoke, D., & Trocme, N. (2005). Reviewing the evidence on assessing risk for child abuse and neglect. *Brief Treatment and Crisis Intervention*, *5*, 310–327.
Laham, S. M., Gonsalkorale, K., & von Hippel, W. (2005). Darwinian grandparenting: Prefential investment in more certain kin. *Personality and Social Psychology Bulletin*, *31*, 63–72.
Lee, L. C., Kotch, J. B., & Cox, C. E. (2004). Child maltreatment in families experiencing domestic violence. *Violence and Victims*, *19*, 573–591.
McBurney, D. H., Simon, J., & Gaulin S. J. C. (2002). Matrilateral biases in the investment of aunts and uncles: Replication in a population presumed to have high paternity certainty. *Human Nature*, *13*, 391–402.
O'Connor, A., & Boag, S. (2010). Do stepparents experience more parental antagonism than biological parents? A test of evolutionary and socialization perspectives. *Journal of Divorce and Remarriage*, *51*, 508–525.
Park, J. H., Schaller, M., & Van Vugt, M. (2008). The psychology of human kin recognition: Heuristic cues, erroneous inferences, and their implications. *Review of General Psychology*, *12*, 215–235.
Perry, G., Daly, M., & Kotler, J. (2012). Placement stability in kinship and non-kin foster care: A Canadian study. *Children and Youth Services Review*, *34*, 460–465.
Pew Research Center. (2011). A portrait of stepfamilies. Pew Social & Demographic Trends. www.pewsocialtrends.org/2011/01/13/a-portrait-of-stepfamilies/. Accessed Sept 2012.
Platek, S. M., Burch, R. L., Panyavin, I. S., Wasserman, B. H., & Gallup, G. G., Jr. (2002). Reactions to children's faces: Resemblance affects males more than females. *Evolution and Human Behavior*, *23*, 159–166.
Platek, S. M., Critton, S. R., Burch, R. L., Frederick, D. A., Myers, T. E., & Gallup, G. G., Jr. (2003). How much paternal resemblance is enough? Sex differences in hypothetical investment decisions but not in the detection of resemblance. *Evolution and Human Behavior*, *24*, 81–87.
Platek, S. M., Raines, D. M., Gallup, G. G., Jr., Mohamed, F. B., Thomson, J. W., Myers, T. E., et al. (2004). Reactions to children's faces: Males are more affected by resemblance than females are, and so are their brains. *Evolution and Human Behavior*, *25*, 394–405.
Pollet, T. V., Nelissen, M., & Nettle, D. (2009). Lineage based differences in grandparental investment: Evidence from a large British cohort study. *Journal of Biosocial Science*, *41*, 355–379.

Pollet, T. V., Nettle, D., & Nelissen, M. (2007). Maternal grandmothers do go the extra mile: Factoring distance and lineage into differential contact with grandchildren, *Evolutionary Psychology, 5*, 832–843.
Prokop, P., Obertova, Z., & Fedor, P. (2010). Paternity cues and mating opportunities: What makes fathers good? *Acta Ethologica, 13*, 101–107.
Ragsdale, G. (2004). Grandmothering in Cambridgeshire, 1770–1861. *Human Nature, 15*, 301–317.
Rubin, D., Downes, K., O'Reily, A., McKonnen, R., Luan, X., & Localio, R. (2008). Impact of kinship care on behavioral well-being for children in out-of-home care. *Archives of Pediatric Adolescent Medicine, 162*, 550–556.
Rumm, P. D., Cummings, P., Krauss, M. R., Bell, M. A., & Rivara, F. P. (2000). Identified spouse abuse as a risk factor for child abuse. *Child Abuse & Neglect, 24*, 1375–1381.
Rycus, J. S., & Hughes, R. C. (2003). *Issues in risk assessment in child protective services: Policy white paper*. Columbus, OH: North American Resource Center for Child Welfare.
Schnitzer, P. G., & Ewigman, B. G. (2005). Child deaths resulting from inflicted injuries: Household risk factors and perpetrator characteristics. *Pediatrics, 116*, 687–693.
Sear, R., & Mace, R. (2008). Who keeps children alive? A review of the effects of kin on child survival. *Evolution and Human Behavior, 29*, 1–18.
Sear, R., Mace, R., & McGregor, I. A. (2000). Maternal grandmothers improve nutritional status and survival of children in rural Gambia. *Proceedings of the Royal Society of London B, 267*, 1641–1647.
Strassmann, B. I., & Garrard, W. M. (2011). Alternatives to the grandmother hypothesis: A meta-analysis of the association between grandparental and grandchild survival in patrilineal populations. *Human Nature, 22*, 201–222.
Sugiyama, L. S. (2005). Physical attractiveness in adaptationist perspective. In D. M. Buss (Ed.), *The Handbook of Evolutionary Psychology* (pp. 292–343). Hoboken, NJ: John Wiley & Sons.
Testa, M. F. (2005). The quality of permanence—lasting or binding? Subsidized guardianship and kinship foster care as alternatives to adoption. *Virginia Journal of Social Policy & Law, 12*, 499–534.
Tooley, G. A., Karakis, M., Stokes, M., & Ozanne-Smith, J. (2006). Generalising the Cinderella effect to unintentional childhood fatalities. *Evolution and Human Behavior, 27*, 224–230.
Trivers, R. (1985). *Social evolution*. Menlo Park, CA: Benjamin/Cummings Publishing Company.
van IJzendoorn, M. H., Euser, E. M., Prinzie, P., Juffer, F., & Bakermans-Kranenburg, M. J. (2009). Elevated risk of child maltreatment in families with stepparents but not with adoptive parents. *Child Maltreatment, 14*, 369–375.
Van Schaik, C. P., & Paul, A. (1997). Male care in primates: Does it ever reflect paternity? *Evolutionary Anthropology, 5*, 152–156.
Voland, E., & Beise, J. (2002). Opposite effects of maternal and paternal grandmothers on infant survival in historical Krummhorn. *Behavioral Ecology and Sociobiology, 52*, 435–443.
Volk, A., & Quinsey, V. L. (2002). The influence of infant facial cues on adoption preferences. *Human Nature, 13*, 437–455.
Volk, A., & Quinsey, V. L. (2007). Parental investment and resemblance: Replications, refinements, and revisions. *Evolutionary Psychology, 5*, 1–14.
Weekes-Shackelford, V. A., & Shackelford, T. K. (2004). Methods of filicide: Stepparents and genetic parents kill differently. *Violence and Victims, 19*, 75–81.
Weithorn, L. A. (2001). Protecting children from exposure to domestic violence: The use and abuse of child maltreatment statutes. *Hastings Law Journal, 53*, 1–156.
Wentz, R. M., & Beck, K. L. (2012). Maintaining family relationships for children in the child welfare system. *Child Law Practice*, 31, 97, 102–108.
Wilson, M., Daly, M., & Weghorst, S. J. (1980). Household composition and the risk of child abuse and neglect. *Journal of Biosocial Science, 12*, 333–340.
Yampolskaya, S., Greenbaum, P. E., & Berson, I. R. (2009). Profiles of child maltreatment perpetrators and risk for fatal assault: A latent class analysis. *Journal of Family Violence, 24*, 337–348.

Zinn, A. (2010). A typology of kinship foster families: Latent class and exploratory analyses of kinship family structure and household composition. *Children and Youth Services Review*, *32*, 325–337.

Zinn, A. (2012). Kinship foster family type and placement discharge outcomes. *Children and Youth Services Review*, *34*, 602–614.

Zvoch, K. (1999). Family type and investment in education: A comparison of genetic and stepparent families. *Evolution & Human Behavior*, *20*, 453–464.

Chapter 5
Warfare and Human Nature

Steven A. LeBlanc

Warfare, as anthropologist Margaret Mead once noted, is an invention.

Harvard University President Drew Gilpin Faust (1992) begins a chapter in her *Southern Stories: Slaveholders in Peace and War* with the above quote. There may be a lot we do not know about human conflict, but one thing we do know is the above sentiment is wrong.[1] The implication is that warfare is a behavior that was thought up for no useful purpose, can be turned on or off at will, and has no great time depth. Why such a set of unfounded beliefs is so widely held is interesting in its own right, but it certainly has made the study of warfare more difficult than need be. While I do not focus on this problem, the reader must remember that there is a strong bias against warfare in the past that pervades much thinking on the topic. Why these ideas are held is an interesting topic, but far more interesting is the role of warfare in the evolution of human nature.

There is considerable pushback to the idea that warfare is an integral part of the human past, much less that such warfare had any impact on our brains. It would appear that the basis for such pushback derives from the "blank slate" attitude, that is, the idea that our minds are not "prewired" and do not have genetically built-in instincts, or predispositions. The blank slate as applied to warfare, in particular, derives from the Pollyanna attitude that if there is not a genetic component to warfare, it will be easier to eliminate. While some of the more vocal promoters of this thinking are men such as Fry (2007, 2012) and Ferguson (1992), and although some very important work has been done by female archaeologists, such as Elizabeth Arkush (Arkush and Allen 2006) and Patricia Lambert (2007), and by female psychologists such as Joyce Berenson, there is a strong female bias in the objections to warfare. A

[1] It is ironic that the particular case Mead makes for a peaceful society, and one that she studied, is the Mountain Arapesh of New Guinea. They were far from peaceful in the past and are a classic case of the anthropologist arriving too late to witness warfare first hand even though it had been present only a few years earlier (Roscoe 2003).

S. A. LeBlanc (✉)
Peabody Museum, Harvard University, Cambridge, MA 02138, USA
e-mail: leblanc@fas.harvard.edu

T. K. Shackelford, R. D. Hansen (eds.), *The Evolution of Violence*,
Evolutionary Psychology, DOI 10.1007/978-1-4614-9314-3_5,

female bias against warfare having any innate component probably plays a role in the attitudes of Mead and Faust noted above. In particular, I have been accused of simply making up much of the evidence for warfare, apparently because I am male, and obviously, the accusation was from a woman. Note I was accused of making up the data, not the far more heinous crime of suggesting there might be a genetic component, although I suspect that was the underlying concern. Since most of the literature espousing that there was not much warfare in the past, or that it was pretend warfare, etc., is little more than drivel, it is not worth further discussion (except one case I discuss below). But the reader should be aware that it is an impediment to honest discussion of this important topic. Currently a mini-series on the History Channel (*Mankind: The story of us all*) claims that warfare began with farming. How such a distortion of reality could be put forth by alleged experts and easily accepted by the show's producers and its audience demonstrates how pervasive this misunderstanding is. I am not addressing the question of whether warfare has declined over time, which still seems to be an issue of debate among some (Lawler 2012), although in my opinion Steven Pinker (2011) has changed the question from whether it has declined to why it has declined. I also do not address the overall level of warfare in the past once there were settled societies—this is dealt with by Keeley (1996), LeBlanc (2003), and Gat (2006).

Background—Or Warfare in Small-Scale Societies

For most of human history we were foragers or, at best, organized into small non-hierarchical societies with no hereditary or permanent leaders. Such societies are also known as acephalous societies. We were mobile, we stored few resources for any time, and group sizes were small. Usually the males in the group were related and the adult women much less so. If there is a genetic component to warfare—and there must be—it evolved while we were such foragers. Thus, understanding the frequency, nature, and outcomes of forager warfare is critical to developing a framework for thinking about warfare and human evolution. It turns out that there are some societies that farm but are otherwise organized very much like true foragers—or at least not very differently. These include the Yanomamo of South America (Chagnon 1968). There are other societies that are organized still more complexly, but are not what would be classed as complex societies, such as the Dani of New Guinea (Heider 1979). To some extent, these societies provide additional, relevant, comparative information on warfare, but just how much to include them in such discussions is tricky. The Yanomamo do not store meaningful amounts of food and move surprisingly often for farmers, and so share many key attributes of foragers. But their community sizes can be in the several hundreds, and they do invest in farming fields. I do include them in my discussion, but try to make clear whenever I extend the discussion beyond true foragers.

It must be made clear that many scholars focus on hunter-gatherers instead of foragers as analogues for our deep past. Overall, such an approach is worthless.

Hunter-gatherers are simply groups that do not farm. Thus, the concept includes the permanent settlement, significant storage, and socially very complex peoples of the Northwest coast, such as the Nootka, Kwakiutl, etc., the horse-riding bison hunters of the Plains, most of the ancient Jomon people of Japan, the Asmat of new Guinea who lived in communities of thousands of individuals, or even the Natufian proto-farmers of the Middle East. That is, the concept of hunter-gatherers is a hodgepodge of people that include the foragers of Tasmania, with very small group sizes and very simple social systems, with the Asmat or Kwakiutl. Many of these hunter-gatherer societies share far more behaviors with tribal or chiefdom farmers than do the Yanomamo who do some farming. Trying to generalize about hunter-gatherers takes one down a blind alley, and that approach is not considered further.

Modern Foragers Our forager society data come from two sources: Recent foragers for whom we have historic and ethnographic information and prehistoric foragers for whom we have only the archaeological record. It is best to consider the recent foragers first. We have some information from most continents about such peoples as the Bushmen, pygmies, Hadza in Africa, all societies of Australia, some societies in New Guinea, a few in Southeast Asia, a few in India, and a number in the Americas from the Eskimo in the north to the Fuegians in the south. One difficulty with the information on these foragers is related to when it was obtained. In many instances, by the time these foragers were studied by anthropologists, their numbers had been decimated, they had access to metal tools and guns, and they even were no longer highly mobile. Equally relevant, some were small societies surrounded by farmers, which in some cases this pattern had gone on for so long that the foragers had lost their indigenous language, such as the pygmies. Teasing out what we know about such peoples as actual foragers, where their neighbors were also foragers (the relevant model for our deep past), is quite difficult. Not impossible, but quite difficult.

It turns out that the anthropological studies by university-trained anthropologists of the twentieth century are much less useful than the early accounts of explorers, patrol officers, missionaries, and the like. Such early accounts have the potential for bias, lack of completeness, etc., and must be used with caution, but such is the case with all such data. Conversely, it is the failure to comprehend the problems with the recent studies that renders the approach of people like Fry and Ferguson virtually worthless, so I look at clear examples of the problems relying on anthropologists below, but first I describe some examples of forager warfare.

Eskimo Perhaps the best information we have on forager warfare comes from the Western Eskimo Inupiat. This is a consequent of Ernst Burch making a concerted effort to obtain such information (Burch 1974, 2005, 2007). His best data came from interviewing old people about what their grandparents, etc., had told them. He was able to collect information that dated to the first half of the nineteenth century. What he found was that warfare was almost constant. Villages were located for defense, children we taught to be very quiet outdoors so as not to give away the community's location, and strangers were killed on sight. Men never left the house unarmed. Revenge played a very large role in fighting. Massacres were more common apparently than with other foragers. The picture he paints is in sharp contrast to later accounts of Eskimos and especially the Netsilik. I will refer to the Inupiat again when I discuss the termination of warfare and the more eastern Netslilik Inuit below.[2]

Andaman Islands These isolated people provide an excellent opportunity to look at forager warfare. The Islanders were definitely foragers in a land of foragers, and the total population was large enough to see what took place between groups. Andaman warfare has been recently well reviewed by Kelly (2000). While he makes every effort to deny the existence of forager warfare in the deep past, the evidence he presents for Andaman warfare is quite substantial.

> … Before they go out for a raid the Jarawa cover their chests with bark armour and paint their faces with patterns of white clay. The bark armour is stitched securely on the body by other persons and can only be removed by cutting off the stitches. These people are in the habit of mutilating their victims. They take out their brains, their eyes, and their bodies are hacked all over…. (Sarkar 1962, p. 675)

The Islanders were able to muster groups in the hundreds to attack the initial British settlements. Given the size of individual groups, this implies the ability to coordinate between groups that would otherwise have been in competition. That is, they formed alliances between polities and were able to coordinate the timing of combining forces. While the descriptions of pitched battles are between the Islanders and the British, the skill with which these battles were fought implies they also took place between Island groups. One section of South Andaman Island was occupied by people, the Jarawa, who, on the basis of linguistics, clearly moved in from an island some 30 miles away. That is, boats must have been used to transport and land a group large enough to survive, which implies planning and coordination of considerable scale. Attacks by people in boats are also known. One of the neighboring groups to the Jarawa was the Bea. It appears they fought whenever they encountered each other, and they killed isolated or indefensible members of the other group on sight, including women and children. Besides the implied boundary change of the Jarawa invasion, historical records show that boundaries among groups did change over time, although Kelly suggests it was a peaceful process. He does however admit that there are independent lines of evidence that show there was fighting over resources and territory did change hands. Territories were certainly defended, and as with most foragers, permission to use the territory of one's allies needed to be obtained. Boundaries were clearly known to each group, but whether buffer zones existed is not clear. Chest guard armor was worn. Conflict within macro-groups could be resolved by means other than fighting, although raiding within these groups did occur. Women were used as interlocutors to arrange peace.

[2]Although some use the term Inuit for all these Arctic people, it is better to use the term Eskimo for all the circum Arctic people who are linguistically related and reserve Inuit for the Eskimo of Central Canada.

!Kung and other peoples of Southern Africa The Bushmen or !Kung of Southern Africa present a particularly difficult case. The classic ethnographies of Lee (1979), Marshall (1976), including the famous movie *The Hunters*, all took place long after any possible warfare had been suppressed. Less well recognized is that herding of sheep, goats and later cattle, had existed in better-watered areas surrounding the desert !Kung for over a thousand years before the earliest European accounts of the region. Moreover, Bantu herder/farmers had arrived in the eastern part of the area in this same time frame. This means that the !Kung would have lived in a land of foragers that included much richer areas earlier, but by the AD 1500–1600s they lived in an area very marginal for herding or farming but were surrounded by such people. The post-Second World War situation, from which all the popular ethnographies are drawn, found the Bushmen often living near government-drilled water wells (boreholes) providing reliable water sources which increased access to resources and essentially eliminated the threat of dying from thirst. Moreover, although carefully ignored in the accounts and photographs, there were numerous Bantu-speaking foragers sharing the same boreholes. Their herders provided buffer food, and, more importantly, young and fertile Bushmen women married into the Bantu, greatly reducing the Bushman-perceived fertility rate. Thus, the peaceful, ecologically balanced Bushmen of the twentieth century are nonrelevant, inaccurately portrayed foragers.

There is ample evidence that these other peoples, including foragers in the richer areas, did engage in warfare, as well as some evidence even for the most marginal groups (Eibl-Eibesfleldt 1975; Parkington 1984; Schapera 1930; Schire 1980), but it is clouded by the presence of the herders, who gave a good account of themselves against the Europeans at very first encounters. Europeans soon learned that the southern coast of Africa was a dangerous place. While accounts vary, it appears that in the early 1500s, Antonio Saldanha landed looking for water and was attacked by some 200 men. In 1510 Indian Viceroy de Almeida's party of over 150 men were successfully attacked and The Viceroy d'Almeida and no fewer than 50 of his men were killed in this battle, and few Europeans ventured ashore for almost 80 years (Colvin 1900, Boonzaier et al. 1996). The attacking force must have been large and well organized to have inflicted such casualties. These herder peoples, probably best termed Khoikhoi, regularly raided each other and what was termed a full-scale war would occasionally occur. That is, for more than a millennium the interior foragers were linked to non-foragers and to see them as totally isolated is a mistake.

Linguistically, the Bushmen do not have smooth linguistic gradients, which is what we would predict if there had not been group replacements. Instead, the Kalahari is a patchwork of unintelligible and even rather unrelated languages. One would expect this pattern to have resulted either from group replacement resulting from successful warfare or from groups failing to survive and being replaced during better times by unrelated ones. That is, the linguistic evidence points to either considerable warfare in the area, or, it was so marginal that from time to time parts of the area were depopulated and then repopulated by different groups.

Deep Past Foragers We do not have such fine-grained information about prehistoric foragers or minimalist farmers. But we do have the ability to look at them over considerable time depths. Just as there is a misconception that recent foragers did not have real warfare, there is misconception that warfare does not go into the deep past. While some of the misconception is simply wishful thinking by some people, much of the rest is produced by misunderstanding of the archaeological record. Put simply, the further one goes back in time the more incomplete the record becomes and the harder it is to interpret. Thus, while there are hundreds of human fossils over 10,000 or 20,000 years old, most are very incomplete. Even when they show evidence of parry fractures, cannibalism, blows to the head and the like, there are always possible explanations other than warfare. Moreover, one has to ask how the remains that are found got there in the first place. Even though people began to be buried some 40,000 years ago, not everyone gets buried. For example, we might expect that individuals killed in a massacre are unlikely to be buried. Who was left alive to undertake the task? Individuals ambushed while hunting, or even some distance from their base camp, are also less likely to be buried than an individual who died peacefully in camp. Spears were being used at least 400,000 years ago, and a lethal spear thrust is quite likely to leave no skeletal evidence especially if the skeletal remains are broken and fragmentary. Moreover, it is always possible to suggest that a violent death was at the hands of a member of the same group, i.e., murder. This is not the place to argue about these data in detail, but it should be made clear that the numbers of individuals who exhibit some trauma are not trivial. There are at least 27 Neanderthals and 19 early modern humans with some evidence of trauma, but only a handful are seen as clearly derived from interpersonal violence. That does not mean some of the other instances are not related to interpersonal violence; however, see Trinkhaus (2012) for a recent summary of the evidence and interpretations. McCall and Shields (2008) also provide a brief summary. But it should be noted that Milner (2005) demonstrated that skeletal evidence for violent death greatly underestimates the actual rate if projectile weapons were being used.

The past is even more complicated than that. One simple example shows how limited our consideration of the archaeological data has been. A relevant piece of information is how many individuals were buried together. It is not always possible to tell if a grave represents a single event or multiple events over time. But there are what appear to be cases in which multiple individuals were buried together at the same time. Sometimes these are a female and infant, but sometimes they are two adults, or even more. People are buried quickly for a variety of reasons, so two individuals buried together must have died within a couple of days of each other at most. So, in groups in which—excluding young children—one expects about one death per year, such multiple burials should be almost nonexistent, but they are not that rare. In such small groups, the likelihood that two individuals died from disease at the same time is extremely remote. Starvation might be an explanation, but the most likely reason is that both individuals were killed in the same raid and were subsequently buried together. Few scholars have ever considered such types of information, because few have ever made an earnest effort to assess death rates from warfare in the deep past.

There certainly are surprisingly common instances of cannibalism, collections of heads (Frayer 1997, Orscheidt 2005), bashed-in skulls, and other such evidence of other-than-peaceful proper deaths and burials, such as the Herto skulls from Ethiopia. These are approximately 160,000-year-old hominid crania with cut marks that indicate postmortem defleshing with stone tools. Polishing and intentional scraping modifications suggest these hominids actively manipulated the crania of the dead.

Cannibalism is far more likely to be of enemies than of family, collections of heads are far more likely to be trophies than venerated ancestors, and bashed-in skulls are more likely to be from warfare than murder based on ethnography and historical accounts. It is harder to demonstrate that the deep past was peaceful than it was filled with warfare. The people who make such claims for a peaceful past have no basis for making such assessments. They can appeal to no supporting data that have been rigorously evaluated.

Another misconception is that once humans had projectile weapons, warfare and killing were done at a distance. This is simply not true. Humans have had spears since at least 400,000 years ago (Thieme 1997). Surely, rocks were thrown before that, and it has been argued that there has been selection for rock throwing (Isaac 1987). Spear throwers have been in use for more than 30,000 years, and some humans have had bows for probably 15,000 years (possibly for 60,000 in a few places). But such distance weapons were not very lethal, and it was not until the recurved bow was developed in the last few thousand years that truly lethal bows existed (and even then over only a small portion of the world). The vision of a man falling instantly dead from an arrow is straight out of Hollywood. All accounts of forager and leaderless society warfare include frequent killing with clubs, knives, axes, and the like. Close combat has, until very recently, always been the norm. Carrying clubs, knives-daggers, and a willingness to get close to the enemy are typical of accounts of such warfare. Warfare was very dangerous and very personal.

Forager Warfare: Deadly and Pervasive

> The next morning the raiders attack the camp and killed all the women and children remaining there.... After shoving sheefish into the vaginas of all the Indian women they had killed, the Noatakers... retreated toward the upper Noatak River....
>
> Some weeks later, the Kobuk caribou hunters returned home to find the rotting remains of their wives and children and vowed revenge. A year or two after that, they headed north to the upper Noatak to seek it. They soon located a large body of Nuataagmiut and secretly followed them. One morning the men in the Nuataagmiut camp spotted a large band of caribou and went off in pursuit. While they were gone, the Kobuk raiders killed every woman in the camp. Then they cut off their vulvas, strung them on a line, and headed quickly toward home.
>
> Iñupiaq Eskimo. (Burch 2005, p. 110).

Forager and other leaderless societies had warfare that did not look to some like "real" warfare. The primary method of attack was the raid, especially the dawn raid. A group of men were recruited—often not all the males in the proximate group (more about recruitment below). Raiding parties could range from a handful of men, to 20–25, with very rare instances in which more than 100 men were involved. Sometimes noncombatants, women or younger boys, accompanied the group to carry food, etc. Usually the individual who recruited the party was the leader, but his leadership role was weak. The goal was to surprise the enemy and kill as many as possible while taking very little risk in the encounter (considerable risks were taken to get to the point of the attack, which is considered below). This well might mean that even after walking for more than a week, a single individual might be killed in the ensuing attack. Such a raid was considered successful. Walker and Bailey (2013) have data on how often attackers were killed for lowland South America, where the societies were noncomplex farming groups and a few foraging groups. Only 2% of the deaths in these raids were of the attackers (5 deaths out of 238, excluding one massacre of defenders).

Less often, formal battles took place. Often these had a somewhat ritual nature, but could still be quite deadly. Again, a single death was a major event. However, the outcomes were often other than what was planned. Sometimes the raiding party would discover that all the men in the target group were away hunting, etc. The attackers were then free to kill all the women, children, and old men. Similarly, the defending males could find themselves outnumbered or otherwise at a great disadvantage and simply flee, leaving the women and children to their fate. That is, occasionally things would go just right for the attacking party and a massacre would take place. Although infrequent, over the long term such massacres were significant. In the New Guinea highlands, over the span of a century about 30% of local groups were extinguished—as a group, individuals often survived by joining other groups (Soltis et al. 1995). Such group extinctions were often the result of massacres.

Even though the number of individuals killed in each raid was typically low, raiding was far more significant than most realize. Raiding could be almost continuous, although often seasonal in some climates. One group might be raiding and be raided by multiple other groups. In such small societies, the number of deaths from raids could be proportionally substantial. Various scholars have tried to estimate the death rates from raiding, including the occasional massacre (e.g., Keeley 1996, Bowles 2009). One of the best sets of data is from lowland South America (Walker and Bailey 2013). Some archaeology has also given us some useful data (Lambert 1997, Lambert and Walker 1991). The somewhat shocking estimates are that between 15 and 25% of males and about 5% of females died from such warfare (about 9% of female deaths for South America). Given these high death rates, the term warfare is appropriate because of the consequences, not the methods.

Most men in these societies slept with, and never went outside without, their weapons. They had nightmares about being killed in attacks. They located their communities for defense and they underutilized vast portions of their territories because it was too dangerous to go there. All this meaningfully reduced the available resources and would have led to deprivation, or even starvation or death. Every male you met who was a not a close relative or member of your local group was a potential threat. Lives in the past were one of fear, worry, and hunger. What some naively think of as occasional, almost play-like, raiding was in fact a very deadly, all-consuming way of life. The exact frequency of deaths due to warfare is not important. Even if the rate was no more than 5–10 %, this was enough to have had a very significant impact on fitness values, and related selection must have been considerable.

Other evidence for the importance of warfare among foragers is the existence of specialized weapons. Foragers used shields, body armor, and daggers, and made and maintained far more spears, arrows, etc., than they needed for hunting. All this came at a price. In a world where everything you owned had to be carried from base camp to base camp many times a year, carrying shields, armor, and the like was a significant cost. High-quality spear points were traded for over great distances. The constant warfare did not come cheap. Although foragers did not construct fortifications, they did locate their settlements in particularly defensive locations, even if these places were not good from other perspectives. Peoples who were slightly more sedentary, constructed fortifications, planted cactus defensive walls, dug pitfalls, and put out sharpened stakes to deter attack.

Chimpanzees as a Model for Proto-Human Warfare

There has been considerable debate on the validity of using what is known about chimpanzee conflict as informative about human, or proto-human, warfare in the extremely deep past. This is far too complicated to consider here. But a couple of points are of note. First, there has been a tendency to pacify the chimpanzee record. Suggestions that the conflict was because the chimps were provisioned, etc., have been more than adequately debunked (Wrangham et al. 2006). The longer the chimpanzees are studied, the clearer it is that intergroup conflict is widespread (Wilson and Wrangham 2003). Chimpanzee deep incursions (how about that for a pleasant, neutral term—not raiding, not warfare) have surprisingly strong parallels to forager raiding behaviors. Once one accepts that foragers have had warfare for hundreds of thousands of years, projecting back to a time when chimpanzee behaviors are a good analogue is not so hard. In each case, the same few behaviors exist. Attack parties do not include all males; instead, there is a recruitment process. There is a clear goal of minimizing risk to the attackers. And when successful, the attackers seem to enjoy it very much. There do seem to be adaptive benefits for this behavior.

Far more difficult to assess is how much is innate and how much is learned. Chimpanzees hunt monkeys. Are the raiding behaviors carried over from behaviors learned from hunting? Do the young males learn to walk quietly in single file, all stopping in unison to listen, etc.? Or are there wired behaviors, or wired learning circuits that make learning raiding behavior easy?

At this point, perhaps the most relevant idea to take from the chimpanzee data is that not only has there been plenty of time for selection for behavioral traits derived from human warfare, but it is quite likely that some behaviors have been selected for over extremely long time spans. That is, we should not reject some hypotheses or fear to formulate hypotheses because there would not have been enough time for natural selection to have acted. This does not mean that any particular hypothesis is true regarding selection and warfare, just that we cannot reject any because of the limits in how much time might have been available for selection to act. For humans and proto-humans, there was plenty of selective pressure in terms of death rates and plenty of time, for significant levels of selection to have taken place.

Warfare—A Male Thing

A final note on what we know about forager warfare: it is a male thing. While it is the case that in certain circumstances women do engage in warfare, essentially all the examples involve complex societies. Not only are such instances rare, they are exceedingly rare to absent among foragers and acephalous societies. In such societies, women do act as enforcers and encouragers for male warfare. "Why haven't you avenged the death of my brother?" They play supporting roles, even going along with raiding parties to carry food, etc. (but always stopping well short of the locality of fighting). They can be involved in the decision to make war and, among somewhat more complex societies, can occupy very important roles in this matter. That, however, is often complicated because women are likely to have relatives in the group being considered for attack and so sometimes they are deliberately left out of planning and decision making. They even can be involved in defense, in particular when fleeing is not possible. However, they are simply not offensive combatants. Any possible examples are too few and too limited to be relevant. Warfare is a male thing. As I will discuss below, this difference has led to different evolutionary outcomes.

The Logic of Peaceful Societies

Several authors have looked to see if there are or have been peaceful societies. I am not aware of anyone who examined the logic of such a search, but it is worth some thought. Let us assume such societies exist (they certainly do in some form) and ignore for a moment just what we mean by peaceful. If the question is simply are there any peaceful societies, what do we gain from that knowledge? Does it mean that we as humans are *not* hopelessly programmed for warfare? Probably not. If 99 % of all societies have a particular trait, warfare being just one example, we would reasonably deduce that we are programmed for that trait in some fashion, and there seem to be some very special circumstances that keep this programming for working in rare cases. This would certainly be the conclusion one would reach for any other general behavior. We would be hard pressed to assume that there was no genetic basis for pair bonding, protecting children, or even smiling, even if only 99 % of all societies did them. We would never assume these behaviors were simply taught and learned with no genetic component. It would be very different if half of all societies were peaceful and the other half warlike. Then we might reasonably hypothesize a learned explanation for such behavior. One could pursue this line of reasoning further except that we know that the overwhelming majority of societies do have war, so there is little benefit in finding a few individual examples in order to refine our percentage estimate.

The search for peaceful societies to provide a counter to the argument that we are programmed for warfare actually has the opposite outcome. How hard the search is demonstrates the pervasiveness of the behavior. This pervasiveness cannot be ignored. It is, however, productive to determine the *circumstances* in which we find peaceful societies. This has the promise of being informative and I consider it below. But before doing so, I need to consider some of the claims for peaceful societies. Almost all such claims are either simply wrong or fail to appreciate the circumstances involved. The question is are they wrong because their proponents were honestly misinformed, or because those that put forth such cases are hopelessly biased and are not proceeding in an objective fashion. This is a major issue in the pursuit of our understanding of warfare and needs to be recognized.

Netsilik Eskimo of Central Canada as a Peaceful Society In his recent challenge to assumptions about war and violence, Douglas Fry looks at five forager societies used as case studies to push the notion of the human potential for peace (Fry 2007, p. 200). He chose these groups because he claimed there appeared to be ample information available to examine data on conflict and conflict management. One of those five societies is the Netsilik of the Central Eskimo grouping. The Netsilik are a classic Eskimo group and the one most used in a comparative fashion and there is good ethnographic data from the twentieth century (Rasmussen 1931, Balikci 1970). In these studies, they are presented as not having warfare, but admittedly a high homicide rate.

In his sample of five simple societies, including the Netsilik, Fry asserts that the level of group violence is minimal in each and that and none of them could be characterized as warlike (Fry 2007, p. 215). He points out that stealing women between bands and group-level fighting over resources are not observed among any of the five groups and the majority of fatalities that are recorded for those five societies are on a personal, not band, level.

Summing up on the patterns of violence among the five groups presented, he considers the kinds of aggression discussed in each group as relatively harmless. Yet, in the case of the Netsilik, as described earlier, we see that these "relatively harmless" acts of aggression include "homicide, revenge killings, executions, and occasionally feuds but not war" (Fry 2007, p. 209). Fry presents material from the literature supporting the notion that there is not and there has never been warfare among the Netsilik, in particular, and the Central Eskimo, in general: the Netsilik language has no word for "war" and even though there are certain places with abundant food resources, no wars have been observed over those resources (Irwin 1990 in Fry 2007, p. 208).

Reality Reality concerning the Netsilik could not be more different. There are no early accounts of the Netsilik compared with the Western Eskimos, but there are accounts that are earlier than the traditional ethnographies of Rasmussen (1931) and Balikci (1970). An early account of these same people paints a very different picture than that of Fry. I excerpt from a much longer account:

> Arriving at a Netsilik camp…
>
> …instead of remaining in their igloos the men were drawn up in line of battle in front of them, and sent out an old woman to find out who we were and what we wanted…
>
> If our designs had been hostile and we had killed the old woman, their fighting strength would not have been reduced, and it would only have been one less old woman to care for….
>
> They carried their bows in their hands, with arrows fixed to the strings; but when the old woman shouted back that we were white men, they laid aside their arms and received us in a friendly manner, striking their breasts and saying, "Many-tu-me," though Joe afterward told me that one of the men wanted a fight anyhow…
>
> They have a custom of killing the first stranger who comes among them after a death in the tribe, and as we filled that requirement, it seems he wanted to carry out the custom. (Gilder 1881, pp. 83–84)

Moreover, there are accounts from the neighboring groups on three borders (there were no neighbors on the remaining side). Each of their neighbors said that they fought with the Netsilik. In particular, both the Copper Eskimo and Iglulik considered the Netsilik an enemy and described relations as hostile.

Fabbro's (1978) assertion for the Copper Eskimo being peaceful also does not hold up under scrutiny, but the argument is redundant and not worth explicating here except for one point. The Copper Eskimo, like most Eskimos, constantly fought with their Indian neighbors wherever the two culturally and linguistically very different groups abutted territories. So, even if the Copper Eskimo had been at peace with all other Eskimos, they would have had to maintain a warlike footing with respect to the Chipewyan (Dene speaking) Indians to the south, as the following well-known account makes clear.

A. Samuel Hearne journeyed to the Coppermine River in 1771 in what was the territory of a subgroup of the Copper Inuit, where his guide and approximately 150 Chipewyan came across Inuit camped in a handful of tents by rapids. The Chipewyan were not spotted and greatly outnumbered the Inuit but still crept up on them while the Inuit slept. After killing all 20, including men, children, and women (including old women), they saw more tents on the other shore and attacked them too. Hearne said the killings were brutal and torturous in some of the cases. Hearne was horrified by the massacre, saying "…and I am confident that my features must have feelingly expressed how sincerely I was affected at the barbarous scene I then witnessed; even at this hour I cannot reflect on the transactions of that horrid day without shedding tears." He subsequently named the location Bloody Falls (Hearne 2007[1796, p. 55]).

I think there are two things going on at the same time. First, and perhaps most important, Burch demonstrates quite convincingly that there was regular, intense and deadly warfare in the early 1800s in western Alaska but that it ended by the late 1800s. As will be discussed below, the best explanation for the cessation of hostilities was the introduction of guns, which caused a shift in trade and carrying capacity. The Netsilik seem to be some of the last Eskimo people to obtain regular access to guns. In the account given above, they did not have guns and they still had warfare. By the time the ethnographers reached them in the early twentieth century, they, like their close relatives to the west, had guns, and warfare had ceased. It should also be noted that almost all other Eskimo societies did have warfare, and one needs to explain why the Netsilik were so different.

The second factor of relevance is that there was considerable variability in the size and social complexity of various Eskimo groups. In fact, Eskimos present a very interesting case of forager warfare. The variance in social complexity and group size seems to correlate with evidence for warfare. There was considerable warfare among the Western Eskimo such as the Iñupiaq (Kotzebue Sound Eskimo) and Yup'ik people further south. There is less warfare evidence for the Mackenzie Delta Eskimo to the east, although the archaeological skeletal sample from the Saunaktuk site in that area has been suggested to provide evidence for massacre, torture, mutilation, and cannibalism (Melbye and Fairgreive 1994). As one goes even further east, groups get still smaller. There were only about 450–500 Netsilik Inuit in the late 1800s, which made them essentially one large social group.[3] Any conflict observed by an ethnographer would be perceived as murder rather than warfare. The opinions of their neighbors to the east and west were not the same as the ethnographers, but it appears that the ethnographers never asked about external relations in previous generations. Finally, and perhaps tellingly, the Netsilik lived at the end of the earth. They had no neighbors to the north as the land was uninhabitable. Burch suspects that their entire range was uninhabitable during the Little Ice Age and it was only recently and barely recolonized prior to visitations by Europeans. Thus, we may have an example of a population that was a demographic sink, or had recently been so, an area so marginal that the death rate from starvation, etc., was so high that there was little conflict over resources, and the infanticide rate so high (focused on girls) that the critical resource was women, leading to within-group male homicide, but little warfare with other social groups.[4]

[3]They are believed to have had 450–500 people in the 1880s, but by 1923 only about 250 were living in the area. When the population decline began is not clear, but by the time of Rasmussen, if not before, they were well below the presumed long-term carrying capacity.

[4]It should be noted that the Eskimo seem to not engage in as much woman-capture as other foragers, so while we would think the scarcity of women would lead to woman-capture raids with adjacent groups, this does not seem to be the case, even for Western Eskimo groups.

The most parsimonious interpretation of all this is that Eskimos had warfare in the early 1800s, that it had terminated almost everywhere by the late 1800s or early 1900s depending on the area, that the Netsilik fit this pattern, and that ethnographies that were done after that date and that did not systematically try to recover information about warfare in earlier periods simply missed what had gone on earlier. It is fair to say that not all ethnographers claimed eternal peace, only that there was no warfare in the era they were studying.

In sum, the example of the Netsilik may tell us a lot about human behavior, but little about warfare. It also demonstrates the danger of knowing the answer before examining the data. Fry could easily have found the same information about Eskimo warfare, but he obviously did not bother to look. In any case, his logic and his data are hopelessly flawed.

The Evolutionary Consequences of Warfare

> On approaching the enemy's quarters, they laid themselves down in ambush until all was quiet, and finding most of them asleep, laying about in groups, our party rushed upon them, killing three on the spot and wounding several others. The enemy fled precipitately, leaving their war implements in the hands of their assailants and their wounded to be beaten to death by boomerangs, three loud shouts closing the victors triumph.
>
> The bodies of the dead they mutilated in a shocking manner, cutting the arms and legs off, with flints, and shells, and tomahawks.
>
> When the women saw them returning, they also raised great shouts, dancing about in savage exstasy. The bodies were thrown upon the ground, and beaten about with sticks – in fact, they all seemed to be perfectly mad with excitement…
>
> South Australia Aborigines. (Morgan (1852), p. 43–44 [Morgan 1979, p. 51])

There are two aspects of a genetic component to warfare. The first is that there are specific genes that might be relevant and the second is that there has been selection for instincts, propensities, or whatever term one wishes, that increase the likelihood of particular behaviors. The first type of genetic component is quite new and the second is a standard evolutionary psychology view of how natural selection built the mechanisms of the mind. Both can be highly controversial with certain audiences. So this is a difficult subject. Again, it would appear useful to lay out the nature of the evidence. One line of evidence is the nature of motivation and risk in leaderless societies. Another is how leadership works, and finally how fighting is terminated. This allows for a discussion of what appears to be rational calculation and what appears to be innate. I then discuss what we know from genetics and psychology. I should note that Walker and Bailey (2013) have approached this question from a somewhat different perspective. They suggest that aggressive male behaviors have been selected for perhaps through the survival of successfully aggressive groups, in both humans and chimpanzees. But, warfare could have, in humans, also resulted in selection for self-sacrifice, strong reciprocity, and revenge seeking. We all seem to be trying to understand the consequences of a long history of warfare and are just approaching it from different perspectives. Their perspective and mine (and many others, such as Boehm (1986) seem to converge on revenge. This revenge behavior deserves far more consideration and research than it has received.

Rational vs. Innate Overall, we find several lines of evidence for rational behavior in leaderless warfare. At the micro-level, there is evidence that warfare can end quite abruptly. The Western Eskimos provide a good example. Their warfare in the first few decades of the 1800s was intense and deadly. Fifty years later it had ceased. The two best explanations for this (and they are not mutually exclusive) are that when they got access to rifles, it greatly increased their carrying capacity. Hunting was much easier than previously, especially for caribou. So, the motivation to fight one's neighbors declined and the benefits of trade with those same individuals increased, as the only way to get bullets was through trade. Your neighbors were no longer competitors but were suddenly valued conduits to goods.

At the time the warfare ended, the Little Ice Age ended, which must have improved conditions overall and would have further increased the carrying capacity. However, the access to bullets (even more critical than the guns themselves) via peaceful relations was probably key. How relevant this is can be seen by noting that the caribou population was decimated within a few decades after obtaining rifles.

At a broader level, however, intensity of warfare does correlate with climate. This is best seen in the archaeological record where there is enough time depth to see such patterns. A very good example is from North America. Populations seem to have grown substantially during the Medieval Warm Period, sometimes termed the Medieval Climate Optimum, or Medieval Climatic Anomaly, and subsequently the carrying capacity appears to have been substantially reduced during the subsequent Little Ice Age. The result was a great increase in warfare over most of the continent, with a population crash in the American Southwest (LeBlanc 1999), and with intense warfare in the Southeast which involved large, empty buffer zones between polities (Milner 1999). These behaviors can be seen to be rational. Because of the Little Ice Age, the population greatly exceeded the carrying capacity and competition for scarce resources resulted in warfare.

When we look at warfare at a closer level, we also see considerable rational behavior. Allies are critical to survival and building alliances is a continuous effort. Allies can be "bought" by exchanging women on terms advantageous to groups you need as allies, or trading for goods you do not really need. Shifting fortunes of your allies can result in calculated shifting of alliances.

There are also social restraints against offensive action when the risk/reward ratio is poor. Groups require consensuses for initiating a raid in many cases and they find reasons to avoid conflict when they are likely to lose in a tit-for-tat exchange of raids. Even though there may be "hotheads" who desire revenge, or young males who see status gains from successful raiding, the group can decide to overrule such interests and rationally assess the potential outcomes. Similarly, many groups have mechanisms for dealing with strong warriors who take advantage of their prowess and fear factor within their own group. (They often get assassinated by their own group.) People get killed in wars, and these deaths generate anger that can keep a war going (see below). Termination of warfare is complicated because younger men are more likely to act in ways that keep war going, while their elders incline more to peace negotiations. Warriorhood is a prime avenue to prestige among young men. War gives young men a chance to prove themselves, which gives them an incentive to start or continue a war. But forager/farmer communities do have solutions to this problem when the costs get too great. They do have established mechanisms for making peace. These seem to be particularly strong within groups—people with whom you exchange wives and who are linguistically related. There is great benefit in stopping what we might consider feuding within groups, as such animosity and loss of life weakens the group against outside threat. But even without outsiders, when the costs are high and the benefit of alliance against others is great, there are means of stopping tit-for-tat or revenge raiding.

There seem to be two principal ways of stopping the fighting: compensation in women (often as an uneven exchange of women) and payment of wergild. It has not been tested, but it appears that women are the medium in low-density societies, with wergild taking their place in high-density societies (Paul Roscoe, personal communication). In any case, this is all rationally thought out, publically debated, and clear to all parties. Such cessation of conflict does not demonstrate our innate peacefulness. Many of the individuals involved see this as buying time. They still consider the score uneven and may wait a generation or two to exact revenge. Peace between independent polities was always fragile and usually short-lived. The benefits of such peace were not typically considered so valuable that once established there were heroic efforts to keep it in place, except under the rarest of circumstances.

So, for all the above reasons and more, it is rather easy to make the case that over the long run, much warfare in the past was rational. However, when asked why warfare, in general, or specific raids were undertaken, etc., the extremely common explanations are women and revenge.

Fighting over women centers on fighting over wives; it is not two men fighting to win the hand of the woman by demonstrating prowess. When women are in short supply, raiding and capturing women is a rational behavior. In South America, Walker and Bailey (2013) found that about 0.6 women were captured per raid, which seems quite significant.[5] Because of selective infanticide and men with multiple wives, there was frequently a shortage of available potential wives in many of these societies. There are also cases in which men enticed women to leave a group with them, or the women left because they were badly treated. This could lead to retaliatory raiding or homicide. But one can see this as calculated behavior, although the responses seem to be close to revenge motivated in some instances.

It is revenge that is the far more interesting behavior. Seeking revenge, especially among men, seems to be close to a human universal. It seems to be closely related to "cultures of honor," where no slight is accepted and reputation is all important

[5] Raiding parties were about 10–15 individuals, but occasionally larger. Assuming the higher 15, and assuming a male went on 10 raids, they had better than one chance in three of obtaining a wife through raiding. Given the low risk of dying in raids, which is less than 2 % for a man going on 10 raids, the risk/reward ratio is very good.

(Boehm 1986). It is easy to see how revenge behavior is rational over the long haul but revenge seems innate and far from rational in the short term (see below). The point here is that the reasons foragers and acephalous farmers give for most of their warfare are not the ones that seem to be driving it from a rational point of view. That is, even when one can clearly see that territory was being annexed, potential competitors eliminated, valuable resource locations secured, or that warfare must have been a response to climate change, the protagonists see it in terms of revenge, upholding honor, or reasons having nothing to do with resources. These responses are so widely given and seem so firmly believed that it is hard not to take them at face value. Long-term rational behavior does not seem driven solely by rational decision making.

Evidence for "Innate," Deeply Emotional, or "Irrational" Behavior in Warfare There is also another behavior component to warfare that is hard to see as consciously determined. We might use the loose term "wired," a polite word for having a genetic basis as I assume innate means. Some of this behavior seems to be irrational, in the sense that that there seems to be little regard for any risk/reward calculation. Does this also imply wired behavior? There are in the literature examples of situations where we see decisions being made out of anger, revenge seeking, or other very emotional "hotheaded" feelings. In spite of the excerpt above, it is hard to evaluate an almost 200-year-old description of a foreign culture in terms of innate or genetically driven behavior.

A place where we can look at these situations more objectively is when we can see how the risk/reward equation works. A rather interesting finding is how much foragers engage in risky behavior. They seem to take risks out of proportion to the potential gains. While they try hard to minimize getting killed in the actual attack phase of raids, or even pitched battles, they take substantial risks in getting to and from the point of attack. This is very different from chimpanzee warfare, where as soon as chimpanzees sense they do not have overwhelming numerical superiority, they retreat (Wilson et al. 2007). It is hard to envision how the attacking party could themselves be overwhelmed. Offensive risk does seem to be very low for chimpanzees.

Such is not the case with foragers and acephalous farmers. They must travel through enemy territory, not knowing for sure where the enemy is or how many there are. They can be spotted and ambushed. From a military perspective, they often had poor situational awareness which could and did lead to massacres of the attack party. Even if the raid was successful, the attack party had to return by traveling back though enemy territory. Here they could be ambushed because the local people could move faster and knew the territory better. They fully realized this because taking female prisoners slowed them down, and it was sometimes felt too dangerous to try and bring them back. They often traversed territory they did not know very well, as seen by entire parties drowning in rivers they were unfamiliar with.

Another example in which what might be rational at one level clearly is not at another level, is the killing of strangers on sight. This is common among foragers. One would think that strangers, as long as they were not a real threat because they were alone, would be seen as a source of information and entertainment. But this does not appear to be the case. Some societies had mechanisms for individuals to approach strange groups to signal that they were not a threat. But an example from the Western Eskimo provides the typical attitude.

An Eskimo man was hunting on the ice for seals. The block of ice broke free and drifted before he could get off. After several days, he was almost dead from exposure and lack of food and water. Fortunately, the ice block drifted back to shore and he was able to get off. However, he landed in foreign territory where he was spotted by its inhabitants. Here he was weak, emaciated, no threat to anyone, and obviously had not intended to be in their territory. They killed him.

Such stories are common. So common that many regions had signals to show that you as a stranger were coming in peace, with the hope that the signal would be recognized before they killed you. While one can argue that killing a stranger meant that there was one less potential enemy in the world, this behavior seems so widespread it appears almost visceral.

Revenge Revenge is an overwhelming emotion for foragers and acephalous farmers. It figures in almost every account of why they fought and the emotional state they were in. If it is important from a long-term perspective to not appear weak, to keep one's enemies off balance, and otherwise not give up, then revenge as a motivation may be evolutionarily rational in the long term. But such long-term calculation is clearly not taking place. On a day-to-day basis, revenge is a very strong emotion that led to much warfare in the past. Simply put, the close kin of warriors killed in the field are commonly motivated to keep a war going until their kinsmen have been avenged. Revenge and kinship are closely related. In some societies this resulted in feuding, which could go on for generations. Societies where such feuding and extremely carefully calculated revenge tallies were pervasive have been termed "honor" societies. But this seems to be a misnomer, much like "warlike" society is. Virtually all forager and acephalous farmers engaged in revenge killing and it seems to always be a strong motivator for warfare. Honor societies are simply those in which it was extreme and in which social mechanisms had been elaborated to moderate it to some degree. Such societies were not qualitatively different from other "leaderless" societies; they were just at one end of the distribution.

It has been argued that herding societies, in which stealing stock was easier than stealing grain or frozen meat, had greater motivation to develop attitudes of honor or reputational revenge. If you know I will avenge any slight and stop at nothing to do so, then you might think twice about stealing my sheep. This well may be true, but foragers with little to steal are also obsessed with revenge.

Treatment of prisoners and captives before killing does seem to be related to the revenge motive. Even if the killing of prisoners is delayed (only among farmers, foragers do not take prisoners and later kill them), it seems to be accompanied by pleasure in the act of killing and seems to be seen as an act of revenge.

It appears that revenge as an important human motivation is considerably understudied. An important factor is that it is costly. One pays a price for exacting revenge in most cases. Either because of increased risk or the time and effort involved.

Casual observation suggests it is more strongly expressed in men than in women. That is, men seem to be willing to pay a higher price to exact revenge than women. I believe revenge can only be understood in terms of its close relationship to warfare in the deep past.

Enjoyment Richard Wrangham has argued that humans, especially men, get a pleasure high from winning, such as in sports. Moreover, it appears to him that it is the same sort of high chimpanzees get when they kill a chimpanzee from another troop. Do foragers get the same sort of high when they are victorious in warfare? The Aboriginal account above and other descriptions of victors' behavior suggest they do, but it is hard to see how one could ever test such a proposition.

One behavior that may indicate an enjoyment factor is what has been termed "overkill." When victory is complete and the winners do not have to retreat promptly to avoid retaliation, they frequently resort to mutilation of the victims or sometimes they continue to spear, shoot arrows into them or otherwise hack them up far beyond what is needed to kill them. This has been referred in some cases to "pincushioning" the dead enemy with arrows. Bodies are repeatedly shot, with perhaps twenty or more arrows. Some Paleolithic art can be interpreted as humans being speared many times. Some of this might be to encourage young, new fighters to shoot the corpse to get them used to the idea, but it seems too common and so excessive that there appears to be an excitement or thrill aspect to it that goes beyond teaching or other calculated behavior.

In summary, humans, especially men, engage in behaviors that involve warfare that cannot be directly explained by short-term conscious calculations. These seem to be wired and must have evolved as adaptive responses to intense warfare through human history.

Ending Warfare People do not always stop fighting even when rational reasons to fight disappear, which seems to be related to revenge. However, humans do sometimes stop fighting very quickly, as in the case of the Eskimos. We also see the intensity of warfare correlate with long-term climate change and even droughts or famines. In these cases, even if revenge became a factor in the nature of response, it did seem to dissipate over time. We also see this in forager and acephalous warfare from a different perspective. Alliances can shift rather remarkably. Groups that are enemies, with revenge as a major motivator, can quickly become allies when the nature of other threats develops. Animosities can disappear swiftly when the motivation is high. Yet we are all too aware of situations even today, where everyone would be far better off with peace than they are with continued conflict. Here is truly an area for research. We need to understand revenge much better and, as part of that, we need to understand why it can be turned off in some situations and why it is so persistent in others. This is a situation in which accepting the reality of warfare and the importance of revenge could lead to a better understanding of warfare that is relevant to today.

I have already noted that when Eskimos obtained rifles their warfare stopped. This seems to be a case of increased carrying capacity combined with the benefits of trade. I have also noted that the intensity of warfare does seem to correlate with climate and it does diminish when climate improves and intensifies when climate deteriorates. But there is a broader pattern with foragers. Many foragers stopped fighting very quickly. This is seen in Australia, Tierra de Fuego, California, and probably South Africa. This seems to relate to the carrying capacity and the impact of Europeans. Impact tended to have two consequences: disease and new tools. Exposure to European diseases greatly reduced the population in many cases. At the same time, the availability of metal for knives, cooking, arrow points, and axes, as well as guns, raised the effective carrying capacity because it made hunting and other activities much more efficient. The combined effect was to change the carrying capacity balance dramatically. Where populations had been near the carrying capacity, they were quickly well below it. Almost invariably, this led to a dramatic decrease in warfare if not its complete cessation. In places like Australia, this process was so rapid that by the time many aboriginal groups were contacted or studied they had already undergone this transition and were quite peaceful.

Some Biological Consequences of Warfare

There are a number of behaviors that seem to be best understood in the context of selection resulting from warfare. After selection derived from male–female reproductive differences, differences derived from warfare in the deep past have had the most important impact on such sex-based behavioral differences. This is clearly not well understood by most evolutionary psychologists. I reviewed several standard textbooks in the field, including their indexes. There was almost no consideration of such factors. Now certainly, the experimental evidence is not as rich as for reproduction-derived differences. But there is some evidence and one can certainly discuss the potential for future research along those lines. I believe the paucity of such discussion is that most evolutionary psychologists do not understand how pervasive and deadly such warfare was and how differently males and females were engaged in it. Even in an otherwise very useful paper on the evolutionary consequences of conflict in developing human's ingroup–outgroup propensities, Culotta (2012) questions the existence of significant warfare in the past. As I am not a psychologist, I only briefly look at some of these differences with a goal to opening a discussion rather than contributing to a deeper understanding.

Male vs. Female behaviors In the 1930s, a group of Yanomamo successfully routed another group. The men fled and the women and children were captured by the victors. One of the captured women recounted what happened next:

> … Meanwhile from all sides the women continued to arrive with their children, whom the other Karawetari had captured…Then the men began to kill the children; little ones, bigger ones, they killed many of them. They tried to run away, but they caught them, and threw them on the ground, and stuck them with bows, which went through their bodies and rooted them to the ground. Taking the smallest by the feet, they beat them against the trees and rocks… All the women wept… Helena Valero, a captive of the Yanomamo (Biocca 1971, p. 35)

Perhaps one of the most overlooked aspects of human warfare is that its evolutionary consequences affect men and women differently. In spite of the politically correct ideas, such as that by not giving boys toy weapons they will be less warlike, these evolutionary consequences are very real and deep. Men did the fighting and suffered the most deaths. Women also suffered both death and social dislocation to a meaningful degree, but the sexes were involved in warfare in very different ways. Surely the clearest and most in-depth consideration of these differences is a forthcoming book by Joyce Benenson—*Warriors and Worriers* (2013). Rather than try and cover all the ground she does, here I simply point out some of the most obvious behavioral differences. Benenson makes the case that males are wired for fighting and competing as well as cooperating with small groups of other males. Females are wired to survive in a very dangerous world and to ensure their children will survive. It is easier to see the impact of warfare on males because they have always done the fighting; hence, the selection has been more direct. To some degree, the female's evolutionary response to warfare is really just a response to an additional threat. Warfare may have been the single biggest threat to a woman's and her offspring's survival, but it was one of many threats, so the female behavioral response is not so easily tied into warfare per se.

To elaborate, Benenson sees evidence for these wiring differences at very young ages. Even young boys compete as groups against other groups, they select friends who would make the best allies, and they are capable of selecting leaders that will make the group successful. Benenson points out that males have, to a considerable degree, solved the very vexing problem of being able to compete with other males over sexual partners, but then be able to cooperate with these males, sometimes at significant cost, to fight with other groups. Women need the support of the community and especially the support of some other women to make sure their children survive. This is seen in their greater focus on social and emotional and interpersonal issues and interactions. They form different size groups than men and have fewer leaders that are not age and kin determined.

To reiterate, men compete for access to women through dominance hierarchies. Everyone wants to be the alpha male. While not nearly so overt as with chimpanzees, human males clearly did and do compete for mates. However, when threatened by an outside threat, males need to stop competing and let another male be the leader. If you do not do this, you are at a terrible disadvantage with respect to the other groups and you will be eliminated. So selection is strong for the ability to work as a team and forget the intragroup competition when the need arises. Conversely, women are very likely to have moved from the group they were born in. This can be due to mate exchange but also due to female capture in warfare. In the latter case, they well could find themselves in a group where they did not even speak the language. The way women form friendships, and their superior ability to read body language, could well derive from being in such situations.

Coming from a very different perspective, Browne (2001) makes a very strong, excellent case for deep differences between men and women when it comes to warfare-related behavior and he also argues that it is deeply wired. The obvious reason is that warfare was a male activity throughout human history. In spite of the strong case these two, among others, make, the evolutionary impact of warfare on behavior remains surprisingly under-considered. Other differences, perhaps less controversial, are also worth reviewing.

Sexual Dimorphism Human males, on average, are universally larger than females and, perhaps most relevant, males have almost double the upper body muscles of women (Lassek and Gaulin 2009). The two standard reasons for this sexual dimorphism are intragroup male competition for women and the need to be larger to hunt large game. The intragroup competition hypothesis may be correct for the deep past, but it does not fit what we know about historic foragers and leaderless farmers. Intragroup marriages tend to be arranged often when the women are still young girls. There is essentially no violent competition for them. This explanation takes on a modern-day form of women being attracted to men with more upper body mass, even to the point of male athletes having more sexual partners that other men (review by Lassek and Gaulin 2009). However, this seems to be a classic case of modern outcomes for older selective processes. In forager and acephalous societies, successful warriors attract and retain mates. And for sports, is it athletes that are attractive or is it males who function well in large aggressive groups that are attractive—is it football players or wrestlers that are attractive to women?

The hunting argument is also weak. Forager and farmer-hunters do not seem to use size to any advantage. Hunters in the Philippines, Bushmen, and pygmies, for example, are all quite small people. And these hunters regularly take on deer, boars, large antelope, and even elephants. Again, hunting megafauna may have required extra muscles. But again, the megafauna of Australia went extinct some 40,000 years ago, and the surviving fauna are not very large. Yet, there is plenty of sexual dimorphism. One would think if hunting large game was the reason for the differences, they would have been greatly diminished in such a long span.

While these reasons may have played a part in sexual dimorphism, a more obvious explanation is warfare. Yet, this explanation is virtually ignored in the literature. If much fighting was at close quarters, size would have been advantageous. Now one must admit that successful warriors seem to be men who are behaviorally aggressive and are not necessarily the largest men. This is certainly possible for offensive raids. However, when attacked, big strong men would have been much more able to defend themselves. For every attack there are defenders and that would seem to provide plenty of selective pressure for the large body size in men. One could argue that it might work for women also, except that most of the time women had small children and the safest course of action is to flee when attacked, or at least try and protect your children. Women are probably optimally sized for the food supply, while males are inefficiently sized based on the ecology but properly sized given the risk of being too small to fight well.

This failure to see sexual dimorphism realistically is another example of the pacification of the past to the detriment of our understanding of warfare.

Male-Biased Sex Ratios Another topic worthy of further consideration but one that is highly speculative and highly charged is male-biased sex ratios. Biased sex ratios are common throughout the world. They invariably result in more males than females. While infanticide was essentially universal, based on carrying capacity limitations, there is no inherent reason why it should be sexually biased. They are usually explained in terms of the value of males as hunters, taking care of elderly parents, etc. Other explanations of sex ratios tend to be around the fact that women are lost to the family in most forager societies. This is always the case for farmers, but my argument is that the essentially universal bias toward males suggests that if this is a built-in human propensity, it must have evolved very long ago. Thus, foragers are the proper model. The problem with the women leaving the group, as an explanation, is that women are essentially traded for other women. No women to trade means no wives for your sons. While that was sometimes the consequent, it is hard to see why it was the underlying reason for such behavior.

Here is a situation in which group selection might have taken place at the cultural level. Any group who differentially selected females over males would quickly be at a numerical disadvantage over contemporary groups who had male-dominated sex ratios. Such groups would have been eliminated. While individual families might have improved their fitness by having excess females, the cost to the group would probably have been quite high. In a world of essentially equally effective competing groups, those with the most males win in an attritional warfare environment, which is what raiding is. Thus, even though males are lost to warfare more often than women are, if you do not have enough males then everyone and everything is lost. Whether the usual arguments about freeloaders apply to this situation is not clear. But such a model should at least be considered as providing a more likely explanation than the "women tend to leave the group" as an explanation for the almost universal "males are more valuable" worldview.

Conclusions

Several points have been made. Warfare in the past was very real and deadly. This warfare would have taken place while humans were foragers and so foragers and, to some degree, acephalous farmers are our best models for how this warfare worked. The evolutionary selection consequences must have been profound. We should expect there to be major differences between men and women in this evolution. Evolutionary consequences should be as profound as for mate selection, but evolutionary psychologists have not devoted nearly as much effort to this aspect of human evolution, probably because they are not fully aware of how important warfare was in the past.

References

Arkush, E., & Allen, M. W. (2006). *The archaeology of warfare: Prehistories of raiding and conquest*. Gainsville: The University of Florida Press.
Balikci, A. (1970). *The Netsilik Eskimo*. Garden City: Natural History Press
Benenson, J. F. (2013). *Warriors and Worriers*. New York: Oxford University Press.
Biocca, E. (1971). *The Yanoama: The narrative of a white girl kidnapped by Amazonian Indians*. New York: Dutton Paperback.
Browne, K. R. (2001). Women at war: An evolutionary perspective. *Buffalo Law Review*, *49*, 51–247.
Boehm, C. (1986). *Blood revenge: The enactment and management of conflict in Montenegro and other tribal societies*. Philadelphia: University of Pennsylvania Press.
Boonzaier, E., Malherbe, C., Smith A., & Berens P. (1996). The cape herders: A history of the Khoikhoi of Southern Africa. Cape Town: D. Philip.
Bowles, S. (2009). Did warfare among ancestral hunter-gatherers affect the evolution of human social behaviors? *Science*, *324*, 1293–1298.
Burch, E. S., Jr. (1974). Eskimo warfare in Northwest Alaska. *Anthropological Papers of the University of Alaska*, *16*(2):1–14.
Burch, E. S., Jr. (2005). *Alliance and conflict: The world system of the Inupiaq Eskimos*. University of Nebraska Press, Lincoln.
Burch, E. S., Jr. (2007). Traditional native warfare in western Alaska. In R. J. Chacon & R. G. Mendoza (Eds.), *North American indigenous warfare and ritual violence* (pp. 11–29). Tucson: The University of Arizona Press.
Chagnon, N. A. (1968) *Yanomamo: The fierce people*. New York: Holt, Reihart and Winston.
Colvin, I. D. (1900). *South Africa*. London, Thomas Nelson and Sons.
Culotta, E. (2012). Roots of racism. *Science*, *336*(May 18), 825–827.
Eibl-Eibesfleldt, I. (1975). Aggression in the! Ko-Bushmen. In M. A. Nettleship, R. D. Givens & A. Nettleship (Eds.) *War, its causes and correlates* (pp. 281–296). Mouton, The Hague.
Fabbro, D. (1978). Peaceful societies: An introduction. *Journal of Peace Research* 15(1):67–83.
Faust, D. G. (1992). *Southern stories: Slaveholders in peace and war*. Columbia Missouri: University of Missouri Press.
Ferguson, R. B. (1992). A savage encounter: Western contact and the Yanomami War Complex. In R. B. Ferguson & N. L. Whitehead (Eds.), *War in the tribal zone: Expanding states and indigenous warfare* (pp. 199–227). Santa Fe: School of American Research Press.
Frayer, D. W. (1997). Ofnet: Evidence for a Mesolithic massacre. In D. L. Martin & D. W. Frayer (Eds.), *Troubled times: Violence and warfare in the past* (pp. 181–216). Amsterdam: Gordon and Breach.
Fry, D. P. (2007). *Beyond war: The human potential for peace*. Oxford: Oxford University Press.
Fry, D. P. (2012). Life without war. *Science*, *336*(May 18), 879–884.
Gat, A. (2006). *War in human civilization*. Oxford: Oxford University Press.
Gilder, W. H. (1881). Schwatka's search: Sledging in the Arctic in quest of the Franklin records. New York: Charles Scribner's Sons.
Hearne, S. (2007) [1795]. *A journey to the Northern ocean: The adventures of Samuel Hearne* by Samuel Hearne. Foreword by Ken McGoogan. Surrey, BC: TouchWood Editions.
Heider, K. (1979). *Grand Valley Dani: Peaceful warriors*. New York: Holt, Rinehart and Winston.
Isaac, B. (1987). Throwing and human evolution. *The African Archaeological Review*, *5*, 3–17.
Keeley, L. H. (1996). *War before civilization*. New York: Oxford University Press.
Kelly, R. C. (2000). *Warless societies and the origin of war*. Ann Arbor: University of Michigan Press.
Lambert, P. M. (1997). Patterns of violence in prehistoric hunter-gatherer societies of coastal Southern California. In D. L. Martin & D. W. Frayer (Eds.), *Troubled times: Violence and warfare in the past* (pp. 77–110). Amsterdam: Gordon and Breach.

Lambert, P. M. (2007). The osteological evidence for indigenous warfare in North America. In R. J. Chacon & R. G. Mendoza (Eds.), *North American indigenous warfare and ritual violence* (pp. 202–221). Tucson: The University of Arizona Press.
Lambert, P., & Walker P. (1991). Physical anthropological evidence for the evolution of social complexity in coastal Southern California. *Antiquity*, *65*, 963–973.
Lassek, W. D., & Gaulin, S. J. C. (2009). Costs and benefits of fat-free muscle mass in men: relationship to mating success, dietary requirements, and native immunity. *Evolution and Human Behavior*, *30*(5), 322–328.
Lawler, A. (2012) The battle over violence. *Science*, *336*(May 18), 829–830.
LeBlanc, S. A. (1999). *Prehistoric warfare in the American Southwest*. Salt Lake City: University of Utah Press.
LeBlanc, S. A. (2003) *Constant battles*. New York: St. Martin's Press.
Lee, R. B. (1979) *The !Kung San: Men, women, and work in a foraging society*. Cambridge: Cambridge University Press.
Marshall, L. (1976). *The!Kung of Nyae Nyae*. Cambridge: Harvard University Press.
McCall, G. S., & Shields, N. (2008). Examining the evidence from small-scale societies and early prehistory and implications for modern theories of aggression and violence. *Aggression and Violent Behavior*, *13*, 1–9.
Melbye, J. & Fairgreive S. I. (1994). A massacre and possible cannibalism in the Canadian Arctic: New evidence from the Saunaktuk site (NgTn-1). *Arctic Anthropology*, *31*(2):57–77.
Milner, G. R. (1999). Warfare in prehistoric and early historic eastern North America. *Journal of Archaeological Research*, *7*(2), 105–151.
Milner, G. R. (2005). Nineteenth-century arrow wounds and perceptions of prehistoric warfare. *American Antiquity*, *70*(144–156).
Morgan, J. (1852) [1979]. *The life and adventures of William Buckley: Thirty two years a wanderer amongst the aborigines*. Hobart, Tasmania: Archibald MacDougall.
Orscheidt, J. A. (2005). The head burials from Ofnet Cave: An example of warlike conflict in the Mesolithic. In M. Parker Pearson & N. Thorpe (Eds.), *Warfare, violence and slavery in Prehistory: Proceedings of a prehistoric society conference at Shefield University* (pp. 67–73). Oxford, BAR 1374.
Parkington, J. E. (1984). Soaqua and Bushmen: Hunters and Robbers. In C. Schrire (Ed.), *Past and present in hunter gatherer studies*. Orlando: Academic Press.
Pinker, S. (2011). *The better angels of our nature: Why violence has declined*. Viking: New York.
Rasmussen, K. (1931). *The Netsilik Eskimos: Social life and spiritual culture*. Report of the Fifth Thule Expedition 1921–1924 Vol. 8(1–2), Copenhagen.
Roscoe, P. B. (2003). Margaret Mead, Reo Fortune, and Mountain Arapesh warfare. *American Anthropologist*, *105*, 581–591.
Sarkar, S. S. (1962). The Jarawa of the Andaman Islands. *Anthropos*, *57*, 670–677.
Schapera, I. (1930). *The Khoisan peoples of South Africa: Bushmen and Hottentots*. London: Routledge.
Schire, C. (1980). An Inquiry into the evolutionary status and apparent identity of San hunter-gatherers. *Human Ecology*, *8*, 9–32.
Soltis, J., Boyd, R., & Richerson, P. J. (1995). Can group-functional behaviors evolve by cultural group selection? An empicral test. *Current Anthropology*, *36*(3), 473–494.
Thieme, H. (1997). Lower Paleolithic hunting spears from Germany. *Nature*, *385*, 807.
Trinkaus, E. (2012). Neandertals, early modern humans, and rodeo riders. *Journal of Archaeological Science*, *39*(12), 3691–3693. doi:10.1016/j.jas.2012.05.039.
Walker, R. S., & Bailey, D. H. (2013). Body counts in lowland South American violence. *Evolution and Human Behavior*.
Wilson, M. L., & Wrangham, R. W. (2003). Intergroup relations in Chimpanzees. *Annual Review of Anthropology*, *32*, 363–392.
Wilson, M. L., Hauser, M. D., & Wrangham, R. W. (2007). Chimpanzees (Pan troglodytes) modify grouping and vocal behavior in response to location-specific risk. *Behavior*, *144*, 1621–1653.
Wrangham, R. W., Wilson, M. L., & Muller, M. N. (2006). Comparative rates of violence in chimpanzees and humans. *Primates*, *47*, 14–26.

Chapter 6
Sexual Selection and the Psychology of Intergroup Conflict

Carlos David Navarrete and Melissa M. McDonald

Sexual Selection and the Psychology of Intergroup Conflict

Violent intergroup conflict is pervasive and has existed throughout history with the available evidence suggesting that it was even more prevalent in the distant past, relative to the present (Pinker 2011). Research also suggests that it is unlikely to have originated in one place or to have spread by cultural diffusion or conquest. The foundational works of world literature such as the *Iliad*, the *Bhagavad Gita*, the *Torah*, and the *Quran* provide a window on the brutality of ancient societies in which conflicts of interests between individuals belonging to differing groups were less often characterized by diplomacy, than by hostile action such as raids, warfare, kidnapping, and rape.

Archeological evidence affirms that this state of affairs likely characterized pr-estate societies predating civilization, with evidence stretching back to at least the Upper Paleolithic (e.g., Keeley 1996; Kelly 2005). This intergroup aggression has almost exclusively been perpetrated by groups of males against other males in contexts ranging from small-scale coalitional skirmishes to regional and geopolitical conflicts (for reviews, see Daly and Wilson 1988; Keegan 1993; Wrangham and Peterson 1996). Evidence for male aggression, going back from deep time to the present, can be inferred from genetic studies comparing the global and regional distribution of the Y-chromosome DNA (inherited from male ancestors) relative to mitochondrial DNA (inherited from female ancestors) in extant humans. Researchers find less variance among Y-chromosome DNA, indicating the presence of fewer male ancestors relative to female ancestors, with estimates of our most

C. D. Navarrete (✉)
Department of Psychology, Michigan State University,
Psychology Building East Lansing, MI 48824 USA
e-mail: cdn@msu.edu

M. M. McDonald
School of Psychology, Interdisciplinary Center,
P.O.Box 167, Herzliya, 46150, Israel
e-mail: m.m.mcdonald32@gmail.com

T. K. Shackelford, R. D. Hansen (eds.), *The Evolution of Violence*,
Evolutionary Psychology, DOI 10.1007/978-1-4614-9314-3_6,

recent female common ancestor having lived 150–200 KYA, whereas our most recent male common ancestor is estimated to have lived only since the Upper Paleolithic era, approximately 30–50 KYA (Makova and Li 2002). Such findings are consistent with a historical explanation in which there was stronger selection on Y-chromosome DNA relative to mitochondrial DNA, as a result of higher male mortality relative to female mortality in the Upper Paleolithic. Evidence of strong selection on Y-chromosome DNA continuing to relatively recent times can be inferred via comparisons where regional conquests perpetrated by a relatively small number of invading males has been documented in detail. For example, extant South American Indian populations show little to no evidence of the persistence of Y-chromosome DNA from native populations in the New World from their most common male ancestor who lived only a few centuries ago (Mahli et al. 2008). However, native mitochondrial DNA is well represented among extant peoples throughout Latin America (e.g., Makova and Li 2002), suggesting strong selection for European male invaders in the last few centuries. Thus, genetic evidence is consistent with both anthropological and historical data suggesting that intergroup violence displacing natal populations has been primarily perpetrated by males against other males.

The presence of differential levels of intergroup aggression between the sexes is expected to be associated with sexual dimorphism, in size and strength, as well as in the design of the psychology of males and females (Daly and Wilson 1988; Tooby and Cosmides 1988), and it is with the latter that this chapter is concerned. The evolutionary approach in which this discussion is framed is referred to as an *adaptationist perspective*, wherein one considers the likely selection pressures that recurred over evolutionary history to frame testable hypotheses regarding human cognition, attitudes, emotions, and behavior (Andrews et al. 2002; Buss et al. 1998; Tooby and Cosmides 1992). An adaptationist approach assumes that psychological systems underlying behavior are "for" functional ends—that is, they exist to solve a problem relevant to one's survival or reproduction. Therefore, research from an adaptationist perspective that seeks to understand the psychology of intergroup conflict is informed by a consideration of the kinds of adaptive problems faced by our Paleolithic ancestors, and how group living helped them address these challenges. In this chapter, examples from recent psychological literature on race bias are used to describe how fundamental aspects of the psychological mechanisms underlying intergroup conflict may operate.

In this chapter, we address a fundamental question regarding a putative evolved psychological system responsible for the mental representation of groups at its most basic level, as well as this system's working mechanisms that generate xenophobic biases. As one might imagine, functional solutions to various problems may require different strategies, which may be generated from distinct psychological systems. Such possibilities include psychological mechanisms evolved to identify social categories (Cheney and Seyfarth 1982; Tajfel 1982) which may then be used to demarcate coalitional groups (Kurzban et al. 2001), familial clans, and cultural or ethnic groups (Gil-White 2001; Hirschfeld 1996)—none of which are mutually exclusive.

Whatever combination of basic cognitive processes underlie how people mentally represent race categories, we believe that a research program that tests hypotheses about when and how race bias is expressed can be enriched by considering the kinds of challenges people face when interacting with individuals from a social group other than one's own (hereafter referred to as the *outgroup*). When studying individual responses to others in intergroup contexts, it is helpful to think of outgroups as posing different kinds of adaptive challenges than are posed by members of one's own group (the *ingroup*). Furthermore, the problems posed by outgroup members differ markedly depending on whether the target or the perceiver is male or female. As such, one might expect that the psychology of intergroup conflict ought to differ considerably between men and women in some domains but not in others. Here we utilize an adaptationist perspective to frame our understanding of the psychology of intergroup conflict, and showcase how this perspective has the potential to provide the conceptual tools for framing interesting hypotheses regarding the psychology of race and ethnic bias and why these biases are so persistent and pervasive in society. In doing so, we draw attention to the fact that our history of intergroup conflict and the unique problems it posed for our male and female ancestors may be responsible for why we tend to be biased when judging and evaluating ingroups and outgroups, and we argue that these biases served functional outcomes for the agents of group-based prejudice and discrimination. An appreciation of this history is crucial to understanding the psychological underpinnings of our propensity for warfare and xenophobia.

A Meta-Theoretical Approach to the Psychology of Intergroup Conflict

In attempting to provide coherent accounts of how the psychology of intergroup conflict operates, it is perhaps most fruitful to stay true to a broader computational approach shared by psychologists of different stripes, and avoid the language of the false dichotomies of *nature versus nurture*, *genes versus culture*, or *personality versus social context*. Rather, a computational approach suggests that the workings of the mind can be understood as the output of psychological systems with working mechanisms designed "for" a purpose or goal of the system (e.g., Tooby and Cosmides 1992). The mechanisms that compose these systems can be understood even without specific knowledge of the contributions made from one's genes versus socially transmitted information. The computational systems devised by natural selection are indifferent to whether information is obtained from one's genes or one's environment (e.g., Dawkins 1982; Kaplan and Gangestad 2005). Rather, the mechanisms that generate behavior operate on decision rules that are shaped by natural selection as a function of their influence on survival and reproduction in a given environment. From this broad, computational understanding of how psychological systems operate, the utility of dichotomous thinking regarding notions such as the relative importance of "persons" versus "social situations" in predicting human behavior and cognition (Mischel 1979) becomes less relevant. This is because an individual's personality and environment are more rightfully conceptualized as informational input into the computational systems of the mind—systems which must yield, as do all replicating systems found in nature, to the forces of selection.

A Theory of the Psychology of Intergroup Conflict: Separate Adaptive Problems between the Sexes and Adaptive Solutions

Our discussion of the workings of the psychological systems relevant to intergroup conflict begins with the acknowledgment that the challenges faced by ancestral men and women, and the solutions to those problems, likely differ as a function of differences in sexual strategies between men and women. As such, we draw heavily on the insights of parental investment and sexual selection theories (Darwin 1871; Bateman 1948; Trivers 1972). We posit that selection has produced psychological systems for managing the cognitive processing of the risks and benefits of physical and sexual aggression in intergroup contexts, which differs between men and women (Thornhill and Palmer 2000; Tooby and Cosmides 1988; Navarrete et al. 2010).

The Roots of a Male-Specific Psychology of Prejudice

Sexual selection is a form of natural selection that operates along two pathways (Darwin 1871; Fisher 1930; Andersson 1994), *intra-* and *intersexual* selection. Intrasexual selection involves competition between members of the same sex, and produces traits that are useful in competition with same-sex rivals in gaining access to mating opportunities (e.g., elongated teeth and horns, large muscles). Intersexual selection describes a feedback process in which the strategies and preferences of one sex give rise to counterstrategies and preferences in the other. Rather than evolving to address same-sex competition, this process typically facilitates the evolution of traits that are useful for attracting members of the opposite sex (e.g., plumage and nuptial gifts), but the process can also be applied to understanding how one sex deals with the sexual strategies of the other sex (e.g., female estrus).

Parental investment theory begins with the observation that the sexes differ in the minimum physiological effort they must exert to produce viable offspring (Clutton-Brock and Vincent 1991). The applications of this theory are wide-ranging and apply to humans and nonhuman animals alike. For example, at minimum, women bear the costs of gamete production, fertilization, placentation, gestation, birthing, and lactation, whereas men are minimally obligated to invest only in the energetic resources required for gamete production and fertilization. Given this asymmetry, the marginal fitness gains from acquiring multiple mates are far greater for men than for women, and the costs of mating with a low-quality mate are far greater for women than for men. In other words, women are physically constrained by their reproductive physiology for a relatively lower reproductive ceiling over their life span; as a result, increasing the number of sexual partners does not increase reproductive success to the same degree as it does for men. In fact, it can place women at higher risk for harmful consequences of sex—such as those arising from infectious disease and low genetic quality of the copulating partner—without the offsetting benefit of steeply increased offspring number as is true for men.

Merging insights from sexual selection and parental investment theory suggests that the fundamental differences in reproductive physiology between the sexes produce an asymmetry in the strength of intrasexual competition, with competition for mates operating more strongly in males (Trivers 1972). For men, risky, aggressive, and physically dangerous tactics used to subdue, debilitate, or eliminate same-sex competitors can greatly increase reproductive output via increased status and its associated fitness benefits, including increased sexual access to the opposite-sex surplus (Griskevicius et al. 2009). For women, however, the same tactics do not increase potential reproductive output given the constraints of women's reproductive physiology.

Given that men have more to gain than women from engaging in interpersonal violence, this logic may be extended to apply to inter*group* violence as well. Assuming that collective action problems characteristic of intergroup conflict are addressed (e.g., Choi and Bowles 2007), the winners of such conflicts may be rewarded with additional territorial and food resources, increased status, and direct acquisition of females from the defeated group (Manson and Wrangham 1991; Mitani et al. 2010; Tooby and Cosmides 1988; Wrangham et al. 2006). Thus, just as interpersonal violence is typically a male affair, when we apply the principles of sexual selection and parental investment to the problem of human intergroup aggression, we should similarly expect males to be both its primary agents as well as its primary targets (Buss and Shackelford 1997; Daly and Wilson 1988; Sidanius and Pratto 1999). This can occur even under conditions of high risk of injury or death, given that the formation of coalitions is typically characterized by mechanisms for effective risk management, such as pooling risk across individuals behind a "veil of ignorance" regarding one's probability of injury or death, and "winner take all" outcomes that create large payoffs for survivors (Choi and Bowles 2007; Tooby and Cosmides 1988). Such incentives explain sex differences in the willingness to engage in risky and aggressive strategies in order to dominate other groups, as well as the motivation to avoid being dominated. As such, with a high-risk, high-reward incentive structure, it is likely that a *male-specific* psychology of intergroup conflict may have evolved to perpetrate or resist intergroup dominance and aggression among males. Thus, to the extent that racial categories can be mentally represented as coalition-like entities to the human mind (Kurzban et al. 2001), we submit that the workings of this psychological system should be detectable in empirical investigations of intergroup bias—including sex differences in behavior, emotional reactions, attitudes, and cognitive processing of group phenomena.

Evidence for a Male-Specific Psychology of Intergroup Conflict

Given that men are willing to accept more risk in competition for valued resources, we predict that in behavioral studies of intergroup conflict, men should be less inhibited to embrace aggressive intergroup strategies. Consistent with this expectation, men report more competitive intergroup interactions than women (van Vugt et al. 2007), and are more likely to engage in "pre-emptive strikes," without provocation, in simulated war games (Johnson et al. 2006). In a recent experimental study, researchers found that men, but not women, were more likely to endorse statements supporting war after they had been primed with attractive members of the opposite sex (Chang et al. 2011). Such results are consistent with the notion that, for men, intergroup conflict may serve the ultimate purpose of gaining access to reproductive resources.

Data from surveys measuring racial attitudes and discrimination support this perspective. Based on the notion that racially prejudiced attitudes can be conceptualized as a type of "low-level" expression of intergroup aggression among males, Sidanius and Veniegas (2000) made the following two predictions: (1) men should express greater racial prejudice and discrimination than women and (2) such prejudice should be more strident against men (compared to women) of the racial outgroup. Survey evidence does in fact suggest that men are, on average, more biased than women on explicit measures of race bias (e.g., Ekehammar 1985; Ekehammar and Sidanius 1980, 1982; Furnham 1985; Marjoribanks 1981; Sidanius et al. 1991; Sidanius and Ekehammar 1980). Archival and audit studies provided some support for the second prediction that men are the targets of greater levels of group-based prejudice. Examples are readily found in audit studies in the educational system (Gordon, Piana and Keleher 2000), the labor market (Arai and Thoursie 2007; Arai, Bursell, and Nekby 2008; Carlsson and Rooth 2007; Stroh et al. 1992), sales pricing of automobiles (Ayres 1991), and criminal sentencing (Bushway and Piehl 2001; Steffensmeier et al. 1998).

Although such outcomes are indicative of "real world" discrimination, such studies have the limitation that, because the gender of the agent of prejudice is anonymous, it is not clear if the male-targeted outcomes are the result of greater discrimination by men or if women also contribute to such negative outcomes for outgroup men. However, several laboratory experiments have demonstrated the greater evocative potential of male outgroup targets in engendering biased reactions. For example, vignettes involving criminal men of racial outgroups elicit greater bias with respect to punitive attitudes about criminal sentencing relative to vignettes involving outgroup women portrayed as criminals (Haley et al. 2004); resistance to extinction of conditioned fear is greater toward outgroup men than women (Navarrete et al. 2009); and angry outgroup male faces facilitate superior detection in visual search tasks akin to the kinds of abilities typically evoked by natural hazards such as snakes or spiders (Ackerman et al. 2007).

More recently, Navarrete et al. (2010) tested a set of predictions informed by a consideration of the specific selection pressures postulated to have shaped the intergroup psychology of men. Namely, that (a) discriminatory outcomes would be greater when men were pitted against other groups of men compared to women and (b) aggression and social dominance would more consistently predict bias for men, relative to women.

The researchers conducted an experiment with male and female participants who were asked to make recommendations for zero-sum resource allocations to ingroups and outgroups composed of all males or all females. They found that when given the option of inflicting a spiteful, costly punishment on another group at the cost of ingroup resources, men elected to punish outgroups composed of men, more so than outgroups composed of women. Interestingly, women showed no bias in punishment, between ingroup and outgroup targets, regardless of their gender composition. In two other studies (Studies 2 and 4; Navarrete et al. 2010), men's racial prejudice, but not women's, was related to individual differences in aggression, particularly when the men's goal of intergroup dominance was chronically salient.

Consistent with the widely documented sex difference in prejudiced attitudes against outgroups, these patterns of sex-specific relationships among target gender, agent gender, aggression, and the goal of social dominance suggest that a meaningful component of racial prejudice may be fundamentally related to recurring intergroup conflict among human males over evolutionary history. Taken together, this collection of findings is consistent with theoretical expectations. However, the selection pressure arising from male–male competition alone does not explain another important aspect of intergroup prejudice: that exhibited by women. Although there is evidence suggesting that women are generally less explicitly prejudiced than men (reviewed in McDonald et al. 2012), they are clearly not free from bias. In studies where the gender of the outgroup target is manipulated, levels of bias displayed by men and women toward outgroup men are often similar (e.g., Haley et al. 2004; Navarrete et al. 2009), or sometimes even greater for women (e.g., Owens et al. 2000; Stets and Straus 1990; Fisman et al. 2008). Such findings suggest that an understanding of the mechanisms underpinning women's intergroup bias cannot rely solely on processes that evolved to manage intrasexual competition among men.

To improve our understanding in this regard, we might ask: what selection pressures have been at play that might have shaped women's psychology of bias? Intrasexual competition among men may have contributed to a conflict of interest between men and women in the choice and timing of mating in intergroup contexts. Below we describe a *female-specific* psychology of intergroup bias that may have evolved in response to the unique problems that women have faced in conflicts of interest with outgroup men.

The Roots of a Female-Specific Psychology of Intergroup Conflict

Female Reproductive Choice and the Problem of Sexual Coercion

Female reproductive choice is a core component of mating strategies for sexually reproducing organisms (Trivers 1972), and maintaining choice of one's mate is critical to the health and wellbeing of offspring. For human females, two general paternal factors influence the survival prospects of their children: the genetic quality of the biological father and the amount of investment the father makes in providing for the offspring. Lower-quality males with genetic predispositions impairing survival prospects or a low social standing have a higher probability of having low-quality offspring who themselves may not survive or may not be able to obtain mates. Women who conceive without paternal investment are at risk of not having the nutritional or protective resources necessary for birthing and raising healthy offspring. Sexual aggression from strangers poses severe risks across both of these factors. Without the important information about the characteristics of the father of one's offspring that comes with familiarity, the opportunity to judge the quality of the father is compromised even more so than when traits of the attacker are known, which is a cost in its own right, to be sure. Moreover, strangers who invade and aggress sexually may be less likely to remain to invest in childcare and protection following birth. Additionally, unfamiliar outgroup males are almost certainly less likely to be held accountable to ingroup norms for the monitoring and sanctioning of deviance.

A point worth making along these lines is that "stranger rape" is less common than rape by those with whom the victim is acquainted in modern societies. However, this is also true of nearly every known kind of violent assault, including murder (Wolfgang 1958), and is due to the logical necessity that most people's social networks are largely a function of their proximity to family, friends, allies, and others with whom they become acquainted (Daly and Wilson 1988). Furthermore, the human proclivity for social interaction along familiar lines is almost certainly due to the fact that we are much better off in proximity to those with shared fates (genetically or otherwise) relative to outsiders whose interests are not closely aligned with ours and who cannot be readily monitored and sanctioned for deviant behavior (Yamagishi 1998; Yamagishi and Kiyonara 2000). As such, the so-called greater "likelihood" of violent or sexual assault by acquaintances or intimate partners relative to strangers may be an artifact of human evolved affiliative preferences serving prophylactic functions, as is suggested by the empirical link between a woman's proximity to her kin and the avoidance of rape (reviewed in McKibbin and Shackelford 2012). Thus, the affordances for victimhood must consider baseline rates of time necessarily spent in proximity to acquaintances/intimates versus that spent among strangers, which almost certainly means that individuals are at a far higher risk of being assaulted by strangers rather than by acquaintances. In other words, the per time unit risk of sexual assault at the hands of unfamiliar outgroup men is likely to be markedly higher than the threat of sexual assault among familiar men from one's own within-group network, if baseline time in proximity were to be held constant. Therefore, the logic underlying female choice implies that the costs associated with the risks of sexual coercion are exacerbated when one is in proximity to an outgroup male.

On Selection Pressures for a Risk Management System

Tying the logic of the costs of sexual coercion to the logic of coalitional conflict among males described above suggests that men on the weaker side of a coalitional conflict are not the only ones who suffer fitness challenges from invaders. Although women may have a lower probability of being the victims of lethal intergroup violence, they have all too often been the targets of nonlethal sexual violence in times of group conflict (Broude and Green 1978; Levinson 1989; Vikman 2005; Thornhill and Palmer 2000). To be sure, the costs for sexual aggression are potentially quite high for men in most within-group contexts (Smith et al. 2001), including the risk of retaliation from the victim, her kin, or mate, as well as the loss of one's reputation and alliances. Thus, it is not surprising that most men, under most circumstances, do not use sexual aggression as a reproductive strategy.

However, the costs to perpetrators of sexual aggression may be markedly lower when committed against outgroups, particularly when intergroup relations are hostile, such as is the case during warfare (Thornhill and Palmer 2000; Wrangham and Peterson 1996; Vikman 2005). This may be due to a combination of several social processes, including the reduced accountability across group boundaries and ethnocentric moral double standards in the value placed on the interests of outgroup members. At the level of proximate causation, there are studies documenting biases in the activation of empathy to ingroup members in pain versus outgroup members (e.g., Avenanti et al. 2010) and the greater likelihood of harming others when in a group than when alone (e.g., Leidner and Castano 2012). Holding aside the question of whether the human *male* psychology has been shaped by selection to seek out opportunities for sexual aggression (Thornhill and Pamer 2000), the available evidence strongly suggests that sexual coercion is likely to have occurred often enough throughout history to have been an important selection pressure on the psychology of human *females*.

That women have been confronted with the problem of maintaining reproductive choice in the face of challenges from coercive males is evidenced in the historical record of intergroup conflict as documented by historians of antiquity as far back as there are records (Vikman 2005). Mass rape of women and girls were among the punitive measures taken by Greek, Persian, Arabic, Jewish, and Roman armies, with ensuing sexual and conjugal slavery condoned and regulated by both secular and religious law. The Hebrew Bible contains numerous references to the ubiquity of gang rape, sexual slavery, and forced marriage of victims to the perpetrators in descriptions of ancient Semitic tribal conflict, and it is described as an almost trivially obvious expectation of the spoils of battle (reviewed in Pinker 2011). Relatively recent examples of sexual aggression during violent conflicts such as those committed in Bosnia, Rwanda, Darfur, and the US engagement in Vietnam highlight the continuing risk of sexual aggression for women on the weaker side of group conflicts.

Regardless of the precise nature of the proximate or functional psychological factors that lead to sexual aggression by men in intergroup contexts, it appears that sexual coercion by outgroup men not only poses unique risks because of the added costs of uncertainty, but also may have historically posed a more probabilistic threat of sexual assault than men from one's own group. Not only has warfare provided greater affordance of opportunities for sexual aggression as far back as the historical record allows (Vikman 2005), but violent intergroup conflict may have been even more common in prehistoric societies than has been the case in historical societies (Bamforth 1994; Chagnon 1996; Daly and Wilson 1988; Ember 1978; Ghiglieri 1999; Keeley 1996; Knauft 1987; Krech 1994; Wrangham and Peterson 1996). In a recent survey of the history and prehistory of violence, Pinker (2011) provides compelling evidence that across cultures and throughout history, physical violence has been reliably correlated with sexual aggression, and physical aggression has substantially declined in modern times. Given the importance of reproductive choice for women, intersexual selection acting on the conflict of reproductive interests between coercive men and discerning women may have favored a female-specific psychology predisposing women to be vigilant against outgroup men to avoid sexual coercion.

Taken together, the observations that (a) sexual aggression is not uncommon among our closest primate cousins, (Smuts 1993) (b) warfare and sexual aggression have been tightly linked as far back as recorded history, (c) physical and sexual aggression are reliably linked across space and time, and (d) intergroup violence was much more common in the past than in modern times, it is not unreasonable to suspect that women have faced recurring threats of sexual assault throughout our evolutionary history, and perhaps threats higher than those encountered in modern Western societies, and that they may have been particularly at risk from men from groups other than their own.

To be sure, by interacting with outgroups, there are potential fitness benefits to broadening the pool of mate choices to include mates of any social group. Although invariant avoidance of outgroup men would drastically decrease the risk of sexual coercion or aggression, there are potential costs to this behavior as well. These costs include diverting attention and energy away from other important tasks and the potential loss of valuable interactions with outgroups, such as trading opportunities or noncoercive mating opportunities. Given that preferences for and against outgroup men have fitness relevant costs, a woman's degree of bias should be expected to vary as a function of her appraised vulnerability to losing control of the maintenance of reproductive choices. As such, we posit that (a) women who perceive themselves to be more vulnerable to sexual coercion and (b) perceive outgroup men as particularly physically formidable (and more capable of overpowering a woman) should be more willing to pay the costs associated with bias (e.g., attention and energy) in order to minimize the probability of sexual aggression and its attendant loss of choice in reproductive partner.

Recent research suggests this may be a productive framework in which to address a female-specific psychology of prejudice. Results from several studies indicate that White women's perceived vulnerability to sexual coercion is positively correlated with negative attitudes toward African Americans (Navarrete et al. 2009; Navarrete et al. 2010, Study 2). One study showed that race prejudice for women was most strongly directed at Black men, not Black women, and that the relationship between perceived vulnerability to sexual coercion and fear toward Black and White men and women was strongest toward Black men (Navarrete et al. 2010, Study 3). Put simply, the degree to which White women were biased against Black men was predicted by how vulnerable White women felt to sexual coercion. Consistent with the notion that a domain-specific link may exist between the avoidance of sexual coercion and the avoidance of outgroup men, this relationship held even when the effect of general fearfulness was statistically controlled.

The link between women's perceived vulnerability to sexual coercion and bias toward outgroup men suggests that outgroup prejudice may be specifically attuned to the costs of sexual aggression, which are not the same throughout the course of a woman's menstrual cycle. Because the reproductive consequences of sexual aggression are strongest during the peri-ovulatory phase of the menstrual cycle (i.e., the window in which a woman can conceive), women should be especially biased toward outgroup males during the fertile part of their cycle. This should be particularly true for women who perceive themselves to be vulnerable to sexual coercion, and for those who view outgroup men as physically formidable. In a test of these specific theoretically derived predictions, Navarrete et al. (2009) reported that the relationship between perceived vulnerability to sexual coercion and multiple measures of prejudice toward outgroups increased in magnitude as fertility increased across the menstrual cycle.

McDonald, Asher, Kerr, and Navarrete (2011) replicated and extended these findings by demonstrating a link between conception risk and implicit prejudice in both racial and nonracial intergroup contexts. In light of the conflict between the potential costs and benefits associated with intergroup interactions, in generating prejudiced evaluations of outgroup men, selection may have favored psychological mechanisms that assess the extent to which such men are perceived as physically formidable, as such traits would increase the effectiveness of a man's attempts to physically overpower and constrain women's behavior, and therefore, reproductive choice. McDonald and colleagues hypothesized that the link between conception risk and implicit intergroup prejudice would be particularly strong for women who associate the outgroup with physical formidability. These findings are not trivial, given that implicit measures of bias have been shown to correlate more strongly with "real-world" behavior than explicit measures (Greenwald et al. 2009).

Two studies were conducted to test this prediction using both White/Black men as targets, as well as men categorized into arbitrarily bifurcated social groups distinguishable solely by shirt colors. Research participants were assigned to groups based on largely arbitrary preferences for one primary color versus another (e.g., yellow vs. blue), after which they completed implicit association tests measuring (a) the extent to which they readily associated outgroup men with physical formidability

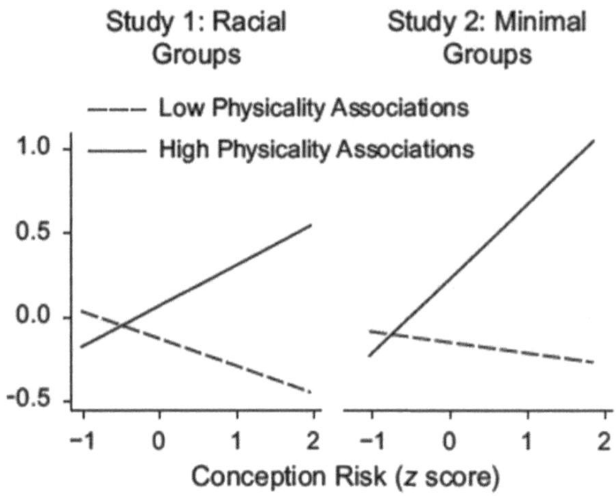

Fig. 6.1 Intergroup prejudice as a function of conception risk and physicality associations (1 S.D. above and below the mean). From McDonald et al., 2011, *Psychological Science*

("physicality") relative to ingroup men and (b) the extent to which outgroup men were more negatively/less positively evaluated on affectively charged semantic terms (e.g., horrible, evil, or good) relative to ingroup men. Across both studies, the results revealed that conception risk was associated with greater prejudice in intergroup evaluations, particularly when outgroup men were perceived as being associated with physicality. These findings suggest that the psychological system by which women's evaluations of outgroup men become more negative, as a function of conception risk, does not depend on a specific racial context (e.g., Black versus White). Instead, the mechanisms within the system likely rely on more basic categorization processes that respond to cues that are not dependent on the race of the target, but on the target's group category—even if largely arbitrary. Such findings are consistent with the notion that our evolved psychology is likely to have been shaped during a time in our evolutionary history when groups were not defined by race but by differences in social alliances marked by nonphysical traits such as linguistic accent, dialect, and social customs or norms (Fig. 6.1).

Overall, these results suggest that women may be equipped with psychological mechanisms designed to protect reproductive choice by avoiding outgroup men, who may have historically posed the greatest reproductive threat, particularly when (a) a women perceives herself as particularly vulnerable to such threats and when (b) the targets are perceived as being most capable of effectively constraining a woman's reproductive choice.

A Summary of Sex Differences in the Psychology of Intergroup Conflict

We have so far argued that the adaptive problems posed by intergroup conflict have been different for men and women throughout human evolutionary history, and that the manner in which natural and sexual selection has provided ways of dealing with these problems may have set the stage for important psychological differences between the sexes. We think these differences reflect the workings of an evolved psychology designed to provide sex-specific solutions to the unique challenges that are posed by outgroup men to each sex. These problems and solutions have produced psychological sex differences in the expression of intergroup bias, likely to have evolved on separate sexually selected avenues of conflict: intrasexual conflict, in which men of separate coalitions have competed with each other for potential access to mates, and intersexual conflict, in which women have attempted to avoid sexually aggressive tactics from outgroup men. These paths to prejudice are psychologically manifested as a predisposition for *aggressive* prejudice for men, and greater proneness to *fearful* prejudice for women—both paths directed most strongly toward male exemplars of the outgroup.

Conclusion

We have described women's bias as primarily targeted toward outgroup men rather than ingroup men or outgroup women because of the costs associated with increased risk of sexual coercion by outgroup men, all else being equal. We have also described men's bias as targeted primarily toward outgroup men, because of the gains to be had by eliminating or dominating other male coalitions. In marshaling empirical support for our claims, we described work that utilized the natural variation existing between individuals on the traits relevant to the function of these biases in order to explain variance in the expression of bias. This is because we do not expect that, as a product of evolution by natural selection, the psychology of prejudice should be characterized by built-in preferences or tastes that are not sensitive to environmental input. Instead, we posit the existence of dynamic, evolved psychological systems that are sensitive to the costs and benefits of any course of action in the face of uncertain outcomes and incomplete information.

The costs of any course of action in response to a given threat are likely to include a risk assessment of one's probability of falling victim to the threat. Highly aggressive and dominant men may feel better able to engage the threat of outgroup men, and therefore express greater prejudice—a syndrome likely to be related to readying oneself for approach-related posturing or violent engagement. On the other hand, women who appraised themselves as highly vulnerable to sexual coercion, and view outgroup men as physically formidable, exhibit more prejudice not because such personality profiles are associated with the need to ready oneself for approach-related contact, but to protect oneself from threats to reproductive choice. Thus, it should be clear that prejudice is not only about approach-related aggression and dominance but also about avoiding danger among those individuals who have appraised themselves as most vulnerable to those dangers. Thus, prejudicial outcomes can arise by opposing strategies of approach and avoidance.

A key limitation with our description of avoidant bias is that there may be overlaps in the psychological mechanisms underlying a female psychology of sexual coercion avoidance with a more general psychology of *disease* avoidance. For example, instead of experiencing fear and engaging in flight and concealment, when presented with a threat of sexual aggression, women may avoid costly mating by experiencing disgust and engaging in a more measured avoidance (Tybur et al. 2009). Although typically thought of as functioning to motivate pathogen avoidance (e.g., Curtis and Biran 2001), disgust is elicited by a number of sexual behaviors that connote costs such as incest and sexual coercion, as well as other sexual behaviors that involve greater potential disease costs (e.g., anal sex). Effectively, the underlying reasons for avoiding such maladaptive sexual interactions are similar to those motivating women's intergroup bias under selection pressure from sexual coercion. Connecting insights from the growing literature on the connection between disease and avoidance and prejudice on the one hand and the links between rape avoidance and prejudice on the other, is a potentially intellectually rich enterprise waiting to be developed.

In closing, we have been careful to avoid claims that all features of the prejudiced mind are reducible to sexual selection, but have done our best to emphasize an often overlooked, but critically important component of the psychology of intergroup conflict, prejudice and discrimination—the sex of the agent and target. However, there are other problems related to group-based prejudice that have not been treated here, some of which are fundamentally related to sex, such as female coalitional alliances and intrasexual aggression in nonphysical forms. Although not likely to be as explicit or as physically aggressive, as is the case among men, a growing body of work suggests that aggression may not be less common among women, but that it may be only less explicit and physically violent in nature (reviewed in Cross and Campbell 2011). As is the case with females of many primate species, coalitions among women and girls against same-sex competitors may be fundamental to the human condition, even if such competition stops short of physical violence (e.g., Fisher, Tran, and Voracek 2008). A full evolutionary account of such dynamics is waiting to be done, and represents a limitation in current theory and research in evolutionary approaches to social psychology, as it is in this present chapter.

Likewise, our current analysis has left out a major thread within the evolutionary literature, and one, which surely must be a key component of the psychological architecture shared by both men and women with respect to thinking about groups: that of the problem of cooperation within groups and how to coordinate collective action. How the problem of cooperation is relevant to the emergence and maintenance of intergroup biases is an under-explored area of inquiry among evolutionary and social psychological researchers (for exceptions see Brewer 1999, and Gil-White 2001). Perhaps humankind's most noble social instincts can also lead to between-group preferences—our capacity for compassion for others like ourselves, our willingness to sacrifice our own comfort and safety for the benefit of others, and our desire to conform in order to not offend others—these may all have a dark side to them if their expression is contingent on anything other than unconditional love. The frontiers of psychological science is ripe for bold perspectives that seek to explain difficult topics, perspectives that cut across disciplinary lines in the search for ever more accurate narratives of topics such as how and why we can too often be so damned tribal.

References

Ackerman, J. M., Shapiro, J. R., Neuberg, S. L., Kenrick, D. T., Becker, V., Griskevicius, V., Maner, J. K., & Schaller, M. (2006). They all look the same to me (unless they're angry): From out-group homogeneity to out-group heterogeneity. *Psychological Science*, *17*, 836–840.

Andersson, M. (1994). *Sexual selection*. Princeton University Press: New Jersey.

Andrews, P., Gangestad, S., & Matthews, D. (2002). Adaptationism, exaptationism, and evolutionary behavioral science. *Behavioral and Brain Sciences, 25*(4), 534–547.

Arai, M., Bursell, M., & Nekby, L. (2008). Between meritocracy and ethnic discrimination: The gender difference. SULCIS Working Papers 2008:2, Stockholm University Linnaeus Center for Integration Studies.

Arai, M., & Thoursie, P. S. (2007). Renouncing personal names: An empirical examination of surname change and earnings. *Journal of Labor Economics*, *27*(1), 127–147.

Avenanti, A., Sirigu, A., & Aglioti, S. (2010). Racial Bias Reduces Empathic Sensorimotor Resonance with Other-Race Pain. *Current Biology*, 20(11), 1018–1022

Ayres, I. (1991). Fair driving. Gender and race discrimination in retail car negotiations. *Harvard Law Review, 104,* 817–872.

Bamforth, D. B. (1994) Indigenous people, indigenous violence: Precontact warfare on the North American Great Plains. *Man*, *29*, 95–115.

Bateman, A. J. (1948). Intra-sexual selection in Drosophila. *Heredity, 2,* 349–368.

Brewer, M. B. (1999). The psychology of prejudice: Ingroup love or outgroup hate? *Journal of Social Issues. Special Issue: Prejudice and intergroup relations: Papers in honor of Gordon W. Allport's centennial*, *55*(3), 429–444.

Broude, G. J., & Greene, J. (1978). Cross-cultural codes on twenty sexual attitudes and practices. *Ethnology*, *15*, 409–430.

Bushway, S. D., & Piehl, A. M. (2001). Judging judicial discretion: Legal factors and racial discrimination in sentencing. *Law & Society Review*, *35*(4), 733–764.

Buss, D. M., & Shackelford, T. K. (1997). Human aggression in evolutionary psychological perspective. *Clinical Psychology Review, 17,* 605–619.

Buss, D. M., Haselton, M. G., Shackelford, T. K., Bleske, A., & Wakefield, J. C. (1998). Adaptations, exaptations, and spandrels. *American Psychologist, 53,* 533–548.

Carlsson, M., & Rooth, D. O. (2007). Evidence of ethnic discrimination in the Swedish labor market using experimental data. *Labour Economics*, *14*, 716–729

Chagnon, N. A. (1996). Chronic problems in understanding tribal violence and warfare. In G. Bock, & J. Goode (Eds.), The genetics of criminal and antisocial behavior. New York: Wiley.

Chang, L., Lu, H. J., Li, H., & Li, T. (2011). The face that launched a thousand ships: the mating-warring association in men. *Personality and Social Psychology Bulletin*, *37*, 976–984.

Cheney, D, & Seyfarth, R. (1982). Recognition of individuals within and between groups of free-ranging Vervet monkeys. *American Zoologist*, *22*, 519–529.

Choi, J., & Bowles, S. (2007). The coevolution of parochial altruism and war. *Science*, *318*(5850), 636–640.

Clutton-Brock, T. H., & Vincent, A. C. (1991). Sexual selection and the potential reproductive rates of males and females. *Nature, 351,* 58–60.

Cross, C., & Campbell, A. (2011). Women's aggression. *Aggression and Violent Behavior*, 16(5), 390–398.

Curtis, V., & Biran, A. (2001). Dirt, disgust, and disease: Is hygiene in our genes? *Perspectives in Biology and Medicine*, *44*, 17–31.

Daly, M., & Wilson, M. (1988). Homicide. Hawthorne: Aldine de Gruyter.

Darwin, C. (1871) *The descent of man and selection in relation to sex*. John Murray: London.

Dawkins, R. (1982). *The Extended Phenotype.* Oxford: Oxford University Press.

Ekehammar, B. (1985). Sex differences in socio political attitudes revisited. *Educational Studies*, *11*, 39.

Ekehammar, B., & Sidanius, J. (1980). Negative similarities versus correlational similarities. *Multivariate Behavioral Research, 15*(1), 95–98.
Ekehammar, B., & Sidanius, J. (1982). Sex differences in sociopolitical attitudes: A replication and extension. *British Journal of Social Psychology, 21*(3), 249–257.
Ember, C. (1978). Myths about hunter-gatherers. *Ethnology, 27*, 239–248.
Fisher, R. A. (1930). *The genetical theory of natural selection.* Oxford University Press; UK.
Fisher, M., Tran, U., & Voracek, M. (2008). The influence of relationship status, mate seeking and sex on intrasexual competition. *Journal of Social Psychology, 148*, 493–508.
Fisman, R., Iyengar, S. S., Kamenica, E., & Simonson, I. (2008). Racial preferences in dating. *Review of Economic Studies, 75*, 117–132.
Furnham, A. (1985). Adolescents' sociopolitical attitudes: A study of sex and national differences. *Political Psychology, 6*, 621 636.
Ghiglieri, M. P. (1999). The dark side of man: Tracing the origins of male violence. Reading, mass.: Perseus Books.
Gil-White, F. J. (2001). Are ethnic groups biological "species" to the human brain? Essentialism in our cognition of some social categories. *Current Anthropology, 42*(4), 515–554.
Gordon, R., Piana, L. D., & Keleher, T. (2000). Facing the consequences: An examination of racial discrimination in U.S. public schools. ERASE Initiative, Applied Research Center, Oakland, CA.
Griskevicius, V., Tybur, J. M., Gangestad, S. W., Perea, E. F., Shapiro, J. R., & Kenrick, D. T. (2009). Aggress to impress: Hostility as an evolved context-dependent strategy. *Journal of Personality and Social Psychology, 96*, 980–994.
Greenwald, A. G., Poehlman, A., Uhlmann, E, Banaji, M. (2009). Understanding and using the Implicit Association Test: III. Meta-analysis of predictive validity. *Journal of Personality and Social Psychology, 97*(1), 17–41.
Haley, H., Sidanius, J., Lowery, B., & Malamuth, N. (2004). The interactive nature of sex and race discrimination: A social dominance perspective. In G. Philogene (Ed.), *Racial Identity in Context: The Legacy of Kenneth B. Clark* (pp. 149–160): American Psychological Association
Hirschfeld L. A. 1996. *Race in the Making: Cognition, Culture and the Child's Construction of Human Kinds*. Cambridge, MA: MIT Press.
Johnson, D. P., McDermott, R., Barrett, E. S., Crowden, J., Wrangham, R., McIntyre, M. H., & Rosen, S. P. (2006) Overconfidence in war games: experimental evidence on expectations, aggression, gender and testosterone. *Proceedings of the Royal Society B, 273*, 2513–2520.
Kaplan, H. S., & Gangestad, S. W. (2005). Life history theory and evolutionary psychology. In D. M. Buss (Ed.), The handbook of evolutionary psychology (pp. 68–96). New York: Wiley.
Keegan, J. (1993). *The history of warfare*. New York: Alfred A. Knopf.
Keeley, L. H. (1996). *War before civilization: The myth of the peaceful savage*. New York: Oxford University Press.
Kelly, R. C. (2005). The evolution of lethal intergroup violence. *Proceedings of the National Academy of Sciences, 102*, 15294–15298.
Knauft, B. (1987). Reconsidering violence in simple human societies. *Current Anthropology, 28*, 457–500.
Krech, S. (1994). Genocide in tribal society. *Nature, 371*, 14–15.
Kurzban, R., Tooby, J., & Cosmides, L. (2001). Can race be erased? Coalitional computation and social categorization. *Proceedings of the National Academy of Sciences, 98*(26), 15387–15392.
Leidner, B., & Castano, E. (2012) Morality shifting in the context of intergroup violence. *European Journal of Social Psychology*, 42, 82–91.
Levinson, D. (1989). *Family violence in cross-cultural perspective.* Newbury Park, CA: Sage Publications.
Makova, K. D., & Li, W.-H. (2002). Strong male-driven evolution of DNA sequences in humans and apes. *Nature, 416*, 624–626.
Manson, J. H., & Wrangham, R. W. (1991). Intergroup aggression in chimpanzees. *Current Anthropology, 32*, 369–390.
Marjoribanks, K. (1981). Sex related differences in socio political attitudes: A replication. *Educational Studies, 7*, 16.

McDonald, M., Asher, B., Kerr, N., & Navarrete, C. D. (2011). Fertility and intergroup bias in racial and in minimal group contexts: Evidence for shared architecture. *Psychological Science, 22*(7), 860–865. Impact Factor: 4.699.

McDonald, M., Navarrete, C. D., & van Vugt, M. (2012). Evolution and the psychology of intergroup conflict: The "warrior male" hypothesis. *Philosophical Transactions of the Royal Society B: Biological Sciences, 367*(1589), 670–679.

McKibbin, W. F., & Shackelford, T. K. (2012). Women's avoidance of rape: An evolutionary psychological perspective. In Beaver, K. M. & Walsh, A. (Eds.). *The Ashgate research companion to biosocial theories of crime*. Farnham: Ashgate.

Mischel, W. (1979). On the interface of cognition and personality: Beyond the person-situation debate. *American Psychologist, 34*(9), 740–754.

Mitani, J., Watts, D., & Amsler, S. (2010). Lethal intergroup aggression leads to territorial expansion in wild chimpanzees. *Current Biology*, 20(12), 507–508.

Navarrete, C. D., Fessler, D. M. T., & Eng, S. J. (2007). Elevated ethnocentrism in the first trimester of pregnancy. *Evolution and Human Behavior, 28*, 60–65.

Navarrete, C. D., Fessler, D. M. T., Santos Fleischman, D., & Geyer, J. (2009). Race bias tracks conception risk across the menstrual cycle. *Psychological Science, 20*(6): 661–665.

Navarrete, C. D., Olsson, A., Ho, A. K., Mendes, W., Thomsen, L., & Sidanius, J. (2009). Fear extinction to an outgroup face: The role of target gender. *Psychological Science, 20*(2), 155–158.

Navarrete, C. D., McDonald, M., Molina, L., & Sidanius, J. (2010). Prejudice at the nexus of race and gender: An out-group male target hypothesis. *Journal of Personality & Social Psychology, 98*(6): 933–945.

Owens, L., Shute, R., & Slee, P. (2000). "Guess what I just heard!": Indirect aggression among teenage girls in Australia. *Aggressive Behavior, 26*, 67–83.

Pinker, S. (2011). *The better angels of our nature*. New York: Viking.

Sidanius, J. & Ekehammar, B. (1980). Sex-related Differences in Socio-political Ideology. *Scandinavian Journal of Psychology, 21*, 17–26.

Sidanius, J., & Pratto, F. (1999). *Social dominance: An intergroup theory of social hierarchy and oppression*. Cambridge: Cambridge University Press.

Sidanius, J., & Veniegas, R. C. (2000). Gender and Race Discrimination: The Interactive Nature of Disadvantage. In S. Oskamp (Ed.). Reducing Prejudice and Discrimination: The Claremont Symposium on Applied Social Psychology. Mahwah, New Jersey: Lawrence Erlbaum Associates, pp 47–69.

Smith, E., Muldc, M., & Hill, K. (2001). Controversies in the evolutionary social sciences: A guide for the perplexed. Trends in Ecology and Evolution, 16(3), 128–135.

Smuts, B. (1993). Male aggression and sexual coercion of females in nonhuman primates and other mammals: Evidence and theoretical implications. Advances in the Scientific Study of Behavior, 22, 1–63.

Steffensmeier, D., Ulmer, J., & Kramer, J. (1998). The interaction of race, gender, and age in criminal sentencing: The punishment cost of being young, black, and male. *Criminology, 36*(4).

Stets, J. E., & Straus, M. A. (1990). Gender differences in reporting of marital violence and its medical and psychological consequences. In M. A. Straus & R. J. Gelles (Eds.), *Physical violence in American families* (pp. 151–165). New Brunswick: Transaction.

Stroh, L. K., Brett, J. M., & Reilly, A. H. (1992). All the right stuff: A comparison of female and male mangers' career progression. *Journal of Applied Psychology, 77*, 251–260.

Tajfel, H. (1981). *Human groups and social categories*. Cambridge: Cambridge University Press.

Thornhill, R., & Palmer, C. (2000). *A natural history of rape: Biological bases of sexual coercion*. Cambridge: MIT Press.

Tooby, J., & Cosmides, L. (1988). *The Evolution of war and its cognitive foundations*: Institute for evolutionary studies: *Technical Report, 88*(1).

Tooby, J., & Cosmides, L. (1992). *The psychological foundations of culture*. In J. Barkow, L. Cosmides, & J. Tooby (Eds.), *The adapted mind: Evolutionary psychology and the generation of culture*. New York: Oxford University Press.

Trivers, R. L. (1972). Parental investment and sexual selection. In B. Campbell (Ed.), *Sexual Selection and the Descent of Man* (pp. 136–179). Chicago: Aldine-Atherton.

Tybur, J. M, Lieberman, D., & Griskevicius, V. (2009). Microbes, mating, and morality: Individual differences in three functional domains of disgust. *Journal of Personality and Social Psychology, 97*, 103–122.

van Vugt, M., De Cremer, D., & Janssen, D. (2007). Gender differences in competition and cooperation: The male warrior hypothesis. *Psychological Science, 18*, 19–23.

Vikman, E. (2005). Ancient origins: Sexual Violence in warfare, part I. *Anthropology & Medicine, 12*(1), 21–31.

Wolfgang, M. (1958). *Patterns of Criminal Homicide*. Philadelphia: Univ. of PA Press.

Wrangham, R. W., & Peterson, D. (1996). *Demonic Males: Apes and the Origins of Human Violence*. Boston: Houghton Mifflin Co.

Wrangham, R., Wilson, M., & Muller, M. (2006). Comparative rates of violence in chimpanzees and humans. *Primates, 47*, 14–26.

Yamagishi, T. (1998). *The structure of trust: The evolutionary game of mind and society*. Tokyo: University of Tokyo Press.

Yamagishi, T., & Kiyonari, T. (2000). The group as the container of generalized reciprocity. *Social Psychology Quarterly, 63*(2), 116–132.

Chapter 7
Evolutionary Behavioral Genetics of Violent Crime

Kevin M. Beaver, Joseph L. Nedelec, Joseph A. Schwartz and Eric J. Connolly

Introduction

Evolutionary psychology typically focuses on universal adaptations that, in some way, at some evolutionary time period, increased reproductive success. While universal adaptations are certainly important in understanding behavioral phenotypes and the selection pressures that spawned their development, an equally important, but often overlooked, level of human nature from an evolutionary framework is individual differences. A focus on individual differences is particularly important for at least two main reasons. First, many of the traits and behaviors that are of interest to evolutionary psychologists show remarkable variation across the human population. Even within phenotypes that are generally considered to be universal adaptations, such as the desire to mate and the capacity for violence, there is considerable variation (Hawley and Buss 2011). Some people, for instance, may be highly sexually active, mating with multiple partners, whereas other people may be more selective and perhaps even monogamous. Similarly, although the capacity for violence is universal, there exists a wide range of phenotypic variation in the actual use of violence with predatory offenders falling at one end of the distribution and other people who would only display violence when attacked or threatened falling near the other end of the continuum. Second, and closely related, variation is what allows universals to evolve. Without phenotypic variation, the trait and/or behavior could

K. M. Beaver (✉) · J. L. Nedelec · J. A. Schwartz · E. J. Connolly
College of Criminology and Criminal Justice, Florida State University,
Tallahassee, FL 32306-1127, USA
e-mail: kbeaver@fsu.edu

J. L. Nedelec
e-mail: joseph.nedelec@uc.edu

J. A. Schwartz
e-mail: jas10t@my.fsu.edu

E. J. Connolly
e-mail: ejc10c@fsu.edu

T. K. Shackelford, R. D. Hansen (eds.), *The Evolution of Violence*,
Evolutionary Psychology, DOI 10.1007/978-1-4614-9314-3_7,

not be actively selected for or under selection pressure. As a result, understanding the processes by which individual differences are produced can provide insight into how human universals arise.

Whether the focus is on human universal adaptations or individual differences in phenotypes, there can be little doubt that genes are partially responsible for producing them. After all, genes and genetic variation are the key ingredients in the evolutionary process. When the focus is on human universals, the overarching assumption is that at some point in human history, there was variation in a given phenotype which was produced by genetic variation. However, because a particular genetic variant conferred a specific evolutionary advantage, this genetic variant spread and wiped out the genetic variation that previously existed at these loci. Part of the reason that human genotypes are exceedingly similar is because of selection pressures that eliminated variation and produced universal adaptations (Plomin et al. 2002). When the focus shifts to studying individual differences, there is an emphasis on identifying parts of the genome that are known to vary and could produce phenotypic variation. Genes, of course, are not deterministic or fatalistic and thus are not the only factors that are involved in producing variation; rather, environmental stimuli are also known to shape and mold certain phenotypes. The extent to which genetic and environmental factors are responsible for producing phenotypic variation is a matter of significant and sometimes contentious debate (Loehlin 2009).

Perhaps nowhere is this debate more pronounced than when it comes to research examining individual variation in violent criminal behaviors. Even today—a decade after the mapping of the human genome—the mere suggestion that violent crime could be partially produced by genetic factors is, in some academic circles (most notably sociology and criminology), still met with resistance, hostility, and outright ridicule (e.g., DeKeseredy 2013; Walby and Carrier 2010). Far too often, the debate centers on *ad hominem* attacks and not on the findings from scientific-based empirical research. Understanding the genetic and environmental causes of individual differences in criminal behavior is important to ascertain why such behavior persists today. In today's society, people who engage in violent criminal behavior face a number of evolutionary obstacles that tend to limit their reproductive success. For example, violent offenders tend to be incarcerated for long periods of time, during which time they cannot gain access to mates capable of reproduction. They are also at a high risk for an early death, they tend to have reduced social standing, they do not accumulate wealth or material assets, and they are plagued by health-related problems (Moffitt 1993). Taken together, the reproductive consequences that flow directly from violent crime should give reason to pause and reconsider whether violent behavior exists today because it conferred reproductive advantages in ancestral environments (i.e., "environment of evolutionary adaptedness"; Alcock and Crawford 2008; Buss 2005). For example, violent persons would be able to move up social and political hierarchies, they would be able to ward off potential attackers or mate poachers, and they might even gain increased access to mates through their successes at wars and/or intrasexual competition (Buss 2005; Buss and Shackelford 1997; Daly and Wilson 1988; Nedelec and Beaver 2012). In other words, if genes were responsible for producing variation in violent tendencies in the ancestral environment, then these violent tendencies should remain with us today even though they are largely maladaptive in contemporary, industrialized societies. This possibility hinges on whether individual variation in violent criminal tendencies is influenced significantly by genetic factors. The remainder of this chapter will explore this possibility.

Estimating Genetic Effects

At the heart of evolutionary behavioral genetics is genetic variation. Without genetic variation, selection at the genetic level would not occur and all phenotypic variation would be attributable to environmental stimuli. For natural selection to operate, genetic variation is required and that variation must correspond to variation in reproductive success (i.e., fitness; Mayr 2001). Genetic variation, for instance, might correspond to increases in strength, beauty, intelligence, and even longevity—all of which can differentially influence reproductive success (Buss 1994; Kanazawa 2004; Lahdenpeä et al. 2004; Symons 1995). Over time, the genetic variants that increase reproductive success will be selected for and those that decrease reproductive success will be selected against. Should the selection pressure be strong enough, eventually genetic variation for that phenotype will be wiped out and the resulting phenotype will become a universal feature of human nature (Mayr 2001). Most of the phenotypes of interest to evolutionary psychologists and social scientists are far from universals and possess a significant amount of phenotypic variation. As a result, trying to figure out the extent to which genetic variation is responsible for producing phenotypic variation has become the source of a considerable amount of research.

One of the key ways in which genetic variation occurs is through mutations—that is, random changes to DNA sequences that can then be passed across generational lines. Genes that vary from person to person (largely because of mutations) are called polymorphisms and alternative copies of the gene are known as alleles. In terms of their fitness-related effects, mutations can be beneficial, harmful, or neutral. Beneficial and harmful mutations are of particular importance to evolutionary genetics as beneficial mutations will tend to spread, whereas deleterious mutations may eventually be purged from the genome. Of course, the spread and/or removal of mutations is much more complex than this, but it does provide the basic foundation for understanding how genetic variation can change over time through evolutionary pressures.

Trying to quantify the extent to which genetic variance is able to account for phenotypic variance is nearly impossible when examining mutations. After all, most phenotypes studied by evolutionary psychologists would be considered polygenic phenotypes, meaning that a relatively large number of genes would be involved in producing phenotypic variance (Beaver 2009a; Tielbeek et al. 2012). For example, suppose that there was a polymorphic gene with two different alleles: **A** and **a**. The **A** allele increased the average life expectancy by 1 month and the **a** allele decreased

Fig. 7.1 Punnett square illustrating the effect on life expectancy of a fictitious polymorphic gene

	A	a
A	**(AA)** 2 month addition to average life span	**(Aa)** No change to average life span
a	**(aA)** No change to average life span	**(aa)** 2 month reduction to average life span

the average life expectancy by 1 month. As illustrated in Fig. 7.1, this single gene could potentially account for a 4-month difference in life expectancy between two people (i.e., one with an **AA** genotype and one with an **aa** genotype), but that is only a small fraction of the entire variation in life expectancy that exists in the human population. Other polymorphic genes are also involved and environmental factors, such as diet, exposure to toxins, and availability of medical treatment, would also play a central role in determining life expectancy. This complexity is compounded by the fact that only a handful of genes thought to affect most phenotypes have been discovered (Plomin et al. 2002). Trying to identify all of the mutations that would account for variance in phenotypes is thus a futile enterprise at this point. This is particularly true for antisocial phenotypes, such as violent crime, as they are thought to be the product of hundreds of genes, an array of environmental pathogens, and interactions between genetic and environmental factors. Moreover, only a few genes have consistently been linked to violence, and so attempting to use mutations as a way of figuring out how much variance in violence is attributable to genetic variance is really a misguided approach (Beaver 2009a).

Fortunately, there are a number of analytical techniques that can be used to estimate the extent to which phenotypic variance in violent criminal behavior is accounted for by genetic variance (mainly through the rise of mutations) without having to identify and measure all of the mutations involved. The first main technique employed to estimate genetic influences on phenotypic variance involves the use of twin pair samples. With twin-based research, two types of twins are compared: monozygotic (MZ) twins and dizygotic (DZ) twins. MZ twins share 100% of their DNA whereas DZ twins share, on average, 50% of their distinguishing DNA. Both types of twins, however, are assumed to share environments that are just as similar to each other (referred to as the equal environments assumption or "EEA"). For example, the environments between MZ twins from the same twin pair are thought to be roughly approximate to the environments between DZ twins from the same twin pair. If the EEA is not violated, then the only reason that MZ twins should be more similar to each other than DZ twins is because they share twice as much genetic material (Medland and Hatemi 2009; Plomin et al. 2013).

In twin-based research, the variance in any measure is then decomposed into three different variance components: a heritability component, a shared environmental component, and a nonshared environmental component. Heritability captures the proportion of variance that is explained by additive genetic variance, and higher heritability estimates reflect greater levels of phenotypic similarity for MZ twins versus DZ twins. The proportion of variance not accounted for by genetic factors is thus explainable by environmental factors. Shared environmental effects capture phenotypic variance that is due to environmental factors that are shared between siblings which make siblings similar to each other. Some common examples of shared environmental factors include family-wide parenting practices, household income, and cultural forces. Nonshared environmental factors, in contrast, include environments that are unique to each sibling which make siblings dissimilar to each other. Different peer groups, child-specific parenting, and prenatal environments are some of the many examples of nonshared environmental influences. Importantly, the effects of error are included in the nonshared environmental estimate as well. In all, 100 % of phenotypic variance is accounted for by some combination of genetic, shared environmental, and nonshared environmental factors (Plomin et al. 2013).

Before moving into a discussion of the results generated from twin-based research, it is important to point out that a number of criticisms have been leveled against research using samples of twins. Briefly, some of the key attacks on this methodology surround the violation of the EEA which would make the findings not generalizable to non-twins. While these arguments are not well grounded (Derks et al. 2006; Medland and Hatemi 2009), they do represent potential threats. Fortunately, there are other methodologies that are not host to these potential limitations. One of the more common of these research designs is the blended-family methodology. This methodology represents a simple variant of the twin-based research design. With the blended-family methodology, all different types of siblings are included in the sample as opposed to just focusing on MZ and DZ twins. A blended-family design, for example, could include regular biological siblings, half-siblings, stepsiblings, and twins. This approach overcomes some of the criticisms of the twin-based approach—mainly, that the findings would not generalize to non-twin populations (Plomin et al. 2013; Posthuma and Boomsma 2000).

There are two other main research designs that have been used to estimate genetic and environmental influences on phenotypic variance. The first is the MZ twins reared apart (MZA) methodology. In these studies, researchers take advantage of the rare (and largely outdated) practice of separating MZ twins at birth and raising them by separate adopted families. Oftentimes the twins would mature into adults without ever knowing that they were part of a twin pair. For various reasons, however, later in life they frequently learn that they have a long-lost twin and thus reunite. MZAs represent perhaps the most powerful way to estimate genetic effects because any similarity that exists between MZAs would be evidence in favor of genetic effects (and the stronger the degree of similarity, the stronger the genetic effect). Although MZAs are exceedingly rare, a laboratory at the University of Minnesota has tracked down more than 100 MZAs and published a great deal of research related to the genetic influence on an array of phenotypes between twins (Bouchard et al. 1990; Tellegen et al. 1988).

As with most of the other research designs used to estimate genetic and environmental influences, the MZA research has also been attacked. Some of these attacks are grounded in logic, such as the findings not generalizing to sample of non-MZAs, and some of these attacks have been more personal, such as accusing the researchers of MZAs of falsifying the data (Segal 2012). Importantly, the researchers were investigated and there was no evidence of misconduct. There is, however, at least one other research design that can be used to estimate genetic and environmental influences on phenotypic variance: the adoption-based research design. The logic of the adoption methodology is relatively straightforward. Basically, if a child is adopted very early in life (e.g., at birth), then their biological parents will have no socializing effect on the child. Rather, socialization will fall squarely on the adoptive parents. If the child does not have any contact with their biological parents, then the only reason that they should resemble their biological parents on any phenotype is because of the genetic material that they share with their parents. Moreover, the only reason that the adoptee should resemble their adoptive parents is because of the environment that they share with them (Plomin et al. 2013). A good deal of research has employed adoption-based research designs to explore the genetic and environmental underpinnings to phenotypic variance. As with all research designs, however, there are limitations associated with the adoption-based methodology. Some of the key attacks on this methodology focus on the generalizability of the results to non-adoptees, the selective placement of adoptees in high-quality families, and the lack of research on adoptees drawn from nationally representative samples in the USA (Plomin et al. 2013).

As the above review makes clear, there are multiple methodologies that can be used to estimate genetic and environmental influences on phenotypes, including violent criminal behavior. While all of the research designs have shortcomings, such shortcomings are not universal across all research designs. Therefore, by using multiple methodologies, it is possible to examine whether the genetic and environmental estimates vary as a function of the research methodology being used. If, for instance, the heritability estimate is exceedingly high in twin-based studies, but nearly absent in adoption-based studies, then it would be likely that heritability is partially a methodological artifact. However, if the genetic and environmental estimates are relatively consistent across research designs, then it is unlikely that these estimates are biased in any significant way. Below we turn to an overview of the findings of studies that have used these research designs to estimate the genetic and environmental influences on variance in measures of violent criminal behaviors.

The Genetic and Environmental Influences on Violent Crime

Hundreds of studies have employed some type of quantitative genetic research design to estimate the heritability of virtually every antisocial phenotype. While the exact heritability estimate varies from study to study and depends on the precise measure that is examined and the sample that is used, the results are nonetheless highly consistent. The results of four meta-analyses can be used to summarize three key findings that flow from these studies (Ferguson 2010; Mason and Frick 1994; Miles and Carey 1997; Rhee and Waldman 2002). First, one of the more consistent findings to emerge from the literature is that genetic factors account for about 50 % of the variance in antisocial phenotypes. These heritability estimates, however, can—and do—vary depending on the severity of the antisocial behavior that is examined. In general, heritability estimates tend to be relatively lower for non-violent and common types of delinquency, such as experimenting with smoking marijuana and skipping school. For more serious types of crime, such as violent criminal behavior and persistent criminality, heritability estimates can top out at around 80–90 %.

Heritability estimates are also known to fluctuate during different stages of the life course. In adolescence, for instance, when antisocial behavior and violent conduct are relatively frequent, heritability estimates are relatively low. As adolescence rolls into adulthood, heritability estimates continue on an upward trend. By the time adulthood is reached, heritability estimates for criminal behavior tend to be at their pinnacle (Ferguson 2010). While it may seem a bit counterintuitive to hear that genetic effects can ebb and flow over time, this is precisely what occurs. The overarching explanation for this variation in heritability estimates centers on the fact that during childhood and adolescence, individuals do not have as much autonomy as they will later in life. During adolescence, parents can instill and enforce certain rules and restrictions that limit their offspring's genetically influenced propensities toward certain behaviors. As adolescents mature into adults, however, they no longer are limited by environmental control (e.g., by their parents or school administrators) and are granted more freedom to follow their own wants, desires, and propensities (all of which are likely genetically influenced). In short, with age, genetic propensities are less likely to be blunted by the environment which ultimately results in a higher heritability estimate. Seen in this way, genetic effects are not fixed, but rather are variable and can change in response to environmental factors and as a result of normal developmental processes (Plomin et al. 2013).

The second main finding to emerge from the meta-analyses is that shared environmental factors account for only a small percentage of the overall variance in antisocial phenotypes, typically somewhere between 0 and 20 %. This finding stands in stark contradiction to the vast amount of criminological and social science theories that focus almost exclusively on the influence of shared environmental factors (e.g., family-wide parenting practices, cultures, neighborhood conditions, etc.). Nonetheless, the lack of a shared environmental effect is in line with a long line of behavioral genetic findings and with some of the current attacks leveled against social science research. Perhaps one of the more insightful findings that has direct bearing on the lack of shared environmental influence comes from research on MZAs. Studies on MZAs have consistently shown that MZ twins who were reared apart are just as phenotypically similar to MZ twins who were reared together. What this highlights is that the similarities that exist among siblings are not the result of shared environmental factors, but rather of genetic factors that are shared among siblings (Plomin et al. 2013).

The third consistent theme to emerge from the meta-analyses is that nonshared environmental factors (plus error) account for approximately 40–50 % of the variance in antisocial phenotypes. What this finding illustrates is that part of the reason siblings differ in terms of their criminal behavior is because of the experiences that are *unique* to each sibling. Precisely what these nonshared environments include is not well known at this point, but they likely include factors such as child-specific parenting, unique peer groups, and even different prenatal conditions (Plomin et al. 2013). When contrasted against the findings for the shared environment, what this appears to indicate is that environmental factors are most salient in explaining differences among siblings, but they have very little, if any, effect on creating similarities among siblings.

Given that these genetic and environmental estimates for a range of antisocial behaviors dovetail with the larger behavioral genetic research examining other traits and behaviors, and given that the findings are highly consistent across different methodologies, it is unlikely that the estimates that flow from this body of research are a result of a methodological or statistical artifacts. Even so, one of the key drawbacks to these quantitative genetic research designs is that the genetic and environmental estimates are modeled as latent factors. What this necessarily means is that these methodologies only provide estimates of the percentage of variance that is accounted for by each factor; they do not provide any information or insight into the specific factors that are involved in explaining the variance. To illustrate, knowing that 50 % of the variance in violent behavior is the result of genetic factors does not reveal anything about the precise genetic polymorphisms that are influencing the violent behavior under examination. In order to unpack the specific genes that are linked to antisocial phenotypes, other types of methodologies must be employed. Below, we review some of the literature that has linked specific genetic polymorphisms to various antisocial phenotypes.

The Molecular Genetic Underpinnings to Violent Behavior

Given that antisocial behaviors have consistently been found to be highly heritable, a new wave of research has set out to identify the specific genetic markers that might account for this variance. While this line of research is still in its infancy, already there has been a suite of genetic polymorphisms that have been linked with certain types of antisocial behaviors. Most of these genes are involved in neurotransmission. In very basic terms, neurotransmission is the process by which neurons (i.e., brain cells) communicate with each other and process information throughout the brain. Neurons are made up of a cell body and long spindly branches—called axons and dendrites—that shoot off from the cell nucleus. The axons and dendrites of each neuron are interconnected with the axons and dendrites of other neurons. For neurons to transmit information, an electrochemical-based action potential moves from the cell nucleus through the axon until it reaches the synapse, which is a small gap that separates each neuron from each other. For the action potential to bridge this gap, neurotransmitters are used. Neurotransmitters are chemical messengers capable of crossing the synapse wherein they can lock into receptors on the postsynaptic neuron. After neurotransmitters successfully bind to the postsynaptic neuron, another action potential will be initiated and this process can thus be repeated.

Once neurotransmitters have locked into the postsynaptic neuron, and after the action potential has been initiated, the neurotransmitters need to be removed from the synapse. This is accomplished in two key ways. The first way in which neurotransmitters are removed from the synapse is by a process known as reuptake. During reuptake, transporter proteins are released into the synapse where they target specific neurotransmitters (e.g., the dopamine transporter protein targeting dopamine) and return them to the vesicles of the presynaptic neuron where they can be used again when needed. In the second process, enzymes are produced where they are then released into the synapse to degrade (i.e., catabolize) neurotransmitters and then flushed from the synapse. Some of the more common types of enzymes that are used in this process are monoamine oxidase A (MAOA), monoamine oxidase B (MAOB), and catechol-O-methyl transferase (COMT), which collectively target multiple neurotransmitters, including dopamine, serotonin, and norepinephrine. Both of these processes are essential to ensure that levels of neurotransmitters are kept within a normal range of variation and that neurotransmission is working efficiently (Anderson 2007; Rowe 2002).

The release of different neurotransmitters, in different quantities, can have different effects on the brain. Some neurotransmitters, for example, are excitatory and increase postsynaptic neuronal activity whereas other neurotransmitters have inhibitory properties and decrease postsynaptic neuronal activity. Although far from universal, in general, excitatory neurotransmitters are thought to increase criminal behaviors while inhibitory neurotransmitters are thought to decrease criminal behaviors (Anderson 2007; Raine 1993; Rowe 2002). Some of the earliest research attempting to examine the link between neurotransmitters and crime focused on levels of certain neurotransmitters, especially dopamine and serotonin (Anderson 2007). Although the evidence is far from clear-cut, there are a significant number of studies showing that variation in levels of serotonin and dopamine is related to involvement in serious types of violent and aggressive behavior (Anderson 2007; Ferguson and Beaver 2009; Raine 1993). These findings set the stage for molecular genetic research to hone in on genes from the dopaminergic and serotonergic systems as potentially influencing the propensity for violence.

Two key types of genes have been the focus of research examining violent criminal behaviors: receptor genes and transporter genes. Broadly speaking, receptor genes are involved in coding for proteins that are involved in the postsynaptic detection of neurotransmitters whereas transporter genes are involved in coding for proteins that are involved in the process of reuptake. There are a number of receptor and transporter genes in the dopaminergic and serotonergic systems that are polymorphic (i.e., there exists more than one variant [allele] of this gene in the population). What is particularly important is that these polymorphic genes have been found to be functional, meaning that different alleles for these genes correspond to differences in neurotransmission.

A handful of receptor genes, principally from the dopaminergic system, have been tied to a range of antisocial and, sometimes, violent behaviors. Polymorphisms in the dopamine D2, D4, and D5 receptor genes (i.e., DRD2, DRD4, and DRD5) have been shown to affect the propensity to engage in an assortment of antisocial behaviors and to display antisocial traits (Beaver 2009b; Vanyukov and Tarter 2000; Vanyukov et al. 1998). To illustrate, the A1 allele of the DRD2 gene has been associated with antisocial personality disorder, alcoholism, and polysubstance abuse (Comings et al. 2001; Munafò et al. 2005; Ponce et al. 2003), while the 7-repeat allele of a polymorphism in the DRD4 gene has been tied to attention-deficit hyperactivity disorder (ADHD), conduct disorder, and externalizing problem behaviors in childhood (Bakermans-Kranenburg and van IJzendoorn 2006; Faraone et al. 2001; Rowe et al. 2001).

In addition, at least two transporter genes have been found to be associated with various antisocial phenotypes. The first transporter gene—the dopamine transporter gene (DAT1)—codes for the production of the dopamine transporter protein and has a polymorphism that is the result of 40-base pair (bp) variable number of tandem repeats. Most research examining the effects of this polymorphism has revealed that the 10-repeat allele (in comparison with the 9-repeat allele) is a risk factor for antisocial behaviors, such as pathological gambling, generalized anxiety disorder, major depression, internalizing disorders, the development of ADHD, and delinquent peer group formation (Beaver et al. 2008a; Comings et al. 2001; Gill et al. 1997; Rowe et al. 1998; Thapar et al. 2005). The other transporter gene that has been linked to antisocial phenotypes is the serotonin transporter gene that is responsible for coding for the production of the serotonin transporter protein. This gene has a polymorphism (5HTTLPR) that results in two alleles: a short allele (*s* allele) and a long allele (*l* allele). The available evidence indicates that the *s* allele, in comparison to the *l* allele confers an increased risk to antisocial and violent behaviors (Beaver 2009b). For example, empirical research has revealed a link between carrying the *s* allele and violent offending, ADHD, excessive alcohol use, nicotine addiction, and conduct disorder during childhood (Cadoret et al. 2003; Feinn et al. 2005; Munafò et al. 2003).

In addition to these receptor and transporter genes, a gene that is involved in the enzymatic breakdown of neurotransmitters has perhaps been the most studied gene in relation to violence: MAOA. The MAOA gene has a polymorphism in the promoter region and different alleles for this polymorphism have been found to have functional differences. In general, the alleles are grouped into two categories: those that correspond to high MAOA activity and those that correspond to low MAOA activity. The high-activity MAOA alleles code for an MAOA enzyme that is more efficient at eliminating neurotransmitters from the synapse whereas the low-activity MAOA alleles code for an MAOA enzyme that is not as efficient at removing neurotransmitters from the synapse. A great deal of research has investigated the effects that these two groups of alleles have on violent behavior, the majority of which has revealed that the low-activity MAOA alleles confer an increased probability of violence and aggression when compared against the high-activity MAOA alleles. For example, the low-activity alleles have been linked to gang membership and weapon use, as well as anger and hostility, delinquent behaviors in adolescents and young adults, likelihood of arrest, and antisocial personality traits (Beaver et al. 2010; Beaver et al. 2011; Guo et al. 2008; Koller et al. 2003; Schwartz and Beaver 2011).

Although these polymorphisms (and others) have been linked to violent behaviors, this should not be interpreted to mean that these are "crime genes." Indeed, a recent genome-wide association study failed to detect a link between any single genetic polymorphism and adult antisocial behavior (Teilbeek et al. 2012). Such a negative finding is not a surprise as genes do not code directly for any type of behavior, but rather simply code for the production of proteins. These proteins are ultimately partially responsible for the manifestation of various phenotypes. When it comes to violent criminal behavior, genetic polymorphisms likely exert their influence by affecting brain structure, brain functioning, and personality (i.e., endophenotypes; Beaver et al. 2011; Plomin et al. 2013). Moreover, violent behavior is a polygenic phenotype which means that there are hundreds or perhaps thousands of genes that influence the propensity to engage in violent crimes. What this necessarily means is that each gene only has a relatively small effect, oftentimes accounting for only around 1 % (or less) of the variance in antisocial behaviors (Beaver 2009a, 2009b). Only when these genetic effects are aggregated across all genes associated with violence will a relatively large proportion of the variance—somewhere around 50 % of the variance—be explained (which, incidentally, is precisely what twin-based studies are able to do). When viewed in this light, it is easy to see that there is nothing deterministic about genes and that genes are not fatalistic. What is also particularly important is that genetic effects are oftentimes amplified or dampened depending on environmental conditions—a process known as gene–environment interaction.

Gene–Environment Interactions and Violent Behaviors

Although there has been a rapidly growing body of research linking specific genetic polymorphisms to criminal behavior, one of the main problems with this area of research is non-replication. It is not uncommon for a study to be published reporting a significant association between an allele and a behavioral phenotype. When follow-up studies attempt to replicate this novel finding, however, there is a failure to replicate the original association. While many explanations have been advanced for non-replication in genetic association studies, one of the more likely possibilities can be found in the logic of gene–environment interactions. In addition to providing an explanation for non-replication, gene–environment interactions also underscore the various ways in which genetic and environmental factors work interdependently to create variation in antisocial phenotypes, including violent criminal behavior.

On a very basic level, gene–environment interactions refer to the idea that the effects that genes have are contingent on the presence of certain environmental stimuli and, conversely, that the effects that environments have are contingent on the presence of certain genetic factors. A focus on gene–environment interactions moves us a long way from the outdated nature versus nurture debate wherein only genes or only environments are thought to matter. With gene–environment interactions, there is an understanding of a dynamic interplay between genetic and environmental factors. Without an environment, for example, genes would cease to have any effects. Likewise, without genes, there would be no organisms to be affected by environmental factors. Of course, there are genes and there are environments, so this is somewhat of a hyperbolic example, but the logic extrapolates to what typically plays out in reality. In the real world, genes may have no effect when paired with one type of environment, but they might have very strong effects when paired with other types of environments. There is a good deal of empirical research underscoring the importance of gene–environment interactions in relation to violent criminal behaviors.

In what is perhaps the most influential gene–environment study, Caspi et al. (2002) were interested in examining the interrelationships among childhood maltreatment, MAOA genotype, and antisocial phenotypes. The results of their analysis based on a sample of males revealed that the low-activity MAOA alleles conferred an increased risk of displaying a range of antisocial outcomes for males who were maltreated as children. This effect was quite large as only about 12 % of males carried the low-activity MAOA allele and had a history of maltreatment, but they accounted for 44 % of all convictions for violent criminal behaviors. For males who were not maltreated, there was not any association between MAOA genotype and antisocial phenotypes. This finding demonstrates what is meant by a gene–environment interaction—that is, that genetic effects (e.g., MAOA) are only visible when combined with certain environmental factors (e.g., childhood maltreatment).

Since Caspi et al.'s (2002) original gene–environment interaction study, there has been a wave of empirical analyses also showing the importance of gene–environment interactions for antisocial, violent, and criminal behaviors. For example, findings from these studies have revealed interactions between polymorphisms in the dopaminergic and serotonergic systems and high-risk environmental factors, such as an alcoholic father, delinquent peers, family adversity, maternal insensitivity, and antisocial parents in the prediction of antisocial and sometimes violent behaviors (Bakermans-Kranenburg and van IJzendoorn 2006; Beaver et al. 2007; DeLisi et al. 2008; Cadoret et al. 2003; Laucht et al. 2007; Vaske et al. 2008). Moreover, there have been other studies showing that MAOA also interacts with environments other than maltreatment to predict antisocial phenotypes (e.g., religiosity, birth weight, and marital status; Beaver et al. 2009; Beaver et al. 2008b; Thapar et al. 2005).

There are at least three key reasons as to why focusing on gene–environment interactions is important. First, without taking into account gene–environment interactions, genetic effects may be masked. If, for instance, Caspi et al. (2002) had not examined MAOA in combination with a history of childhood maltreatment, the effect of MAOA would have been non-significant. Given that samples used in genetic association studies are often differentially exposed to environmental liabilities, there is good reason to believe that gene–environment interactions may account for some of the reason why there is often difficulty in replicating genetic associations.

Consider the hypothetical case of non-replication in two studies. In the first study, the sample is exposed to an array of risk factors (e.g., a high-risk sample) and a genetic effect was detected between a certain polymorphism and violent behavior. A follow-up study is then conducted in an attempt to replicate the results. This time, however, the sample is drawn from a nationally representative sample of all youth and no genetic effect was detected. Part of the reason for non-replication could, therefore, be differential exposure to risk factors. Perhaps if the follow-up study had examined the potential interaction between the polymorphism and exposure to risk factors, the genetic effect may have emerged. Of course, these are empirical questions that can be tested using quantitative methods, but it is important to recognize that non-replication may be driven partially—or even largely—by failure to fully examine gene–environment interactions.

The second key reason to focus on gene–environment interactions is because they reveal that genetic effects are not fixed, but rather are flexible and can change in response to a range of different environmental conditions. Viewing genotype as being somewhat plastic (but still only varying within certain inherited parameters) allows for a more dynamic understanding of how the genotype can adapt to ever-changing environmental influences. No longer does a specific genotype have to match the environment for optimal reproductive success, but rather the manifestations of genotypic influence can ebb and flow depending on the type of environment that is encountered. This type of phenotypic plasticity, which flows partially from genotypic plasticity, can help to explain how humans are able to adapt to environments that change much faster than genes.

Third, focusing on gene–environment interactions allows for a more thorough and scientific understanding of why people respond to the same environments in very different ways. Most environmental stimuli—including those that are considered potent risk factors for violence—typically only have relatively small effects (Beaver 2009a). What this means is that there is a lot of variation in how people respond to these deleterious environments. As it applies to violent criminal behavior, bear in mind that in today's industrialized nations there are codified laws that most citizens follow. Even when there is some type of criminal conduct, most of the time the offense is relatively minor (e.g., theft) or non-physical in nature (e.g., burglary). Therefore, a looming question would be why a small segment of the population engages in violent criminal behavior. While the answer to this question is complex, a focus on gene–environment interactions could help shed some light on this answer. To illustrate, even though there are laws in place, some people will violate those laws simply because of their genetic tendencies that make them more likely to act out and become violent. The vast majority of people, however, lack such genetic tendencies and thus are able to follow the policies, procedures, and rules that script behavior. In other societies where codified laws do not exist, more people are likely to engage in violence even though they lack such genetic tendencies. In short, just focusing on the environment or just focusing on genes would not allow for a comprehensive understanding of why people act violently in different types of societies.

Simply showing through statistical models that genetic and environmental factors work interactively unfortunately does not provide much insight into the underlying mechanisms that give rise to gene–environment interactions. For the most part, gene–environment interactions have been interpreted through the well-known diathesis–stress model. With the diathesis–stress model, for a genetic predisposition for a certain behavioral phenotype to emerge, there must be some type of environmental stimuli present in order to "trigger" the genetic effect. If the environmental pathogen is lacking, then the genetic predisposition simply remains a potential effect that will only surface if the environmental trigger is ultimately encountered (Belsky and Beaver 2011).

More recently, however, Belsky (Belsky and Beaver 2011; Belsky and Pluess 2009; Belsky et al. 2009) has advanced another interpretation for gene–environment interactions known as the differential-susceptibility hypothesis. According to this explanation, conceptualizing certain alleles as risk alleles in gene–environment interactions is likely misguided. Rather, he argues that risk alleles should be viewed as "plasticity alleles" that indicate how susceptible each person is to environmental stimuli. People with more plasticity alleles will be more likely to be affected by their environments—both positive and negative environments—when compared to people with fewer plasticity alleles. Gene–environment interactions thus occur because environments are more likely to shape, mold, and affect people who possess a greater number of plasticity alleles. Given the same environmental conditions, people with more plasticity alleles will be differentially affected by the interaction of the alleles with the environment (Belsky and Beaver 2011; Belsky et al. 2009).

Of course, all of this leads to a debate over whether the diathesis–stress model or the differential-susceptibility model is better able to explain gene–environment interactions. Simply examining a statistical interaction that tests for a gene–environment interaction does not provide enough information to distinguish between evidence in support of the diathesis–stress model versus evidence in favor of the differential-susceptibility model. To distinguish between the two models, the environmental and outcome measures must be measured in a bipolar fashion, such that low scores represent extreme negative outcomes and high scores represent extreme positive outcomes (or vice versa). All too often in criminological research, the measures of interest focus only on the negative side and a low score represents the absence of a negative environment or a negative outcome. The absence of a negative environment or outcome, however, does not necessarily indicate the presence of a positive environment or outcome. For example, scoring low on a measure of childhood maltreatment does not indicate that the rearing environment was a positive one—it could still include high levels of parental detachment which were not measured. Similarly, if the outcome measure is whether the subject has been arrested for a violent crime, not being arrested for a violent crime does not mean that the person is prosocial. Once again, the person could have escaped detection or lived a parasitic lifestyle.

In studies where environmental measures and outcome measures are measured in a bipolar way, it is possible to distinguish between the two theoretical models.

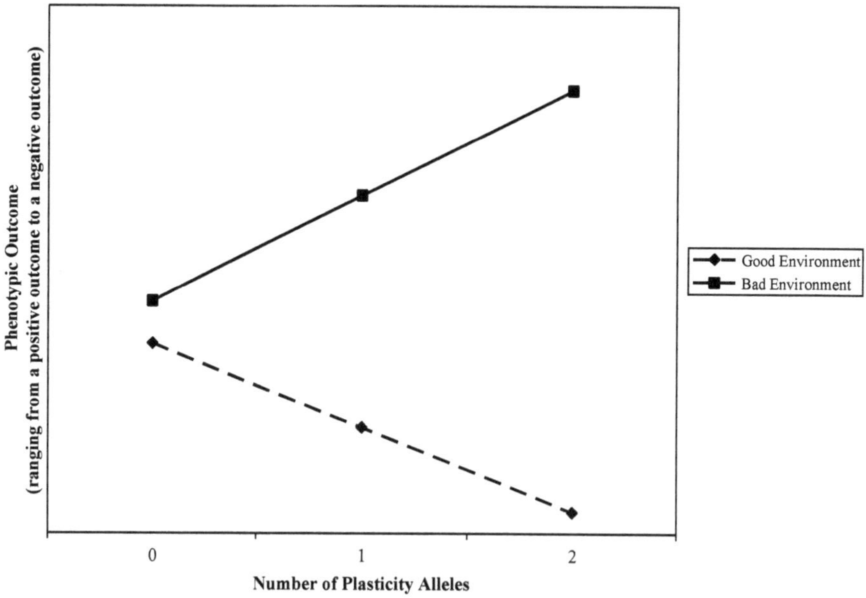

Fig. 7.2 Graphical depiction of a gene-environment interaction according to the differential-susceptibility model

The differential-susceptibility model makes a unique hypothesis—it states that people with the greatest number of plasticity alleles will exhibit the most negative outcomes in the presence of negative environments, but these same individuals will also exhibit the most positive outcomes in the presence of positive environments. In this way, the plasticity alleles work in a "better-or-for-worse" fashion, which is most often determined by plotting the gene–environment interaction (Belsky et al. 2009). If the interaction is a crossover interaction, then this typically is viewed as evidence in favor of the differential-susceptibility thesis (Fig. 7.2). The diathesis–stress model, in contrast, predicts only that the allele will be related to negative outcomes in the presence of negative environmental conditions. According to this perspective, the allele should not be associated with positive outcomes because it is conferring an increased risk of the negative phenotype (as illustrated in Fig. 7.3; Belsky et al. 2009).

Although the differential-susceptibility thesis was advanced a relatively short time ago, there is already a good deal of evidence in support of it. Studies have found, for instance, that gene–environment interactions operate in a "better-or-for-worse" fashion for self-control/self-regulation, for crime, and for other types of violent aggression (Belsky and Beaver 2011; Belsky and Pluess 2009). There also has been support garnered for the diathesis–stress model (Nederhof et al. 2012). Clearly, more research is needed to test these two mechanisms that might potentially account for gene–environment interactions on violent behavior, but for now the available evidence tentatively suggests that both are involved in some capacity.

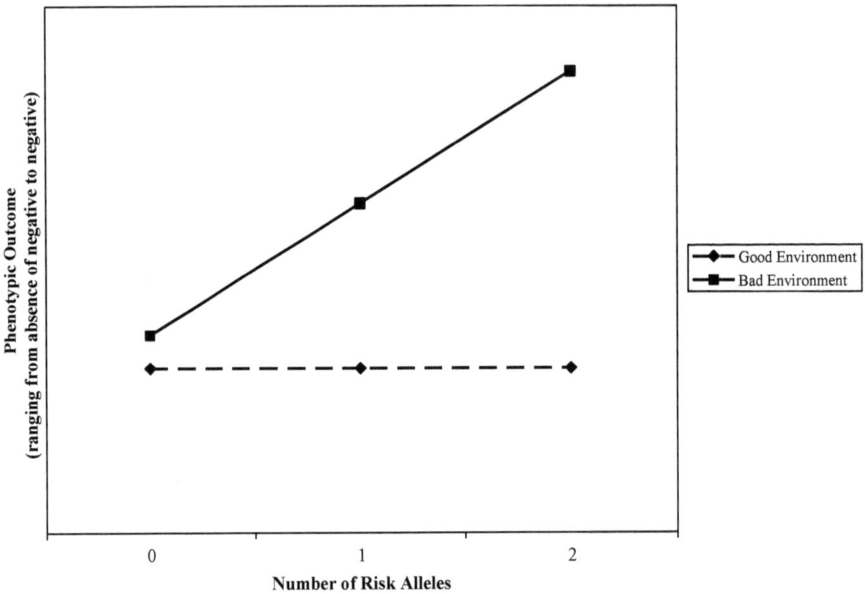

Fig. 7.3 Graphical depiction of a gene-environment interaction according to the diathesis-stress model

Conclusion

Whether focusing on universal adaptations or individual differences, there is ample evidence to indicate that genes are involved. This is especially true when the focus is on violent criminal behaviors. Given that serious violent criminal behavior is largely maladaptive and can siphon off opportunities for successful reproduction, the obvious question is why it continues to exist. As this chapter revealed, one potential explanation centers on the genotype. Given that violent behavior was likely more adaptive in the ancestral environment than it is today, alleles related to violence likely were relatively common. Since the distribution of alleles moves at a relatively low rate, the alleles that conferred an advantage in the ancestral environment will remain in existence today even if they are somewhat maladaptive. This could explain part of the reason why violent, predatory criminals remain in the population today despite the negative reproductive consequences associated with it. With that said, there is also emerging evidence to indicate that genetic influences may be moderated by environmental conditions. If this is the case, then the alleles associated with criminal behavior should not be viewed as deterministic, but rather as propensities that prime a person to act in a certain way given a certain environment. To fully unpack the factors that account for violent criminal behavior, evolutionary psychology needs to place a significant emphasis on the study of individual differences in antisocial behavior. By doing so, a great deal of progress will likely be made in better understanding the evolutionary pressures that ultimately produced and continue to produce hardened, violent criminals.

References

Alcock, J., & Crawford, C. (2008). Evolutionary questions for evolutionary psychologists. In C. Crawford & D. Krebs (Eds.), *Foundations of evolutionary psychology* (pp. 25–45). New York: Taylor & Francis.

Anderson, G. S. (2007). *Biological influences on criminal behavior*. New York, NY: CRC Press.

Bakermans-Kranenburg, M. J., & van IJzendoorn, M. H. (2006). Gene-environment interaction of the dopamine D4 receptor (DRD4) and observed maternal insensitivity predicting externalizing behavior in preschoolers. *Developmental Psychobiology, 48*, 406–409.

Beaver, K. M. (2009a). *Biosocial criminology: A primer*. Dubuque, IA: Kendall/Hunt Publishing.

Beaver, K. M. (2009b). Molecular genetics and crime. In A. Walsh & K. M. Beaver (Eds.), *Biosocial criminology: New directions in theory and research*. New York: Taylor and Francis.

Beaver, K. M., Wright, J. P., DeLisi, M., Walsh, A., Vaughn, M. G., Boisvert, D., et al (2007). A gene × gene interaction between DRD2 and DRD4 is associated with conduct disorder and antisocial behavior in males. *Behavioral and Brain Functions, 3*, 30–38.

Beaver, K. M., Wright, J. P., & DeLisi, M. (2008a). Delinquent peer group formation: Evidence of a gene X environment correlation. *The Journal of Genetic Psychology, 169*, 227–244.

Beaver, K. M., Wright, J. P., DeLisi, M., & Vaughn, M. G. (2008b). Desistance from delinquency: The marriage eï¬ect revisited and extended. *Social Science Research, 37*, 736–752.

Beaver, K. M., Gibson, C. L., Jennings, W. G., & Ward, J. T. (2009). A gene X environment interaction between DRD2 and religiosity in the prediction of adolescent delinquent involvement in a sample of males. *Biodemography and Social Biology, 55*, 71–81.

Beaver, K. M., DeLisi, M., Vaughn, M. G., & Barnes, J. C. (2010). Monoamine oxidase A genotype is associated with gang membership and weapon use. *Comprehensive Psychiatry, 51*, 130–134.

Beaver, K. M., Nedelec, J. L., Wilde, M., Lippoff, C., & Jackson, D. (2011). Examining the association between MAOA genotype and incarceration, anger and hostility: The moderating influences of risk and protective factors. *Journal of Research in Personality, 45*, 279–284.

Belsky, J., & Beaver, K. M. (2011). Cumulative-genetic plasticity, parenting and adolescent self-regulation. *Journal of Child Psychology and Psychiatry, 52*, 619–626.

Belsky, J., & Pluess, M. (2009). Beyond diathesis stress: Differential susceptibility to environmental influences. *Psychological Bulletin, 135*, 885–908.

Belsky, J., Jonassaint, C., Pluess, M., Stanton, M., Brummett, B., & Williams, R. (2009). Vulnerability genes or plasticity genes? *Molecular Psychiatry, 14*, 746–754.

Bouchard, T. J. Jr., Lykken, D. T., McGue, M., Segal, N. L., & Tellegen, A. (1990). Sources of human psychological differences: The Minnesota study of twins reared apart. *Science, 250*, 223–228.

Buss, D. M. (1994). The strategies of human mating. *American Scientist, 82*, 238–249.

Buss, D. M. (2005). *The murderer next door: Why the mind is designed to kill*. New York: Penguin Books.

Buss, D. M., & Shackelford, T. K. (1997). Human aggression in evolutionary psychological perspective. *Clinical Psychology Review, 17*, 605–619.

Cadoret, R. J., Langbehn, D., Caspers, K., Troughton, E. P., Yucuis, R., Sandhu, H. K., et al (2003). Associations of the serotonin transporter promoter polymorphism with aggressivity, attention deficit, and conduct disorder in an adoptee population. *Comprehensive Psychiatry, 44*, 88–101.

Caspi, A., McClay, J., Moffitt, T. E., Mill, J., Martin, J., Craig, I. W., et al (2002). Role of genotype in the cycle of violence in maltreated children. *Science, 297*, 851–854.

Comings, D. E., Gade-Andavolu, R., Gonzalez, N., Wu, S., Muhleman, D., Chen, C., et al (2001). The additive effect of neurotransmitter genes in pathological gambling. *Clinical Genetics, 60*, 107–116.

Daly, M., & Wilson, M. (1988). *Homicide*. New York, NY: Aldine De Gruyter.

DeKeseredy, W. S. (2013). The myth that "criminals" are fundamentally different from "non-criminals.". In R. M. Bohm & J. T. Walker (Eds.), *Demystifying crime & criminal justice* (2nd ed., pp. 13–24). New York: Oxford University Press.

DeLisi, M., Beaver, K. M., Wright, J. P., & Vaughn, M. G. (2008). The etiology of criminal onset: The enduring salience of nature and nurture. *Journal of Criminal Justice, 36*, 217–223.

Derks, E. M., Dolan, C. V., & Boomsma, D. I. (2006). A test of the equal environment assumption (EEA) in multivariate twin studies. *Twin Research and Human Genetics, 9*, 403–411.

Faraone, S. V., Doyle, A. E., Mick, E., & Biederman, J. (2001). Meta-Analysis of the association between the 7-repeat allele of the dopamine D4 receptor gene and attention deficit hyperactivity disorder. *American Journal of Psychiatry, 158*, 1052–1057.

Feinn, R., Nellissery, M., & Kranzler, H. R. (2005). Meta-analysis of the association of a functional serotonin transporter promoter polymorphism with alcohol dependence. *American Journal of Medical Genetics Part B (Neuropsychiatric Genetics), 133B*, 79–84

Ferguson, C. J. (2010). Genetic contributions to antisocial personality and behavior: A meta-analytic review from an evolutionary perspective. *The Journal of Social Psychology, 150*, 160–180.

Ferguson, C. J., & Beaver, K. M. (2009). Natural born killers: The genetic origins of extreme violence. *Aggression and Violent Behavior, 14*, 286–294.

Gill, M., Daly, G., Heron, S., Hawi, Z., & Fitzgerald, M. (1997). Confirmation of association between attention deficit hyperactivity disorder and a dopamine transporter polymorphism. *Molecular Psychiatry, 2*, 311–313.

Guo, G., Ou, X.-M., Roettger, M., & Shih, J. C. (2008). The VNTR 2 repeat in MAOA and delinquent behavior in adolescence and young adulthood: Associations and MAOA promoter activity. *European Journal of Human Genetics, 16*, 626–634.

Hawley, P. H., & Buss, D. M. (2011). Introduction. In D. M. Buss & P. H. Hawley (Eds.), *The evolution of personality and individual differences* (ix–xix). New York: Oxford University Press.

Kanazawa, S. (2004). General intelligence as a domain-specific adaptation. *Psychological Review, 111*, 512–523.

Koller, G., Bondy, B., Preuss, U. W., Bottlender, M., & Soyka, M. (2003). No association between a polymorphism in the promoter region of the MAOA gene with antisocial personality traits in alcoholics. *Alcohol and Alcoholism, 38*, 31–34.

Lahdenpeä, M., Lummaa, V., Helle, S., Tremblay, M., & Russell, A. F. (2004). Fitness benefits of prolonged post-reproductive lifespan in women. *Nature, 428*, 178–181.

Laucht, M., Skowronek, M. H., Becker, K., Schmidt, M. H., Esser, G., Schulze, T. G., et al (2007). Interacting effects of the dopamine transporter gene and psychosocial adversity on attention-deficit/hyperactivity disorder symptoms among 15-year-olds from a high-risk community sample. *Archives of General Psychiatry, 64*, 585–590.

Loehlin, J. C. (2009). History of behavior genetics. In Y. K. Kim (Ed.), *Handbook of behavior genetics*. New York: Springer Science.

Mason, D. A., & Frick, P. J. (1994). The heritability of antisocial behavior: A meta-analysis of twin and adoption studies. *Journal of Psychopathology and Behavioral Assessment, 16*, 301–323.

Mayr, E. (2001). *What evolution is*. New York: Basic Books.

Medland, S. E., & Hatemi, P. K. (2009). Political science, biometric theory, and twin studies: A methodological introduction. *Political Analysis, 17*, 191–214.

Miles, D. R., & Carey, G. (1997). Genetic and environmental architecture of human aggression. *Journal of Personality and Social Psychology, 72*, 207–217.

Moffitt, T. E. (1993). Adolescence-limited and life-course-persistent antisocial behavior: A developmental taxonomy. *Psychology Review, 100*, 674–701.

Munafò, M. R., Roberts, K., Johnstone, E. C., Walton, R. T., & Yudkin, P. L. (2005). Association of serotonin transporter gene polymorphism with nicotine dependence: No evidence for an interaction with trait neuroticism. *Personality and Individual Differences, 38*, 843–850.

Nedelec, J. L., & Beaver, K. M. (2012). The association between sexual behavior and antisocial behavior: Insights from an evolutionary analysis. *Journal of Contemporary Criminal Justice, 28*, 329–345.

Nederhof, E., Belsky, J., Ormel, J., & Oldehinkel, A. J. (2012). Effects of divorce on Dutch boys' and girls' externalizing behavior in gene X environment perspective: Diathesis stress or differential susceptibility in the Dutch Tracking Adolescents' Individual Lives Survey study? *Development and Psychopathology*, *24*, 929–939.
Plomin, R., DeFries, J. C., Craig, I. W., & McGuffin, P. (2002). Behavioral genetics. In R. Plomin, J. C. DeFries, & I. W. Craig (Eds.), *Behavioral genetics in the postgenomic era* (pp. 3–15). Washington, DC: American Psychological Association.
Plomin, R., DeFries, J. C., Knopik, V. S., & Neiderhiser, J. M. (2013). *Behavioral genetics* (6th Ed.). New York: Worth Publishers.
Ponce, G., Jimenez-Arriero, M. A., Rubio, G., Hoenicka, J., Ampuero, I., Ramos, J. A., et al (2003). The A1 allele of the DRD2 gene (TaqIA polymorphisms) is associated with antisocial personality in a sample of alcohol-dependent patients. *European Psychiatry*, *18*, 356–360.
Posthuma, D., & Boomsma, D. I. (2000). A note on the statistical power in extended twin designs. *Behavior Genetics*, *30*, 147–158.
Raine, A. (1993). *The psychopathology of crime: Criminal behavior as a clinical disorder*. San Diego: CA: Academic Press.
Rhee, S. H., & Waldman, I. D. (2002). Genetic and environmental influences on antisocial behavior: A meta-analysis of twin and adoption studies. *Psychological Bulletin*, *128*, 490–529.
Rowe, D. C. (2002). *Biology and crime*. Los Angeles, CA: Roxbury.
Rowe, D. C., Stever, C., Card, J. M. C., Cleveland, H. H., Sanders, M. L., Abramowitz, A., et al (1998). The relation of the dopamine transporter gene (DAT1) to symptoms of internalizing disorders in children. *Behavior Genetics*, *28*, 215–225.
Rowe, D. C., Stever, C., Chase, D., Sherman, S., Abramowitz, A., & Waldman, I. D. (2001). Two dopamine genes related to reports of childhood retrospective inattention and conduct disorder symptoms. *Molecular Psychiatry*, *6*, 429–433.
Schwartz, J. A., & Beaver, K. M. (2011). Evidence of a gene × environment interaction between perceived prejudice and MAOA genotype in the prediction of criminal arrests. *Journal of Criminal Justice*, *39*, 378–384.
Segal, N. L. (2012). Personality similarity in unrelated look-alike pairs: Addressing a twin study challenge. *Personality and Individual Differences*, *54*, 23–28.
Symons, D. (1995). Beauty is in the adaptation of the beholder: The evolutionary psychology of human female sexual attractiveness. In P. R. Abramson & S. D. Pinkerton (Eds.) *Sexual nature, sexual culture*. Chicago, IL: The University of Chicago Press.
Tellegen, A., Lykken, D. T., Bouchard, T. J. Jr., Wilcox, K. J., Segal, N. L., & Rich, S. (1988). Personality similarity in twins reared apart and together. *Journal of Personality and Social Psychology*, *54*, 1031–1039.
Thapar, A., O'Donovan, M., & Owen, M. J. (2005). The genetics of attention deficit hyperactivity disorder. *Human Molecular Genetics*, *14*, R275–R282
Tielbeek, J. J., Medland, S. E., Benyamin, B., Byrne, E. M., Heath, A. C., Madden, P. A. F., et al (2012). Unraveling the genetic etiology of adult antisocial behavior: A genome-wide association study. *PLOS One*, *7*, e45086.
Vanyukov, M. M., & Tarter, R. E. (2000). Genetic studies of substance abuse. *Drug and Alcohol Dependence*, *59*, 101–123.
Vanyukov, M. M., Moss, H. B., Gioio, A. E., Hughes, H. B., Kaplan, B. B., & Tarter, R. E. (1998). An association between a microsatellite polymorphism at the DRD5 gene and the liability to substance abuse: Pilot study. *Behavior Genetics*, *28*, 75–82.
Vaske, J., Beaver, K. M., Wright, J. P., Boisvert, D., & Schnupp, R. (2008). An interaction between DAT1 and having an alcoholic father predicts serious alcohol problems in a sample of males. *Drug and Alcohol Dependence*, *104*, 17–22.
Walby, K., & Carrier, N. (2010). The rise of biosocial criminology: Capturing observable bodily economies of 'criminal man'. *Criminology and Criminal Justice*, *10*, 261–285.

Chapter 8
The Evolutionary Psychology of Sibling Conflict and Siblicide

Catherine A. Salmon and Jessica A. Hehman

There is a little boy inside the man who is my brother... Oh, how I hated that little boy. And how I love him too.

—Anna Quindlan

When brothers agree, no fortress is so strong as their common life.

—Antisthenes

The Rule of Sibs: If your sibling gets something you want, you (1) try to take it; (2) break it; or (3) say it's no good

—Patricia Fleming

Introduction

Our brothers and sisters are often our closest allies, but they can also be our greatest competitors. Some of the time we adore them; some of the time they can drive us to despair if not violence. What factors influence the course of sibling rivalry, whether brothers band together against all others or become deadly enemies as in the biblical story of Cain and Abel? This chapter focuses on the evolutionary roots of sibling solidarity and conflict not just in humans but in nonhumans as well, as there is a long and rich history of studying sibling conflict in many other species that can inform our understanding of the human case. Siblicide is an excellent example of a topic much better studied in nonhuman species, due to the fact that it is much

C. A. Salmon (✉) · J. A. Hehman
Department of Psychology, University of Redlands,
1200 E Colton Ave, Redlands, CA 92373, USA
e-mail: Catherine_Salmon@redlands.edu

J. A. Hehman
e-mail: jessica_hehman@redlands.edu

T. K. Shackelford, R. D. Hansen (eds.), *The Evolution of Violence*,
Evolutionary Psychology, DOI 10.1007/978-1-4614-9314-3_8,

more frequent in nonhumans and yet shares many of the same root causes. Siblicide is rare in humans, not surprisingly as it is the most extreme expression of sibling competition.

Siblicide can be defined as the killing of one sibling by another and includes both fratricide (the killing of a brother) and sororicide (the killing of a sister). As will be discussed later, sibling violence is the most frequent type of nonlethal familial violence (Wiehe 1997). With siblicide being relatively rare in humans, there is scant research on the topic. The majority of research on familial violence has focused on spousal abuse/homicide and child abuse/infanticide in which deaths are much more common (Statistics Canada 2004; Underwood and Patch 1999).

Despite its current low rate, historical data, biographies, and fictional stories tell the story of siblicidal conflict. In the Bible, Cain slew his brother Abel (a version of conflict over parental favoritism) after God showed a preference for Abel and his animal offerings over Cain's crops. Sultan Mehmet II of the Ottoman Empire imprisoned his brothers and killed them all once he had produced an heir to protect his "territory" and offspring. The fact that such events and tales of events keep cropping up across time and cultures suggests that siblicidal conflict has been a concern and that not all sibling rivalries end peacefully during or after childhood. Of course, when sibling rivalry is examined in humans, it is typically of the nonlethal variety. Even if conflict between human children escalates beyond the verbal to punching and shoving, parents have an emotional and fitness interest in quickly intervening. But the fact is that such conflict does occur despite the shared genetic interests of siblings, even if human siblings are less likely to cause their siblings' deaths, as is seen in many other animal sibships.

Evolutionary perspectives have been productively applied to the study of familial conflict across a number of contexts including spousal homicide (Daly and Wilson 1988; Wilson and Daly 2004), infanticide (Daly and Wilson 1984, 1994a), child abuse (Daly and Wilson 1986, 1994b), parent–offspring conflict (Salmon 2007; Schlomer et al. 2011), and sibling relationships in general (Pollet 2007; Salmon 2003; Salmon and Daly 1998), as well as siblicide (Daly et al. 2001; Michalski et al. 2007).

Sibling Conflict Theory

Sibling relationships are the most enduring relationships of the life span (Cicirelli 1995). Within those relationships, there is potential for conflict as well as cooperation. Explaining motivation for cooperation and altruism (even that directed toward one's kin) from an evolutionary perspective presented a problem, until Hamilton (1964) proposed *kin selection theory*. With this theory, Hamilton redefined classic Darwinian fitness (i.e., survival and successful reproduction, hence the transmission of one's own genes into subsequent generations) into the concept of *inclusive fitness* (i.e., encompassing not only one's own survival and reproduction, but also that of genetically related individuals in whom one has invested). According to 'Hamilton's rule' (1964), the likelihood an individual will behave altruistically toward another depends on whether the degree of relatedness and the potential fitness benefit to the other person outweigh the potential fitness cost to oneself (i.e., $r * b > c$). Thus, altruistic behavior directed toward kin serves as an indirect way to increase one's own inclusive fitness. In addition, kin selection theory predicts that genetic relatedness should influence the likelihood of conflict and cooperation between individuals. Specifically, according to this theory, we expect to see more cooperation (and less conflict) between genetically related individuals, with greater relatedness leading to greater cooperation (and even less conflict) when all other things are equal. These predictions have been supported by numerous studies investigating feelings of subjective closeness and received support across adult relationships as a function of degree of relatedness, with higher levels directed to kin versus nonkin and to more closely related kin (e.g., a sibling) than more distantly related kin (e.g., a cousin) (Neyer and Lang 2003).

Genetic relatedness, however, does not guarantee that those that are related will share the same interests or be motivated to behave altruistically toward each other. A clear example of this comes from *parent–offspring conflict theory* (Trivers 1974). The genetic interests of parents and their offspring are not identical. Offspring will be selected to manipulate their parents in order to ensure higher investment, and parents will be selected to manipulate their offspring to suit their own (i.e., the parents') genetic interests. When two parties have differing interests, there is a possibility of conflict. From an offspring's perspective, the more parental investment (e.g., resources such as time, energy, food, etc.), the better. From a parent's point of view, the more he/she invests in any one offspring, the less he/she can invest in other current or future offspring (Trivers 1972). According to *parental investment theory*, the amount and allocation of parental investment depends on the amount of resources available to parents, the quality of the offspring, and the potential for future offspring (Trivers 1972). Assuming availability of resources and equal quality of offspring, it would be expected that parents value each offspring equally and would encourage them to value their siblings more than they would be naturally inclined to do. Each offspring, however, being more closely genetically related to itself than to its sibling, values itself over its siblings. This brings about the possibility for sibling conflict as siblings compete for parental resources. Therefore, it could be expected that each sibling would try to receive more than their "fair share" of parental investment. An extreme outcome of this conflict is siblicide, which, although rare in humans, is not uncommon in nonhuman animals.

Sibling Competition in Nonhuman Animals

Sibling conflict in nonhumans shares many features with such a conflict in humans. Its intensity is influenced by the sex of siblings, their birth order (which often translates into size and strength differences), the number of siblings, and the available resources. Inclusive fitness theory also suggests greater conflict between nonkin (as in human step-siblings) than between kin over food or territory, and the greater the levels of conflict, the lesser the degree of relatedness (half siblings experiencing greater conflict than full biological siblings, for example). The Holmes and Sherman (1982) well-known studies of the role of kinship in reducing territorial aggression examined its impact on the social behavior of Belding's ground squirrels (*Spermophilus beldings*). In this species of ground squirrel, females tend not to disperse, staying in close proximity to their natal burrow. As a result, sisters are likely to occupy adjacent territories. Holmes and Sherman found half-sisters to exhibit greater aggression toward each other than full sisters and to be less likely to band together to defend each other's burrow from nonkin invaders even though they grew up in the same natal nest. Full sisters engaged in more cooperation and less antagonism than half-sisters.

More familiar to some than adult conflicts over territory, scramble competition among young siblings occurs in many mammals over access to milk. Typically, the number of offspring influences the intensity of this competition. In guinea pigs (*Cavia aperea f. porcellus*), for example, when litters are experimentally manipulated such that they have more or less offspring than available teats to nurse (Fey and Trillmich 2008), the pups from larger litters experience slower growth rates due to competition for milk and the resulting longer wait for access to teats. Aggression toward siblings in this study was only seen among the larger litters.

Competition for maternal milk can also be seen in domestic pigs. Sows may not have enough milk to feed all their piglets, especially when litters are very large. The teats nearest to the front of the sow's body have the best supply of milk. Competition for access to the best teats is direct and piglet dentition (sharp incisors) is specialized to facilitate aggressive attacks on siblings. As a result of such direct competition, some low birth weight piglets do not survive. Piglets also compete indirectly by stimulating milk production at the teats most used, with the remaining teats producing less milk (Drake et al. 2008). The more restricted the supply of food, the more intense the sibling aggression to the point where some piglets die of sibling-induced starvation (Andersen et al. 2011).

Competition for food provided by parents can also be intense in a variety of avian species. Competition between barn swallow (*Hirundo rustica*) chicks is influenced by offspring sex, sex of competing siblings, and hatching order. Chicks engage in vocalizations, gaping, and posturing such that parents provide more food to the chicks that beg more intensely (Lotem 1998). Studies examining how factors influence the outcome of such sibling competition indicate that junior chicks and males beg more vigorously (perhaps signally greater need) and, as a result, receive more feedings (Bonisoli-Alquati et al. 2011). In this case, the parents appear to be compensating male junior chicks for the disadvantage of asynchronous hatching.

One mammalian species (familiar to many from zoos and television shows) with nontrivial sibling rivalry is the cooperatively breeding meerkat. Meerkats (*Suricata suricatta*) commonly engage in aggression between littermates that can be fierce, though rarely resulting in serious injury and never lethal (Hodge et al. 2007).

In a meerkat group, one female monopolizes reproduction with an average of three to four litters per year with a typical litter size of four pups, though there can be as few as one and as many as seven (Hodge et al. 2008). While in the beginning, pups are fed in the burrow, as they mature they travel with the adults in the group, begging for food from helpers. As cooperative breeders, meerkat groups contain nonreproductive helpers who feed and protect pups. There are benefits to being the only pup around a helper because helpers tend to feed whichever begging pup is closest to them. Pups, therefore, try to deny other pups' access to a specific helper that they are shadowing by attacking any littermate who comes close to the helper. Such attacks mainly consist of snaps and lunges and the other pup is usually quickly driven off. Fights do sometimes occur, with the loser retreating in search of another helper. Most meerkat sibling aggression occurs between juveniles and dissipates as they become adults.

Unsurprisingly, meerkat pup littermate aggression increases when food availability decreases, usually due to a lack of rain or a low number of helpers. Hodge et al. (2009) tested the impact of food availability on levels of sibling aggression with short-term feeding experiments. Researchers decreased a pup's hunger by provisioning with a small amount of food before a foraging excursion. Pups that had been fed exhibited less aggression during foraging/begging than the unfed control pups.

As the above examples might suggest, siblicide in many species is often a result of substantial resource shortages that produce extreme sibling competition. This final outcome can be influenced by the degree of relatedness between offspring and the impact of such aggression on parental fitness. It is important, as well, to distinguish between cases in which competition between siblings is always fatal to the subordinate (obligate siblicide) and cases in which the consequences of competition are highly variable, influenced largely by environmental conditions (facultative siblicide).

Why do parents produce more offspring than they are able to successfully raise? There are several possibilities or ways in which overproduction of offspring can lead to greater parental fitness. "Overproduction allows: (1) efficient 'resource-tracking' (where the extra offspring actually turn out to be affordable because of an unpredictable upswing in ecological conditions); (2) the possibility of 'sibling facilitation' (e.g. some offspring serving as helpers or critical meals for others); and/or (3) the use of extras as 'replacement offspring' when one or more members of the core brood proves defective or happens to die" (Mock and Parker 1998, p. 2). There are also circumstances in which parents may be able to provide enough resources for all their offspring but chose not to, instead keeping some portion of resources in reserve for other uses, including opportunities for future reproduction (Williams 1966). Parents may, rather than prevent competition and possible siblicide, encourage brood reduction through asynchronous hatching, selective care of offspring, or infanticide (St. Clair et al. 1995). When considering whether siblicide is more likely to be obligate or facultative, evidence suggests that we should expect obligate siblicide or aggression to evolve where resources are most often limited and siblings can present a serious drain on scarce resources. Facultative siblicide is more likely to be found in circumstances in which resources are not always limited (Mock et al. 1990). In the obligate species, the extra sibling can serve as a replacement if the first offspring dies. In the facultative species, the extra sibling will survive and contribute to both parental and sibling fitness when conditions are favorable.

Siblicide in Nonhuman Animals

There is an extensive literature on siblicide in nonhuman species, particularly avian ones. Many organisms regularly produce more offspring than they can afford to raise to maturity, from insects with massive broods in which only one or two survive to marsupials who produce more young than they have teats to feed them with (Mock and Parker 1998). In a majority of such species, the reduction in offspring occurs through differential starvation. But in other cases, brood reduction occurs via siblicide, the elder offspring (the "A" chick, for example) killing its younger sibling (the "B" chick) directly or by forcing it from the nest. As previously mentioned, food availability is a driving factor in the intensity of sibling competition, the one that moves the competition to a deadly level. A great deal of research on sibling competition for food has focused on birds as they tend to lend themselves well to such observations. Siblings are confined to the close proximity of a nest. They are dependent on their parents for small packets of food that are easily quantified, and their nests are often easily observable (in trees, ground nests, etc., as opposed to underground burrows).

Avian Siblicide

Boobies. Siblicidal behavior has been examined in a number of booby species. The Nazca booby (*Sula granli*) fledges just one nestling regardless of clutch size and the elder "A" chick always eliminates its younger rival. This species therefore practices obligate siblicide (Anderson 1990). Despite the fact that only one nestling survives to fledge, two eggs are typically laid. This surplus production of offspring is sometimes explained with the insurance egg hypothesis, which suggests that the second egg can serve as a replacement or backup egg in case the first egg fails to hatch or the chick dies soon after hatching. As a result of such insurance, booby parents who produce two eggs will have greater reproductive success than those that lay one egg (as one-egg nests would be more likely to fail to fledge).

Clifford and Anderson (2000) tested this insurance hypothesis experimentally by manipulating clutch sizes. Natural one-egg clutches were increased to two-egg ones and natural two-egg clutches were reduced to one-egg ones. In both cases, parents with two-egg clutches produced more hatchlings and fledglings than the one-egg clutches. The insurance benefit of the extra egg was clear—those booby parents with two eggs experienced greater reproductive success. Why do all natural clutches not consist of two eggs? The most reasonable answer is that parents who are strongly limited by their own resource condition (or food availability as the time of laying) are only able to produce one egg.

Possible proximate mechanisms that enable obligate or facultative siblicide have also been examined, with particular regard to androgen levels. An examination was conducted of perinatal androgen levels in two species of booby, the previously mentioned obligate Nazca and the facultative blue-footed booby (*Sula nebouxii*) which, unlike the Nazca, often raises more than one chick (Muller et al. 2008). Blue-footed booby parents do favor the eldest chick in terms of their own feeding behavior when food is scarce.

But patterns of chick aggression are quite different between the two species. The Nazca elder chick unconditionally attacks its younger sibling, when possible ejecting it from the nest. Blue-footed chicks exhibit aggression but it is conditional on food availability, and is highly focused on getting access to, or monopolizing, whatever food is available. When androgen levels were examined, obligate Nazca chicks were found to hatch with higher circulating androgen levels than the facultative blue-footed chicks. The role of high levels of androgens in facilitating sibling aggression is revisited in the section on mammalian siblicide.

However, in the obligate brown booby (*Sula leucogaster*), there is no evidence of the role of androgens in facilitating sibling aggression (Drummond et al. 2008). Rather, in this case it appears that brown booby mothers make their junior chicks vulnerable to siblicide by hatching them 5 days after their nestmates, not by differential allocation of egg androgens or nutrients. Drummond and colleagues (2008) also found that facultative blue-footed booby mothers hatched their subordinate chicks 4 days after their nestmates and with 10 % less yolk to ensure their low status.

Kittiwakes. The food amount hypothesis (FAH) proposes that sibling aggression is negatively correlated with the amount of food parents provide to the aggressor (Mock 1987). Evidence that supports the FAH has been found in a number of species including cattle egrets and osprey (both discussed below) and the black-legged kittiwake.

White et al. (2010) tested the FAH in a colony of black-legged kittiwakes in the Gulf of Alaska that had been experiencing long-term food shortages. As part of a large-scale food supplementation project examining the impact of food supply on kittiwake breeding, the amount of food available to parents was manipulated. Breeding pairs raising two chicks were split into two groups: one was given supplemental fish and the other was not. The supplementation was started approximately 1 month before hatching and was ended once the majority of chicks had fledged.

"A" chicks received substantially more food when their parents were supplemented than those with unsupplemented parents such that they gained more weight. There was no difference in the amount fed to "B" chicks between groups. While the aggression exhibited by "A" chicks in both groups decreased over time, the "A" chicks in the supplemented group were less aggressive (in terms of frequency of attacks and intensity of them) than those in the unsupplemented group. This corresponds to field-study reports that chick aggression in kittiwakes is greater during seasons of food shortage (Irons 1992), supporting the adaptive view of sibling aggression.

Cattle egrets. The cattle egret (*Bubulcus ibis*), unlike most herons, is typically found feeding in fields and other dry grassy habitats. They seem to follow the insurance chick model to a certain extent, with a clutch size that ranges from one to five eggs but is typically three. Frequently, the third (and fourth or fifth) chicks do not survive and the nestlings exhibit intense sibling rivalry. If we consider a brood of three, the "A", "B", and "C" chicks hatch asynchronously, giving the "A" chick the size advantage, as usual. After winning some early skirmishes, the "A" chick is usually free to enjoy the dominant position with its first dibs on food delivered by parents. The "C" chick gets about half the food the older siblings do and loses the majority of fights to the "B" chick. When the nestlings are very young, attacks do not do serious damage but as they get larger, they will raise their heads up and drive down on their opponents, often drawing blood, and fighting is most intense when food is arriving. The "C" chick inevitably surrenders by lowering its head (making access to food brought from above by a parent difficult). With food being monopolized by the "A" and "B" chicks, the "C" chick loses weight and strength so that by their third week, one-third to one-half of all "C" chicks would have died (Mock 2004). If a senior chick is lost to defect, disease, or predation, the "C" chick is more likely to survive to fledge.

Ospreys. The osprey (*Pandion haliaetus*) is a large fish-eating raptor found worldwide, typically nesting on lakeshores and in coastal areas. They typically lay two to four eggs asynchronously and appear to experience facultative brood reduction during food shortages (Jamieson et al. 1983; McLean and Byrd 1991). An experimental study designed to test the FAH in ospreys was conducted in southwest British Columbia in which the researchers removed broods from their nests, exposed them to a starvation period, and then either fed them or did not (sham feeding) in order to manipulate the hunger level of the nestlings (Machmer and Ydenberg 1998). They were then placed in a nest with food and their behavior was observed. Broods were more aggressive when food was introduced after sham feeding, with senior siblings being the most aggressive and claiming the larger share of the food. It appears that the competitive asymmetries established through sibling aggression facilitate brood reduction in ospreys to a level matching the prevailing food supply.

Black eagles. Unlike most of the avian species previously discussed, the black eagle (*Aquila verreauxi*) is a species with obligate siblicide. Rather than exhibiting support for the FAH, they are an example of the extra offspring as insurance model. Their range includes the mountains of southern and northeastern Africa and parts of the Middle East. Black eagles nest on cliff ledges, laying two eggs which hatch asynchronously, typically 3 days apart. The resulting "A" chick is larger, typically attacking the "B" chick from the day it hatches with its very sharp beak. The older chick usually prevents the younger one from gaining access to parentally provided food until it finally dies of starvation. It is unusual for more than one chick to fledge from a black eagle nest (Simmons 1988).

Laughing kookaburras. The laughing kookaburra (*Dacelo novaeguineae)* is a cooperatively breeding member of the kingfisher family. Being carnivorous, they live in forested areas of Australia, in family groups with a monogamous pair breeding between September and January supported by older offspring. Three eggs are laid at 2-day intervals which then hatch asynchronously, giving an advantage, as usual, to the larger, older "A" chick. Laughing kookaburra chicks have a hooked bill specialized for sibling competition which is used to grasp and shake their victim. Such an aggressive competition is common when the food supply is limited. There is typically a bump in "C" chick deaths in the first week as a result of physical injuries. A week or two later, there will be another increase in mortality with less visible causes, mainly due to starvation (Legge 2000; Legge and Cockburn 2000). The hooked bill seen in nestlings disappears by the time they fledge.

Legge (2002) examined the extra offspring as insurance model and the resource-tracking model in a population of laughing kookaburras in the Canberra Nature Park. While she found that nests with no mortality resulted in more independent fledglings, those nests that experienced brood reduction by siblicide had higher-quality surviving siblings (as measured by weight and feather development) than nests where brood reduction occurred by starvation. If there is an inability to raise all three offspring, early siblicide seems to produce the best result from the perspective of parental fitness.

Mammalian Siblicide

Spotted hyenas. Siblicide is relatively rare among mammals. The spotted hyena (*Crocuta crocuta*) has received a great deal of attention with regard to its intense sibling competition; much of it focused on whether siblicide in this species is obligate or facultative.

Observational evidence suggests that siblings kill approximately one-quarter of cubs, half of those born to same-sex litters in which sibling competition is increased compared to opposite-sex litters (Frank et al. 1991).

Spotted hyenas are found in sub-Saharan Africa and their cubs are born in underground dens. In addition to their siblicidal behavior, the species is also well known for the strong degree to which females are masculinized, anatomically and behaviorally, by exposure to high levels of androgens during development. Neonates also show high levels of androgens. Cubs also experience precocial motor development. At birth, their eyes are open and they have fully erupted front teeth. These teeth are used to bite and shake their sibling rivals. Spotted hyenas usually give birth to a pair of cubs. Aggressive fighting peaks in the 48 hours immediately after birth (Frank et al. 1991; Smale et al. 1995). By this time, dominance has been clearly established. In same-sex litters, the subordinate sibling may die, but in mixed-sex litters, both usually survive. When three cubs are born, the third almost always perishes. While some researchers thought this might be an example of obligate siblicide, recent evidence from wild and captive populations indicates that facultative siblicide is the more likely explanation (Smale et al. 1999; Wahaj et al. 2007). When food resources are insufficient to raise two cubs, the early aggression to establish dominance can be deadly to the subordinate cub, if not by direct siblicide, then indirectly by starvation when the dominant cub monopolizes the food supply.

A long-term study of maternal provisioning and cub survival in the Serengeti (Hofer and East 2008) found an increase in the incidence of siblicide as the average cohort growth rate declined (due to fluctuations in prey abundance). In siblicidal litters, the dominant cub's growth rate increased substantially once their other cub died. The result was a siblicidal-cub growth rate similar to that of a singleton cub with a corresponding increase in expected survival. It was a clear example of a facultative response to fluctuating nutritional resources.

Galapagos fur seals. Like the hyena, the Galapagos fur seal (*Arctocephalus galapagooensis*) experiences high resource uncertainty. In addition, they take a long time to wean and, as a result, can often have overlapping successive young with 5–23 % of pups born while an older sibling is still being nursed. Such younger siblings have a lower birth weight, grow less, and suffer higher early mortality than those without a currently nursing older sibling. Many of these sibling pairs are also half-siblings, sharing a mother but with different fathers and about half of the older siblings will harass the younger ones, biting them and/or chasing them away from the mother (Trillmich and Wolf 2008). Mothers frequently interfere in such disputes, using threats or biting the older sibling to discourage attacks on the younger one. However, even without direct attacks, scramble competition for a limited milk supply can sometimes be lethal, with the older pup leaving insufficient milk for the younger one.

Sibling Conflict in Humans

As illustrated by the quotes at the beginning of this chapter, sibling relationships in humans are often complicated. Indeed, most sibling relationships can be characterized as treading a fine line between love and hate, especially during childhood and adolescence. Animosity and conflict among siblings, although it can be quite intense at times, is thought to be a normal part of development (Cicirelli 1995). As such, this conflict has been shown to hold both potential benefits as well as potential costs for psychosocial and cognitive development. Potential benefits of sibling conflict may include greater empathy and perspective taking (Dunn and Brown 1994; Dunn and Slomskowski 1992) as well as valuable practice in social negotiation, producing greater problem-solving and conflict-resolution skills (Azmitia and Montgomery 1993; Campione-Barr and Smetana 2010). Especially coercive, unresolved, and intense sibling conflict may lead to psychological, behavioral, and academic problems by early and middle adolescence including peer rejection and delinquent behavior (Bank et al.2004; Cohen 2004). Also, in extreme cases, sibling conflict can lead to siblicide, although this is rare in human siblings, as discussed later.

From an evolutionary perspective, sibling conflict (among human and other nonhuman species) stems from rivalry over limited resources. Specifically, for human siblings, this means competition over limited parental resources (e.g., attention, time, and money in modern societies versus limited food and basic resources such as shelter across our evolutionary past). As such, more conflict would be expected in families that have more limited parental resources as well as larger numbers of siblings. In relation to family size, evidence suggests that while fewer siblings are associated with more severe acts of violence, more siblings are associated with more overall incidents of violence (Straus et al. 2006). Investigations of proximate explanations have found the most common sources of sibling conflict to involve issues of relative power, self-interest (e.g., sharing of personal items), violation of rules (e.g., perceived immaturity and inappropriate behavior), and interests outside the family (McGuire et al. 2000). The most commonly cited source of conflict by both older and younger siblings has been the sharing of personal possessions, and the least commonly cited source has been competition over parental attention. This has been a consistent finding in studies conducted with toddlers and preschool-aged siblings (Dunn and Munn 1987; Stenimetz 1977), school-aged siblings (McGuire et al. 2000), as well as adolescent siblings who noted conflict over personal space and possessions as not only the most frequent source of conflict, but also the most intense one (Campione-Barr and Smetana 2010). Given the consistency of these findings, it has been suggested that sibling conflict may be a process by which children learn their place in the world, learn how to set personal boundaries, and (especially for young adolescents) learn to assert their independence and claim autonomy over their personal choices (McGuire et al. 2000).

In a recent study conducted in our lab, participants were asked to describe the times when they fantasized about aggressive encounters with a sibling. Many reported conflicts over personal possessions and a sense that they were treated differently, or rather that their sibling got special treatment. For example:

> When she becomes violent, I sometimes wish that I could retaliate. If I come away with a broken nose, obviously it was my fault because I provoked her but if she comes away with so much as a scratch it becomes assault and I'm the villain for not being the bigger person.
>
> I also imagined myself beating him up…unrealistic since he was so much bigger in size than me.
>
> My sister has been so frustrated with my sarcasm and back-sass that she claimed she wanted to kill me with several different details involving weapons blood and gore.
>
> …there were so many revenge thoughts going through my head…I wished that he didn't exist.

Relative to other types (e.g., parent–child and spousal violence), sibling violence is the most common form of family violence. Interestingly, since it is considered to be a normal part of family life, sibling violence seems to be acceptable, whereas violence between nonrelated individuals is not. Indeed, many accounts of sibling violence would likely be considered criminal assault if they had occurred outside the sibling relationship, while within the sibling relationship the acts of violence are often considered to be minor offenses. A national study of family violence in two-parent households found that approximately 80 % of American children between the ages of 3 and 17 years reported at least one act of violence against a sibling in a typical year (Straus et al. 2006). Within this sample, 74 % of siblings reported pushing or shoving a sibling, 48 % reported slapping a sibling, 42 % reported kicking, biting, or punching a sibling, 40 % reported hitting a sibling with an object, and 16 % reported beating up a sibling. The only act of violence that was shown to be more prevalent in parent–child and spousal relationships was the use of weapons (e.g., a gun or knife), which is consistent with siblicide rates being the lowest of family homicides. Although the rates of physical violence decline across development (i.e., with age of the children), it is estimated that nearly two-thirds of teenagers aged 15–17 years still engage in physical aggression with their siblings (Straus et al. 2006).

Factors that Influence the Intensity of Sibling Conflict

The prevalence as well as the intensity of sibling conflict is influenced by many factors. Some proximate influences include temperament and differential parental treatment, while some ultimate or evolutionary influences include relatedness, gender, birth order, and birth spacing. We discuss both sets of factors.

Temperament. Personality differences—or differences in temperament of younger children—have been associated with sibling conflict (Brody et al. 1987). In female sibling pairs, both older and younger sisters with higher activity and emotional intensity levels were found to direct more aggressive (and less prosocial) behavior toward their sibling. In male sibling pairs, however, high activity levels of the younger brother and high emotional intensity of the older brother predicted more conflictual interaction between the siblings. In the male sibling pairs, any aggressive behavior from the younger brother resulted in reciprocation of aggression by the older brother. While the difference in temperament predicted sibling conflict, it should also be noted that the sibling pairs in which both children exhibited high levels of activity and/or emotional intensity exhibited even greater conflict than those pairs in which only one sibling had those temperament traits.

Differential parental treatment. Given that sibling conflict can be construed as rivalry over limited parental resources, it makes sense that (1) siblings would be conscious of differential treatment, and (2) noticeable differences in parental treatment between siblings would lead to an increase in sibling conflict. By the age of 3 years, children are sensitive to differences in parental treatment between themselves and their siblings and actively monitor their siblings' relationships with their parents relative to their own (Dunn and Munn 1985). Not only are children sensitive to these differences from a young age, but this differential treatment has also been associated with higher levels of negativity in sibling relationships (Brody et al. 1992a, 1992b). The effect of differential parental treatment on the sibling relationship is moderated by birth order (Shanahan et al. 2008). Specifically, firstborns who recognize differential maternal treatment in favor of their sibling exhibit withdrawal from the relationship. That is, instead of directing aggression at the younger sibling, they tend to decrease levels of warmth and emotional closeness directed to the sibling. Secondborn children, however, respond to differences in maternal treatment in favor of the older sibling by directing more aggression toward that sibling.

Relatedness. Hamilton's kin selection theory (1964) predicts that greater genetic similarity should lead to increased levels of cooperation and altruism, whereas less genetic similarity would lead to increased competition. Consistent with the kin selection theory, findings from twin studies have shown that monozygotic (i.e., identical) twins have higher levels of cooperation across different tasks as well as closer relationships throughout childhood and into adulthood relative to dizygotic (i.e., fraternal) twins (for review, see Segal 2005). Although relatively few studies have investigated the effect of relatedness on sibling relationships, the results of studies that have been conducted are also consistent with the finding of kin selection theory that there is less conflict in full-sibling relationships relative to half-sibling and step-sibling relationships (Hetherington 1988; Pollet 2007).

Gender. Boys have more conflict with siblings than do girls (Brody et al. 1985) and opposite-sex siblings have more conflict (although not physical violence) than same-sex siblings (Dunn and Kendrick 1982; Campione-Barr and Smetana 2010). Older female siblings are more likely to help take care of younger siblings, and as a result have less conflictual relationships with younger siblings than do older male siblings (Cicirelli 1994; Hrdy 2005). Gender differences in closeness of sibling pairs continue into adulthood with sister–sister pairs having closer and stronger relationships relative to brother–brother and brother–sister pairs (Campione-Barr and Smetana 2010; Pollet 2007). Investigations of sibling violence have found that boys are more violent toward siblings than are girls and the highest level of violence occurs between brothers (Straus et al. 2006). Across all ages, girls are less likely to use physical violence than are boys, regardless of the sex of their siblings. Boys, however, are less violent with sisters relative to brothers or brother–sister mixes, and girls with brothers tend to be more violent than girls with sisters.

Birth order. Evidence suggests that middleborn children perceive their parents in a less positive light than do first- and lastborns, preferring to have a close relationship with a friend over kin (Salmon 2003; Salmon and Daly 1998). Firstborns are more likely to maintain a close contact with siblings and invest more in siblings relative to laterborns (Pollet and Nettle 2009). There are also birth-order differences in terms of sources of sibling conflict. Older siblings report issues centering around the younger sibling's immaturity, whereas younger siblings report issues centering around rejection by (and aggression from) the older sibling (Buhrmester and Furman 1990; Ross et al. 1994).

Birth spacing. The effects related to birth-order effects are of birth spacing. During childhood, greater birth spacing leads to a reduction in conflict; however, in adulthood, greater birth spacing is associated with less contact and less close relationships between siblings (Pollet 2007). Close birth spacing has been associated with not only increased conflict over parental resources, but also detrimental effects on development and health (Miller et al. 1992; Powell and Steelman 1993; Rustein 2005). It has been noted that most sibling conflict occurs between siblings who are within two years of age, presumably because they have similar need of parental resources (Cicirelli 1995).

Siblicide in Humans

The most extreme form of sibling conflict is siblicide, in which one sibling kills another. While siblicide is much more common in many other animal species, as discussed previously (Mock and Parker 1998), it is rare in humans. In fact, family homicides (e.g., intimate partner homicides, filicides—parents killing their offspring, parricide—children killing their parents, and siblicides) in general are not common, and siblicide is the rarest form of family homicide (Diem and Pizarro 2010). Siblicides have been estimated to make up only 1.4–2 % of all homicides in Detroit and Canada (Daly and Wilson 1988; Bourget and Gagne 2006)with the majority (over 70 %) of siblicides being brother-killing-brother (Gebo 2002; Underwood and Patch 1999). Consistent with these focused samples, national studies on homicide rates in the USA have estimated that approximately 1.5 % of all homicides are siblicides (Sussman and Steinmetz 1987). Evidence from investigations of siblicide has indicated that when they do occur, siblicides are typically due to competition over very limited resources (Daly and Wilson 1988; Pollet and Hoben 2011). Some cultures (e.g., some Islamic societies) condone "honor killings" of females by male family members, most commonly committed by her brother, which center around protecting a family's honor by ridding itself of a female whose sexual reputation is not chaste and pure. Overall, consistent with predictions from Hamilton's kin selection theory (1964), it is more likely that siblings will form alliances to protect their common interests from nonkin rather than kill each other.

While the developmental literature indicates that most siblings grow out of intense conflict and rivalry when they reach adulthood and leave their parents' home (Buhrmester and Furman 1990), siblicide is most likely to occur when this is not the case. Therefore, although rare, siblicides do occur and have been proposed to be a result of sibling rivalry, stress, unresolved conflicts, mental illness, and substance abuse (Ewing 1997). The majority of siblicides are committed by adult siblings who are still living together in intense competition for parental resources, status, and power. Furthermore, there is an increased risk of siblicide occurring with unemployment and/or substance abuse of the adult siblings. Based on homicide data from 1988 covering 33 counties across the USA, it was found that alcohol was involved in approximately 50 % of siblicides and mental illness was involved in approximately 20 % of the incidents (Dawson and Langan 1994).

Factors that Influence the Likelihood of Siblicide

There are several factors that may influence the likelihood that one sibling would kill another. Some proximate influences (a few of which were mentioned above) include poverty, mental illness, substance abuse, and social disorganization (Diem and Pizarro 2010; Ewing 1997). From an evolutionary perspective, ultimate influences include age (or birth order), gender, and degree of relatedness, which we focus on in this section.

Age and Birth Order. Siblicide is most likely to occur in early and middle adulthood, not in adolescence as might be expected (Underwood and Patch 1999). Indeed, according to United States Federal Bureau of Investigation Supplementary Homicide Reports from 1976 to 1994, 78% of siblicides that occurred in the USA involved adult victims and perpetrators (Gebo 2002). Analysis of siblicide data from 1993 to 1995 found the mean age of siblicide victims to be 33.3 years and the mean age of perpetrators to be 34.4 years (Underwood and Patch 1999). Other analyses have indicated that 86% of victims of siblicide are between the ages of 20 and 59 years (Dawson and Langan 1994).

There is also a convergence of evidence indicating that, consistent with the majority of all homicides, the perpetrators of siblicide tend to be younger than their victims. That is, younger siblings tend to murder older siblings (Daly et al. 2001; Gebo 2002; Marleau and Saucier 1998; Underwood and Patch 1999). Siblicides are most likely to occur when the victim and perpetrator are within 5 years of age of each other. This pattern is reversed, however, for juvenile siblicides in which both the victim and perpetrator are under the age of 18. In juvenile siblicides, older siblings are more likely to murder their younger sibling, a pattern that emerged in 65% of juvenile siblicides in one study (Daly et al. 2001; Gebo 2002).

What could account for a younger sibling being more likely to kill an older sibling? A cross-cultural investigation of siblicide found the most common sources of conflict leading to siblicide included arguments over familial property, money, authority (i.e., specifically an older adult sibling asserting authority over a younger adult sibling), and entitlement (Daly et al. 2001). These findings were consistent across Japanese, American, British, Canadian, and tribal society samples in which the older sibling has privileged status over the younger sibling. Therefore, siblicides in which a younger sibling kills an older sibling appear to revolve around a power struggle, with the younger sibling defying the presumed authority of the older sibling and asserting his own dominance in the relationship.

Gender. Male-on-male homicide is most common, overall, and the same is true for siblicide. Males are more likely to kill their brother and are, therefore, much more likely to be both the perpetrators and victims of siblicide than are females (Daly et al. 2001; Gebo 2002; Underwood and Patch 1999). Females are more likely to be the victims of siblicide than they are perpetrators. Indeed, it has been found that 76.1% of siblicides were brother killing brother, 11.9% were brother killing sister, 8.2% were sister killing brother, and 3.9% were sister killing sister (Underwood and Patch 1999). This same distribution in frequency of gender-dyad siblicides has been found across several studies (Daly et al. 2001; Gebo 2002; Marleau and Saucier 1998). This is consistent with the expectation that same-sex sibling rivalry would be more intense than opposite-sex sibling rivalry, as there would likely be more direct competition over the same parental resources and attention, especially when the siblings are closer in age.

Relatedness. Although the predictions for the role of relatedness in siblicide are clear from an evolutionary perspective, the existing literature on the relationship is somewhat unclear. This is due to two main reasons: (1) the relationship has been greatly understudied (i.e., there have only been a couple studies on this issue) and (2) the lack of clear relatedness information in the available homicide data sets. An evolutionary perspective would suggest that degree of genetic relatedness would moderate sibling relationships such that higher relatedness would lead to less conflict (and hence less incidence of siblicide). That is, siblicides involving full siblings would be expected to be less prevalent than siblicides involving half-siblings and step-siblings. The existing data to date, however, do not seem to support this prediction.

In the first investigation of the relationship between relatedness and siblicide, approximately 93 % of siblicides were found to involve full siblings, approximately 4 % involved half-siblings, and approximately 3 % involved step-siblings (Russell et al. 2007). Although this finding was contrary to what would be expected, there was a trend in the data suggesting that siblicides among full siblings were less brutal than those among half-siblings and step siblings. Specifically, it was found that 6 % of full-sibling siblicides involved brutal beating murders relative to 12.5 % of the half-sibling and step-sibling siblicides. This trend is consistent with findings that stepparents (acting out of anger and resentment) typically use more brutal methods to murder children than do genetic parents (Daly and Wilson 1994a). It would be expected that half-siblings and step-siblings would not experience the same level of closeness that full siblings would and therefore would be more likely to act out of anger and resentment of the half/step-sibling receiving parental resources they feel should be directed more toward themselves.

In an attempt to increase the sample size, a second follow-up study investigated the relationship between relatedness and siblicide in a 60-year period in Chicago (Michalski et al. 2007). This study, however, did not really address relatedness of siblings but rather looked at homicides committed by full siblings versus siblings-in-law (no genetic relatedness at all, but rather affinal kin). Again due to a small sample size, the result did not reach significance, but the authors did find a trend of more accidental deaths among full siblings and more deliberate, intentional siblicides among siblings-in-law.

Therefore, the question of the relationship between genetic relatedness and siblicide remains largely unanswered, and more studies are desperately needed in this area (also pointed out by Gebo 2002). One major problem (and obstacle) leading to the apparent lack of support for the evolutionary prediction of fewer siblicides occurring among full siblings is the lack of clear relatedness information in the homicide records. For example, analysis of this topic would require information not only about degree of relatedness, but also about how long the children lived together in the same household, the history and degree of their interactions, as well as information about the population of full-sibling households versus half-sibling and step-sibling households overall. Without detailed information, we are unlikely to be able to get a clear answer regarding the role of relatedness on siblicide.

Conclusion

In this chapter, we discussed factors that influence sibling conflict and (in its most extreme form) siblicide among human and nonhuman animals. Although siblicide is much more rare in humans than in many nonhuman animals, to some extent they share the same underlying cause—that is, availability of resources. Whereas siblicide among nonhuman animals is more likely to occur at younger ages with the older sibling killing the younger sibling, siblicide among humans is more likely to occur in adulthood with the younger sibling killing the older sibling. Proximate factors that contribute to intensified conflict among human siblings include temperament (with more conflict among siblings when at least one has high activity and/or high emotional intensity levels) and differential parental treatment (with recognition of more favorable parental treatment toward one's sibling leading to greater conflict). Ultimate factors that contribute to intensified conflict among human siblings include gender (with males being more aggressive toward siblings and brother–brother pairs experiencing the greatest conflict), birth spacing (with more conflict between siblings close in age as they compete over similar parental resources), and relatedness (with greater conflict and competition among half- and step-siblings relative to full siblings). Although available research on this topic seems consistent with predictions from the evolutionary theories of parent–offspring conflict and kin selection, conflict within human sibling relationships (especially siblicide) is still understudied and not fully understood. One key area that requires further investigation is the influence of genetic relatedness on human siblicide as a main effect, as well as potential interactions between degree of relatedness and other factors known to lead to greater conflict among siblings.

References

Andersen, I. L., Naevdal, E., & Boe, K. N. (2011). Maternal investment, sibling competition, and offspring survival with increasing litter size and parity in pigs (*Sus scrofa*). *Behavioral Ecology and Sociobiology, 65,* 1159–1167.

Azmitia, M., & Montgomery, R. (1993). Friendship, transactive dialogues, and the development of scientific reasoning. *Social Development, 2,* 202–221.

Bank, L., Burraston, B., & Snyder, J. (2004). Sibling conflict and ineffective parenting as predictors of adolescent boys' antisocial behavior and peer difficulties: Additive and interactional effects. *Journal of Research on Adolescence, 14,* 99–125.

Bonisoli-Alquati, A., Boncoraglio, G., Caprioli, M., & Saino, N. (2011). Birth order, individual sex and sex of competitors determine the outcome of conflict among siblings over parental care. *Proceedings of the Royal Society B, 278,* 1273–1279

Bourget, D., & Gagne, P. (2006). Fratricide: A forensic psychiatric perspective. *Journal of American Academy of Psychiatry Law, 34,* 529–533.

Brody, G. H., Stoneman, Z., & Burke, M. (1987). Child temperaments, maternal differential behavior, and sibling relationships. *Developmental Psychology, 23,* 354–362.

Brody, G. H., Stoneman, Z., MacKinnon, C. E., & MacKinnon, R. (1985). Role relationships and behaviors between preschool-aged and school-aged sibling pairs. *Developmental Psychology, 21,* 124–129.

Brody, G. H., Stoneman, Z., & McCoy, J. K. (1992a). Associations of maternal and paternal direct and differential behavior with sibling relationships: Contemporaneous and longitudinal analyses. *Child Development, 63,* 82–92.

Brody, G. H., Stoneman, Z., & McCoy, J. K. (1992b). Parental differential treatment of siblings and sibling differences in negative emotionality. *Journal of Marriage and the Family, 54,* 643–651.

Buhrmester, D., & Furman, W. (1990). Perceptions of sibling relationships during middle childhood and adolescence. *Child Development, 61,* 1387–1398.

Campione-Barr, N., & Smetana, J. G. (2010). "Who said you could wear my sweater?" Adolescent siblings' conflicts and association with relationship quality. *Child Development, 81*(2), 464–471.
Cicirelli, V. G. (1994). Sibling relationships in cross-cultural perspective. *Journal of Marriage and the Family, 56,* 7–20.
Cicirelli, V. G. (1995). *Sibling relationships across the life span*. New York: Plenum Press.
Clifford, L. D., & Anderson, D. J. (2000). Experimental demonstration of the insurance value of extra eggs in an obligately siblicidal seabird. *Behavioral Ecology, 12,* 340–347.
Cohen, S. (2004). Social relationships and health. *American Psychologist, 59,* 676–684.
Daly, M., & Wilson, M. (1984). A sociobiological analysis of human infanticide. In G. Hausfater & S. B. Hrdy (Eds.), *Infanticide: Comparative and evolutionary perspectives* (pp. 487–502). New York: Aldine Press.
Daly, M., & Wilson, M. (1986). Child abuse risk and household composition in Hamilton. *Journal of the Ontario Association of Children's Aid Societies, 31*(Oct), 11–15
Daly, M., & Wilson, M. (1988). *Homicide*. Hawthorne: de Gruyter.
Daly, M., & Wilson, M. (1994a). Some differential attributes of lethal assaults on small children by stepfathers versus genetic fathers. *Ethology and Sociobiology, 15,* 207–217.
Daly, M., & Wilson, M. (1994b). Stepparenthood and the evolved psychology of discriminative parental solicitude. In S. Parmigiami & F. S. vom Saal (Eds.), *Infanticide and parental care* (pp. 121–134). Chur: Harwood Academic Publishers.
Daly, M., Wilson, M., Salmon, C. A., Hiraiwa-Hasegawa, M., & Hasegawa, T. (2001). Siblicide and seniority. *Homicide Studies, 5,* 30–45.
Dawson, J. M., & Langan, P. A. (1994). *Murder in families*. Washington, DC: Department of Justice, Bureau of Justice Statistics.
Diem, C., & Pizarro, J. M. (2010). Social structure and family homicides. *Journal of Family Violence, 25,* 521–532.
Drake, A., Fraser, D., & Weary, D. M. (2008). Parent-offspring resource allocation in domestic pigs. *Behavioral Ecology and Sociobiology, 62,* 309–319.
Drummond, H., Rodriguez, C., & Schwabl, H. (2008). Do mothers regulate facultative and obligate siblicide by differentially provisioning eggs with hormones? *Journal of Avian Biology, 39,* 139–143.
Dunn, J., & Brown, J. (1994). Affect expression in the family, children's understanding of emotions, and their interactions with others. *Merrill-Palmer Quarterly, 40,* 120–137.
Dunn, J., & Kendrick, C. (1982). *Siblings: Love, envy, and understanding*. Cambridge: Cambridge University Press.
Dunn, J., & Munn, P. (1985). Becoming a family member: Family conflict and the development of social understanding in the second year. *Child Development, 56,* 764–774.
Dunn, J., & Munn, P. (1987). The development of justifications in disputes. *Developmental Psychology, 23,* 791–798.
Dunn, J., & Slomskowski, C. (1992). Conflict and the development of social understanding. In C. U. Shantz & W. W. Hartup (Eds.), *Conflict in child and adolescent development* (pp. 70–92). New York: Cambridge University Press.
Ewing, C. P. (1997). *Fatal families: The dynamics of intrafamilial homicide*. London: Sage.
Frank, L. G., Glickman, S. E., & Licht, P. (1991). Fatal sibling aggression, precocial development, and androgens in neonatal spotted hyaenas. *Science, 252,* 702–704.
Gebo, E. (2002). A contextual exploration of siblicide. *Violence and Victims, 17,* 157–168.
Hamilton, W. D. (1964). The genetic evolution of social behavior, I and II. *Journal of Theoretical Biology, 7,* 1–52.
Hetherington, E. M. (1988). Parents, children, and siblings: Six years after divorce. In R. A. Hinde & J. Stevenson-Hinde (Eds.), *Relationships within families: Mutual influences* (pp. 311–331). Oxford: Oxford University Press.
Hodge, S. J., Flower, T. P., & Clutton-Brock, T. H. (2007). Offspring competition and helper associations in cooperative meerkats. *Animal Behaviour, 74,* 957–964.

Hodge, S. J., Manica, A., Flower, T. P., & Clutton-Brock, T. H. (2008). Determinants of reproductive success in dominant female meerkats. *Journal of Animal Ecology, 77,* 92–102.
Hofer, H., & East, M. L. (2008). Siblicide in Serengeti spotted hyenas: A long-term study of maternal input and cub survival. *Behavioral Ecology and Sociobiology, 62,* 341–351.
Holmes, W. G., & Sherman, P. W. (1982). The ontogeny of kin recognition in two species of ground squirrels. *American Zoologist, 22,* 491–517.
Hrdy, S. B. (2005). Evolutionary context of human development: The cooperative breeding model. In S. C. Carter, L. Ahnert, K. Grossman, S. B. Hrdy, M. E. Lamb, S. W. Porges & N. Sachser (Eds.), *Attachment and bonding: A new synthesis* (pp. 9–32). Cambridge: MIT Press.
Irons, D. B. (1992). *Aspect of foraging behavior and reproductive biology of the black-legged kittiwake.* PhD thesis. University of California, Irvine
Jamieson, I. G., Seymour, N. R., Bancroft, R. P., & Sullivan, R. (1983). Sibling aggression in nestling ospreys in Nova Scotia. *Canadian Journal of Zoology, 61,* 466–469.
Legge, S. (2000). Siblicide in the cooperatively breeding laughing kookaburra (*Dacelo novaeguineae*). *Behavioral Ecology and Sociobiology, 48,* 293–302.
Legge, S. (2002). Siblicide, starvation, and nestling growth in the laughing kookaburra. *Journal of Avian Biology, 33,* 159–166.
Legge, S., & Cockburn, A. (2000). Social and mating system of cooperatively breeding laughing kookaburra (*Dacelo novaeguineae*). *Behavioral Ecology and Sociobiology, 47,* 220–229.
Lotem, A. (1998). Differences in begging behavior between barn swallow, *Hirundo rusitica*, nestlings. *Animal Behaviour, 55,* 809–818.
Machmer, M. M., & Ydenberg, R. C. (1998). The relative roles of hunder and size asymmetry in sibling aggression between nestling ospreys, *Pandion haliaetus*. *Canadian Journal of Zoology, 76,* 181–186.
Marleau, J. D., & Saucier, J. (1998). Birth order and fratricidal behavior in Canada. *Psychological Reports, 82,* 817–818.
McGuire, S., Manke, B., Eftekhari, A., & Dunn, J. (2000). Children's perceptions of sibling conflict during middle childhood: Issues and sibling (dis)similarity. *Social Development, 9*(2), 173–190.
McLean, P. K., & Bryd, M. A. (1991). Feeding ecology of Chesapeake bay ospreys and growth and behavior of their young. *Wilson Bulletin, 103,* 105–111.
Michalski, R. L., Russell, D. P., Shackelford, T. K., & Weekes-Shackelford, V. A. (2007). Siblicide and genetic relatedness in Chicago, 1870–1930. *Homicide Studies, 11,* 231–237.
Miller, J. F., Trussel, J., Pebley, A. R., & Vaughan, B. (1992). Birth spacing and child mortality in Bangladesh and the Philippines. *Demography, 29,* 305–318.
Mock, D. W. (1987). Siblicide, parent-offspring conflict, and unequal parental investment by egrets and herons. *Behavioral Ecology and Sociobiology, 20,* 247–256.
Mock, D. W. (2004). *More than kin and less than kind: The evolution of family conflict.* Cambridge: Belknap Press.
Mock, D. W., Drummond, H., & Stinson, C. H. (1990). Avian siblicide. *American Scientist, 78,* 438–449.
Mock, D. W., & Parker, G. A. (1998). Siblicide, family conflict, and the evolutionary limits of selfishness. *Animal Behaviour, 56,* 1–10.
Muller, M. S., Brennecke, J. F., Porter, E. T., Ottinger, M. A., & Anderson, D. J. (2008). Perinatal androgens and adult behavior vary with nesting social system in siblicidal Boobies. *PLoS One, 3,* e2460. doi:10.1371/journal.pone.0002460.
Neyer, F. J., & Lang, F. R. (2003). Blood is thicker than water: Kinship orientation across adulthood. *Journal of Personality and Social Psychology, 84,* 310–321.
Pollet, T. V. (2007). Genetic relatedness and sibling relationship characteristics in a modern society. *Evolution and Human Behavior, 28,* 176–185.
Pollet, T. V., & Hoben, A. D. (2011). An evolutionary perspective on siblings: Rivals and resources. In C. A. Salmon & T. K. Shackelford (Eds.), *The Oxford Handbook of Evolutionary Family Psychology* (pp. 128–148). New York: Oxford University Press.

Pollet, T. V., & Nettle, D. (2009). Birth order and family relationships in adult life: Firstborns report better sibling relationships than laterborns. *Journal of Social and Personal Relationships, 26,* 1029–1046.
Powell, B., & Steelman, L. C. (1993). The educational benefits of being spaced out: Sibship density and educational progress. *American Sociological Review, 58,* 367–381.
Ross, H. S., Filyer, R. E., Lollis, S. P., Perlman, M., & Martin, J. L. (1994). Administering justice in the family: Special section: Siblings, family relationships, and child development. *Journal of Family Psychology, 8,* 254–273.
Russell, D. P., Michalski, R. L., Shackelford, T. K., & Weekes-Shackelford, V. A. (2007). A preliminary investigation of siblicide as a function of genetic relatedness. *Journal of Forensic Sciences, 52,* 738–739.
Rustein, E. (2005). Effects of preceding birth intervals on neonatal, infant and under-five years mortality and nutritional status in developing countries: Evidence from the demographic and health surveys. *International Journal of Gynecology and Obstetrics*, *89*, S7–S24
Salmon, C. A. (2003). Birth order and relationships: Family, friends, and sexual partners. *Human Nature, 14,* 73–88.
Salmon, C. A. (2007). Parent-offspring conflict. In C. A. Salmon & T. K. Shackelford (Eds.)., *Family relationships: An evolutionary perspective* (pp. 145–161). New York: Oxford University Press.
Salmon, C. A., & Daly, M. (1998). Birth order and familial sentiment: Middleborns are different. *Evolution and Human Behavior, 19,* 299–312.
Schlomer, G. L., Del Guidice, M., & Ellis, B. J. (2011). Parent-offspring conflict theory: An evolutionary framework for understanding conflict within human families. *Psychological Review, 118*(3), 496–521.
Segal, N. L. (2005). Evolutionary studies of cooperation, competition, and altruism: A twin-based approach. In R. L. Burgess & K. B. MacDonald (Eds.), *Evolutionary perspectives on human development* (2nd ed, pp. 265–304). Thousand Oaks: Sage.
Shanahan, L., McHale, S. M., Crouter, A. C., & Osgood, D. W. (2008). Linkages between parents' differential treatment, youth depressive symptoms, and sibling relationships. *Journal of Marriage and Family, 70,* 480–494.
Simmons, R. (1988). Offspring quality and the evolution of Cainism. *Ibis, 130,* 339–357.
Smale, L., Holekamp, K. E., Weldele, M., Frank, L. G., & Glickman, S. E. (1995). Competition and cooperation between littermates in the spotted hyaena, *Crocuta crocuta*. *Animal Behaviour, 50,* 671–682.
Smale, L., Holekamp, K. E., & White, P. A. (1999). Siblicide revisited in the spotted hyaena: Does it conform to obligate or facultative models? *Animal Behaviour, 58,* 545–551.
St Clair, C. C., Waas, J. R., St Clair, R. C., & Boag, P. T. (1995). Unfit mothers? Maternal infanticide in royal penguins. *Animal Behaviour, 50,* 1177–1185.
Statistics, C.: Homicide in Canada. (2004). Ottawa, ON, Canada: Canadian Centre for Justice Statistics, Catalogue 85–002-XPE 25(6), 2005
Steinmetz, S. K. (1977). The use of force for resolving family conflict: The training ground for abuse. *The Family Coordinator, 26,* 19–26.
Straus, M., Gelles, R. J., & Steinmetz, S. K. (2006). *Behind closed doors: Violence in the American family*. Piscataway: Transaction Publishers.
Sussman, M. B., & Steinmetz, S. K. (1987). *Handbook of marriage and family*. New York: Plenum Press.
Trivers, R. L. (1972). Parental investment and sexual selection. In B. Campbell (Ed.), *Sexual section and the descent of man* (pp. 136–179). Chicago: Aldine Publishing Company.
Trivers, R. L. (1974). Parent-offspring conflict. *American Zoologist, 14,* 249–264.
Underwood, R. C., & Patch, P. C. (1999). Siblicide: A descriptive analysis of sibling homicide. *Homicide Studies, 3,* 333–348.
Wahaj, S. A., Place, N. J., Weldele, M. L., Glickman, S. E., & Holekamp, K. E. (2007). Siblicide in the spotted hyena: Analysis with ultrasonic examination of wild and captive individuals. *Behavioral Ecology, 18,* 974–984.

White, J., Leclaire, S., Kriloff, M., Mulard, H., Hatch, S. A., & Danchin, E. (2010). Sustained increase in food supplies reduces broodmate aggression in black-legged kittiwakes. *Animal Behaviour, 79,* 1095–1100.

Williams, G. C. (1966). Natural selection, the costs of reproduction, and a refinement of Lack's principle. *American Naturalist, 100,* 687–690.

Wilson, M., & Daly, M. (2004). Marital cooperation and conflict. In C. B. Crawford & C. A. Salmon (Eds.), *Handbook of evolutionary psychology* (pp. 197–215). New York: Erlbaum.

Chapter 9
Aggression Grows Up: Looking Through an Evolutionary Developmental Lens to Understand the Causes and Consequences of Human Aggression

David F. Bjorklund and Patricia H. Hawley

Aggression is typically defined simply as behavior intended to harm another person. Usually, the target of aggression also perceives that he or she has been hurt (Underwood 2002). At present, the public conversation regarding childhood aggression is at an all-time high, in large part due to highly publicized—and in many cases filmed—bullying incidents which, in the extreme, have led to death of the victim, sometimes at the hands of the assailant and at other times as a result of suicide. Most intervention efforts have historically focused on the "bully," with the assumption that there is something "wrong" with the child who needs to be fixed. Here, aggressive behavior is seen as the result of the developmental process gone wrong. An evolutionary perspective sheds a slightly different light on childhood aggression, and accordingly contributes to the national conversation in different ways. The main component of an evolutionary perspective is that aggression has been naturally selected over the course of human evolution and has provided the aggressor fitness benefits, albeit often at the expense of his or her victims. Moreover, it is not only adults who sometimes reap the benefits of aggressive behavior, but also children, and individual differences in the propensity to behave aggressively have not only deep phylogenetic roots but also deep ontogenetic roots.

In the present chapter, we look at the form and function of aggression during childhood and adolescence, first examining research and theory from a classic developmental perspective followed by a look of childhood aggression from an evolutionary perspective. We then look at the development of aggression from infancy through young adulthood, followed by an examination of aggression as a possible *facultative adaption*, with children's sensitivity to early environmental conditions

D. F. Bjorklund (✉)
Department of Psychology, Florida Atlantic University, Boca Raton, FL 33431-0991, USA
e-mail: dbjorklu@fau.edu

P. H. Hawley
Educational Psychology & Leadership College of Education, Texas Tech University, Box 41071 3008 18th Street, Lubbock, TX 79409, USA
e-mail: Patricia.Hawley@TTU.edu

T. K. Shackelford, R. D. Hansen (eds.), *The Evolution of Violence*, Evolutionary Psychology, DOI 10.1007/978-1-4614-9314-3_9,

directing their development toward certain adaptive paths, some of which may include high levels of aggression. We conclude with an evolutionary developmental look at bullying, asking "What's in it for the bullies?," and suggest how such a perspective may be applied to reduce the incidence of bullying.

Developmental Perspective on Aggression

Childhood aggression has long been of interest to developmental psychologists, dating back at least to G. Stanley Hall's 1904 book *Adolescence*, and has always been of concern to parents. Various theories of childhood aggression have been in vogue over the last century, including drive reduction, social learning, psychoanalytic, ethological, and social cognitive (see Dodge et al. 2006). Independent of theoretical differences, developmental psychologists have differentiated various types of aggressive behavior, as well as contexts in which they are likely to be displayed, providing a useful framework for assessing the development of aggression and its possible causes and consequences.

Instrumental vs. Reactive Aggression

Lay discussions of childhood aggression can often be needlessly confused by overlooking important distinctions long made in the developmental literature. Namely, it makes no sense to talk about "mitigating aggression" unless one knows what "type" of aggression one is talking about. With deep theoretical roots (e.g., Bandura 1973; Dollard et al. 1939), there are at least two *functions* of aggression: aggression that serves to attain some goal of the perpetrator (i.e., *instrumental aggression*, which can be considered planful and cool-headed) and aggression that is impulsively enacted in response to some provocation, real or imagined (i.e., *reactive aggression*, which can be considered unplanned and hot-headed). A simple example of instrumental aggression is an attack on the victim for some material reward, such as money or an iPhone. Reactive aggression is exemplified by an outburst to a perceived or actual slight. For child developmentalists, the distinction is important because each is associated with a unique developmental trajectory and consequent socio-emotional outcomes. For example, reactively aggressive children are more apt to display poor psychological adjustment because their dysregulation leads to related social difficulties such as peer rejection (Coie and Koeppl 1990). By contrast, instrumentally aggressive children are not necessarily dysregulated. Moreover, their success at goal attainment may even lead to positive peer regard (Hawley et al. 2008; see discussion later in this chapter). When measured carefully using best-practice analytic techniques, the functions of aggression are actually orthogonal to one another (Little et al. 2003).

Social vs. Physical Aggression

Independent of function is the form aggression takes, that is, its phenomenological manifestation. The aggressive act may manipulate the social standing of the victim (e.g., through rumor spreading; Underwood 2002) or may be overtly physical. Physical aggression is relatively straightforward, reflected in hitting, kicking, or other physical assaults on another person. However, some of these behaviors are also observed in rough-and-tumble play and play fighting (Pellegrini and Smith 1998), making the context of the acts important when classifying them. Unlike real fighting, play fighting—most typically engaged in by boys—is usually done with a play face and participants remain together after the bout is over. Although children sometimes do get hurt during play fighting, most researchers do not consider such activity as aggression.

In contrast to physical aggression, social aggression had long been overlooked, primarily because it is more difficult to see. How do you identify the source of a damaging rumor? Social aggression has also been described as *relational aggression* (Crick and Grotpeter 1995) and *indirect aggression* (Kaukiainen et al. 1999), and defined as "a noxious behavior in which the target person is attacked not physically or directly through verbal intimidation but in a more circuitous way, through social manipulation" (Kaukiainen et al. 1999, p. 83).

Bullying

Research and conversation about bullying lie somewhat outside this simple classification system. In large part, bullying is defined by repeated acts of aggression against someone with lesser social standing. As such, bullying should be seen as a subcategory of the wider domain of aggression (behavior that intends to harm). This definition, credited to Dan Olweus (1978, 1993), preceded more recent representations of form and function (e.g., Little et al. 2003). It appears that bullying is best understood to be a manifestation of power (Olweus 1978; Vaillancourt et al. 2003; Vaillancourt and Hymel 2006). At the same time, it is not clear what the function of bullying is (a good deal of it seems to be for pleasure; educators often treat it in terms of conflict between kids) or whether it must be physical to "count." Educators, researchers, and popular-press authors are nowhere near being of one mind (Stassen Berger 2007). These latter points are emerging in earnest in the bullying literature at present in both educational and evolutionary developmental (e.g., Volk et al. 2006) domains. We have more to say about bullying later in this chapter

Aggression as Incompetence

Common to most developmental views not of evolutionary origin is the perception that aggression is a maladaptive manifestation of a perturbed developmental process.

In accordance with a medically derived model (see Ellis et al. 2012; Hawley 2011, for extended discussions), behavior that disrupts the well-being of others is seen to be consequent to some "infection," not unlike a disease process, from environmental perturbation such as harsh parenting or poor urban environments. This view is challenged at length below. For now, suffice it to say that common to developmental views is the assumption that aggression is a problem to be fixed in the aggressive child, that no good will come from an aggressive profile, and that aggression lies outside the boundaries of normal and healthy human social functioning. Consistent with these assumptions, aggressive children of a certain ilk (see more below) are targeted with therapeutic intervention strategies designed to reduce said behavior.

Evolutionary Perspectives: Aggression as Adaptation

Counter to traditional developmental perspectives of aggression, evolutionary developmental perspectives examine the potential benefits as well as costs of aggression at different times in ontogeny. Although child aggression is viewed negatively by most adults, it can be effective for children in gaining resources and manipulating social relations, both of which are useful in competing with other children (Campbell 2005; Pellegrini and Archer 2005). Individuals can gain an advantage by aggressing against others, especially if the risk is low. Aggression, of course, is often associated with negative psychological consequences. For example, high levels of aggression in school-age children are associated with rejection and low social status (e.g., Bierman et al. 1993; Coie and Koeppl 1990). Yet overall rates of aggression are *positively* correlated with popularity for preschool children (e.g., Hawley 2003a), and sometimes for older children as well (e.g., Hawley et al. 2008; Rose et al. 2004). Although aggression is typically viewed negatively, children who use it effectively for personal goal attainment can indeed gain benefits with respect to popularity and social status (e.g., Cillessen and Mayeux 2004; Hawley et al. 2007a; Vaillancourt and Hymel 2006).

An evolutionary developmental perspective of aggression also assumes that natural selection has provided children the ability to be sensitive to early environmental conditions that are predictive of later, adult environments and to entrain development to pattern behavior consistent with the likely future environment. In some cases, this can mean children learn to use aggression rather than (or perhaps in addition to) more prosocial techniques to solve problems, which, from an inclusive-fitness perspective, has proved to be an adaptive strategy and may continue to be a successful strategy for contemporary youth. This in no way implies that bullying or other forms of youthful coercion should be tolerated; but it does suggest alternative ways of viewing such socially problematic behavior (e.g., it serves some adaptive purpose for the perpetrator and is not a form of pathology) and may suggest alternative ways to counteract such behavior (see e.g., Ellis et al. 2012; Hawley 2011).

With respect to the distinction of function and form, the evolutionist and developmentalist John Bowlby (1969) recognized early on that different forms of behavior could serve similar functions in an evolutionary sense. That is, infants come into the world with reflexes and early-developing behaviors shaped by selection to serve the same function, namely, to extract caregiving from parents. These reflexes and behaviors include sucking, rooting, grasping, separation anxiety, vocalizing, smiling (positive affect), and crying (negative affect), and are universal across humans (and in many other species to some degree). In other words, positive and negative social cues in the infant, though different in *form* (phenomenal manifestation), serve similar *function* (purpose), here, maintaining proximity to the primary caregiver. On this latter point, evolutionists are well versed; in the natural world there are several ways (forms) to solve similar problems (function). A mammal's weapons may jut from its mouth (elephants), be on the top of its head (moose), or protrude from the top of its face (rhinoceros), yet serve a similar purpose. One purpose for such weaponry in many social animals is the attainment and subsequent maintenance of high status in a social hierarchy (often achieved via aggressive means), with individuals higher in the hierarchy being described as "dominant" and achieving benefits in terms of mating opportunities and access to resources.

The pecking order of chickens inspired the first treatments of social-dominance hierarchies in the early twentieth century (Schjelderup- Ebbe 1922); hens compete for desired resources predominantly by pecking each other. This work quickly gave rise to an aggression-based view (form-focused) of social dominance that persists to this day across species and taxa (e.g., Alonso et al. 2012; Krebs and Davies 1997). Alcock (2009), for example, refers to dominance as a "sexually selected manifestation of conflict" (p. 332) in his animal behavior textbook. Moreover, the pecking order construal quickly impacted work in child development (e.g., Bühler 1927) and has left a legacy of the continued focus on the *form* of behavior (agonistic contests, fighting ability, and submissive gestures), even though the *function* of such contests was always understood to be resource control. For example, Abramovitch (1976) defined dominance as property fights, involving "struggles" or "tussles," in her work with children.

Resource Control Theory

Evolutionary perspectives generally explicitly adopt function-driven approaches, that is, what is a behavior *for*, what function does it play that it might have been favored by selection? Function-driven approaches (cf., form-driven approaches) lead one to see the world through different lenses. For example, from a function-driven perspective, prosocial behavior (behavior intended to benefit another, though for varying underlying psychological motivations, some "selfish," some "altruistic"; Eisenberg and Fabes 1998) can be viewed as generated by mechanisms common to sociality. That is, living in groups wins one resources unattainable on one's own, and cooperating and otherwise behaving in prosocial ways with group members can be one means of acquiring resources. Thus, prosocial behavior can be considered an indirect resource control strategy. That is, a variety of mechanisms, including kin selection (cooperative aid to genetic relatives), reciprocal altruism (aid dispensed to those who are in a position to reciprocate in the long run), or indirect reciprocity (aid given to others that wins approval from group members, and consequently an increased probability that aid will be given in return), can eventually lead to aid (resources) received. Resource control theory (Hawley 1999) explicitly incorporates this theoretical point into its measurement model; we have gathered via observed interactions (in children; Hawley 2002), others' reports (Hawley 2003a), and self-reports (Hawley 2003b), that children and adults behave prosocially to achieve a material goal. Moreover, we socialize our children to do this. In fact, research with toddlers and preschool children makes it clear that young humans are predisposed toward prosocial interactions with other humans (see Tomasello 2009; Warneken and Melis 2012). However, humans have not totally changed the resource-acquisition game, becoming fully cooperative and eschewing more "negative" means of gaining what they need and want. Coercion also functions as an effective resource control strategy. That is, resources can be obtained through deception, social manipulation, or physical force. Social response to these behaviors is much different from social responses to prosocial behaviors; children tend to be censured for using them. At the same time, they are less censured (at least by peers) than traditional developmental approaches would have us believe (see Hawley 2003b).

The Well-Adapted Machiavellian

From a life history perspective—which postulates that important developmental events in an animal's life are shaped by selection to promote inclusive fitness—the modal pattern is to use both prosocial and coercive strategies to some extent (Hawley 2011) to attain some degree of average effectiveness (most of us are average, after all). Those who are especially effective at obtaining resources in the presence of others—or, in other words, are effective competitors—have been shown to be those who use both prosocial and coercive strategies to a high degree (and hence are referred to as *bistrategic controllers*) and, thus, from a *functional* view, are socially dominant. This stands to reason; both strategies, gainfully employed, yield success. Mono-strategists (i.e., those who use predominantly prosocial or coercive strategies, but not both) are more effective than "average" individuals, but less effective than bistrategic controllers. These latter two groups (i.e., *prosocial controllers* and *coercive controllers*) are well captured by the extant literature in developmental psychology; prosocial controllers are highly skilled, well-liked, and well-regulated peer leaders, whereas coercive controllers are impulsive, hostile, and rejected by peers. People falling into each of the categories have been identified at all ages, from preschoolers (e.g., Hawley 2003a; Pellegrini et al. 2007) and school-age children (e.g., Garandeau et al. 2011; Hawley et al. 2008; Rose et al. 2004) through adults (Hawley et al. 2009). These patterns are by now quite intuitive.

What is less intuitive from this approach, however, is that bistrategic controllers not only are instrumentally successful, but also possess social competence (Hawley

2002), in large part because they appear to be able to use the social group to access resources in some contexts while at the same time being willing to bypass or confront the social group in others. Consistent with our predictions, Hawley and colleagues have generally found bistrategic controllers to possess attributes associated with social skills; that is, they tend to be extroverted, socially perceptive, and morally astute (Hawley 2003a; Hawley and Geldhof 2012). Both male and female bistrategic controllers are high on traditional measures of aggression (i.e., social and physical), and even direct this aggression toward their best friends (Hawley et al. 2007b). In this regard, they are much like coercive controllers. Yet, despite their high levels of aggression, and in contrast to expectations from most theoretical perspectives (e.g., Coie and Dodge 1998), they are socially attractive to peers (Hawley 2003a, 2003b) and demonstrate relationship skills (e.g., intimacy; Hawley et al. 2007a). This complex constellation of skills, including those of social manipulation, invites comparisons to Machiavelli's treatise on effective leaders.

Machiavellianism through the Lens of Life History Theory

Little is known at this point about what "makes" an effective Machiavellian. Developmental approaches, however, have shown early ecological factors that precede and perhaps calibrate lifelong patterns of aggression and prosociality. With respect to aggression, children with physically abusive parents are more aggressive than children with nonabusive parents, both at home and in school (Dodge et al. 2008; Trickett and Kuczynski 1986).[1] The effects of parental maltreatment on aggression vary somewhat for boys and girls, with maltreated boys showing elevated levels of physical aggression, whereas maltreated girls display heightened levels of relational aggression (Cullerton-Sen et al. 2008). Similarly, children who view their parents as warm and loving (and who generally display authoritative parenting styles) are more generous, supportive, comforting, and cooperative than other children (Hoffman 1975; Krevans and Gibbs 1996; Robinson et al. 1994). Yet this literature has not, as a rule, looked at how these behavioral patterns act in concert. Thus, these literatures are likely talking mainly about prosocial and coercive controllers, and not about the most effective bistrategic controllers. We do, however, know something about the attachment relationships of these resource control types, and attachment processes are thought to be a primary context for early social calibration (see Del Giudice 2009; Del Giudice et al. 2009). Bistrategic controllers (in a college

[1] Most of the published studies on the effects of parenting on aggression have not been genetically sensitive in that they do not control for shared genes. Aggression has been investigated in more than 100 behavioral genetic studies using a variety of measures (see Dodge et al. 2006; Rhee and Wildman 2002). In a meta-analysis of twin and adoption studies, Rhee and Wildman (2002) reported that approximately 41 % of individual differences in levels of aggression could be accounted for by genetic effects, 16 % by shared environmental influences, and 43 % by nonshared environmental influences. Thus, although shared genes clearly have an influence on levels of aggression, behavioral genetic studies indicate an even greater proportion of the variance can be accounted by environmental factors, which include parenting style.

sample), for example, report a potent mix of relationship confidence, high anxiety, and high avoidance (and, especially, see their relationships as secondary to their material goals; Hawley et al. 2009). Bear in mind that avoidance does not entail evasion of social interactions, but rather avoidance of intimacy. One can have many relationships and use one's social network effectively without forming deep and meaningful ties to others. Consistent with this pattern is the fact that although bistrategic controllers report viewing both the material and social world as resources, they value the material world more. Their high social anxiety (a "hyperactivation" of the attachment system; Bartholomew and Horowitz 1991; Mikulincer and Shaver 2003) suggests that they are at the same time preoccupied with relationships and concerned with pleasing others to avoid social rejection. Indeed, the evidence suggests that bistrategics do this very well; they appear to benefit from rather accurate thermostats that can gauge social temperature. Consequently, bistrategics as a group adjust their behavior accordingly and in ways that coercive controllers cannot or do not (e.g., Hawley 2003b).

Conversely, coercive controllers have the avoidance but not the anxiety or confidence of bistrategics. They report negative expectations of social relationships (they do not view relationships as resources), which may explain the fact that they react to perceived threats of not obtaining goals with frustration and hostility (Hawley 2003b; Little et al. 2003). Unlike bistrategic controllers, coercive controllers tend to repel others. Their lack of social skills (e.g., knowing how they make others feel) and poor regulation (e.g., low conscientiousness) make them qualitatively different from the bistrategic controllers. Prosocial controllers, on the other hand, have an attachment profile that fits most similarly to descriptions of security: high confidence and low avoidance. Prosocial controllers, because they are socially invested, see social ties as resources more so than other groups, and expect (and get) positive social interactions. Consequently, they can achieve their goals through prosocial channels without the need to resort to coercion. Even though they prize both social and material resources, they appear to assign a different significance to their interpersonal relationships than do bistrategic controllers, one that psychologists tend to evaluate more positively.

Though not as yet studied directly with developmental methods (i.e., early attachment through observational methods), the findings above are suggestive; schemas about the role other humans play in resource attainment are calibrated by the early parent–child relationship, the first ecological condition one is exposed to. Life history theory would also suggest important roles for harshness, predictability, and resource richness. These questions are just beginning to be pursued, and we look at some of this emerging literature later in this chapter.

A Note on "Risk"

The existence of bistrategic resource controllers confounds predominant developmental-psychopathology models that construe aggressive behavior as a risk factor in development through its associations with negative developmental outcomes (e.g., peer rejection and delinquency). In developmental circles, "risk" has been largely influenced by epidemiological disease models that attempt to "locate agents or conditions that are associated with an increased probability of outcomes that compromise health, quality of life, or life itself" (Jessor 1991, p. 597). These medical-model-inspired approaches have been applied fruitfully to youth aggression, unsafe sex, and substance use. Yet, even the originator of problem behavior theory (PBT) cautioned that the medical-model metaphor can only go so far; namely, unlike most pathogens and viruses, many adolescent "risk behaviors" have positive outcomes, and the goals that adolescents formulate for such behaviors can be rational (Jessor 1991). Benefits associated with alcohol use, for example, include the foundational human need for social connectedness (e.g., Shim and Maggs 2005). At the same time, others have characterized risk as "normal behavior gone awry" (Dodge and Albert 2012, p. 625), and that costs, though not perhaps evident in the short run, may emerge eventually (e.g., incarceration or dysfunction; Dodge and Albert 2012). From these perspectives, low-risk behaviors are good for one's behavioral portfolio.

In contrast, evolutionary models are more similar to those in economics; here, risk is defined in terms of the variance of outcomes distributed about an expected outcome average (Figueredo and Jacobs 2010). Behaviors that yield benefits and costs are high risk from this perspective. Unlike developmental psychopathology models, cost is not unduly weighted; an accumulation of short-term benefits may outweigh costs that may or may not manifest in the distant future. Such calculations are anything but controversial in biological circles, especially if "costs" manifest post reproduction.

What does the risk distribution look like for aggressive behavior? Traditional developmental models have assumed that social costs (e.g., ostracism) associated with aggression outweigh any benefits. At the same time and as outlined in this chapter, evolutionary and non-evolutionary scholars have recently documented sizable social advantages associated with some forms of aggression, such as status attainment (Hawley 2003a; Pellegrini 2001; Rodkin et al. 2000) and mating opportunities (Ellis et al. 2012; Volk et al. 2012a). Aggressive behavior appears to be a strategy that can pay handsome dividends, especially if it is balanced with other strategies connoting social skills and prosociality.

The Development of Aggression

Aggression in children is often labeled as "antisocial," and this is unfortunate because aggression is a social behavior. In fact, as early as children are able to interact with one another, a significant proportion of their interaction is aggressive, making aggression a highly frequent and salient social behavior. Also somewhat counterintuitive to most people, aggressive behavior decreases in frequency with age, although both the benefits (e.g., status, resources) and costs (e.g., incarceration, damage inflicted on others) of aggression in older children and adolescents are greater than in childhood.

Physical Aggression

Peer-directed aggression is observed as soon as infants have the physical ability and opportunity to inflict harm on another individual (e.g., Hay et al. 2011; Hay et al. 1983). For example, in one study (Hay et al. 2011), researchers observed the use of physical force by 12-month-olds interacting with unfamiliar infants of the same age during a 20-minute make-believe birthday party. Hay et al. reported that infants made an average of nearly 3.5 forceful actions against peers (2.32 incidents of instrumental force, e.g., tugging on peer's toys; 1.16 incidents of the use of bodily force, e.g., hitting a peer), with children whose mothers had a history of conduct problems and/or mood disorders engaging in more aggressive actions than other infants. Although such actions might often bring tears and vocal protests, the consequences are rarely serious, and 12-month-olds only occasionally have opportunities for direct, unsupervised interaction with one another. Physical aggression among toddlers is substantially higher than in infancy (Alink et al. 2006), often involving disputes over toys. In fact, nearly 50% of interactions among toddlers can be described as conflictual, though not necessarily aggressive (see Dodge et al. 2006). We should not necessarily view this as all negative, however. Hawley (1999) suggests that, given toddlers' limited cognitive and negotiation abilities, "taking" a toy is an effective means of acquiring resources and "may in fact indicate a healthy assertive approach to the world that may lead to material rewards that ultimately foster growth and survival" (p. 121).

Longitudinal studies have found that physical aggression decreases over the preschool years, peaking at 2 or 3 years of age and declining substantially by age five (e.g., Côté et al. 2006; Cummings et al. 1989). The incidence of physical aggression continues to decline over childhood into adolescence (Cairns et al. 1989; NICHD Early Child Care Research Network 2004; Tremblay et al. 1999). However, although most children show decreases in physical aggression over the preschool and early school years, individual differences in degree of aggression tend to be stable, at least for boys (Broidy et al. 2003; Cummings et al. 1989), and a subgroup of children tend to maintain elevated levels of aggression at least to age 11 (Côté et al. 2006). The 16.6% of children in the Côté et al. (2006) study who displayed stable levels of high physical aggression were more likely to be boys from lower socioeconomic status (SES) families whose parents used hostile/ineffective parenting styles. In other research, Cleverely et al. (2012) reported that both males and females who displayed increasing levels of physical and indirect aggression over childhood and adolescence had higher levels of delinquency and depression than other individuals in emerging adulthood.

Boys are, on average, more physically aggressive than girls at every age, beginning in toddlerhood (see Baillargeon et al. 2007; Dodge et al. 2006; Tremblay et al. 1999). Archer (2009) and Benenson (2009) independently argued that these robust sex differences can be explained by sexual selection theory (Trivers 1972) in which females, as the primary caregivers of children, avoid physical risk (see Campbell 1999), and males, as the sex that invests less in parenting, are more competitive and use aggression selectively to attain status and access to mating opportunities. Although sex differences in physical aggression are found at all ages, they are perhaps most notable in adolescence and young adulthood, when the aggression can lead to serious physical harm and even death. We discuss this idea in greater detail later in the section on "The Young Male Syndrome."

Social/Indirect Aggression

Although physical aggression declines over the preschool and school years into adolescence, it is often replaced by social, or indirect, aggression. Although both sexes engage in indirect aggression, it typifies the type of aggression used by girls (e.g., Crick and Grotpeter 1995; Österman et al. 1998), in large part because girls engage in less physical aggression than boys (Card et al. 2008). Archer and Coyne (2005) proposed that indirect aggression is an alternative strategy to direct (usually physical) aggression that is used when the costs of direct aggression are high. Just as physical aggression can be used to the benefit of the aggressor, so too can indirect aggression. For example, in a 2-year longitudinal study of children between grades 6 and 8, high levels of indirect aggression predicted increases in positive friendship quality 1 year later (Banny et al. 2011).

Indirect aggression has been hypothesized to be produced by evolved mechanisms that support female mating strategies (Vaillancourt 2005; Vaillancourt et al. 2010). More specifically, it is a form of intrasexual competition that involves mainly harming the reputation and devaluing the physical appearance of other girls/women. In support of this, in one study, adolescents girls and young women (age range 16—29 years, mean age = 20 years) who more frequently made negative comments about other women's appearance showed high levels of aggression toward their romantic partner and their peers (Arnocky et al. 2011). The authors interpreted their findings as young women's attempts to ward off potential rivals and to minimize the risk of partner defection by reducing the rivals' mate values.

Effective indirect aggression requires verbal and cognitive abilities not available to toddlers and young preschoolers, and one reason for the decline in direct physical aggression over the preschool and school years is children's increasing communicative and intellectual skills (Archer and Coyne 2005). The decrease in physical aggression over these years is mirrored by an increase in indirect aggression (Björkqvist et al. 1992; Côté et al. 2007). Recently, Ingram and Bering (2010; Ingram 2014) proposed that tattling is one form of indirect aggression used by preschoolers. Unlike gossiping behind someone's back, tattling is typically overt and used to punish a peer and/or to keep social order. Tattling is a relatively common activity among preschool children (e.g., den Bak and Ross 1996; Ingram and Bering 2010). For example, in one naturalistic study, preschool children tattled about 1.25 times per day (Ingram and Bering 2010). Children's negative reports of other children's behavior to adults were generally truthful; tattling was used most often by dominant children, and was positively related to measures of indirect aggression. Ingram and Bering (2010) proposed that tattling can be viewed as an adaptive behavior in preschool children and as a precursor to gossiping, both of which are forms of indirect aggression that increase as physical aggression declines. Hawley and Geldhof (2012) observed analogous patterns of behavior to likewise be associated with dominance and observed the likeness of these behaviors to "selective moral engagement"—moral behavior conditionally enacted to further one's own cause.

The Young-Male Syndrome

Although physical aggression decreases over childhood into adolescence, the consequences of aggression in adolescence and young adulthood are often especially damaging. For instance, arrests for violent crimes and assaults for males increase sharply between the ages of 10 and 19 years (Cairns and Cairns 1986), the rate of men's involvement in violent crimes and same-sex homicides is the highest between 18 and 30 years, and the probability of being the victim or perpetrator of homicide peaks in adolescence and young adulthood. This phenomenon has been found in all cultures and time periods studied (see Daly and Wilson 1988, 1990).

Daly and Wilson (1988) referred to this phenomenon as the *young-male syndrome* and explained it in terms of Trivers' (1972) parental investment and sexual selection theory. Males and females differ in the effort they put into mating and parenting. Like most mammals, human females are the more investing sex with respect to parenting, starting with 9 months gestation and an obligatory period of lactation and nursing (obligatory for most of human history anyway, before the advent of baby formula). Although human males invest in their mates and offspring more than do most mammals (95% of male mammals invest nothing in their offspring; Clutton-Brock 1991), the human male investment necessary to produce successful offspring varies with ecological conditions (see Geary 2005), such as availability of social support for the mother and physical resources needed to rear a child to adulthood. As the more-investing sex, females are choosier in consenting to sex, whereas males engage in greater intrasexual competition for access to females. There is greater reproductive variability in males than females. Whereas most females will find and secure a mate (albeit perhaps a low-quality one), many low-quality males (e.g., those without substantial resources, physically unhealthy) risk never reproducing. In contrast, higher-quality males (e.g., physically robust, high resource holding potential) may monopolize multiple females, and certainly the most valuable ones in terms of evolutionarily relevant characteristics (e.g., youthful, fertile, and healthy). It is during the time when young men enter the "mating market" that male-on-male aggression increases, much of it over status and the opportunity to impress and secure access to fertile women. Fights and deaths among adolescent males and young men often occur over what can appear on the surface to be minor slights, such as insults to one's reputation or masculinity. Despite the risk of injury and the societal penalties associated with assault and murder, *Homo sapiens'* male psychology has evolved to be sensitive to competitive conditions and threats to status, which, in the ancestral past, have been associated with inclusive fitness. Failing to compete, even via violence, can result in being shut out of the mating game. Some young men, depending on the ecological conditions in which they were raised, may perceive the use of aggression as a functional strategy. We discuss such conditions in the next section.

Facultative Adaptations: Early Childhood Environment as a Predictor of Later Environments and Aggression

Behavioral Plasticity

Aggression can have both adaptive and maladaptive consequences for children and adolescents, consistent with an evolutionary perspective involving cost–benefit analysis (CBA). However, there are substantial individual differences in the expression of aggression, dependent, to a large extent, on environmental (particularly social) conditions. Humans have evolved a large brain and with it the ability to modify behavior, including aggression. Yet, some individuals are more prone to aggression and violence than others. Some of this may be attributed to differences in temperament. However, children seem to be especially sensitive to early (the first 5–7 years) environmental conditions. In a pioneering paper in evolutionary developmental psychology, Belsky et al. (1991) combined aspects of attachment theory with new ideas from the then emerging field of life history theory to propose that evolved mechanisms detect and respond to features of early environments and entrain patterns of development to produce adult behaviors best suited to anticipated future environments (anticipated based on early environments). These are *contingent* strategies that enable organisms to succeed in a variety of contexts and are referred to as *facultative adaptations*, or sometimes *conditional adaptations* (Boyce and Ellis 2005). According to Belsky et al.:

> A principal evolutionary function of early experience—the first 5 to 7 years—is to induce in the child an understanding of the availability and predictability of resources (broadly defined) in the environment, of the trustworthiness of others, and of the enduringness of close interpersonal relationships, all of which will affect how the developing person apportions reproductive effort (p. 650).

Belsky et al. proposed that children growing up in low-stress, resource-rich environments with secure attachments to caretakers learn that significant others in one's life are dependable, relationships are stable, and resources likely to be available in the future. These children adopt what has been termed a *slow life history strategy*, delaying pubertal maturation and sexual debut compared to children growing up in high-stress, resource-poor environments with insecure attachments to caretakers. These latter children adopt a *fast life history strategy*, with accelerated onset of puberty and sexual activity. Moreover, as adults, children following a slow life history

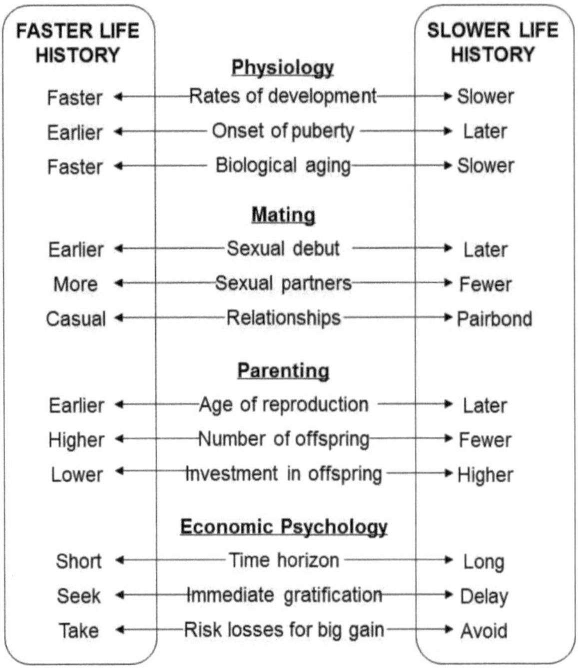

Fig. 9.1 *Faster versus slower life history strategies* (from Ellis, B. J. Del Giudice, M., Dishon, T. J., Figueredo, A. J., Gray, P., Griskevicius, V., Hawley, P. H., Jacobs, W. J., James, J., Volk, A. A., & Wilson, D. S. (2012). The evolutionary basis of risky adolescent behavior: Implications for science, policy, and practice. *Developmental Psychology, 48, 598–623.*)

strategy tend to have fewer offspring and invest more in them than those following a fast life history strategy. There are also differences in economic psychology, with a slower life history strategy being associated with taking a long-term perspective, delaying gratification, and avoiding risk, compared to people following a faster life history strategy (see Fig. 9.1).

Although from the point of view of contemporary Western society, a slow life history strategy is more favorable, presumably because it inflicts fewer costs on others, including society as a whole. Costs on others, however, are not an obstacle from an evolutionary perspective. Human rearing environments are and always have been variable: some children experience supportive environments and others stressful ones. Early environments are predictive (albeit imperfectly) of later environments, and developmental systems have been shaped by natural selection to adjust to both putatively "positive" and "negative" developmental contexts. Although negative developmental contexts are today associated with "poor psychological adjustment" from a mental-health perspective, "maladaptation" from an evolutionary perspective does not necessarily ensue. Rather, for many of our ancestors, a fast life history strategy was associated with reproductive benefits for children in stressful, high-risk environments, and likely is for many children today (see e.g., Ellis and Bjorklund 2012; Ellis et al. 2011; Ellis et al. 2012).

One consequence of a fast life history strategy and accelerated pubertal development is increased levels of aggression, delinquency, and crime (see e.g., Ellis 2004; Mishra and Lalumière 2008; Wang et al. 2009). This association was recently demonstrated using data from the Minnesota Longitudinal Study of Risk and Adaptation (Simpson et al. 2012). Simpson et al. examined how two separate features of environments—harshness (e.g., rates of morbidity–mortality in the local environment) and unpredictability (fluctuations in the harshness of environmental conditions over time)—in early childhood (0—5 years) and later childhood (6—16 years)—predicted risky behavior, including aggression and delinquency (based on self-report scales) and involvement in criminal behavior in adulthood (see also Ellis et al. 2009). Simpson et al. reported that children exposed to more unpredictable environments during their first 5 years self-reported higher levels of aggression and delinquency and engaged in more criminal activities at age 23 than did children exposed to more predictable early environments. These relationships did not hold for the children exposed to harsh and unpredictable environments in later childhood.

These findings suggest that environmental unpredictability during the first 5 years of life has long-term influences on subsequent delinquent behaviors, which, as mentioned previously, may yield benefits especially for those living in harsh and unpredictable environments. Note that neither harshness nor degree of unpredictability later in childhood (6—16 years) uniquely predicted subsequent delinquent behavior. That is to say, children exposed *early* to unpredictable environments may adopt an accelerated life history strategy characterized by aggression, delinquency, and criminality. Expanding on this idea, Belsky (2012) recently proposed that children may have evolved developmental programs that are sensitive to extreme violence, such as war and ethnic cleansing, with those exposed to these harsh environmental features developing insecure attachment, a more anxious phenotype, and a faster life history strategy than children not exposed to such early violence.

Gene–Environment Interactions

However, not all children who experience stressful or unpredictable early environments necessarily engage in elevated levels of aggression or come to the attention of local law enforcement. For developmentalists, it is important to identify individual-level factors that either protect or make children vulnerable to environmental effects. Indeed, there is research showing that the quality of early environment interacts with a child's genotype in predicting such behavior in adolescence. For example, an abusive early environment was shown to be associated with later delinquent behavior, but only for children with particular genetic-based physiological characteristics. In a longitudinal study conducted in New Zealand, the delinquent behavior of adolescent boys was examined as a function of the likelihood of childhood maltreatment (none, probable, severe) and their level of the enzyme *monoamine oxidase A* (*MAOA*) that metabolizes several types of neurotransmitters (Caspi et al. 2002). Low levels of MAOA are associated with increased levels of aggression in both laboratory animals and humans (e.g., Guo et al. 2008a). Caspi et al. reported that the prevalence of delinquent behavior was especially high for adolescents who experienced severe maltreatment as children *and* had low levels of MAOA. Although levels of delinquent behavior were also high for children with high MAOA activity who experienced severe maltreatment, by far the most influenced group was adolescents who had both low MAOA levels and experienced severe childhood maltreatment. Other studies have similarly shown that quality of home environments is mediated by genotypes in expressing aggressive and violent behavior, clearly pointing to the interaction of early rearing environment and genetics (e.g., Foley et al. 2004; Guo et al. 2008b).

Predictive Adaptive Responses

Other research has demonstrated that childhood and adolescent levels of aggression and conduct disorder are predicted by certain *prenatal* experiences. Gluckman and Hanson (2005) identified experiences during the prenatal period, such as poor nutrition, as influencing subsequent functioning later in life in beneficial ways, termed *predictive adaptive responses*. With respect to poor prenatal nutrition, children develop "thrifty phenotypes," storing more fat than children whose prenatal diets were more nutritious. Several researchers have noted a connection between maternal stress and anxiety as reported by pregnant women and subsequent externalizing and conduct disorders in their children after controlling for other variables (e.g., SES, smoking, obstetric risk) (e.g., O'Connor et al. 2002a, b; O'Connor et al. 2003; Van den Bergh and Marcoen 2004; see Glover 2011 for a review). Although few of these studies controlled for direct genetic influences, Glover (2011) and others (e.g., O'Connor Heron et al. 2002; Van den Bergh and Marcoen 2004) have argued that a genetic explanation is not likely the entire story; namely the effects of maternal stress and anxiety on later behavior of offspring have been repeatedly found when the stress was reported for the prenatal development period, but not if the stress was reported during the immediate postnatal development. If individual differences in genes were the principal factor governing the relationship, then the relationship would be evident for both the pre- and postnatal groups. In an innovative study that attempted to tease apart genetic from prenatal experiential factors, researchers used a prenatal cross-fostering design, in which pregnant women were either genetically related or unrelated to their child as a result of in vitro fertilization (IVF) (Rice et al. 2010). Between 4 and 10 years of age, children's "antisocial" behavior was significantly related to stress experienced by their birth mothers, whether they were genetically related to them or not.

What's in it for the Bullies?

Bullying is a serious problem worldwide, with up to 600 million children being directly involved in bullying each year (Volk et al. 2006). As we mentioned in the opening paragraph of this chapter, the problem of bullying in childhood and adolescence has caught the attention of the public, with loud calls to end it. Yet, despite the efforts of school systems and the obvious physical and psychological harm to its many victims, bullying persists and has been resistant to intervention efforts (Stassen Berger 2007). As many species-universal behaviors, bullying may be associated with some adaptive outcomes, making its eradication difficult. An evolutionary perspective on bullying may provide some novel insights and possible solutions to this social problem.

About 10% of elementary school children can be classified as bullies (Boulton and Underwood 1992, in the UK; Olweus 1993, in Scandinavia; Pellegrini and Bartini 2000, in the U.S.). Although bullying can begin as early as 5—7 years of age (e.g., Synder et al. 2003), it tends to increase in frequency and intensity during the early school years, usually decreases over the elementary school years, and often then increases in early adolescence (e.g., Stassen Berger 2007; Rigby 2002; Salmivalli and Peets 2009). Both boys and girls bully and are equally likely to be victims of bullies, although boys are more apt to experience physical aggression from other boys and girls to experience indirect, or social, aggression from other girls (Veenstra et al. 2010).

Although bullying was once viewed as a case of "boys being boys" (and "girls being girls") and generally tolerated as a necessary part of childhood, its prevalence and negative consequences on its victims have brought it to a new level of public awareness. Bullying can result in low self-esteem, sleeping problems, bedwetting, headaches, self-harm, and depression for victims (e.g., Arsenault et al. 2010; Boulton and Smith 1994; Ladd et al. 1997; see Rigby 2002), and can sometimes lead to suicide or homicide.

There are surely many reasons why children bully. When 8- to 11-year-old Australian children were asked why they bullied particular children, the most frequent answer was that the victims "annoyed" them, with "getting even" being a close second (Rigby 2002). However, might there be an unstated reason? Rather than viewing bullying as a maladaptive strategy used by children with underdeveloped social skills and the result of faulty development, an evolutionary perspective suggests that some forms of bullying may represent a facultative adaptation, as described in the previous section. Under some conditions, some children use bullying to successfully gain resources and status when other strategies are not available to them (e.g., Pellegrini and Long 2002). This is a view recently presented by Anthony Volk et al. (Book et al. 2012; Volk et al. 2012a, 2012b), who propose that bullying can be an effective strategy to gain resources and status, particularly during adolescence. In support of their argument, they note that bullying: (1) is found across cultures; (2) has its analogue in social mammals, in which a stronger individual repeatedly attacks or takes resources away from a weaker one (see Archer 1988); (3) is highly heritable (in one study, genetic factors accounted for 61% of variation in bullying and 73% of the variation in victimization (Ball et al. 2008)); and (4) although some bullies display adjustment problems, many others experience positive outcomes.

Although bullies had traditionally been viewed as oafish, socially incompetent individuals, others have suggested that some bullies possess average, or perhaps above average, social-cognitive skills (Sutton et al. 1999a). While some researchers report deficits in social cognition (e.g., theory of mind, understanding empathy) in bullies (e.g., Shakoor et al. 2012), others report no social-cognitive deficits (e.g., Gini 2006; Caravita et al. 2010; Renouf et al. 2010), or even greater than average social-cognitive abilities (Sutton et al. 1999b). (Other research shows that although social cognition is not related to bullying, it is positively associated with defending victims of bullies (Caravita et al. 2009; Caravita et al. 2010).)

As we noted earlier, some children who frequently use aggression are also rated high in popularity (e.g., Hawley 2003b; Hawley et al. 2008). Bullies are likely to be leaders of their groups (both aggressive and nonaggressive groups; Estell et al. 2007) and, in adolescence, may be positively regarded by members of the opposite sex and have greater dating opportunities. For example, Connolly et al. (2000) interviewed nearly 200 self-reported bullies in grades 5 through 8 about their dating experiences and compared them to a matched group of adolescents. Children identified as bullies were oriented toward opposite-sex relationships and started dating earlier and engaged in more advanced dating experiences (e.g., having a boyfriend or girlfriend) than control children. Other research has found similar patterns. For example, in one longitudinal study of 11- to 14-year-old adolescents, both boys and girls who had higher levels of indirect aggression at Time 1 had more dating opportunities than their less aggressive peers 1 year later (Arnocky and Vaillancourt 2012). Using a retrospective design, Gallup et al. (2011) reported that college women who engaged in elevated levels of indirect aggression in adolescence began dating earlier than their less aggressive peers (see also White et al. 2010), whereas college men who engaged in more aggression in middle- and high-school reported having more dating partners than their less-aggressive peers. Several studies have also shown the inverse—that victimized adolescents have fewer dating opportunities and (eventual) sex partners than nonvictimized adolescents (e.g., Arnocky and Vaillancourt 2012; Gallup et al. 2009, 2011). These documented patterns hint at the possibility that bullying privileges perpetrators in terms of proximal variables (e.g., winning attention from the opposite sex) presumably associated with reproductive success.

Although levels of aggression were generally positively related with current and subsequent dating opportunities in these studies, there is some indication that the quality of dating relationships differs between children high versus low in aggression. For example, in the study by Connolly et al., bullies reported that their relationships with their boyfriends or girlfriends were less intimate, affectionate, and stable than control children, and bullies were more likely to report acts of aggression with a boyfriend or girlfriend than control children. Although characteristics of children's early lives (e.g., harsh and/or unpredictable environments) were not assessed in these studies, the bullies examined here display behavioral characteristics associated with children who follow a fast life history strategy (as described in the previous section), which is associated with elevated levels of aggression and delinquent behavior (e.g., Simpson et al. 2012).

Viewing bullying as an evolutionary adaptation does not mean that it is cost free; indeed, "adaptive" (i.e., functional) bullies, despite often being viewed as popular and of high status (i.e., benefits), are not typically socially preferred by their peers (e.g., Caravita et al. 2009, 2010; see Stassen Berger 2007), and their aggressive behavior can attract negative responses from adults in authority. And bullying certainly produces often serious, deleterious consequences for victims, which is reason enough to eliminate it. Bullying, however, need not be viewed solely as an aberration, but for some children in some contexts can be viewed as an adaptive solution to social problems, especially those contexts concerning power hierarchies. When developing interventions to reduce bullying, one must ask "What's in it for the kids?" who engage in such behavior (Ellis et al. 2012; Volk et al. 2012a). Bullying and other risky adolescent behaviors (e.g., drinking games, reckless driving) often confer status and mating opportunities to the youth who engage in them, and programs aimed at reducing bullying will be more likely to succeed when this is taken into consideration.

Implications for Intervention

Modern public sentiment—in large part as a reaction to a recent spate of teen suicides—characterizes the problem of bullying (perhaps correctly) as a national health concern. Without informed guidance and support from the scientific community, this outpouring of emotion can lead to well-meaning yet ill-informed policy statements that give the appearance of immediacy and effectiveness (e.g., implementing laws proclaiming zero tolerance or "criminalizing" bullying), but in fact have little evidence to suggest that such measures alone would be effective, and some evidence to suggest they may make the problem worse (Skiba and Knesting 2001).

Even when the scientific community weighs in, outcomes associated with bullying intervention programs have been described in their collective as "disappointing" (Stassen Berger 2007). Although contemporary bullying intervention programs have moved well beyond reactionary zero-tolerance policies, efficacy studies reveal mixed results, showing modest to no effect of examined interventions (e.g., Baldry and Farrington 2004; Frey et al. 2005; Merrell et al. 2008). Indeed, even Olweus's (1993) program, commonly considered the gold standard for American intervention, has not been rigorously tested in ways consistent with high standards of program evaluation. At the same time, however, derivative programs coming from Finland (e.g., KiVa) are showing more promise in regard to changing behavior of Finnish youth (Kärnä et al. 2011; Salmivalli et al. 2010). This program, however, has not been tested in the diverse American ecology.

In looking at KiVa through evolutionary lenses, we believe the program holds a great deal of promise in large part because it assumes that if one changes the ecology, one changes fundamentally the behaviors that will be adaptive in that ecology. This of course is a foundational principle of natural selection; behaviors are adaptive only insofar as they are selected by the local ecology.

As previously discussed, bullies had long been thought to be incompetent and disliked. By contrast, at present there appears to be some agreement that bullying yields several social rewards, including power, status, mating opportunities, and, perhaps more controversially, positive esteem from peers (e.g., Hawley et al. 2007b; Perren and Alsaker 2006; Vaillancourt et al. 2003). Thus, in school contexts where bullies thrive, there appears to be some selective advantage.

The grounding principles of KiVa recognize the functionality of bullying as a means of obtaining social rewards. Accordingly, the program seeks to alter reward structures for bullying behavior by, for example, focusing intervention efforts on other constituents in the social ecology, namely, the bystanders of bullying, or the majority of children who either explicitly (e.g., laughter, esteem) or implicitly (e.g., tolerance, resignation) reward the aggression of others even if they are not aggressive themselves. The success of this intervention appears to lie in the fact that it recognizes the functional nature of bullying and that it can be mitigated by altering the cost–benefit ratio so that it is no longer an adaptive strategy in the school ecology.

Conclusion

That aggression has ancestrally adaptive benefits is likely not a surprise for readers of this volume; evolutionary theorists have typically had a more difficult time explaining the presence of prosocial behaviors than of aggressive ones. Yet, mainstream developmental psychologists have traditionally viewed aggression in children as socially dysfunctional, and in many cases it certainly is. Even if it is not detrimental for the aggressor, it is for the victim and frequently for the harmony of the group. Viewing aggression in children from an evolutionary perspective gives developmentalists and social interventionists a new way of looking at the perpetrators of these harmful and often disruptive behaviors, one that may result in more positive outcomes when dealing with highly aggressive children or situations. An evolutionary approach is not necessary to develop an appreciation of the functional value of childhood aggression. However, such an approach is the foundation of evolutionary perspectives, and we believe that it is one that provides a better understanding of phenomena such as bullying and thus affords a greater chance of developing successful interventions than approaches that neglect a functional approach.

An evolutionary developmental approach may also alter how mainstream evolutionary psychologists view aggression. It seems clear today that both aggression and prosociality are universal features of human nature, both shaped by natural selection over *Homo sapiens'* evolutionary history. However, neither highly prosocial nor highly aggressive behavior is inevitable. Children have also evolved the developmental plasticity to be sensitive to early local environments that contingently entrain the course of ontogeny. In some situations, especially when early environments are harsh and unpredictable, children may display behavior patterns consistent with a fast life history strategy, which may include using aggression in ways that benefit the aggressor, at least in the short term. Of course, this, in a sense, is the function of a fast life history strategy—the early attainment of developmental milestones in anticipation that life may be short and/or opportunities few. From this perspective, much of adult aggression can be viewed through an evolutionary developmental lens. Which adults will use violence or excessive force in certain contexts is related not only to immediate conditions, but also to a childhood that biased the individual to be differentially sensitive to certain environmental contexts and to respond in certain ways (some aggressively) to achieve goals. From this viewpoint, a developmental perspective may not be necessary to understand adult use of violence, but we believe that is can greatly facilitate such an understanding.

References

Abramovitch, R. (1976). The relation of attention and proximity rank in preschool children. In M. Chance & R. Larsen (Eds.), *The social structure of attention* (pp. 154–176). London: Wiley.

Alcock, J. (2009). *Animal behavior: An evolutionary approach* (9th ed.). New York: Sinauer Associates.

Alink, L. R. A., Mesman, J., van Zeijl, J., Stolk, M. N., Juffer, F., Koot, H. M., Bakermans-Kranenburg, M. J., & van IJzendoorn, M. H. (2006). The early childhood aggression curve: Development of physical aggression in 10- to 50-month-old children. *Child Development, 77*, 954–966.

Alonso, F., Honji, R. M., Guimarães Moreira, R., & Pandolfi, M. (2012). Dominance hierarchies and social status ascent opportunity: Anticipatory behavioral and physiological adjustments in a Neotropical cichlid fish. *Physiology and Behavior, 106*, 612–618

Archer, J. (1988). *The behavioral biology of aggression*. Cambridge, UK: Cambridge University Press.

Archer, J. (2009). Does sexual selection explain human sex differences in aggression? *Behavioral and Brian Science, 32*, 249–311.

Archer, J., & Coyne, S. M. (2005). An integrated review of indirect, relational, and social aggression. *Personality and Social Psychology Review, 9*, 212–230.

Arnocky, S., & Vaillancourt, T. (2012). A multi-informant longitudinal study on the relationship between aggression, peer victimization, and adolescent dating status. *Evolutionary Psychology, 10*, 253–270.

Arnocky, S., Sunderani, S., Miller, J. L., & Vaillancourt, T. (2011). Jealousy mediates the relationship between attractiveness comparison and females' indirect aggression. *Personal Relationships, 19*, 290–303.

Arsenault, L., Bowes, L., & Shakoor, S. (2010). Bullying victimization in youths and mental health problems: 'Much ado about nothing'? *Psychological Medicine, 40*, 717–729.

Baillargeon, R. H., Zoccolillo, M., Keenan, K., Côté, S. M., Pérusse, Wu, H-X., Boivin, M., & Tremblay, R. E. (2007). Gender differences in physical aggression: A prospective population-based survey of children before and after 2 years of age. *Developmental Psychology, 43*, 13–26.

Baldry, A., & Farrington, D. P. (2004). Evaluation of an intervention program for the reduction of bullying and victimization in schools. *Aggressive Behavior, 30*, 1–15.

Ball, H. A., Arsenault, L., Taylor, A., Maughan, B., Caspi, A., & Moffitt, T. E. (2008). Genetic influences on victims, bullies, and bully-victims in childhood. *Journal of Child Psychology and Psychiatry, 49*, 104–112.

Bandura, A. (1973). *Aggression: A social learning analysis*. Englewood Cliffs, NJ: Prentice Hall

Banny, A., Heilbron, N., Ames, A., & Prinstein, M. J. (2011). Relational benefits of relational aggression: Adaptive and maladaptive associations with adolescent friendship quality. *Developmental Psychology, 47*, 1153–1166.

Bartholomew, K., & Horowitz, L. M. (1991). Attachment styles among adults: A test of a four-category model. *Journal of Personality and Social Development, 61*, 226–244.

Belsky, J. (2012). An evolutionary perspective on child development in the context of war and political violence. In T. K. Shackelford & V. Weekes-Shackelford (Eds.), *The Oxford handbook of evolutionary perspectives on violence, homicide, and war* (pp. 393–409). New York: Oxford University Press.

Belsky, J., Steinberg, L., & Draper, P. (1991). Childhood experience, interpersonal development, and reproductive strategy: An evolutionary theory of socialization. *Child Development, 62*, 647–670.

Benenson, J. F. (2009). Sex differences in aggression from an adaptive perspective. In M. J. Harris (Ed.), *Bullying, rejection, and peer victimization: A social cognitive neuroscience perspective* (pp. 171–198). New York: Springer.

Bierman, K. L., Smoot, D. L., & Aumiller, K. (1993). Characteristics of aggressive-rejected, aggressive (nonrejected), and rejected (nonaggressive) boys. *Child Development, 64*, 139–151.

Björkqvist, K., Österman, K., & Kaukiainen, A. (1992). The development of direct and indirect aggressive strategies in males and females. In K. Björkqvist & P. Niemela (Eds.), *Of mice and women: Aspects of female aggression* (pp. 51–63). San Diego: CA: Academic Press.

Book, A. S., Volk, A. A., & Hosker, A. (2012). Adolescent bullying and personality: An adaptive approach. *Personality and Individual Differences, 52*, 218–223.

Boulton, M. J., & Smith, P. K. (1994). Bully/victim problems in middle school children: Stability, self-perceived competence, peer-perceptions and peer acceptance. *British Journal of Developmental Psychology, 12*, 315–329.

Boulton, M. J., & Underwood, K. (1992). Bully/victim problems among middle school children. *British Journal of Educational Psychology, 62*, 73–87.

Bowlby, J. (1969). *Attachment and loss: Vol. 1: Attachment.* London: Hogarth.

Boyce, W. T., & Ellis, B. J. (2005). Biological sensitivity to context: I. An evolutionary-developmental theory of the origins and functions of stress reactivity. *Development and Psychopathology, 17*, 271–301.

Broidy, L. M., Nagin, D. S., Tremblay, R. E., Bates, J. E., Brame, B., Dodge, K. A., Fergusson, D., Horwood, J. L., Loeber, R., Laird, R., Lynam, D. R., Moffitt, T. E., Pettit, G. S., & Vitaro, F. (2003). Developmental trajectories of childhood disruptive behavior and adolescent delinquency: A six-site, cross-national study. *Developmental Psychology, 39*, 222–245.

Bühler, C. (1927). Die ersten sozialen Verhaltensweisen des Kindes. In C. Bühler, H. Hetzer & B. Tudor-Hart (Eds.), *Soziologische und psychologische Studien über das erste Lebensjahr (Social and psychological studies of the first year of life)* (pp. 1–102). Jena: Gustav Fischer.

Cairns, R. B., & Cairns, B. D. (1986). The developmental-interactional view of social behavior: Four issues of adolescent aggression. In D. Olweus, J. Block, & M. Radke-Yarrow (Eds.), *Development of antisocial and prosocial behavior: Research, theories, and issues* (pp. 315–342). New York: Academic Press.

Cairns, R. B., Cairns, B. D., Neckerman, H. J., Ferguson, L. L., & Gariépy, J. (1989). Growth and aggression: 1. Childhood to early adolescence. *Developmental Psychology, 25*, 320–330.

Campbell, A. (1999). Staying alive: Evolution, culture, and women's intrasexual aggression. *Behavioral and Brain Sciences, 22*, 203–252.

Campbell, A. (2005). Aggression. In D. Buss (Ed.), *Handbook of evolutionary psychology* (pp. 628–652). New York: John Wiley.

Caravita, S. C. S., Di Blasio, P., & Salmivalli, C. (2009). Unique and interactive effects of empathy and social status on involvement in bullying. *Social Development, 18*, 140–163.

Caravita, S. C. S., Di Blasio, P., & Salmivalli, C. (2010). Early adolescents' participation in bullying: Is ToM involved? *Journal of Early Adolescence, 30*, 138–170.

Card, N. A., Stucky, B. D., Sawalani, C. M., & Little, T. D. (2008). Direct an indirect aggression during childhood and adolescence: A meta-analytic review of gender differences, intercorrelations, and relations to maladjustment. *Child Development, 79*, 1185–1229.

Caspi, A., McClay, J., Moffitt, T. E., Mill, J., Martin, J., Craig, I. W., Taylor, A., & Poulton, R. (2002). Role of genotype in the cycle of violence in maltreated children. *Science, 297* (2 August), 851–854

Cillessen, A. H. N., & Mayeux, L. (2004). From censure to reinforcement: Developmental changes in the association between aggression and social status. *Child Development, 75*, 147–163.

Cleverely, K., Szatmari, P., Vaillancourt, T., Boyle, M., & Lipman, E. (2012). Developmental trajectories of physical and indirect aggression from late childhood to adolescence: Sex differences and outcomes in emerging adulthood. *Journal of the American Academy of Child and Adolescent Psychiatry, 51*, 1037–1051.

Clutton-Brock, T. H. (1991). *The evolution of parental care*. Princeton, NJ: Princeton University Press.

Coie, J. D., & Dodge, K. A. (1998). Aggression and antisocial behavior. In W. Damon (Series, Ed.) & N. Eisenberg (Vol. Ed.), *Handbook of child psychology, Vol. 3. Social, emotional, and personality development* (5th ed., pp. 779–862). New York: Wiley.

Coie, J. D., & Koeppl, G. K. (1990). Adapting intervention to the problems of aggressive and disruptive rejected children. In S. R. Asher & J. D. Coie (Eds.), *Peer rejection in childhood* (pp. 309–337). Cambridge University Press

Connolly, J., Pepler, D., Craig, W., & Taradash, A. (2000). Dating experiences of bullies in early adolescence. *Child Maltreatment, 5*, 299–310.

Côté, S. M., Vaillancourt, T., Leblanc, J. C., Nagin, D. S., & Tremblay, R. E. (2006). The development of physical aggression from toddlerhood to pre-adolescence: A nation wide longitudinal study of Canadian children. *Journal of Abnormal Child Psychology, 34*, 71–85.

Côté, S., Vaillancourt, T., Barker, E. D., Nagin, D. S., & Tremblay, R. E. (2007). The joint development of physical and indirect aggression: Predictors of continuity and change during childhood. *Development and Psychopathology, 19*, 37–55.

Crick, N. R., & Grotpeter, J. K. (1995). Relational aggression, gender, and social psychological adjustment. *Child Development, 66*, 710–722.

Cullerton-Sen, C., Cassidy, A. R., Murray-Close, D., Cicchetti, D., Crick, N. R., & Rogosch, F. A. (2008). Childhood maltreatment and the development of relational and physical aggression: The importance of a gender-informed approach. *Child Development, 79*, 1736–1751.

Cummings, E. M., Iannotti, R. J., & Zahn-Waxler, C. (1989). Aggression between peers in early childhood: Individual continuity and developmental change. *Child Development, 60*, 887–895.

Daly, M., & Wilson, M. (1988). *Homicide*. New York: Aldine.

Daly, M., & Wilson, M. (1990). Killing the competition: Female/female and male/male homicide. *Human Nature, 1*, 81–107.

Del Giudice, M. (2009). Sex, attachment, and the development of reproductive strategies. *Behavioral and Brain Sciences, 32*, 1–21.

Del Giudice, M., Angeleri, R., & Manera, V. (2009). The juvenile transition: A developmental switch point in human life history. *Developmental Review, 29*, 1–31.

den Bak, I. M., & Ross, H. S. (1996). "I'm telling!" the content, context, and consequences of children's tattling on their siblings. *Social Development, 5*, 292–309.

Dodge, K. A., & Albert, D. (2012). Evolving science in adolescence. *Developmental Psychology, 48*, 624–627.

Dodge, K. A., Coie, J. D., & Lynam, D. (2006). Aggression and antisocial behavior in youth. In W. Damon & R. M. Lerner (Gen, Eds.), *Handbook of child psychology (6th edition),* N. Eisenberg (Vol. Ed.), *Vol. 3, Social, emotional, and personality development* (pp. 719–788). New York: Wiley.

Dodge, K. A., Greenberg, M. T., Malone, P. S., & Conduct Problems Prevention Research Group (2008). Testing an idealized cascade model of the development of serious violence in adolescence. *Child Development, 79*, 1907–1927.

Dollard, J., Doob, C. W., Miller, N. E., Mowrer, O. H., & Sears, R. R. (1939). *Frustration and aggression*. New Haven, CT: Yale University Press.

Eisenberg, N., & Fabes, R. (1998). Prosocial development. In W. Damon & R. M. Lerner (Gen, Eds.), *Handbook of child psychology (6th edition),* N. Eisenberg (Vol. Ed.), *Vol. 3, Social, emotional, and personality development* (pp. 701–778). New York: Wiley.

Ellis, B. J. (2004). Timing of pubertal maturation in girls: An integrated life history approach. *Psychological Bulletin, 130*, 920–958.

Ellis, B. J., & Bjorklund, D. F. (2012). Beyond mental health: An evolutionary analysis of development under risky and supportive environmental conditions: An introduction to the special section. *Developmental Psychology, 48*, 591–597.

Ellis, B. J., Figueredo, A. J., Brumbach, B. H., & Schlomer, G. L. (2009). Fundamental dimensions of environmental risk: The impact of harsh versus unpredictable environments on the evolution and development of life history strategies. *Human Nature, 20*, 204–268.

Ellis, B. J., Boyce, W. T., Belsky, J., Bakermans-Kranenburg, M. J., & van IJzendoorn, M. H. (2011). Differential susceptibility to the environment: An evolutionary–neurodevelopmental theory. *Development and Psychopathology*, *23*, 7–28.

Ellis, B. J., Del Giudice, M., Dishon, T. J., Figueredo, A. J., Gray, P., Griskevicius, V., Hawley, P. H., Jacobs, W. J., James, J., Volk, A. A., & Wilson, D. S. (2012). The evolutionary basis of risky adolescent behavior: Implications for science, policy, and practice. *Developmental Psychology, 48, 598–623*

Estell, D. B., Farmer, T. W., & Cairns, B. D. (2007). Bullies and victims in rural African American youth: Behavioral characteristics and social network placement. *Aggressive Behavior*, *33*, 145–159.

Figueredo, A. J., & Jacobs, W. J. (2010). Aggression, risk-taking, and alternative life history strategies: The behavioral ecology of social deviance. In M. Frias-Armenta & V. Corral-Verdugo (Eds.), *Biopsychosocial perspectives on interpersonal violence* (pp. 3–27). Hauppauge, NY: Nova Science Publishers

Foley, D. L., Eaves, L. J., Wormley, B., Silberg, J., Maes, H., Kuhn, J., et al. (2004). Childhood adversity, monoamine oxidase A genotype, and risk for conduct disorder. *Archives of General Psychiatry*, *61*, 738–744.

Frey, K. S., Hirschstein, M. K., Snell, J. L., Edstrom, L. V., MacKenzie, E. P., & Broderick, C. J. (2005). Reducing playground bullying and supporting beliefs: An experimental trial of the Steps to Respect program. *Developmental Psychology*, *41*, 479–491.

Gallup, A. C., O'Brien, D. T., White, D. D., & Wilson, D. S. (2009). Peer victimization in adolescence has different effects on the sexual behavior of male and female college students. *Personality and Individual Differences*, *46*, 611–615.

Gallup, A. C., O'Brien, D. T., & Wilson, D. S. (2011). Intrasexual peer aggression and dating behavior during adolescence: An evolutionary perspective. *Aggressive Behavior*, *37*, 258–267.

Garandeau, C. F., Ahn, H. J., & Rodkin, P. C. (2011). The social status of aggressive students across contexts: The role of classroom status hierarchy, academic achievement, and grade. *Developmental Psychology*, *47*, 1699–1710.

Geary, D. C. (2005). Evolution of paternal investment. In D. M. Buss (Ed.), *The handbook of evolutionary psychology* (pp. 483–505). New York: Wiley.

Gini, G. (2006). Social cognition and moral cognition in bullying: What's wrong? *Aggressive Behavior*, *32*, 528–539.

Glover, V. (2011). Annual research review: Prenatal stress and the origins of psychopathology: An evolutionary perspective. *Journal of Child Psychology and Psychiatry*, *52*, 356–367.

Gluckman, P., & Hanson, M. (2005). *The fetal matrix: Evolution, development, and disease*. Cambridge, UK: Cambridge University Press.

Guo, G., Ou, X.-M., Roettger, M., & Shih, J. C. (2008a). The VNTR 2-repeat in *MAOA* and delinquent behavior in adolescence and young adulthood: Associations and *MAOA* promoter activity. *European Journal of Human Genetics*, *16*, 626–634.

Guo, G., Roettger, M., & Cai, T. (2008b). The integration of genetic propensities into social control models of delinquency and violence among male youths. *American Sociological Review*, *73*, 543–568.

Hall, G. S. (1904). *Adolescence: Its psychology and its relations to physiology, anthropology, sociology, sex, crime, religion and education*. Vol. 1. New York: Appelton.

Hawley, P. H. (1999). The ontogenesis of social dominance: A strategy-based evolutionary perspective. *Developmental Review*, *19*, 97–132.

Hawley, P. H. (2002). Social dominance and prosocial and coercive strategies of resource control in preschoolers. *International Journal of Behavioral Development*, *26*, 167–176.

Hawley, P. H. (2003a). Strategies of control, aggression and morality in preschoolers: An evolutionary perspective. *Journal of Experimental Child Psychology*, *85*, 213–235.

Hawley, P. H. (2003b). Prosocial and coercive configurations of resource control in early adolescence: A case for the well-adapted Machiavellian. *Merrill-Palmer Quarterly*, *49*, 279–309.

Hawley, P. H. (2011). The evolution of adolescence and the adolescence of evolution: The coming of age of humans and the theory about the forces that made them. *Journal of Research on Adolescence, 21*, 307–316.

Hawley, P. H., & Geldhof, J. G. (2012). Preschoolers' social dominance, moral cognition, and moral behavior: An evolutionary perspective. *Journal of Experimental Child Psychology, 112*, 18–35.

Hawley, P. H., Card, N. A., & Little, T. D. (2007a). The allure of a mean friend: Relationship quality and processes of aggressive adolescents with prosocial skills. *International Journal of Behavioral Development, 31*, 22–32.

Hawley, P. H., Card, N. A., & Little, T. D. (2008). The myth of the alpha male: A new look at dominance related beliefs and behaviors among adolescent males and females. *International Journal of Behavioral Development, 32*, 76–88.

Hawley, P. H., Little, T. D., & Rodkin, P. C. (Eds.) (2007b). *Aggression and adaptation: The bright side to bad behavior*. Mahwah, NJ: Erlbaum.

Hawley, P. H., Shorey, H. S., & Alderman, P. M. (2009). Attachment correlates of resource control strategies: Possible origins of social dominance and interpersonal power differentials. *Journal of Social and Personal Relationships, 26*, 1097–1118.

Hay, D. F., Nash, A., & Pedersen, J. (1983). Interaction between 6-month-old peers. *Child Development, 54*, 557–562.

Hay, D., Mundy, L., Roberts, S., Carta, R., Waters, C. S., Perra, O., Jones, R., Jones, I., Goodyer, I., Harold, G., Thapar, A., & van Goozen, S. (2011). Known risk factors for violence predict 12-month-old infants' aggressiveness with peers. *Psychological Science, 22*, 1205–1211.

Hoffman, M. L. (1975). Altruistic behavior and the parent-child relationship. *Journal of Personality and Social Psychology, 31*, 937–943.

Ingram, G. P. D. (2014). From hitting to tattling to gossip: An evolutionary rationale for the development of indirect aggression. *Evolutionary Psychology*.

Ingram, G. P. D., & Bering, J. M. (2010). Children's tattling: The reporting of everyday norm violations in preschool settings. *Child Development, 81*, 945–957

Jessor, R. (1991). Risk behavior in adolescence: A psychosocial framework for understanding and action. *Journal of Adolescent Health, 12*, 597–605.

Kärnä, A., Voeten, M., Little, T. D., Poskiparta, E., Kaljonen, A., & Salmivalli, C. (2011). A large-scale evaluation of the KiVa antibullying program: Grades 4–6. *Child Development, 82*, 311–330.

Kaukiainen, A., Björkqvist, K., Lagerspertz, K., Österman, K., Salmivalli, C., Rothberg, S., & Ahlbo, A. (1999). The relationship between social intelligence, empathy, and three types of aggression. *Aggressive Behavior, 25*, 81–89.

Krebs, J. R., & Davies, N. B. (Eds.). (1997). *Behavioural ecology: An evolutionary approach* (4th ed). Oxford: Blackwell.

Krevans, J., & Gibbs, J. C. (1996). Parents' use of inductive discipline: Relations to children's empathy and prosocial behavior. *Child Development, 67*, 3263–3277.

Ladd, G. W., Kochenderfer, B. J., & Coleman, C. C. (1997). Classroom peer acceptance, friendship, and victimization: Distinct relational systems that contribute uniquely to children's school adjustment? *Child Development, 68*, 1181–1197.

Little, T. D., Jones, S. M., Henrich, C. C., & Hawley, P. H. (2003). Disentangling the 'whys' from the 'whats' of aggressive behavior. *International Journal of Behavioral Development, 27*, 122–133.

Merrell, K. W., Gueldner, B. A., Ross, S. W., & Isava, D. M. (2008). How effective are school bullying intervention programs? A meta-analysis of intervention research. *School Psychology Quarterly, 23*, 26–42.

Mikulincer, M., & Shaver, P. R. (2003). The attachment behavioral system in adulthood: Activation, psychodynamics, and interpersonal processes. *Advances in Experimental Social Psychology, 35*, 53–152.

Mishra, S., & Lalumière, M. L. (2008). Risk-taking, antisocial behaviour, and life histories. In J. Duntley & T. K. Shackelford (Eds.), *Evolutionary forensic psychology: Darwinian foundations of crime and law* (pp. 176–197). New York: Oxford University Press.
NICHD Early Child Care Research Network. (2004). Trajectories of physical aggression from toddlerhood to middle childhood: Predictors, correlates, and outcomes. *Monographs of the Society for Research in Child Development* (*69*, Serial No. 278)
O'Connor, T. G., Heron, J., & Glover, V. (2002a). Antenatal anxiety predicts child behavioral/emotional problems independently of postnatal depression. *Journal of the American Academy of Child and Adolescent Psychiatry, 41*, 1470–1477.
O'Connor, T. G., Heron, J., Golding, J., Beveridge, M., & Glover, V. (2002b). Maternal antenatal anxiety and children's behavioural/emotional problems at 4 years. Report from the Avon Longitudinal Study of Parents and Children. *British Journal of Psychiatry, 180*, 502–508.
O'Connor, T. G., Heron, J., Golding, J., Glover, V., and the ALSPAC Study Team (2003). Maternal antenatal anxiety and behavioural/emotional problems in children: A test of a programming hypothesis. *Journal of Child Psychology and Psychiatry, 44*, 1025–1036.
Olweus, D. (1978). *Aggression in the schools: Bullies and whipping boys*. New York: Hemisphere.
Olweus, D. (1993). *Bullying at school: What we know and what we can do*. Malden, MA: Blackwell.
Österman, K., Björkqvist, K., & Lagerspetz, K. M. J., Kirsti, M. J., Kaukianen, A., Landau, S. F., Fraczek, A., & Caprara, G. V. (1998). Cross-cultural evidence of female indirect aggression. *Aggressive Behavior, 24*, 1–8.
Pellegrini, A. D. (2001). The roles of dominance and bullying in the development of early heterosexual relationships. *Journal of Emotional Abuse, 2*, 63–73.
Pellegrini, A. D., & Archer, J. (2005). Sex differences in competitive and aggressive behavior: A view from sexual selection theory. In B. J. Ellis & D. F. Bjorklund (Eds.), *Origins of the social mind: Evolutionary psychology and child development* (pp. 219–244). New York: Guilford.
Pellegrini, A. D., & Bartini, M. (2000). An empirical comparison of methods of sample aggression and victimization in school settings. *Journal of Educational Psychology, 92*, 360–366.
Pellegrini, A. D., & Long, J. D. (2002). A longitudinal study of bullying, dominance, and victimization during the transition from primary school through secondary school. *British Journal of Developmental Psychology, 20*, 259–280.
Pellegrini, A. D., & Smith, P. K. (1998). Physical activity play: The nature and function of a neglected aspect of play. *Child Development, 69*, 577–598.
Pellegrini, A. D., Long, J. D., Roseth, C., Bohn, K., & Van Ryzin, M. (2007). A short-longitudinal study of preschoolers' (*Homo sapiens*) sex segregation: The role of physical activity, sex, and time. *Journal of Comparative Psychology, 121*, 282–289.
Perren, S., & Alsaker, F. D. (2006). Social behavior and peer relationships of victims, bully-victims, and bullies in kindergarten. *Journal of Child Psychology and Psychiatry, 47*, 45–57.
Renouf, A., Brendgen, M., Séguin, J. R., Vitaro, F., Boivin, M., Dionne, G., Tremblay, R. E., & Pérusse, D. (2010). Interactive links between theory of mind, peer victimization, and reactive and proactive aggression. *Journal of Abnormal Child Psychology, 38*, 1109–1123.
Rhee, S. H., & Wildman, I. D. (2002). Genetic and environmental influences on antisocial behavior: A meta-analysis of twin and adoption studies. *Psychological Bulletin, 128*, 490–529.
Rice, F., Harold, G. T., Boivin, J., van den Bree, M., Hay, D. F., & Thapar, A. (2010). The links between prenatal stress and offspring development and psychopathology: Disentangling environmental and inherited influences. *Psychological Medicine, 40*, 335–345.
Rigby, K. (2002). Bullying in childhood. In P. K. Smith & C. H. Hart (Eds.), *Blackwell handbook of childhood social development* (pp. 549–568). Oxford, UK: Blackwell.
Robinson, J. L., Zahn-Waxler, C., & Emde, R. N. (1994). Patterns of development in early empathic behavior: Environmental and child constitutional influences. *Social Development, 3*, 125–145.
Rodkin, P. C., Farmer, T. W., Pearl, R., & Van Acker, R. (2000). Heterogeneity of popular boys: Antisocial and prosocial configurations. *Developmental Psychology, 36*, 14–24.

Rose, A. J., Swanson, L. P., & Waller, E. M. (2004). Overt and relational aggression and perceived popularity: Developmental differences in concurrent and prospective relations. *Developmental Psychology, 40*, 378–387.
Salmivalli, C., & Peets, K. (2009). Bullies, victims, and bully-victim relationships in middle childhood and early adolescence. In K. H. Rubin, W. M. Bukowski & B. Laursen (Eds.), *Handbook of peer interactions, relationships, and groups* (pp. 322–340). New York: Guilford.
Salmivalli, C., Kärnä, A., & Poskiparta, E. (2010). Development, evaluation, and diffusion of an anti-bullying program, KiVa. In B. Doll, W. Pfohl & J. Yoon (Eds.), *Handbook of youth prevention science* (pp. 238–252). New York: Routledge.
Schjelderup-Ebbe, T. (1922). Beiträge zur Sozialpsychologie des Haushuhns (Contributions to the social psychology of domestic chickens). *Zeitschrift für Psychologie, 88*, 225–252.
Shakoor, S., Jaffee, S. R., Bowes, L., Ouellet-Morin, I, Andreou, P., Happé, F., Moffitt, T. E., & Arsenault, L. (2012). A prospective longitudinal study of children's theory of mind and adolescent involvement in bullying. *Journal of Child Psychology and Psychiatry, 53*, 254–261.
Shim, S., & Maggs, J. L. (2005). A psychographic analysis of college students' alcohol consumption: Implications for prevention and consumer education. *Family and Consumer Sciences Research Journal, 33*, 255–273.
Simpson, J. A., Griskevicius, V., Kuo, S. I.-C., Sung, S., & Collins, W. (2012). Evolution, stress, and sensitive periods: The influence of unpredictability in early versus late childhood on sex and risky behavior. *Developmental Psychology, 48*, 674–686.
Skiba, R. J., & Knesting, K. (2001). Zero tolerance, zero evidence: An analysis of school disciplinary practice. *New Directions for Mental Health Services, 92*, 17–43.
Snyder, J., Brooker, M., Patrick, M. R., Synder, A., Schrepferman, L., & Stoolmiller, M. (2003). Observed peer victimization during elementary school: Continuity, growth, and relation to risk for child antisocial and depressive behavior. *Child Development, 74*, 1881–1898.
Stassen Berger, K. (2007). Update on bullying at school: Science forgotten? *Developmental Review, 27*, 90–126.
Sutton, J., Smith, P. K., & Swettenham, J. (1999a). Bullying and theory of mind: A critique of the social skills deficit view of anti-social behavior. *Social Development, 8*, 117–127.
Sutton, J., Smith, P. K., & Swettenham, J. (1999b). Social cognition and bullying: Social inadequacy or skilled manipulation? *British Journal of Developmental Psychology, 17*, 435–450.
Tomasello, M. (2009). *Why we cooperate*. Cambridge, MA: MIT Press.
Tremblay, R. E., Japel, C., Pérusse, D., McDuff, P., Boivin, M., Zoccolillo, M., & Montplaisir, J. (1999). The search of the age of "onset" of physical aggression: Rousseau and Bandura revisited. *Criminal Behavior and Mental Health, 9*, 8–23.
Trickett, P. K., & Kuczynski, L. (1986). Children's misbehavior and parental discipline strategies in abusive and nonabusive families. *Developmental Psychology, 22*, 115–123.
Trivers, R. (1972). Parental investment and sexual selection. In B. Campbell (Ed.), *Sexual selection and the descent of man* (pp. 136–179). New York: Aldine de Gruyter.
Underwood, M. (2002). Sticks and stones and social exclusion: Aggression among boys and girls. In P. K. Smith & C. H. Hart (Eds.), *Blackwell handbook of childhood social development* (pp. 533–548). Oxford, UK: Blackwell.
Vaillancourt, T. (2005). Indirect aggression among humans: Social construct or evolutionary adaptation? In R. E. Tremblay, W. W. Hartup & J. Archer (Eds), *Developmental origins of aggression* (pp. 158–177). New York: Guilford Press.
Vaillancourt, T., & Hymel, S. (2006). Aggression and social status: The moderating roles of sex and peer-valued characteristics. *Aggressive Behavior, 32*, 396–408.
Vaillancourt, T., Hymel, S., & McDougall, P. (2003). Bullying is power: Implications for school-based intervention strategies. *Journal of Applied School Psychology, 19*, 157–176.
Vaillancourt, T., Miller, J. L., & Sharma, A. (2010). "Tripping the Prom Queen": Female intrasexual competition and indirect aggression. In K. Österman (Ed.), *Indirect and direct aggression* (pp. 17–32). Frankfurt, Germany: Peter Lang Publishing.

Van Den Bergh, B. R., & Marcoen, A. (2004). High antenatal maternal anxiety is related to ADHD symptoms, externalizing problems, and anxiety in 8- and 9-year-olds. *Child Development, 75*, 1085–1097.

Veenstra, R., Lindenberg, S., Munniksma, A., & Dijkstra, J. K. (2010). The complex relation between bullying, victimization, acceptance, and rejection: Giving special attention to status, affection, and sex differences. *Child Development, 81*, 480–486.

Volk, A., Camilleri, J., Dane, A., & Marini, Z. (2012a). If, when, and why bullying is adaptive. In T. K. Shackelford & V. Weekes-Shackelford (Eds.), *Oxford handbook of evolutionary perspectives on violence, homicide, and war (pp. 270–288)*. NY: Oxford University Press.

Volk, A., Camilleri, J., Dane, A., & Marini, Z. (2012b). Is adolescent bullying an evolutionary adaptation? *Aggressive Behavior, 38*, 222–238.

Volk, A., Craig, W., Boyce, W., & King, M. (2006). Adolescent risk correlates of bullying and different types of victimization. *International Journal of Adolescent Medicine and Health, 18*, 375–386.

Wang, X. T., Kruger, D. J., & Wilke, A. (2009). Life history variables and risk-taking propensity. *Evolution and Human Behavior, 30*, 77–84.

Warneken, F., & Melis, A. (2012). The ontogeny and phylogeny of cooperation. In J. Vonk & T. K. Shackelford (Eds.), *The Oxford handbook of comparative evolutionary psychology* (pp. 399–418). New York: Oxford University Press.

White, D. D., Gallup, A. C., & Gallup, G. G. Jr (2010). Indirect peer aggression in adolescence and reproductive behavior. *Evolutionary Psychology, 8*, 49–65.

Chapter 10
Adaptation and Coherence: Evolutionary and Dynamical Perspectives on Human Violence

Robin R. Vallacher and Christopher Brooks

Adaptation and Coherence: Evolutionary and Dynamical Perspectives on Human Violence

The potential for violence is a universal feature of social life that leaves no realm of human interaction untouched. As such, violent behavior qualifies as a central domain of human psychology, on par with far loftier domains like language, music, love, and procreation. To be sure, the frequency and intensity of violence show variability across cultures and historical periods. But even in the most peaceful societies and during the least stressful times, violence between individuals, groups, and societies is an ever-present possibility, primed to surface in response to a wide variety of triggers. The ubiquity of violent behavior at different levels of social reality suggests that its occurrence is not an aberration or a result of idiosyncratic factors, but rather represents the expression of basic psychological mechanisms. The question is, what are these mechanisms?

Evolutionary psychology provides a reasonable way to think about this issue, and considerable evidence has been amassed in recent years in support of this account. We suggest, however, that the dynamical systems perspective in social psychology (e.g., Guastello et al. 2009; Vallacher and Nowak 2007; Vallacher et al. 2002) is worthy of consideration as well. This perspective on the nature of human experience represents an adaptation of the work on complexity science and nonlinear dynamical systems that revolutionized the natural sciences in the 1970s (e.g., Eckmann and Ruelle 1985; Haken 1982; Strogatz 1994; Thompson and Stewart 1986; Waldrop 1992; Weisbuch 1992). The attempt to conceptualize social psychology in these terms is relatively new and thus has not yet produced a track record to match that of evolutionary psychology. Like evolutionary psychology, however,

R. R. Vallacher (✉) · C. Brooks
Department of Psychology, Florida Atlantic University, Boca Raton, FL, 33431, USA
e-mail: vallacher@fau.edu

C. Brooks
e-mail: chrisabrooks11@gmail.com

T. K. Shackelford, R. D. Hansen (eds.), *The Evolution of Violence*,
Evolutionary Psychology, DOI 10.1007/978-1-4614-9314-3_10,

the dynamical perspective holds promise for integrating the highly fragmented field of social psychology, and the evidence to date suggests that it may fulfill this role.

Our aim in this chapter is to make the case for both points of view, both in general terms and with respect to the specific issue of human violence. Beyond comparing the respective merits of the evolutionary and dynamical perspectives, we intend to show how these seemingly distinct models of human psychology can be integrated to promote a higher-order frame for human violence that is both integrative and heuristic. To set the stage for this analysis, we first clarify the issue of human violence and document the need for a comprehensive theory concerning its origins and functions.

Human Violence: The Need for Comprehensive Theory

The phenomenon of violence is at once simple and complex. Its simplicity is captured in the definition provided by the World Health Organization: "the intentional use of physical force or power, threatened or actual, against oneself, another person, or against a group or community, that either results in or has a high likelihood of resulting in injury, death, psychological harm, maldevelopment or deprivation" (Dahlberg and Krug 2002, p. 5). Simple enough, but things become complicated when one considers the various forms that violence can take and the various factors that can activate or inhibit these forms. Violence can occur between individuals, between groups, and between nation-states. It commonly represents antagonistic feelings, yet it can emerge in the most intimate of relationships. It can be a one-off experience, lasting mere seconds, or it can unfold on timescales ranging up to years, even decades. It can involve direct physical contact or it can take place by means of a button press that launches missiles to a location thousands of miles away.

Nor is violence simple with respect to its normalcy and adaptive value. It is tempting to view violent behavior that causes harm as an aberration of normal psychological processes. Violent behavior that results in long-term suffering and death seems especially pathological and thus unique in its underlying psychological and social forces. However, uniqueness could be claimed for blind obedience to authority, racial prejudice, and self-defeating behavior—or of heroism and altruism, for that matter. Yet each of these topics has been successfully framed in terms of basic processes that are manifest in far more banal realms of human experience. Perhaps violence, too, is a manifestation of fundamental psychological processes.

A great deal has been learned over the years about the potential for violence in human affairs. For the most part, though, the focus in this research has been on the proximate causes—the triggers—of hostile intent and aggressive behavior. So despite the ubiquity and universality of violence, the distal causes of this phenomenon have yet to be unequivocally established. What is needed, then, is a comprehensive account that can establish the invariant features of violence, while accounting for its myriad forms of expression. If evolutionary psychology and nonlinear dynamical systems aspire to be the foundational science for human psychology, they should be able to provide the conceptual integration that is lacking for violent behavior. Accordingly, we consider each perspective in turn in the following sections.

The Case for Evolutionary Psychology

Traditional social psychology has done a fine job of cataloguing the various domains of human experience and identifying the proximate causes and situational triggers associated with each. This fine-grained approach to understanding personal and social processes, however, has resulted in a fragmented field populated by numerous mini-theories, each with a narrow range of application, and many self-contained research paradigms that share few assumptions, methods, and tools (e.g., Gergen 1973; Vallacher and Nowak 1994). There is clearly a need in psychology for a comprehensive yet parsimonious theory that can put the field back together. Evolutionary psychology has emerged in recent years as a strong contender for fulfilling this role.

Overview of the Evolutionary Perspective

At the time evolutionary theory was proposed in the mid-nineteenth century, no one was aware that the earth was 4.5 billion years old, there was no understanding of genetics, and few suspected that the ground in certain parts of the world was littered with fossils of extinct species—including species that were transitional between primitive apes and modern humans. For that matter, most people had never seen a monkey. All that has changed, of course, since Darwin's time. Science has made enormous strides in our knowledge of the earth, genetics, the fossil record, and the diversity of species that have lived on this planet. In every instance, these strides have provided confirmatory evidence for evolution by natural selection. Emboldened by the success of evolutionary theory in biology, scientists over the past few decades have applied evolutionary principles to human psychology (e.g., Buss 2005, 2011; Kenrick 2012; Barkow et al. 1992)—and once again, the evidence amassed has provided strong confirmation for this perspective on the nature of human experience.

The central idea of evolutionary psychology is that the human mind evolved many millennia ago under conditions that are dramatically different in many respects from the conditions in which we now live. The world was dangerous, unpredictable, and no doubt quite mysterious for the first modern humans, who first appeared in Southern Africa about 150,000 thousand years ago. There was no medical care, advanced technology, sophisticated weaponry, agricultural systems, governments, laws, emergency warning systems, history books, or anger management courses. The selection pressures were intense, and mortality rates were very high, with few people living into their 30s and even fewer surviving childhood. On top of this, human ancestors were frail compared to other species and thus defenseless as individuals against predators.

Against this backdrop, evolution by natural selection built a suite of adaptations in humans to solve these varied adaptive problems. This does not mean the survival of every individual, however. Indeed, evolution requires uneven mortality, such that only those individuals who display the “right” characteristics have a chance of reaching adulthood, securing a mate, and passing on their genes to their offspring. The differential survival rates of human ancestors effectively eliminated traits that less successfully solved adaptive problems than alternative traits, while selecting for traits that more successfully solved adaptive problems. What were these adaptive or evolved traits? Some general traits were selected for, including big and powerful brains, a strong desire to form social bonds, and attachment to offspring.

But evolutionary psychologists go further than this. They argue that a large number of specific preferences and motives were selected for and these became ingrained as information processing “modules” in the human brain. These mental modules underlie kin selection (preferential helping for close relatives), reciprocal altruism (exchanging help and favors with others), selective sexual preference (attraction to opposite-sex people with specific facial and bodily features signaling reproductive fitness and fertility), pair bonding (monogamous male–female sexual relations), sexual jealousy (expressed differently in males and females), sensitivity to injustice (expressed as revenge), and an astute ability to perceive the intentions of other people (including deceptive intent).

The evolutionary perspective has emerged as a major paradigm in social psychology, in part because it provides insight into behavior patterns that do not seem personally adaptive or socially useful. Extreme risk-taking by adolescent males is unnecessary and certainly dangerous in today’s world, but such behavior may have been adaptive in dealing with the dangers and uncertainties that were facts of life in our ancestral environment. Those males who were more willing to take on difficult and risky challenges may also have had an advantage in establishing their dominance in the group, thereby gaining access to young women for mating opportunities. Revenge, intolerance, prejudice, and hostility toward people with different beliefs and values, and unthinking conformity in group settings all pose problems in the modern world, but these tendencies may represent the lingering legacy of adaptations to different circumstances tens or hundreds of thousands of years ago. Violence certainly fits this bill as well.

The Evolutionary Perspective on Violence

Although violence is a species-wide phenomenon with deep roots in animal behavior (e.g., Campbell 2005; Maynard-Smith and Price 1973; Wrangham et al. 2006), it is not considered an end-state or a goal but rather a readily available means by which higher-order concerns can be redressed or goals can be achieved. Presumably, when other means are made available—particularly if these means incur fewer costs—they can supplant violent behavior as the salient instrumental behavior. In understanding violence, then, the focus is on its functional value in service of basic evolutionary mandates.

Several mandates have been proposed and verified (cf. Liddle et al. in press). Most are self-evident and do not warrant detailed consideration here. These uncontroversial bases for violence include intra-sex battles for dominance and mating opportunities, territory acquisition and protection, protection of offspring, defense against predation, and victory in competition between groups (e.g., Archer 1988; Buss and Shackelford 1997; Campbell 2005; Durrant 2011; Maynard-Smith and Price 1973). Some bases for violence are less obvious, however, and are commonly considered symptoms of pathology rather than the product of adaptations. Domestic violence, for example, is widely (and appropriately) condemned, and those who perpetrate such behavior are deemed criminal, if not pathological.

Even here, however, one can find an evolutionary rationale. The most commonly invoked argument centers on male's uncertainty about paternity and the feelings of proprietary jealousy evoked by this uncertainty (e.g., Buss 1996; Daly et al. 1982). Because ovulation in women is concealed and fertilization occurs internally, men face the adaptive problem of uncertainty of paternity in offspring. If they fail to resolve this uncertainty, men risk investing resources in children to whom they are genetically unrelated. Beyond this risk, cuckoldry can jeopardize a man's mating opportunities in two ways: foregoing other mating opportunities in the present and incurring reputational damage that can hinder mating opportunities in the future (cf. Buss 2000; Daly and Wilson 1994). The jealousy motivated by these concerns motivates men to guard their mates to prevent them from having sex with other men and to prevent them from leaving the relationship. This motivation can promote a range of abusive behaviors (Daly et al. 1982; Malamuth 1996) that are commonly labeled domestic violence and that serve to circumvent women's choices regarding sexual behavior (Buss 1996; Geary et al. 1995; Smuts 1996).

There is considerable archival evidence in support of this rationale (e.g., Buss 1996, 2000; Buss and Malamuth 1996; Buss and Shackelford 1997; Daly and Wilson 1993; Wilson and Daly 1993). Sexual proprietariness is found worldwide (Buss 1996; Daly et al. 1982). In men, it occurs in response to threats (real or imagined) of sexual infidelity or defection by a mate (e.g., Daly and Wilson 1993; Shackelford et al. 2000). The risk of domestic violence is ten times greater for younger, reproductive age women than it is for older, post-reproductive age women (Peters et al. 2002). Experimental evidence in support of the evolutionary account of domestic violence is difficult to obtain for obvious ethical and practical reasons, although laboratory research has confirmed that simply imagining sexual infidelity by one's partner can generate emotional and physiological distress in men (e.g., Buss et al. 1992).

It is important to note that such distress, and the potential for domestic violence it generates, is not motivated in a *proximate* sense by men's concerns over paternity uncertainty and investing in children who do not share their genes. Men simply do not want their mates to have sex with other men. All the birth control in the world would not mitigate this concern. The *distal cause* specified by evolutionary psychology—ensuring the survival of one's genes—may be totally lost in men or even inaccessible to conscious awareness, as it is in other species. The distinction between distal causes that exist outside of awareness and the proximate causes that provide conscious motivation is an important feature of evolutionary psychology.

Evolutionary psychology thus provides a compelling rationale for different manifestations of human violence. Although violence is frowned upon in everyday life and is viewed as a problematic feature of human psychology by social scientists and psychologists, it represents a cross-species and cross-cultural means of achieving basic evolutionary mandates. Because it is a means to an end rather than a goal *per se*, however, violence can admit to considerable variability as a function of culture, history, and demography (e.g., Campbell 2005; Cohen and Nisbett 1994; Keeley 1996; Letendre et al. 2010; Nisbett 1993; Pinker 2011; Shackelford 2005). The evolutionary perspective, in short, qualifies as a highly credible and well-documented theory of human violence.

Commentary on the Evolutionary Perspective

There is much to recommend evolutionary psychology as a foundational science for social thought and behavior. It provides a coherent and parsimonious set of principles with which to integrate the enormous diversity of human behavior. It establishes a bridge between biology and psychology. It develops a clear rationale for domains of behavior that are hard to understand with recourse to traditional models of motivation and that seem dysfunctional if not pathological in today's world. In addition, because it does not rely on people's awareness of their evolved mechanisms, it allows for distal causes of behavior that are inaccessible to introspective access. People feel as though they are acting in accordance with proximate causes that are identifiable, but lack insight into the basic evolutionary adaptations that give rise to these recognizable forces and conscious considerations.

Caution is warranted, though, in viewing violence through only an evolutionary prism. Aggressive behavior is associated with territorial defense, intra-sex competition for mate selection, and the risk of paternity uncertainty, but such behavior is not an inevitable consequence of these factors. Most conflicts over resources and territory are resolved without violent confrontation (e.g., Coleman 2011). In addition, intra-sex competitions for dominance are commonly waged in a nonviolent manner. The same is true for the antagonism that develops between groups. These factors are triggers for spontaneous aggression and physical confrontation in other species, but that is because the motive at issue—resource protection, dominance, mate protection, and so forth—cannot be satisfied in any other manner. Humans, in marked contrast, have a variety of alternative means for satisfying these motives (e.g., wealth acquisition, social status, and lawyers), and need only resort to violence when these channels are unavailable or blocked.

Even when one considers the biological bases for violence, the expression of such behavior is not inevitable under conditions that activate concerns with dominance, mate selection, and the like. Historically, the proclivity for interpersonal aggression and intergroup violence has been a tendency associated largely with males (cf. Daly and Wilson 1994). Across many mammalian species, there is a connection between levels of testosterone and aggressive behavior (Ellis 1986; Monaghan and Glickman 1992). The immediate effect of testosterone, however, is seeking and maintaining dominance—not aggression *per se*. Aggression, of course, is a basic means of establishing dominance in many species. But among humans in today's world, dominance can be established by nonaggressive means—economic success, leadership in business and industry, reputation in science, and so forth. Research on this point has established that the relationship between testosterone and aggression exists primarily for men in lower socioeconomic classes, for whom opportunities for achieving dominance by other means is limited (Dabbs and Morris 1990). The fact that violence has decreased steadily for decades with the rise of urban living, international trade, democracy, and societal laws (e.g., Pinker 2011) is further testament to the non-essential nature of violence. Evolutionary mandates create the precondition for violence, but do not guarantee that it will be expressed.

The Case for Dynamical Social Psychology

The development of the dynamical perspective can be traced in part to the same factors that inspired efforts to develop the evolutionary foundations of intrapersonal, interpersonal, and group-level processes. The range of topics covered by social psychology is enormous, from those that are intrapersonal (e.g., attitudes, self-concept) to those that are interpersonal (e.g., attraction, persuasion) and collective (e.g., ingroup–outgroup relations, social change) in nature. Much has been learned on a topic-by-topic basis, but the resultant theories have unclear points of contact and are tested within specialized paradigms employing very different tools and procedures. A central aim of the dynamical systems approach is to provide the conceptual and paradigmatic integration that is lacking in the field (Vallacher and Nowak 1994). To accomplish this aim, a new set of assumptions, principles, and methods is called for.

Distinctions Between the Dynamical Approach and the Canonical Approach

The dynamical perspective is based on the noncontroversial assumption that every domain of human experience is inherently dynamic. Actions, judgments, emotions, interactions, and relationships all exhibit continual change on various timescales. In part, the dynamic nature of human experience reflects the number and variety of factors that can promote change in the way people think and behave. But people are not blank slates, responding in a simple proportional manner to the forces they experience. Rather than "causing" a one-step response, external factors interact with the internal dynamics of the person or group to trigger a response that unfolds over time. Consider the difference between kicking a soccer ball (an inanimate object) and kicking a dog (an animate object). The ball will move proportionately in response to the kick, but the dog's response will depend on its internal state—its fear, anger, or confusion, for example. Thus, the same cause (kicking) can provoke different responses—running away (fear), biting (anger), or freezing (confusion).

Beyond that, the response to an external force can conform to one of several distinct temporal patterns. A person who is insulted, for example, may initially experience anger or intimidation, but over time his or her response may move in different directions—intensified anger with a corresponding increase in a desire for retaliation, perhaps, or diminished anger with an increasing sense that the insult was warranted. For that matter, the person's response may show a pattern of oscillation between these conflicting emotional states. The traditional approach in social psychology—focusing on a response (the dependent variable) at one point in time after exposure to an external factor (the independent variable)—may produce misleading results and conclusions that overlook the dynamics defining the process in question.

The dynamical perspective takes seriously the fact that external forces rarely operate in isolation but rather interact to promote temporal patterns of thought and behavior. Traditional psychology recognizes the potential for interactions among independent variables, of course, but the playing field is typically reduced to a small number of factors. No psychologist wants to decompose the statistical interaction among more than three independent variables. Clearly, however, the effect of a restricted set of variables can change when other relevant factors are thrown into the mix. A person who is insulted, for example, may display different trajectories of thoughts and feelings depending on a wide range of other relevant factors—the status differential between the "insulter" and the "insultee," the mood of the insultee, the presence of other people, the way in which the insult is delivered, and so on.

Overview of the Dynamical Perspective

The explicit focus on internal dynamics and the complex interplay of factors that influence internal dynamics represents a paradigm shift in the way social processes are understood and investigated. This new approach, however, has deep roots. As noted at the outset, it is informed by the principles, methods, and tools developed in the study of nonlinear dynamical systems in the natural sciences. But it can also be traced to the formative years of social psychology in the early and mid-twentieth century—decades before the focus on nonlinear dynamics and complexity emerged as a dominant paradigm in the natural sciences. Such prominent figures as William James (1890), Charles Horton Cooley (1902), and Kurt Lewin (1936) provided important insights into the dynamic nature of human experience and the complex constellation of internal and external forces that shape people's thoughts and actions over time. It was not until appropriate tools and methods (e.g., time-series analysis, phase space construction, and computer simulations) were developed, however, that social psychology could return to its roots and exploit the insights of the field's founding fathers (Vallacher and Nowak 1997).

Dynamical Principles and Processes

In its most basic sense, a dynamical system is simply a set of interconnected elements that evolve in time, with the elements continually influencing each other to achieve a coordinated state that characterizes the system as a whole. Elements can represent anything from atoms and molecules to animals and planets. The task of dynamical systems theory is to specify how the elements interact with each other over time to promote properties and behavior at a higher level of functioning. In physics and chemistry, a fundamental question is how subatomic particles interact to produce visible matter and forces; in ecology, a central concern is how animals interact to generate and maintain a balance between predator and prey; in cosmology, the focus is how celestial bodies such as planets influence each other to produce stable orbits.

The higher-order property or behavior that results from the mutual influence among elements has emergent properties, which simply means that the higher-level property or behavior cannot be reduced to the properties of the elements (cf. Holland 1995). The stable pattern of planetary orbits in the solar system, for example, depends on the mutual gravitational influences among the planets, not on the properties of the planets in isolation. Because emergence is due to the interactions among elements over time, the process is referred to as *self-organization*. Rather than being imposed on the system from above or from outside the system altogether, the higher-level properties and behaviors emerge from the internal workings of the system itself. The emergence of coherent system-level properties by means of self-organization provides an important link between distinct areas of science. The synchronized flashing of fireflies (Strogatz 2003), for example, is different from the synchronized firing of neurons associated with pattern recognition and consciousness (cf. Hopfield 1982; Tononi and Edelman 1998), but both phenomena represent the tendency for the elements of a system to become coordinated and promote the emergence of coherent system-level properties and behavior.

Once a higher-level state emerges in a dynamical system, it constrains the behavior of the elements that give rise to it. When a stable orbit emerges in a planetary system, for example, new elements (e.g., a passing asteroid) are captured by the orbit and lose their original trajectory. Because a system-level property or behavior "attracts" the behavior of both existing and new elements, it is referred to as an *attractor*.[1] In complex systems—systems composed of many interconnected elements—attractors develop as the elements influence each other to achieve

[1] Three types of attractors have been identified in dynamical systems: fixed-point, periodic (including multi-periodic and quasi-periodic), and deterministic chaos. Because we have found fixed-point attractors to have the greatest relevance for issues of interpersonal and intergroup conflict, they provide the focus of our discussion.

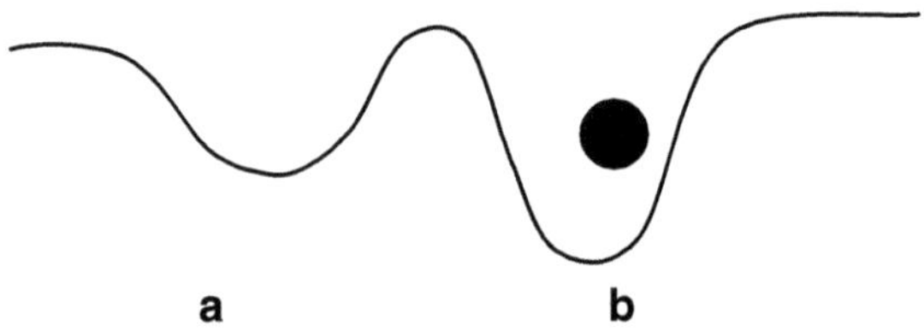

Fig. 10.1 A dynamical system with two attractors, **a** and **b**

a relatively coherent state or pattern of changes that provides coordination for the elements (cf. Haken 1982; Hopfield 1982; Strogatz 2003). An attractor is thus similar to the notion of equilibrium or homeostasis (cf. Cannon 1932; Miller 1944).[2]

A dynamical system may have more than one attractor, each corresponding to a different coherent state. Which attractor governs a system's dynamics in a particular instance depends on the initial states or starting values of the system's evolution. The set of initial states converging on each attractor represents the *basin of attraction* for that attractor. This means that for a person or a group characterized by multiple attractors, the process in question can display different equilibrium tendencies, each associated with a distinct basin of attraction. Within each basin, different initial states will follow a trajectory that eventually converges on the same stable value. However, even a slight change in the system's initial state will promote a large change in the system's trajectory if this change represents a state that falls just outside the original basin of attraction and within a basin for a different attractor.

The attractor concept is captured by a gravity metaphor, depicted in Fig. 10.1. The ball represents the current state of the system and the valleys represent two attractors for the system. The ball will roll down the hill and come to rest at the bottom of the valley, which represents a local energy minimum. The width of each valley represents the basin of attraction. A system with a wide basin "attracts" a broad range of states, including information and events that seem inconsistent with the attractor. A system with a narrow basin "attracts" a smaller range of states and thus is less able to absorb inconsistent ideas and events. In Fig. 10.1, the basin of attraction for Attractor A is somewhat wider than the basin of attraction for Attractor B. This means that a wider variety of states will evolve toward A than toward B.

An attractor can also be characterized in terms of its *strength* or resistance to change. This feature is represented by the depth of each valley in Fig. 10.1. It is difficult to dislodge a system from a strong attractor, even when perturbed by strong external influences, whereas a relatively weak influence can dislodge a system from a weak attractor. In Fig. 10.1, Attractor B is stronger than Attractor A. This means that once a system is at Attractor B, it is more difficult for it to be dislodged by external influence.

In psychological and social systems, an attractor can be described as a restricted range of mental states and actions that is commonly experienced by a person or group. At the individual level, the thoughts and feelings that arise in the stream of

[2] More precisely, a fixed-point attractor corresponds to a stable equilibrium. An unstable equilibrium, referred to as a repellor, represents a state that the system tries to avoid.

thought can influence each other to take on a common meaning and promote the emergence of a coherent higher-order belief or social judgment (Vallacher et al. 1994). Once a global mental state develops, it resists subsequent input that threatens to undermine it. In the context of a positive view of someone, for example, information that the person is "critical" may be interpreted as a virtue ("constructive") rather than a vice ("mean-spirited").

Similar dynamics operate in the emergence and maintenance of norms, attitudes, and fashions in a social system. Individuals, who may differ initially in their personal preferences, influence each other to adopt a shared reality (cf. Kenrick et al. 2003; Nowak et al. 1990). Once a collective state comes to characterize the thought processes of interconnected individuals, there is strong resistance to new information or forces that threaten to undermine it. Thus, discrepant information is discounted or reinterpreted to fit the prevailing view and individuals holding deviant ideas are subject to intense influence from the local majority or are ostracized.

Attractors do not necessarily represent desired states. People with low self-esteem, for example, initially embrace flattering feedback from others, but over time they tend to discount or reinterpret this feedback, displaying a pattern of self-evaluative thought that converges on a negative state (Swann et al. 1990; Vallacher et al. 2002). At an interpersonal level, some people display a persistent pattern of antagonistic behavior in their social relations, despite efforts to avoid behaving in this manner. In an inter-group context, warring factions may display conciliatory gestures when prompted to do so, but then revert to a pattern of antagonistic thought and behavior when the outside interventions are relaxed (Vallacher et al. 2010). When a system's dynamics are governed by an attractor, the system will consistently evolve to a particular state, even if this state is not pleasant, and will return to this state despite experiencing forces that would promote a more pleasant state.

The dynamical systems perspective has shown promise for identifying the common features of topics that are typically investigated separately. Thus, self-organization and the emergence of progressively higher-order states have been demonstrated for self-concept (Nowak et al. 2000), self-evaluation (Vallacher et al. 2002), self-regulation (Vallacher and Nowak 1999), action identification (Vallacher et al. 1998), social judgment (Vallacher et al. 1994), personality development (Nowak et al. 2005), the emergence of public opinion (Nowak et al. 1990), and societal change (Nowak and Vallacher 2001). The system elements are obviously different for each phenomenon (e.g., self-relevant thoughts, individual actors), but the basic principles at work are the same. Both self-concept and the social change, for instance, have been simulated using the same formalism (cellular automata) and the same rules of interaction among the elements in question.

Dynamical Methods

No one would argue with the suggestion that human social experience is complex and dynamic, nor would most observers deny the potential relevance and utility of nonlinear dynamical systems to personal and interpersonal phenomena. What is less clear to many researchers, though, is how to implement this approach in their own research agendas. Many of the methods and tools developed to investigate the dynamic properties of complex systems are foreign to social psychologists, and it is not self-evident that learning to adapt such tools will have added value in theory construction or real-world application.

This concern has abated in recent years with the advent of several research programs employing dynamical concepts and methods. Some have used experimental methods to track the temporal trajectories of basic processes, including social interaction (e.g., Beek and Hopkins 1992; Buder 1991; Newtson 1994), personality expression (e.g., Brown and Moskowitz 1998; Mischel and Shoda 1995), mood (e.g., Schuldberg and Gottlieb 2002), self-evaluation (e.g., Vallacher et al. 2002), attitude change (Kaplowitz and Fink 1992; Latané and Nowak 1994), group dynamics (e.g., Arrow 1997; Losada 1999), close relationships (e.g., Gottman et al. 2002), and social judgment (e.g., Vallacher et al. 1994). In a few research programs, experimental methods have been supplemented by analytical tools designed to identify the formal properties of the observed dynamics. Newtson (1994) has shown that the periodic flow of social interaction has a fractal (i.e., self-similar) structure, for example, and Vallacher et al. (1994) have shown that the moment-to-moment dynamics of social judgment reflect the operation of a low-dimensional cognitive–affective system.

For the most part, however, computer simulation is the tool of choice in investigating intrapersonal, interpersonal, and societal dynamics. The most frequently employed simulation platforms in this work are cellular automata and neural networks (cf. Liebrand et al. 1998; Nowak and Vallacher 1998; Read et al. 1997). These approaches have proven especially useful in modeling the emergence of global properties in a system from the interactions of the lower-level elements comprising the system in question.

With respect to intrapersonal processes, elements correspond to components of the cognitive system, such as specific thoughts and pieces of information, and the emergent global properties refer to decisions, judgments, and self-concepts. The press for coherence in social judgment (e.g., dissonance reduction, impression formation, stereotype formation, and change), for example, has been analyzed as constraint satisfaction processes within a connectionist or neural network framework (e.g., Kunda and Thagard 1996; Read et al. 1997; Shultz and Lepper 1996; Smith 1996). The emergenceof global properties of self-concept (e.g., self-esteem, self-concept clarity) from the self-organization of specific elements of self-relevant information, meanwhile, has been modeled within a cellular automata framework (Nowak et al. 2000).

Computer simulations are widely employed to model the emergence of global properties in social systems. In this approach, the elements correspond to individuals and the system-level properties refer to various group-level phenomena that emerge through social interactions among the individuals. This approach has proven successful in modeling the emergence of public opinion (Nowak et al. 1990), the development of social networks (Nowak et al. 1998), the emergence of cooperation in social dilemma situations (e.g., Messick and Liebrand 1995), and the conditions that promote incremental versus nonlinear (sudden, catastrophic) economic and political transitions in society (Nowak and Vallacher 2001).

Computer simulations have two noteworthy advantages in investigating the dynamics of intrapersonal, interpersonal, and societal processes. This approach, first of all, enables one to investigate the relationship between micro- and macro-levels of social reality. The investigator equips individual elements in the system with rules of behavior and observes how these rules give rise to global properties for the set of elements as a whole. For example, very simple rules of social interaction (e.g., adopt the point of view held by the majority of one's neighbors) can promote the emergence of shared norms and attitudes in a group. In a reversal of this procedure, the investigator starts with knowledge of the system's global properties (e.g., the distribution of public opinion in a society) and reverse engineers the system to discover what rules on the level of individual elements are necessary to produce the system-level phenomena.

The second advantage of computer simulations is their capacity to reveal the temporal patterns associated with the emergence of global properties in a system. For many intrapersonal, interpersonal, and societal processes, the effects of a given cause are unlikely to be revealed immediately. An insult may produce hate, for example, but this feeling develops on a relatively long timescale and may not be immediately apparent. Love at first sight, meanwhile, may be a popular theme in literature and movies, but in reality many interactions and prolonged contact may be necessary for a romantic attraction to develop. The computer simulation approach is ideal for investigating the effects of multiple iterations of a given process. Thousands of interactions and decades of real time can be compressed into seconds of computer time, revealing delayed consequences that simply cannot be observed in real time.

The use of computers is not an alternative to experimental research. Indeed, these approaches have been used in a complementary fashion, providing cross-validation for one another in theory construction and testing. Through computer visualization, first of all, an investigator can discover patterns that are predicted by theory, generated in experiments, or exist in reality (e.g., archival or historical data). The investigator can literally see the emergence of temporal and spatial patterns in a social psychological process, whether the polarization and clustering of public opinion through social influence (Nowak et al. 1990) or the progressive differentiation of self-concept through social feedback on one's qualities (Nowak et al. 2000).

Perhaps more importantly, comparing the patterns and outcomes identified in experimental data with the patterns and outcomes produced by computer simulation provides a new means of verifying a theory. The results of experimental research can be implemented in a computer program to assess the feasibility and long-term consequences of the process being investigated. The results of a computer simulation, in turn, may suggest a new set of causal factors that can then be investigated in subsequent experimental work. With repeated iterations of the reciprocal feedback between simulation and experiment, the investigator is able to gain greater clarity and precision in theoretical understanding.

The Dynamical Perspective on Violence

To date, theory and research informed by the dynamical perspective have not focused specifically on the issue of human violence. Dynamical models have been developed, however, for destructive social conflicts that have become protracted and seemingly impossible to resolve (e.g., Bartoli et al. 2010; Liebovitch et al. 2008; Liebovitch et al. 2010; Nowak et al. 2010; Vallacher et al. 2010). These *intractable conflicts* hold tremendous potential for triggering violent behavior between individuals, groups, and nations. Our discussion of the relevance of dynamical systems to violence, then, is limited to this particular source and expression of violent social behavior.

Traditional theories of motivation are hard pressed to explain the persistence of destructive conflict. Beyond being intrinsically unpleasant and generating negative emotion, protracted conflicts destroy lives, tear apart families and communities, and divert attention and energy from more productive pursuits. In addition, the goals maintaining such conflicts are rarely achieved, particularly for conflicts that persist through many generations with no end in sight. Hedonism, enlightened self-interest, achievement motivation, and other traditional motives fall short in accounting for this aspect of human social behavior. Even if reasonable motives could be identified (e.g., ingroup solidarity afforded by outgroup antagonism), they could be satisfied by other means without experiencing the costs and adverse consequences of intractable conflict.

There are many well-documented proximate causes of intractable conflict, including competition over scarce resources, territorial disputes, past humiliation, perceived injustice, and ideological disputes (cf. Deutsch et al. 2006). In the dynamical account, these factors mask a more fundamental tendency expressed in nature—the progressive integration of basic elements of a system into a higher-order state that lends stability and coherence to the system. Once a coherent state has emerged, it becomes self-sustaining and thus can trump the usual taxonomy of human motives (e.g., hedonism, self-esteem, achievement, long-term self-interest). The self-organizing nature of intractable conflict, moreover, provides a framework within which proximate causes and local triggers can be understood and investigated.

In the dynamical account, a protracted destructive conflict is conceptualized as a strong attractor that maintains a negative, but coherent cognitive, affective, and behavioral orientation among the parties to the conflict. When destructive conflict is associated with a deep attractor, an attempt to address the current state of the conflict corresponds to pushing the ball uphill in Fig. 10.1. Even with considerable effort, this attempt is likely to be futile. Once the pushing force is relaxed, the ball will roll back to the attractor. In international conflict, this futility is exemplified by peace agreements that eventually collapse after the fanfare of the initial breakthroughs subsides.

If the attractor for destructive conflict has a wide basin of attraction, a broad range of ideas and action possibilities will eventually evolve toward the dominant mental and behavioral pattern characterizing the parties to the conflict. Even positive information that contradicts the negative view of members of an outgroup is transformed by a variety of cognitive and social mechanisms until it fits the predominant view. A peaceful overture, for example, might initially be taken at face value but over time it will become reframed until it provides evidence in support of, rather than in opposition to, the predominant response tendency of the person or group. Instead of being seen as good faith effort to resolve conflict and reduce hostilities, the overture might be seen as a deceptive move designed to lull one's group into a false sense of security.

As noted earlier, a system may have two (or more) attractors, each promoting a different pattern of dynamics. In conflict scenarios, these alternative modes of thought and action correspond to negativity and aggression versus neutrality (or positivity) and benign relations (or conciliation). Hence, minimal differences in the circumstances associated with the conflict can promote dramatically different behaviors, with no response that can integrate the two tendencies (Vallacher et al. 2010). A seemingly trivial event (e.g., a negative comment by an outgroup member), for example, can transform a peaceful relationship into a contentious one with outbursts of violence. But by the same token, an unremarkable positive event (e.g., an apology for a disparaging comment) can reposition the parties to a conflict within the basin of an attractor for positive relations. Knowing the attractors associated with a social relationship, and identifying the basins of attraction associated with each, is critical for understanding the effect that various events are likely to have on the nature of a social relationship.

When the system is in the basin of one attractor, the parties to the conflict may be oblivious to the existence of the other attractor. But these *latent attractors* may play a critical role in the transformation of social relations from destructive and violent to benign and peaceful—or vice versa—because they identify which states are possible when conditions change. Peaceful overtures, for example, may do little to dampen intergroup hostility, but they may strengthen a latent attractor for conciliation. The new mode of interaction may remain latent for an extended period of time, but suddenly become manifest in response to an external influence or event that functions as a tipping point. So even if an intervention does not have an immediate impact on the relationship between warring parties, it may have the longer-term effect of creating or deepening a latent positive attractor for the system. Of course, the opposite scenario can be envisioned—a benign relationship can show a sudden and catastrophic transition to a relationship characterized by mistrust, animosity, and violence.

Commentary on the Dynamical Perspective

The driving force in dynamical systems is achieving and maintaining coherence and coordination among interconnected elements. Even if the coherent state that emerges by means of self-organization runs counter to the self-interest of a person or group, external forces that threaten to undermine that state will be actively resisted. People with a coherent but negative view of themselves resist positive feedback, for example, and groups embroiled in a never-ending destructive conflict resist efforts to terminate the conflict and bring about peace. In addition, once a coherent state has emerged, it exists autonomously and no longer needs support from the factors that were initially responsible for it. The issues that launched a protracted social conflict, for example, can be resolved without changing the antagonistic feelings or potential for violence among the parties involved (Vallacher et al. 2010). Knowledge of a system's attractor dynamics is more important than knowledge of the specific issues and events that sparked the conflict.

The higher-order coherent state that emerges from the self-organization of lower-level system components may not always be experienced as pleasant or desirable, but it is often adaptive. A person with well-integrated sense of self can act more decisively and feel more certain about his or her social standing than can someone whose self-relevant thoughts contradict one another. Likewise, a coordinated social group can engage in collective tasks and maintain a shared reality more effectively than a group whose members cannot synchronize their mental states and actions. In this sense, the press for coherence in dynamical systems is consistent with the central role of adaptation in evolutionary psychology.

But coherence can also prove to be highly maladaptive. The potential for violence in a relationship where the dynamics are governed by a strong negative attractor is a case in point. Neither party to the conflict is acting in its best self-interest and the antagonism characterizing the relationship is hardly conducive to joint endeavors, let alone peaceful coexistence. Adaptation, moreover, requires flexibility in order to accommodate changing circumstances, but in a system with strong attractors such changes are reacted to as if they were threats. Instead of profiting from new information and events, individuals and groups whose dynamics are governed by a strong attractor are likely to demonstrate defensiveness and rigidity.

Because nonlinear dynamical systems are investigated with respect to formal models that are not tied to specific content or a particular level of social reality, they hold potential for identifying the invariant processes characterizing very different social phenomena. This virtue, however, could also be viewed as a weakness. In particular, the minimalist nature of the dynamical approach leaves it open to the "blank slate" critique (e.g., Pinker 2002). Assuming only that human minds and groups develop mental and behavioral repertoires on the basis of content-free dynamical principles may not be sufficient to predict the specific ways in which people across time and culture think and behave. Knowing the demands faced by our ancestors throughout the course of human history, and recognizing the extent to which psychological processes are encoded in the human genome, provides the needed specificity that is lacking in dynamical accounts.

This critique is not entirely warranted, however. In true blank-slate theories, virtually any type of mental or behavioral process can be envisioned. With nothing more than a general learning mechanism at work, people could go through life without a set of coherent values or they could consistently fail to suspend their personal interests when interacting with others. The dynamical perspective does not allow for such idiosyncrasy. No matter how an individual is reinforced (as long as the training does not produce pathology), he or she is destined to integrate specific thoughts and feelings into higher-order states that reflect broad attitudes, beliefs, and values. Nor can an individual easily escape self-organization dynamics in his or her interactions with other individuals, and thus avoid achieving some level of coordination with respect to others' mental and behavioral states.

Evolutionary Dynamics: The Promise of Higher-Order Integration

Evolutionary psychology and the dynamical perspective have merits in common that qualify each as a potential foundational science for human psychology. They both provide a unified and parsimonious set of principles that can accommodate the enormous complexity and diversity of human experience, and they both can account for features of human experience that cannot be explained with the usual motives offered in canonical psychology, such as hedonism, self-interest, competence, and personal survival. Furthermore, both perspectives recognize the limited role of consciousness in human affairs. People act consciously on the basis of proximate considerations while often totally out of touch with distal causes and dynamical forces that operate outside of consciousness.

The evolutionary and dynamical systems account may turn out to be complementary, with each providing an important piece of the puzzle. The topic of human violence may provide a vehicle for establishing this complementarity. The dynamical account captures the intractability of human conflicts characterized by violence, as well as the potential for catastrophic change between violence and benign relations in such conflicts. For its part, the evolutionary account provides the constraints within which these dynamic processes are likely to be observed. After all, violence does not erupt without reason. Evolutionary psychology spells out the distal causes (e.g., limited resources, competition for dominance, interpersonal and intergroup rivalry, paternity uncertainty) that set the stage for violent interactions between individuals and groups. Once the stage is set, scenarios of violence can unfold in accordance with dynamical processes.

Some principles associated with dynamical systems have a natural fit with evolutionary mechanisms. Self-organization and the emergence of coordination, for example, is a defining principle of complex systems throughout nature. In human systems, self-organization can be observed at all levels of psychological and social reality, from the formation of neural networks in the brain to the emergence of social networks in society (Vallacher and Nowak 2007). Coordination may play a fundamental role in evolutionary psychology as well. Some models, for example, suggest that the proclivity for social coordination is critical for group survival and thus a prime target for natural selection (e.g., Caporael 1997). This idea is consistent with the contemporary (albeit controversial) emphasis on group selection (e.g., indirect reciprocity, multi-level selection), which holds that the selection pressure for cooperation and altruism goes beyond kin selection and inclusive fitness (Hamilton

1964) to include cooperation with genetically unrelated members of an individual's group (e.g., Nowak and Highfield 2011; Wilson 2011).

Recent years have witnessed attempts to test evolutionary hypotheses using platforms developed in the study of nonlinear dynamical systems. Most notably, cellular automata—computer programs that are essentially programmable dynamical systems (cf. Nowak and Vallacher 1998; Wolfram 2002)—have been employed to model the evolution of life generally, and of diversity in particular (cf. Sigmund 1993). Kenrick and his colleagues, for example, have used this approach to simulate the emergence of different behavior patterns in a population composed of individuals who differ in their preferences for such patterns (e.g., Kenrick 2001; Kenrick et al. 2002; Kenrick et al. 2003). Key evolutionary mandates have been investigated in this manner, including self-protection, coalition formation, status seeking, mate choice, relationship maintenance, and care of offspring. In a sense, the use of cellular automata to model these domains is tantamount to modeling the evolution of culture.

Consider mating strategies, for example. People vary in their preference for restricted and unrestricted mating strategies, with males typically showing a stronger preference for the latter. As in the cellular automata models of public opinion and social change (Nowak et al. 1990; Nowak and Vallacher 2001), individuals compare their personal preference with those of their neighbors (i.e., the nearest and most frequent interaction partners) and adopt the strategy that is preferred by the majority in this local neighborhood. Thus, each individual will either maintain his or her initial preference (if surrounded by like-minded neighbors) or change his or her preference to match that of the local majority (if it represents the opposite preference). This simple rule is iterated for successive rounds of interaction until a more-or-less stable preference structure is achieved at the population level. The resultant structure looks very much like the structure observed in the Nowak et al. public opinion and social change simulations. A slight initial preference for one mating strategy becomes stronger over time (polarized), but the minority preference survives in local clusters of like-minded people.

There are no doubt other ways in which evolutionary and dynamical psychology can benefit one another and promote a synthesis that is more integrative than either perspective alone. Consider, for example, the tendency of self-organization dynamics to promote two very different coherent states to which the system can converge over time. This bi-stability can make it difficult to predict how the people will respond to new information or external forces. Suspected infidelity, for example, is a well-documented risk factor for jealousy, mate guarding, and even violence (e.g., Buss 1996; Daly et al. 1982). But the same "cause" could also promote a far different response—a heart-to-heart discussion, perhaps, or an increase in the frequency of displays of affection. The emergence of bi-stability in physical systems is fairly well understood (e.g., Ruelle 1989), but such insight has yet to be established for many social phenomena (Nowak and Vallacher 1998). Nor have the factors been identified that determine which attractor in a bi-stable social system is likely to become manifest. Identifying the factors that promote bi-stability in various types of social relations and that determine which coherent state will function as the manifest attractor would enhance the predictive value of evolutionary models of human behavior. Such a research agenda would seem to hold considerable promise.

Looking Ahead

Clearly, both evolutionary psychology and dynamical systems theory have integrative and heuristic value for identifying the basic principles underlying seemingly diverse domains of social experience. A higher-order perspective that combines their respective insights might prove especially enlightening about human nature. To date, however, few integrations of this form have been attempted, and none with respect to issues centering on violence. This promissory note is well worth fulfilling. In a broader sense, evolutionary psychology and dynamical social psychology can be viewed as basic elements in a system of conceptual understanding. Under the right selection pressures, the interaction between these two ways of framing human psychology may well promote the emergence of a new synthesis. This synthesis, modified to incorporate succeeding generations of research, could prove adaptive in the ongoing struggle for insight into the human condition.

References

Archer, J. (1988). *The behavioural biology of aggression*. Cambridge: Cambridge University Press.

Arrow, H. (1997). Stability, bistability, and instability in small group influence patterns. *Journal of Personality and Social Psychology*, *72*, 75–85.

Barkow, J. H., Cosmides, L., & Tooby, J. (Eds.). (1992). *The adapted mind*. New York: Oxford University Press.

Bartoli, A., Bui-Wrzosinska, L., & Nowak, A. (2010). Peace is in movement: A dynamical systems perspective on the emergence of peace in Mozambique. *Peace and Conflict: Journal of Peace Psychology*, *16*, 211–230.

Beek, P. J. & Hopkins, B. (1992). Four requirements for a dynamical systems approach to the development of social coordination. *Human Movement Science*, *11*, 425–442.

Brown, K. W. & Moskowitz, D. S. (1998). Dynamic stability of behavior: The rhythms of our interpersonal lives. *Journal of Personality*, *66*(1), 105–134.

Buder, E. H. (1991). A nonlinear dynamic model of social interaction. *Communication Research*, *18*, 174–198.

Buss, D. M. (1996). Sexual conflict: Evolutionary insights into feminism and the "battle of the sexes." In D. M. Buss & N. M. Malamuth (Eds.), *Sex, power, conflict* (pp. 296–318). New York: Oxford University Press.

Buss, D. M. (2000). *The dangerous passion*. New York: Free Press.

Buss, D. M. (2011). *Evolutionary psychology: The new science of the mind* (4th ed.). Boston: Pearson.Buss, D. M., & Malamuth, N. M. (1996). *Sex, power, conflict*. New York: Oxford University Press.

Buss, D. M., & Shackelford, T. K. (1997). From vigilance to violence: Mate retention tactics in married couples. *Journal of Personality and Social Psychology*, *72*, 346–361.

Buss, D. M., & Shackelford, T. K. (1997). Human aggression in evolutionary psychological perspective. *Clinical Psychology Review, 17*, 605–619.

Buss, D. M., Larsen, R. J., Westen, D., & Semmelroth, J. (1992). Sex differences in jealousy: Evolution, physiology, and psychology. *Psychological Science, 3*, 251–255.

Campbell, A. (2005). Aggression. In D. M. Buss (Ed.), *The handbook of evolutionary psychology* (pp. 628–652). Hoboken, NJ: Wiley.

Cannon, W. B. (1932). *The wisdom of the body*. New York: Norton.

Caporael, L. R. (1997). The evolution of truly social cognition: The core configurations model. *Personality and Social Psychology Review, 1*, 276–298.

Cohen, D., & Nisbett, R.E. (1994). Self protection and the culture of honor: Explaining southern homicide. *Personality and Social Psychology Bulletin, 20*, 551–567.

Coleman, P. T. (2011). *The five percent: Finding solutions to (seemingly) impossible conflicts.* New York: Public Affairs, Perseus Books.

Cooley, C. H. (1902). *Human nature and the social order*. New York: Scribner.

Dabs, J. M., Jr., & Morris, R. (1990). Testosterone, social class, and antisocial behavior in a sample of 4462 men. *Psychological Science, 1*, 209–211.

Dahlberg, L. L., & Krug, E. G. (2002). Violence—a global public health problem. In E. G. Krug, L. L. Dahlberg, J. A. Mercy, A. B. Zwi, & R. Lozano (Eds.), *World report on violence and health.* Geneva: World Health Organization.

Daly, M., & Wilson, M. (1993). An evolutionary psychological perspective on male sexual proprietariness and violence against wives. *Violence and Victims, 8*, 271–294.

Daly, M., & Wilson, M. (1994). Evolutionary psychology of male violence. In J. Archer (Ed.), *Male violence* (pp. 253–288). New York: Routledge.

Daly, M., Wilson, M., & Weghorst, S. J. (1982). Male sexual jealousy. *Ethology and Sociobiology, 3*, 11–27.

Deutsch, M., Coleman, P. T., & Marcus, E. (Eds.) (2006). *The handbook of conflict resolution: Theory and practice* (2nd ed.). San Francisco: Jossey Bass.

Durrant, R. (2011). Collective violence: An evolutionary perspective. *Aggression and Violent Behavior, 16*, 428–436.

Eckmann, J. P., & Ruelle, D. (1985). Ergodic theory of chaos and strange attractors. *Review of Modern Physics, 57*, 617–656.

Ellis, L. (1986). Evidence of neuroandrogenic etiology of sex roles form a combined analysis of human, non-human primate and nonprimate mammalian studies. *Personality and Individual Differences, 7*, 519–552.

Geary, D. C., Rumsey, M., Bow-Thomas, C. C., & Hoard, M. K. (1995). Sexual jealousy as a facultative trait: Evidence from the pattern of sex difference in adults from China and the United States. *Ethology and Sociobiology, 16*, 355–383.

Gergen, K. J. (1973). Social psychology as history. *Journal of Personality and Social Psychology, 26*, 309–320.

Gottman, J., Swanson, C., & Swanson, K. (2002). A general systems theory of marriage: Nonlinear difference equation modeling of marital interaction. *Personality and Social Psychology Review, 6*, 326–340.

Guastello, S., Koopmans, M., & Pincus, D. (Eds.) (2009). *Chaos and Complexity in Psychology: The Theory of Nonlinear Dynamical Systems*. New York: Cambridge University Press.

Haken, H. (Ed.) (1982). *Order and chaos in physics, chemistry, and biology*. Berlin: Springer.

Hamilton, W. D. (1964). The genetical evolution of social behaviour, I, II. *Journal of Theoretical Biology, 7*, 1–52.

Holland, J. H. (1995). *Emergence: From chaos to order*. Reading, MA: Addison-Wesley.

Hopfield, J. J. (1982). Neural networks and physical systems with emergent collective properties. *Proceedings of the National Academy of Sciences, USA, 81*, 3088–3092.

James, W. (1890). *Principles of psychology*. New York: Holt.

Kaplowitz, S. A., & Fink, E. L. (1992). Dynamics of attitude change. In R. L. Levine & H. E. Fitzgerald (Eds.), *Analysis of dynamic psychological systems* (Vol. 2, pp. 341–369). New York: Plenum.

Keeley, L.H. (1996). *War before civilization: The myth of the peaceful savage*. New York: Oxford University Press.
Kenrick, D. T. (2001). Evolutionary psychology, cognitive science, and dynamical systems: Building an integrative paradigm. *Current Directions in Psychological Science, 10*, 13–17.
Kenrick, D. T. (2012). Evolutionary theory and human social behavior. In P. A. M. Van Lange, A. W. Kruglanski, & E. T. Higgins (Eds.), *Handbook of theories of social psychology* (pp. 11–31). London: Sage.
Kenrick, D. T., Li, N. P., & Butner, J. (2003). Dynamical evolutionary psychology: Individual decision rules and emergent social norms. *Psychological Review, 110*, 3–28.
Kenrick, D. T., Maner, J. K., Butner, J., Li, N. P., & Becker, D. V. (2002). Dynamical evolutionary psychology: Mapping the domains of the new interactionist paradigm. *Personality and Social Psychology Review, 6*, 347–356.
Kunda, Z., & Thagard, P. (1996). Forming impressions from stereotypes, traits, and behaviors: A parallel-constraint-satisfaction theory. *Psychological Review, 103*, 284–308.
Latané, B., & Nowak, A. (1994). Attitudes as catastrophes: From dimensions to categories with increasing involvement. In R. R. Vallacher & A. Nowak (Eds.), *Dynamical systems in social psychology* (pp. 219–249). San Diego: Academic Press.
Letendre, K., Fincher, C. L., & Thornhill, R. (2010). Does infectious disease cause global variation in the frequency of intrastate armed conflict and civil war? *Biological Reviews, 85*, 669–683.
Lewin, K. (1936). *Principles of topological psychology*. New York: McGraw-Hill.
Liddle, J. R., Shackelford, T. K., & Weekes-Shackelford, V. A. (in press). Why can't we all just get along? Evolutionary perspectives on violence, homicide, and war. *Review of General Psychology*, 16(1), 24–36
Liebovitch, L. S., Naudot, V., Vallacher, R., Nowak A, Bui-Wrzosinska, L., & Coleman, P. T. (2008). Dynamics of two-actor cooperation–competition conflict models. *Physica A, 387*, 6360–6378.
Liebovitch, L. S., Vallacher, R., & Michaels, J. (2010). Dynamics of cooperation-competition interaction model. *Peace and Conflict: The Journal of Peace Psychology, 16*, 175–188.
Liebrand, W. B. G., Nowak, A., & Hegselman, R. (Eds.) (1998). *Computer modeling of social processes*. London: Sage.Losada, M. (1999). The complex dynamics of high performance teams. *Mathematical and Computer Modelling, 30*, 179–192.
Malamuth, N. M. (1996). The confluence model of sexual aggression: Feminist and evolutionary perspectives. In D. M. Buss & N. M. Malamuth (Eds.), *Sex, power, conflict* (pp. 269–295). New York: Oxford University Press.
Maynard-Smith, J., & Price, G. R. (1973). The logic of animal conflict. *Nature, 246*, 15–18.
Messick, D. M., & Liebrand, V. B. G. (1995). Individual heuristics and the dynamics of cooperation in large groups. *Psychological Review, 102*, 131–145.
Miller, N. E. (1944). Experimental studies of conflict. In J. M. Hunt (Ed.), *Personality and the behavior disorders* (pp. 431–465). New York: Ronald.
Mischel, W., & Shoda, Y. (1995). A cognitive-affective system theory of personality: Reconceptualizing situations, dispositions, dynamics, and invariance in personality structure. *Psychological Review, 102*, 246–268.
Monaghan, E., & Glickman, S. (1992). Hormones and aggressiveness behavior. In J. Becker, S. Breedlove, & D. Crews (Eds.), *Behavioral endocrinology* (pp. 261–285). Cambridge, MA: MIT Press.
Newtson, D. (1994). The perception and coupling of behavior waves. In R. R. Vallacher & A. Nowak (Eds.), *Dynamical systems in social psychology* (pp. 139–167). San Diego: Academic Press.
Nisbett, R.E. (1993). Violence and U.S. regional culture. *American Psychologist, 48*, 441–449.
Nowak, A., Szamrej, J., & Latané, B. (1990). From private attitude to public opinion: A dynamic theory of social impact. *Psychological Review, 97*, 362–376.
Nowak, A., & Vallacher, R. R. (1998). *Dynamical social psychology*. New York: Guilford.

Nowak, A., Vallacher, R. R., & Burnstein, E. (1998). Computational social psychology: A neural network approach to interpersonal dynamics. In W. Liebrand, A. Nowak, & R. Hegselman (Eds.), *Computer modeling and the study of dynamic social processes*. New York: Sage.
Nowak, A., Vallacher, R. R., Tesser, A., & Borkowski, W. (2000). Society of self: The emergence of collective properties in self-structure. *Psychological Review, 107*, 39–61.
Nowak, A., & Vallacher, R. R. (2001). Societal transition: Toward a dynamical model of social change. In W. Wosinska, R. B. Cialdini, D. W. Barrett, & J. Reykowski (Eds.), *The practice of social influence in multiple cultures* (pp. 151–171). Mahwah, NJ: Lawrence Erlbaum.
Nowak, A., Vallacher, R. R., & Zochowski, M. (2005). The emergence of personality: Dynamic foundations of individual variation. *Developmental Review, 25*, 351–385.
Nowak, A., Deutsch, M., Bartkowski, W., & Solomon, S. (2010). From crude law to civil relations: The dynamics and potential resolution of intractable conflict. *Peace and Conflict: Journal of Peace Psychology, 16*, 189–209.
Nowak, M. A., & Highfield R. (2011). *SuperCooperators: Altruism, evolution, and why we need each other to succeed.* New York: Free Press.
Peters, J., Shackelford, T. K., & Buss, D. M. (2002). Understanding domestic violence against women: Using evolutionary psychology to extend the feminist functional analysis. *Violence and Victims, 17*, 255–264.
Pinker, S. (2002). *The blank slate: The modern denial of human nature*. New York: Viking.
Pinker, S. (2011). *The better angels of our nature: Why violence has declined.* New York: Penguin.
Read, S. J., Vanman, E. J., & Miller, L. C. (1997). Connectionism, parallel constraint satisfaction processes, and Gestalt principles: (Re)Introducing cognitive dynamics to social psychology. *Personality and Social Psychology Review, 1*, 26–53.
Ruelle, D. (1989). *Elements of differentiable dynamics and bifurcation theory*. New York: Academic Press.
Schuldberg, D., & Gottlieb, J. (2002). Dynamics and correlates of microscopic changes in affect. *Nonlinear Dynamics, Psychology, and the Life Sciences, 6*, 231–257.
Shackelford, T. K. (2005). An evolutionary psychological perspective on cultures of honor. *Evolutionary Psychology, 3*, 381–391.
Shultz, T. R., & Lepper, M. R. (1996). Cognitive dissonance reduction as constraint satisfaction. *Psychological Review, 103*, 219–240.
Sigmund, K. (1993). *Games of life: Explorations in ecology, evolution, and behaviour*. New York: Oxford University Press.
Smith, E. R. (1996). What do connectionism and social psychology offer each other? *Journal of Personality and Social Psychology, 70*, 893–912.
Smuts, B. (1996). Male aggression against women: An evolutionary perspective. In D. M. Buss & N. M. Malamuth (Eds.), *Sex, power, conflict* (pp. 231–268). New York: Oxford University Press.
Strogatz, S. (1994). *Nonlinear Dynamics and Chaos*. Cambridge, MA: Perseus Books Group.
Strogatz, S. (2003). *Sync: The emerging science of spontaneous order*. New York: Hyperion Books.
Swann, W. B., Jr., Hixon, J. G., Stein-Seroussi, A., & Gilbert, D. (1990). The fleeting gleam of praise: Cognitive processes underlying behavioral reactions to self-relevant feedback. *Journal of Personality and Social Psychology, 59*, 17–26.
Thompson, J. M. T., & Stewart, H. B. (1986). *Nonlinear dynamics and chaos*. New York: Wiley.
Tononi, G., & Edelman, G. M. (1998). Consciousness and complexity. *Science, 282*, 1846–1851.
Vallacher, R. R., & Nowak, A. (1994). The chaos in social psychology. In R. R. Vallacher & A. Nowak (Eds.), *Dynamical systems in social psychology* (pp. 1–16). San Diego: Academic Press.
Vallacher, R. R., & Nowak, A. (1997). The emergence of dynamical social psychology. *Psychological Inquiry, 8*, 73–99.
Vallacher, R. R., & Nowak, A. (1999). The dynamics of self-regulation. In R. S. Wyer (Ed.), *Advances in social cognition* (Vol. 12, pp. 241–259). Mahwah, NJ: Erlbaum.
Vallacher, R. R., & Nowak, A. (2007). Dynamical social psychology: Finding order in the flow of human experience. In A. W. Kruglanski & E. T. Higgins (Eds.), *Social psychology: Handbook of basic principles* (2nd ed., pp. 734–758). New York: Guilford Publications.

Vallacher, R. R., Nowak, A., & Kaufman, J. (1994). Intrinsic dynamics of social judgment. *Journal of Personality and Social Psychology, 67*, 20–34.
Vallacher, R. R., Nowak, A., Markus, J., & Strauss, J. (1998). Dynamics in the coordination of mind and action. In M. Kofta, G. Weary, & G. Sedlek (Eds.), *Personal control in action: Cognitive and motivational mechanisms* (pp. 27–59). New York: Plenum.
Vallacher, R. R., Nowak, A., Froehlich, M., & Rockloff, M. (2002). The dynamics of self-evaluation. *Personality and Social Psychology Review, 6*, 370–379.
Vallacher, R. R., Read, S. J., & Nowak, A. (Eds.) (2002). The dynamical perspective in social psychology. *Personality and Social Psychology Review, 6*, 264–388.
Vallacher, R. R., Coleman, P. T., Nowak, A., & Bui-Wrzosinska, L. (2010). Rethinking intractable conflict: The perspective of dynamical systems. *American Psychologist, 64*, 262–278.
Waldrop, M. M. (1992). *Complexity: The emerging science at the edge of order and chaos*. New York: Schuster.
Weisbuch, G. (1992). *Complex systems dynamics*. Redwood City, CA: Addison-Wesley.
Wilson, E. O. (2011). *The social conquest of earth*. New York: Liveright Publishing Corporation.
Wilson, M., & Daly, M. (1985). Competitiveness, risk-taking and violence: The young male syndrome. *Ethology and Sociobiology, 6*, 59–73.
Wilson, M., & Daly, M. (1993). An evolutionary psychological perspective on male sexual proprietariness and violence against wives. *Violence and Victims, 8*, 271–294.
Wilson, M., Johnson, H., & Daly, M. (1995). Lethal and nonlethal violence against wives. *Canadian Journal of Criminology, 37*, 331–361.
Wolfram, S. (2002). *A new kind of science*. Champaign, IL: Wolfram Media, Inc.
Wrangham, R.W., Wilson, M.L., & Muller, M.N. (2006). Comparative rates of violence in chimpanzees and humans. *Primates, 47*, 14–26.

Chapter 11
Violence and Aggression in Women

Catharine P. Cross and Anne C. Campbell

That women, as a sex, are less aggressive than men is relatively uncontroversial. Until evolutionary theory was incorporated into psychologists' thinking, the widely accepted reason for this was evident and wrong: While we reward little boys for conforming to male adult stereotypes incorporating aggression, agency, and dominance, we reward little girls for conforming to female adult stereotypes of care, empathy, and compromise. This answer, however, simply pushes the explanatory problem back one step to asking why such stereotypes exist. Sex differences in aggression cross cultural boundaries and transcend historical periods. Moreover, as evolutionary biologists have noted, they are not confined to humans.

This led evolutionary psychologists to argue that the correlation between gender stereotypes and gendered behaviour results from a causal connection precisely opposite to that proposed by the Standard Social Science Model: Stereotypes reflect our accurate appraisal of behavioural sex differences that we see around us. Evolutionary psychologists argue that these are a consequence of our mammalian heritage, characterised by asymmetry in parental investment.

In the first part of this chapter, we will examine this evolutionary argument and suggest that female competition has been underestimated and under-theorised. In the second section, we will explore some of the proximate psychological mechanisms that might underlie sex differences in aggression. In the third section, we will introduce the "special case" of intimate partner aggression and argue that cultural effects might shape sex differences in aggression to a greater extent than previously acknowledged by evolutionary psychology.

C. P. Cross (✉)
School of Psychology & Neuroscience, University of St Andrews, KY16 9JP, St Andrews, UK
e-mail: cpc2@st-andrews.ac.uk

A. C. Campbell
Department of Psychology, Durham University Science Site, DH1 3LE, Durham, UK
e-mail: a.c.campbell@durham.ac.uk

T. K. Shackelford, R. D. Hansen (eds.), *The Evolution of Violence*,
Evolutionary Psychology, DOI 10.1007/978-1-4614-9314-3_11,

From Investment Asymmetry to Sex Differences in Aggression

In about 90% of mammals, males limit their reproductive input to the supply of easily replaceable sperm and make no contribution to the care of infants (Clutton-Brock 1991). Eggs are costly, carrying the necessary nutrients to sustain a zygote (should one be formed) until it can sequester resources through the placenta directly from the mother's bloodstream. The majority of parental investment, beginning with anisogamy and continuing through gestation, lactation, and infant care, was firmly imposed on females in most mammalian species. This simple fact is argued to have had immense ramifications for the evolutionary bifurcation of male and female behaviour (Trivers 1972).

This is because the strategies for maximising reproductive success differ between the sexes depending on who invests more. For males, inseminating multiple females became the holy grail of reproductive success. The more females a male could inseminate, the more offspring he could leave behind (Bateman 1948, but see Brown et al. 2009; Gowaty et al. 2012). Of course, this was also the optimal strategy for his similarly parentally unencumbered rivals, raising the levels of intra-male competition. Male reproductive winners won big: In our own species, Moulay Ismail the Bloodthirsty (1672–1727) of Morocco is alleged to have fathered 888 children. Losers left no descendants and it is this fact which is most critical to evolutionary accounts of sex differences in aggression. The greater male variance in human reproductive success continues today even under ostensible monogamy (Jokela et al. 2010). This disparity between reproductive winners and losers made the stakes high and consequently increased male willingness to take risks for mating success (Wang 2002).

Females were freed from the need to compete with one another for male insemination. This was the upside to their heavy burden of parental investment: Males were only too happy to monopolise female investment at the cost of a modest sperm deposit. Females, it was argued, did not benefit from "superfluous" copulations. Once inseminated, why would a female risk the chance of disease, predation, physical injury, and possible coercive aggression from males that are associated with further copulations (Arnqvist and Rowe 2005)?

The simplicity of this argument has recently been questioned in relation to human behaviour. Although reproductive variance is higher in men, the sex difference is more marked in polygynous and serially monogamous societies than under strict monogamy (Brown et al. 2009). Mathematical models suggest that traditional sex roles (the extent to which females prioritise parenting and males prioritise mating) can vary as a function of numerous factors such as operational and adult sex ratio, mortality rates, variance in mate quality, and population density (Kokko and Jennions 2008). Finally, benefits to females of mating with multiple males have been documented in humans (Mesoudi and Laland 2007) and other species (Jennions and Petrie 2000).

These three points all demonstrate the need for recent work in evolutionary biology to be integrated into the work of evolutionary psychologists (see also Laland and Brown 2011). Our focus, however, is on rectifying what we see as an androcentric bias in previous evolutionary thinking on aggression. For many theorists, it was assumed that because females did not fight for copulations there was nothing of consequence for them to fight about. High levels of male aggression were treated as the focus of interest and low levels of women's aggression were dismissed as a default option—only the former was thought to warrant explanation. However, there is more to life than copulation—mating is only one component of reproductive success.

Although at an individual level the most successful male will always out-reproduce the most successful female, every offspring has one father and one mother, so ultimately the two sexes are equal in their output (the "Fisher condition"; see Kokko and Jennions 2008, for a consideration of how this affects models of sex role evolution). Although women are more tightly bunched together in terms of offspring *number*, differences in offspring *quality* have the potential to produce large variance in numbers of grandchildren which are not captured by most existing empirical studies of reproductive success. We have already seen that males in poor condition might well fail to produce any offspring; similarly producing poor-quality children carries a very real cost in terms of potential grandchildren. As Sarah Hrdy put it: "behind every wildly reproductively successful male there must also be, one generation back, a mother" (Hrdy 1987: 109). There should, therefore, be strong selection for any factor that bestows even a small advantage in bearing, raising, and protecting offspring who themselves are reproductively successful.

Mothers need food resources to raise their offspring. Pregnancy raises a women's metabolic rate by 15–26% (Butte et al. 2004). Lactating mothers need approximately 670 extra calories and 20 g of additional protein per day (Dewey 1997). Like most primates, humans are a group-living species, which means that food can be a contested resource and females must compete to feed themselves and their offspring. At the same time, they must supervise and protect their offspring from ecological dangers, potentially infanticidal males, and harassment by other females. These tasks can be achieved more easily by a dominant female because her status elicits deference and compliance from lower-ranking females. Dominant female primates typically have higher infant survival rates and more rapid production of offspring (Pusey et al. 1997), which is, at least in part, a function of better access to food resources (Stockley and Bro-Jørgenson 2011).

This suggests that dominance should be worth fighting for among females as well as males. Yet female dominance hierarchies are primarily restricted to female-bonded species in which females are philopatric, remaining in their natal group while males disperse (Sterck et al. 1997). In these species, dominance hierarchies are organised around matrilines. Dominance follows three clear rules. First, females inherit their mother's rank relative to other members of the group. Second, mothers dominate daughters for life: Daughters can rise to their mother's position in the matriline only upon her death. Third, as adults, younger sisters dominate older sisters which removes incentives for younger daughters to form alliances with their older sisters. The point is that females, unlike males, rarely risk their lives to achieve dominance. They simply accept it when lineage and fate confer it on them.

A female's reluctance to engage in direct attack is particularly puzzling because a successful challenge would not only immediately increase her food intake, freedom from harassment, and reproductive success, but all of these advantages would be passed down to her daughters as well. Matrilines remain remarkably stable over time. Walters (1980)found that a juvenile female's rank at the time of her birth correctly predicted her adult rank in 97% of cases. In a 400-day study of yellow baboons, Hausfater (1975)did not find a single instance of an agonistically induced change of status among females. In non-female-bonded species, in which female group members emigrate from their natal group, dominance hierarchies are "weak or undiscernible, unstable, and non-linear" (Isbell and Young 2002, p. 188; Van Hoof and van Schaik 1992)and agonistic interactions are rare. Dominance behaviour is "uncommon and is never observed among some dyads" (Pusey et al. 1997). So, while dominance offers manifest rewards, fighting for dominance has not been strongly selected for in females. This suggests that it was offset by higher costs (see also Sharp and Clutton-Brock 2011).

We outline here two ways in which competition carries higher costs for females than for males. First, success in aggressive competition appears to be a double-edged sword for female primates: Dominant females are better nourished and reproduce faster, but they also have a higher risk of miscarriage. Some of the most successful female competitors show suppressed fertility and have few, or no, successful pregnancies (Packer et al. 1995). This suggests that dominance competition is a risky 'hit and miss' strategy for females as it is for males, with some individuals winning big rewards and some suffering reproductive death. This suppression of fertility represents a direct trade-off between parenting and competition which constrains competition to a greater degree in females than in males (Stockley and Bro-Jørgenson 2011).

Second, we turn to the most obvious cost of aggression—the possibility of injury or death. At an experiential level, this is doubtless welcomed no more by males than by females. However, recall that costs are calculated in terms of the number of surviving descendants who themselves go on to reproduce. Here the costs differ by sex. Even scholars exploring the idea of humans as "cooperative breeders"—with children benefiting from the help of kin—acknowledge that "the consequences of losing a mother very early in life are catastrophic" (Sear and Mace 2008, p. 5). If she dies while her offspring are young, they will likely die too. In the end, a woman's massive investment in her offspring will shorten her life (Penn and Smith 2007) but, until that day comes, the critical dependence of the young on her for their survival means she must stay away from danger and the possibility of injury or death. For a male, death removes the possibility of future matings but is less likely to compromise the reproductive success he has achieved to date because he can rely on the mother to ensure the survival of his offspring.

Sear and Mace (2008) examined the impact of parental survival on offspring survival in populations ranging from eighteenth-century China to twentieth-century Nepal; from Burkina Faso to New York State. In every case, a mother's survival reduced the likelihood of her children dying. The percentage of children surviving a mother's death ranged from 2 to 50 %. The beneficial effects are stronger before children are weaned: In rural Gambia, a mother's death multiplies the odds of her child's death by 6.2 in infancy, 5.2 in toddlerhood, and 1.4 in childhood (Sear et al. 2002). Pavard et al. (2005) examined data from seventeenth-century Quebec, controlling for a range of variables including the possibility of transmitted infection and shared genetic vulnerability. If a mother died while her infant was still a neonate, the odds of the child dying in the neonatal period were multiplied by 5.52, dropping to 1.27 when the child was aged 5–15 years.

But what about fathers? In 68 % of cases, across 22 populations, the death of a father had no effect on the survival of his children (Sear and Mace 2008). Because there is always variation within populations, this finding suggests that some fathers have a positive effect on infant survival, while some are *detrimental* to a child's chances of living to adulthood. This stands in stark contrast to the consistent and marked effect of mothers on child survival: Mothers, all things considered, are more important to their offspring, and there is therefore an increased selection pressure on females to safeguard their own lives to raise their offspring (Campbell 1999). Sex differences in aggression could be thought of not just as the result of selection pressures on males to compete for dominance, but pressures selecting for the avoidance of dangerous competition in women.

To summarise this section: Our understanding of sex differences in aggression can never be complete if we only ask the question: "Why are males so aggressive?" For a complete picture of sex differences in aggression we must also ask, "Why do females refrain from aggression?" As we shall see later, however, we also need to consider circumstances in which the sex difference in aggression diminishes or reverses.

The Proximal Mechanisms of Sex Differences in Aggression

We have seen that the fitness rewards and costs of aggression differ for males and females. Evolutionary psychologists are interested in the evolved psychological processes that calibrate them and thus mediate the sex difference in behavioural response to these long-haul sexual selection pressures. It is important to emphasise that when we speak of rewards and costs, in relation to the use of aggression, we do not mean to imply that individuals consciously calculate the pros, cons, and respective probabilities of different courses of action, choosing the one with the highest positive net value. Instead, our actions are guided by the "whisperings within" of emotion (Barash 1981) and unbidden impulses (Berkowitz 2008). We do not dismiss conscious decision-making and higher cortical processes as unimportant, and we acknowledge that explicit cost–benefit perceptions do correlate with aggressive behaviour (Archer and Southall 2009). However, the role of emotion in general decision-making has been increasingly recognised in recent years (Loewenstein et al. 2001) and this is likely to be particularly true of aggression, which is often an unpremeditated and reactive behaviour. In this section, we briefly review research on sex differences in emotion (fear and anger) and personality traits (impulsivity and sensation seeking) with a view to identifying the psychological infrastructure that supports sex differences in aggressive behaviour.

Aggressive behaviour can be thought of as a trade-off between prospective rewards (which motivate approach and attack) and potential costs (which motivate avoidance and withdrawal). The basic emotions of anger and fear align neatly with *approach* and *avoidance* motivation, respectively. Angry people make optimistic estimates of risk and favour risk-seeking choices, while fearful people make pessimistic risk estimates and risk-averse choices (Lerner and Keltner 2000; 2001). A sex difference in the threshold for experiencing one or both of these emotions might underlie the sex difference in aggression. Fear and anger are differentially associated with aggressive responses to provocation in the context of hypothetical aggressive conflicts, suggesting that "anger functions as aggression facilitator whereas fear functions as aggression inhibitor" (Winstok 2007, p. 131).

In situations of threat, anger and fear can and do co-occur. In some situations, the scales are tipped strongly in favour of anger so that fear barely registers as an emotion. In others, despite our fury, fear overpowers us and we retreat. While men and women experience both emotions, we argue that the relative balance between them is tipped more strongly in favour of overt aggression in men. But is this because men experience greater anger or lower fear?

Anger

It used to be thought that positive emotions were associated with approach motivation and negative emotions with avoidance motivation (Davidson 2000; Lang et al. 1992; Watson et al. 1999). By this logic, anger should be associated with avoidance, but this is not the case (Carver and Harmon-Jones 2009). In common with other emotions associated with approach motivation, anger activates left frontal brain activity more strongly than right hemisphere activity (Murphy et al. 2003). Anger correlates positively with psychometric scales measuring approach motivation and negatively with avoidance motivation scales (Harmon-Jones 2003; Smits and Kuppens 2005). In typically developing children, infant approach tendencies predict increased anger at later ages (Rothbart et al. 2000) and toddlers with externalising problems, including aggression, show high levels of behavioural approach in laboratory tasks (Putnam and Stifter 2005). Anger increases muscle tension, heart rate, blood pressure, muscular blood flow, and body temperature; these are the hallmarks of the sympathetic nervous system activity preparing us for exertion and combat.

Therefore, anger represents the accelerator pedal for aggressive behaviour. Is the more frequent and severe aggression of males a result of their propensity to experience greater anger? It seems not. A narrative review by Kring (2000) concluded there was a marked absence of sex differences in anger and this was confirmed by Archer (2004), who reported an effect size of $d=-0.004$ in his meta-analysis of data from 46 samples. In a poll of over 2000 Americans, women reported more episodes of anger during the last 7 days than men, even after controlling for sex differences in emotional expressiveness (Mirowsky and Ross 1995). Simon and Nath's (2004) analysis of data from the US General Social Survey found no difference in the frequency of anger, but women exceeded men in the intensity and duration of the emotion, controlling for sociodemographic factors. The evidence suggests, therefore, that men do not experience greater anger than women.

Fear

Unlike anger, there is much evidence that the sexes differ in the frequency and intensity of fear (Else-Quest et al. 2006). Developmentally, girls express fear earlier than boys (Gartstein and Rothbart 2003) and, in a large longitudinal study of personality development, more girls than boys were on a high fearfulness trajectory (Cote et al 2002). In adulthood, women experience fear more intensely (Brody and Hall 1993; Fischer 1993; Fischer and Manstead 2000; Gullone 2000) and more frequently (Brebner 2003) than men. Women also show more intense verbal and non-verbal expression of fear than men (Madden et al. 2000). Behaviourally, women show greater increases in skin conductance and a more marked startle reflex to physically threatening scenes (McManis et al. 2001). Women who receive a single dose of testosterone show a reduced potentiated startle response to anticipated electric shock (Hermans et al. 2006), implicating testosterone as a mediator of this sex difference.

Women make more risk-averse decisions than men do, especially when the risks are physical or life-threatening and when actual risky behaviour (rather than hypothetical choice) is examined (Hersch 1997). The sex difference in fear "may explain gender differences in risk taking more adequately than the cognitive processes involved in the reflective evaluation of options" (Byrnes et al. 1999, p. 378). Loewenstein et al. (2001)also identified women's higher level of fear as particularly relevant to sex differences in risk taking.

Neuropsychological research supports women's greater sensitivity to fear. Although both sexes recruit frontal, limbic, and neural structures when processing emotion, women show stronger activation in these areas when processing fear (Williams et al. 2005). Furthermore, men show more effective automatic modulation of negative emotion, with stronger parieto-temporal activation and weaker activation of limbic and subcortical areas (Whittle et al. 2011). In response to negative stimuli, women report greater negative emotion and show stronger activation in a number of areas, including anterior cingulate cortex and insula (Hofer et al. 2007). These two areas are jointly activated by fear-inducing stimuli and have been implicated in the experience of emotion. The anterior cingulate mediates consciousness of affective state and the insula is associated with interoception (Craig 2009). Stronger activity in these regions may explain why women experience fear more intensely (Ordaz and Luna 2012).

Consistent sex differences in fear, but not anger, strongly suggest that women's desistance from aggression, which becomes more marked as the degree of danger increases, results from their stronger fear responses. We now turn to sex differences in the personality traits of impulsivity and sensation seeking, which are evaluated here as complementary, rather than competing, explanations for sex differences in aggression.

Impulsivity and Sensation Seeking

Impulsivity has been proposed as a mediator of sex differences in aggression: Perhaps women are simply more successful than men in controlling their behavioural impulses, including aggression (Campbell 2006; Strüber et al. 2008). Given developmental evidence that fear underlies the acquisition of self-control and behavioural inhibition (Rothbart and Bates 2006), women might be expected to show lower impulsivity. Consensus on the definition of impulsivity has proved elusive in psychology, though most academics broadly agree that it refers to a "tendency to act spontaneously and without deliberation" (Carver 2005, p. 313). Sensation seeking has also been proposed as another relevant personality factor, measuring as it does the "taste for risk" that Wilson & Daly (1985) argued underlies male participation in aggressive competition. We conducted a meta-analysis of sex differences from 277 studies of impulsivity and sensation seeking (Cross et al. 2011). In summarising our results here, we note important distinctions between higher- and lower-order theories of impulsivity, and between impulsivity and sensation seeking.

Impulsivity Lower-order theories of impulsivity view impulsive actions not as the result of a cognitive deficit but as manifestations of basic affective and temperamental reactions (e.g., Fowles 1988; Gray and McNaughton 2000). According to this view, impulsivity can arise either from over-attraction to reward ("I want it so much I can't tolerate a delay") or from under-sensitivity to punishment ("There may be a price to be paid for this decision but I don't care about it"). In our analysis, women and men did not differ consistently in their sensitivity to reward ($d=-0.02$, with effect sizes strongly modulated by how sensitivity was measured), but women were consistently more sensitive than men were to punishment ($d=-0.33$). This dovetails with our argument that women have evolved greater sensitivity to negative outcomes than men, manifested in their lower threshold for fear (Campbell 1999; 2006).

Higher-order theories of impulsivity see it as a failure of the cognitive control over behaviour that is typically acquired with age (e.g., Rothbart and Bates 2006). Researches who conceptualise impulsivity in this way often measure it as the inability to withhold a prepotent response or to plan for the future. Here, there are very few differences between men and women ($d=0.08$). This finding provides further evidence that cognitive processes, while important in developing a complete understanding of aggression, are not a likely candidate for mediating the sex difference.

Sensation seeking In our review of the literature on impulsivity and sensation seeking, we found that one is frequently measured as a proxy for the other. We strongly caution against this. Empirically, the two constructs consistently appear as orthogonal factors in factor analytic studies (Depue and Collins 1999). Sensation seeking is defined as "the seeking of varied, novel, complex, and intense sensations and experiences and the willingness to take physical, social, legal, and financial risks for the sake of such experience" (Zuckerman 1994, p. 27). The central defining feature of impulsivity—namely, acting without deliberation—is absent from the definition of sensation seeking. Questionnaires that measure sensation seeking typically ask about the respondent's preference for risky but exciting activities—such as parachute jumping—over safe but tedious ones. However, the items make no reference to the failure of deliberation which is the hallmark of impulsive action. Parachute jumpers do not jump from planes on impulse; they plan carefully, checking their equipment, drop site, parachute, and timings. When we analysed sensation seeking and risk taking separately from impulsivity, we found a marked sex difference in the male direction ($d=0.41$). This was in stark contrast to the weak, inconsistent differences in measures of impulsivity. Men seek risk to a much greater extent than women, but are not more impulsive in general.

In summary, women are not consistently less impulsive than men, but they are more punishment-sensitive and more risk-averse. While impulsivity and sensation seeking are distinct personality traits, the overlap between them is an area in need of further research (Campbell and Muncer 2009). Actions such as running across a road to beat the traffic, having sex with a stranger, or accepting an offer of drink or drugs can be considered both risky and impulsive. The tendency to engage in these actions—risky impulsivity—is likely to be of most relevance to understanding sex differences in aggressive behaviour.

When, Why, and How do Women Use Aggression?

Although women engage in physical confrontations less frequently and less seriously than men, fights between women do occur. In a victimisation survey of 1,455 British respondents, 7% of women reported an actual assault by another woman and a further 4% reported a threat of assault during the preceding 5 years (George 1999). Approximately three-quarters of adolescent girls' attacks are on other girls (Bureau of Justice Statistics 1999; Campbell 1986). In the USA and Britain, the perpetrators and victims of female assault are usually 15–24 years old and known to one another. The most common forms of attack are pushing, shoving, grabbing, tripping, slapping, kicking, and punching (Campbell 1986; Ness 2004).

Women's aggression is sensitive to the same environmental and social factors as men's. Girls, like boys, show a marked age–violence relationship, rising in the early teenage years and falling in the mid-20s. The age–violence relationship is very similar in both sexes, although male violence is more prevalent than female violence and peaks slightly later, corresponding to girls' 2-year-earlier attainment of sexual maturity. For both sexes, the post-pubertal years are a time of high stakes: Entry into the arena of mating brings with it increased competition. The reasons for the evolution of monogamy in our species are still debated (Henrich and Richardson 2012), but that monogamy brought with it a two-way sexual selection is not disputed (see, e.g., Kokko and Johnstone 2002). When a man commits himself to a single woman, he becomes considerably more selective in his choice of mate. Under monogamy, women gain male support that can ease the burden of childcare, but the price is greater competition between women for access to the best male partners.

The reasons for fighting between females are often connected directly or indirectly to young men (Burbank 1987; Campbell 1995; Ness 2004; Schuster 1985). As with male aggression, ecological and demographic factors concentrate female aggression among the young in the poorest communities (Campbell 1999). For example, women are most likely to find a partner in the immediate neighbourhood and, to the extent that the local male–female ratio drops below unity (as a function, for example, of early male mortality or more frequent incarceration), competition between women increases. High variation in men's resources also intensifies female competition. Among middle-class young women, the risk of direct aggressive competition is rarely worth it: The difference between marrying this doctor or that accountant is not sufficiently great. However, in deprived areas, the difference between the desperate poverty of "dope fiends" and the conspicuous consumption of "high rollers" is extreme (Campbell 2011). Men who can be a source of support, rather than a drain on resources, are worth fighting for.

A common cause of female fights is defending a sexual reputation. Gossip about a girl's promiscuity, while an indirect form of attack (see later), can act as a trigger for direct physical attack when a victim attempts to reclaim her threatened reputation. Cues to potential infidelity can be used by men as a means of ruling out potential long-term partners (Buss and Schmitt 1993), so women can gain an advantage by undermining their rivals' sexual reputation while defending their own. That is why terms such as "slag," "tart," or "whore" are powerful sources of reputation challenge among women (Campbell 1982, 1995; Marsh and Patton 1986). Because it is not possible to publicly prove that such an accusation is false, women might seek to deter rivals from making such accusations with a credible threat of violence.

Despite these episodes of outright aggression, female aggression is still less frequent and less likely to be lethal than that of males. Weapons are rarely used, with fights confined overwhelmingly to fists and feet (Ness 2004). The majority of women's violent offences are simple rather than aggravated assaults (Greenfeld and Snell 1999). Even when women do use physical aggression, they are less accepting of risk to their lives than men.

The sex difference in aggression has been the focus of hundreds of studies using a range of techniques including laboratory experiments, observation, personality assessment, and self- and peer-reported behaviour. The results fit a clear pattern: The less risky the form of aggression measured, the smaller the sex difference (see Archer 2009, and Campbell 2006, for cross-cultural reviews). For physical acts such as hitting, punching, and kicking, the effect size lies between $d=0.59$ and $d=0.91$, while for verbal acts such as abuse and threats, the effect size is between $d=0.28$

and $d=0.46$ (Knight et al. 1996; Knight et al. 2002). The sex difference in indirect aggression is negligible, $d=-0.02$ (Archer 2004) and it is this form of aggression to which we now turn.

Indirect or relational aggression (see Archer and Coyne 2005, for a discussion of terminology) is a means by which women can compete without risking their safety. Acts that stigmatise, ostracise, and otherwise exclude others from social interaction can be used without direct physical confrontation. Such acts do not eliminate or physically injure the target, but they do inflict stress and diminish the opponents' reputation and social support. The target is attacked circuitously—the aggressor can often remain unidentified and safe from retaliation, at least in the short term. Targets that discover the identity of an indirect aggressor might, however, reply with direct aggression, for example in the case of derogation of sexual reputation (see above).

A key component of indirect aggression is the use of gossip to undermine an opponent's reputation and decrease their social capital. Physical attractiveness is another topic of gossip used to derogate competitors (Hall 2002). Of the 28 tactics that participants reported using to make same-sex rivals undesirable to the opposite sex, Buss and Dedden (1990)found that "derogate competitor's appearance" was used more often by women than men. Naturalistic studies concur that pejorative comments about other girls' appearance rank high in girls' topics of gossip (Duncan 1999; Simmons 2002).

We have seen the potential prizes that can incite female competition. We have also seen how, relative to men, women's aggressive competition is suppressed by pressures acting on women to safeguard their bodily integrity to support offspring. We move now into an area in which—in Western samples—aggression shows no sex difference: Intimate partner aggression. We note how this form of aggression is a particularly potent demonstration of the interactions between evolved psychology and culture.

Intimate Partner Aggression

Intimate partner aggression is one of the most emotive topics in the social sciences and empirical demonstrations of gender symmetry in rates of partner-directed aggressive acts have been the subject of controversy and resistance (see, e.g., Archer 2000, 2006; Johnson 2011; Straus and Ramirez 2007). We note here that gender symmetry is found only in Western samples (Archer 2006) and is confined to acts rather than outcomes (Archer 2000). In this brief overview, we first highlight the distinction between *situational* couple aggression and *intimate terrorism*. Intimate terrorism (hereafter IT) is a form of unilateral intimate violence, coupled with controlling behaviour (see Graham-Kevan and Archer 2003; Johnson 2011). Scholars are currently divided on whether intimate terrorism is gender-symmetric or perpetrated predominantly by men (see Johnson 2011, and Straus 2011, for opposing views). However, it is clear that the majority of people who are injured (Archer 2000) or killed (Coleman et al. 2007) by intimate partners are female. The most severe consequences of intimate aggression therefore affect women more frequently.

Our empirical work (Cross and Campbell 2012; Cross et al. 2011)focuses on what is known as "situational" (Johnson 2006), "ordinary" (Straus 2011), or "common" (Milardo 1998) couple violence. We will adapt Johnson's terminology and call it situational couple aggression (SCA). This is the—usually bilateral—result of an escalation of conflict rather than part of a systematic pattern of unilateral control (Johnson 2006). Importantly, most of what is detected in self-report studies is SCA, rather than IT (Johnson 2011). We highlight the distinction between SCA and IT because while the former shows strong evidence of being gender-symmetric (Archer 2000, 2009; Cross and Campbell 2012; Robertson and Murachver 2007; Straus 2011; Straus and Ramirez 2007), the latter does not. Perhaps more importantly, SCA and IT likely require different psychological explanations.

Evolutionary Approaches to Intimate Aggression

Early evolutionary approaches to intimate aggression focused almost exclusively on male violence towards female partners, and male jealousy was the main explanatory factor (see Dobash et al. 1992; Kaighobadi et al. 2009). The argument is as follows: Because fertilization takes place inside the female body, men can be deceived into investing in children who were sired by other males—at the expense of their own fitness. Males can reduce their risk of being cuckolded by "mate guarding"—controlling their partners' behaviour and restricting their movement so that they cannot consort with other males. Men's partner aggression, therefore, is a tactic for ensuring paternity (Wilson and Daly 1996). According to this argument, patriarchal societies perpetuate this evolved pattern, upholding the belief that men have the right to control their partners, which leads to police and judicial reluctance to intervene in "domestic" disputes and allows male abuse of partners to go unchecked. In short, patriarchal societies positively foster a culture of "wife-beating"—unilateral violence suffered by women at the hands of men. Proponents of this view argue that women's aggression towards male partners is rare and, in cases where it does occur, is "almost always… in response to cues of imminent assault" (Dobash et al. 1992, p. 80).

We welcome this acknowledgement that culture and evolutionary factors can interact, a perspective that has been missing from some evolutionary accounts of human behaviour but that is now gaining prominence (Bolhuis et al. 2011). However, we also suggest that this argument has only limited applicability to SCA because it focuses entirely on male perpetration. Hence, it cannot account for the gender-symmetric rates of SCA found in most Western self-report studies. While we touch on the issue of specific male adaptations for jealousy elsewhere (Campbell and Cross 2012), here we focus on the role of societal norms in accounting for the gender-symmetric pattern of SCA.

Women in UK samples raise their aggression in the context of an intimate relationship, relative to friends of either the same or the opposite sex. This is true in self-report studies of actual aggressive acts (Cross and Campbell 2012) and in a study in which participants were asked about their likely aggression in response to the same hypothetical provocations by partners and others (Cross et al. 2011). It is also very different from men's responses in such studies, which suggest that men would engage in less aggression towards female than male targets and that partners are no exception.

This pattern of results appears paradoxical in light of our explanation of women's lower aggression as resulting from their lower threshold for experiencing fear. If women have evolved to place a premium on their own safety, why take the risk of attacking a man, given the male advantage in size and strength? And why does this effect appear to be restricted to Western samples? Here, we consider cultural variation in whether women's fear of men is likely to be modulated in line with social norms of male behaviour. As we have noted, parity between the sexes in intimate aggression appears to be unique to "WEIRD" societies (i.e., Western, Educated, Industrialised, Rich, and Democratic; Henrich et al. 2010). Cross-cultural findings are hard to compare directly, so what we present here is intended to illustrate the scope of the problem rather than to provide comprehensive answers.

Western Culture and Women's Intimate Aggression

Do Western social norms, as some have argued, encourage or tolerate male aggression towards partners? At present, the answer appears to be no. A man's aggression towards a female partner is deemed more serious and more deserving of police intervention than a woman's aggression towards a male partner (Felson and Feld 2009; Sorenson and Taylor 2005). Men who assault their partners are more likely to be convicted (Felson 2008) or incarcerated (Smith and Farole 2009) than their female counterparts. A review published in the early 1990s (Dobash et al. 1992) reported that male violence towards female partners is unlikely to be punished by police. However, both sexes are less likely to be convicted for assaulting a known person than a stranger, regardless of whether they are a partner, a friend, or a family member (Felson and Pare 2007). Furthermore, penalties for partner assault have been more stringently applied for assailants of both sexes in recent years. While those who assault partners are less likely to be convicted than those who assault strangers, this effect is diminishing over time, is not confined to partners, and is not confined to male assailants. A snapshot of the social norms of modern wealthy industrialised societies, therefore, suggests that men who assault their female partners are "breakers, not bearers, of society's norms" (Felson 2002: 70).

We argue that the prevailing cultural framework radically alters the costs–benefit analysis of aggression—including women's aggression towards intimate partners. The reduced likelihood of male aggression means that women's appraisals of fear are also reduced, weakening their inhibition of aggressive impulses. For example, Fiebert and Gonzalez (1997)reported that women who strike their partners believe that they are not in danger of being struck in retaliation, and social norms in the USA proscribe male aggression towards women even in response to an attack (Feld and Felson 2008). Cultural context alters the likely consequences and the cognitive appraisal of costs and benefits which, in turn, influence levels of aggression.

Cultural Variation in Intimate Aggression

A large-scale review by Archer (2006)found an impressive correlation of $r = -0.79$ between the United Nations' Gender Empowerment Measure (GEM) and the magnitude of sex differences in intimate aggression in community samples. Countries with lower GEM showed a male-biased perpetration and countries with higher GEM showed a more gender-symmetric pattern. In high GEM societies, this appears to be a function both of men hitting female partners less frequently and of women hitting male partners more frequently. Women's victimisation, in particular, is inversely correlated with gender equality and positively correlated with sexist attitudes (Archer 2006). This, in turn, alters the risk of retaliation in response to female aggression towards male partners.

WEIRD societies with high GEM tend also to be more individualist than collectivist, and the construal of women as individuals rather than as parts of a family unit might be an important factor in predicting rates of partner aggression. For example, in cultures in which there is a strong societal emphasis on "honour," women are expected not to report intimate partner aggression to the authorities (Clark et al. 2010). Haj-Yahia (2011) describes how the functioning of the family unit is considered more important than the well-being of individual members in some collectivist societies: Women are defined primarily as members of their family unit rather than as autonomous individuals. When intimate aggression occurs, it is not generally considered to be a criminal problem—indeed, the prevention of partner aggression is seen as the responsibility of the wife (Clark et al. 2010; Haj-Yahia 2000). Where men's use of physical aggression towards partners is condoned, women's aggression is likely to be constrained—to a greater extent than in WEIRD societies—by a realistic fear of retaliation.

The cultural dynamics of a particular society, therefore, can have strong effects on the levels of male- and female-perpetrated intimate aggression[1], and are strong predictors of the sex differences therein. We must appreciate that, while sex-specific selection pressures appear to have influenced male and female minds differently, culture is also important. Our suggestion is that the sexes differ relatively consistently in their sensitivity to the costs and benefits of aggression, but that these costs and benefits vary considerably cross-culturally. But how and why do these cultural effects come about?

[1] Note also that the proportions of reported intimate aggression that reflect SCA as opposed to IT might also be expected to vary cross-culturally.

Gene–Culture Co-Evolution

Researchers working in the area of gene–culture co-evolution explicitly address the interactions between culturally transmitted behaviour and humans' evolved psychological characteristics, treating both of these as essential to any complete explanatory account (see, e.g., Henrich et al. 2012; Laland and Brown 2011). Gene–culture co-evolution research has already developed useful models of the cultural evolution and proliferation of beliefs relating to reproduction. For example, evolutionary accounts of intimate partner aggression often treat male-perpetrated jealousy-induced aggression as a consequence of paternity uncertainty stemming from internal fertilisation in humans. Yet evidence that this behaviour is not a human universal comes from "partible paternity" societies. In such societies, men are believed to be a father (either "primary" or "secondary") to any child whose mother he had sex with in the year before the child was born. Children with both a primary and a secondary father have increased survivorship to age 10, compared to children with only one father. This is contrary to what would be expected if males who were uncertain of sole paternity routinely attacked or deserted their wives or offspring (Beckerman and Valentine 2002).

Mesoudi & Laland (2007) used a gene–culture co-evolution approach to model the origin and proliferation of partible paternity beliefs. Different configurations of sex ratio and control over mate choice were modelled. The critical scenarios were those in which the sex ratio was strongly female-biased (highly plausible in small populations, especially where many males die in intergroup aggression, for example). In these cases, beliefs and mating strategies diverged into one of two stable states according to which sex had more control over mating: Where females (i.e., the majority sex) controlled mating, partible paternity beliefs and polygynandrous mating became fixed. Where males (i.e., the minority sex) controlled mating, singular paternity beliefs and monogamous mating became fixed (Mesoudi and Laland 2007). Phylogenetic analysis of populations in lowland South America also supports Hrdy's (2000) argument that polyandry is more likely when women have more societal power and kin support (Walker et al. 2010). Internal fertilisation and uncertainty of paternity are human universals, but adaptive responses to them vary depending on cultural constraints.

Gene–culture co-evolution can also be applied to cultural variation in beliefs about the status of women (e.g., Smuts 1995). For example, Henrich et al. (2012) argue that the socially imposed monogamy prevalent in many societies is the result of cultural group selection: It benefits the groups in which it is held by reducing the numbers of unattached adult males, thereby reducing male–male aggression and age discrepancies between husbands and wives. In turn, it increases gender equality in a society (Henrich et al. 2012). Cultural changes such as this could in turn affect sex differences in intimate partner aggression: For example, large discrepancies in partner ages are positively correlated with intimate homicide by both sexes (Daly and Wilson 1988). Because baseline rates of perpetration are male biased, reducing age discrepancies could affect the rates of partner homicide committed by men more than it affects partner homicide committed by women. More generally, we have already noted that gender empowerment is strongly correlated with sex symmetry in intimate aggression (Archer 2006). This illustrates how cultural beliefs prevalent in a society, which can evolve in complex reciprocal interaction with our evolved psychology, can affect patterns of sex differences observed in intimate aggression.

Conclusion

In closing, we hope that researchers in the near future will examine more closely the interactions between evolved mechanisms and cultural factors in producing sex differences in aggression. Calls for an integrated approach which grants agency to both evolved psychology and cultural processes are not new (see, e.g., Boyd and Richerson 1985; Feldman and Cavalli-Sforza 1979; Lumsden and Wilson 1981; Tooby and Cosmides 1992), although the importance of the roles of biological and cultural evolution remains contentious. We close by highlighting three lines of questioning that could be particularly fruitful.

First, the nature of hypothesised species-typical evolved mechanisms needs to be elucidated further. Low-level affective mechanisms such as fear and punishment sensitivity have utility in explaining sex differences in behaviour. Researchers in a number of psychological disciplines are recognising the need for dual process theories which emphasise the interaction between the evolutionarily ancient limbic structures which humans share with other species and our higher-level reasoning capabilities (Bolhuis et al. 2011; Evans 2008). Neuroimaging studies are especially useful in identifying connectivity (which sometimes shows sex differences) between these neural structures (Li et al. 2012; Whittle et al. 2011).

Second, the extent to which evolved sex differences might interact with contextual factors is empirically tractable: Vignette studies have already proved useful in examining the effects of context on sex differences in aggression (e.g., Richardson and Green 2006, Cross et al. 2011) and could be used to examine contextual factors relating to societal norms that influence the perceived risks associated with aggression and the extent to which impelling and inhibitory forces are felt. Finally, it would be informative to model the conditions under which specific beliefs relating to the status of women and the (un)acceptability of controlling them could evolve, comparing these results with patterns in cross-cultural observations. Integrating different levels of explanation with an evolutionary perspective is the best way to gain a fuller understanding of women's aggression.

References

Archer, J. (2000). Sex differences in aggression between heterosexual partners: A meta-analytic review. *Psychological Bulletin, 126*, 651–680.

Archer, J. (2004). Sex differences in aggression in real world settings: A meta-analytic review. *Review of General Psychology, 8*, 291–322.

Archer, J. (2006). Cross-cultural differences in physical aggression between partners: A social role analysis. *Personality and Social Psychology Review, 10*, 133–153.
Archer, J. (2009). Does sexual selection explain human sex differences in aggression? *Behavioural and Brain Sciences, 32*, 249–311.
Archer, J., & Coyne, S. M. (2005).An integrated review of indirect, relational, and social aggression.*Personality and Social Psychology Review, 9*(3), 212–230. doi:10.1207/s15327957pspr0903_2.
Archer, J., & Southall, N. (2009). Does cost-benefit analysis or self-control predict involvement in bullying behavior by male prisoners? *Aggressive behavior, 35*(1), 31–40. doi:10.1002/ab.20283.
Arnqvist, G. & Rowe, L. (2005) *Sexual conflict*. Princeton: Princeton University Press.
Barash, D. P. (1981). *Whisperings within: Evolution and the origin of human nature*. London; Penguin.
Bateman, A. J. (1948). Intrasexual selection in *Drosophila. Heredity, 2*, 349–368.
Berkowitz, L. (2008). On the consideration of automatic as well as controlled psychological processes in aggression. *Aggressive behavior, 34*(2), 117–129. doi:10.1002/ab.20244
Bolhuis, J. J., Brown, G. R., Richardson, R. C., & Laland, K. N. (2011). Darwin in Mind: New Opportunities for Evolutionary Psychology. *PLoS Biology, 9*(7), e1001109. doi:10.1371/journal.pbio.1001109.
Boyd, R., & Richerson, P. J. (1985). *Culture and the evolutionary process*. Chicago: Chicago University Press.
Brebner, J. (2003). Gender and emotions.*Personality and Individual Differences, 34*, 387–394.
Brody, L. R., & Hall, J. A. (1993).Gender and emotion. In M. Lewis, & J. M. Haviland (Eds.), *Handbook of emotions* (pp. 447–460). New York: Guildford Press.
Brown, G. R., Laland, K. N., & Mulder, M. B. (2009).Bateman's principles and human sex roles. *Trends in Ecology & Evolution, 24*(6), 297–304. doi:10.1016/j.tree.2009.02.005.
Burbank, V. (1987).Female aggression in cross-cultural perspective.*Behavioral Science Research, 21*, 70–100.
Bureau of Justice Statistics (1999).*Special report: Women offenders*. http://www.ojp.usdoj.gov/bjs/pub/pdf/wo.pdf. Accessed 21 Oct 2010
Buss, D. M. & Dedden, L. A. (1990).Derogation of competitors.*Journal of Personal and Social Relationships, 7*, 395–422.
Buss, D. M. & Schmitt, D. (1993). Sexual strategies theory: An evolutionary perspective on human mating. *Psychological Review, 100*, 204–232.
Butte, N. F., Wong, W. W., Treuth, M. S., Ellis, K. J., & Smith, E. O. B. (2004).Energy requirements during pregnancy based on total expenditure and energy deposition. *American Journal of Clinical Nutrition, 79*, 1078–1087.
Byrnes, J. P., Miller, D. C., & Schafer, W. D. (1999). Gender differences in risk taking: A meta-analysis. *Psychological Bulletin, 125*, 367–383.
Campbell, A. (1982). Female aggression.In P. Marsh and A. Campbell (Eds.), *Aggression and violence* (pp. 137–150). Oxford: Blackwell.
Campbell, A. (1986). Self report of fighting by females. *British Journal of Criminology, 26*, 28–46.
Campbell, A. (1995). A few good men: Evolutionary psychology and female adolescent aggression. *Ethology and Sociobiology, 16*, 99–123.
Campbell, A. (1999). Staying alive: Evolution, culture, and women ' s intrasexual aggression. *Behavioral and Brain Sciences*, 203–252.
Campbell, A. (2006). Sex differences in direct aggression: What are the psychological mediators? *Aggression and Violent Behavior, 11*, 237–264.
Campbell, A. (2011) Ladies, choose your weapons. *The Evolutionary Review, 2*, 106–112.
Campbell, A., & Cross, C. P. (2012).Evolution, culture, and women's aggression. In T. Shackelford and V. Weekes-Shackelford (Eds.).*The Oxford Handbook of Evolutionary Perspectives on Violence, Homicide, and War*, Oxford University Press
Campbell, A., & Muncer, S. (2009). Can 'risky' impulsivity explain sex differences in aggression? *Personality and Individual Differences, 47*, 402–406.

Carver, C. S. (2005). Impulse and constraint: Perspectives from personality psychology, convergence with theory in other areas and potential for integration. *Personality and Social Psychology Review*, *9*, 312–333.
Carver, C. S., & Harmon-Jones, E. (2009). Anger is an approach-related affect: Evidence and implications. *Psychological Bulletin*, *135*, 183–204.
Clark, C. J., Silverman, J. G., Shahrouri, M., Everson-Rose, S., & Groce, N. (2010).The role of the extended family in women's risk of intimate partner violence in Jordan.*Social Science & Medicine*, *70*, 144–151. 10.1016/j.socscimed.2009.09.024.
Clutton-Brock, T. H. (1991).*The evolution of parental care*. Princeton: Princeton University Press.
Coleman, K., Jansson, K., Kaiza, P., & Reed, E. (2007).*Homicides, Firearm Offences and Intimate Violence, 2005/2006*. Home Office Statistical Bulletin.
Cote, S., Tremblay, R. E., Nagin, D., Zoccolillo, M., & Vitaro, F. (2002). The development of impulsivity, fearfulness and helpfulness during childhood: Patterns of consistency and change in the trajectories of boys and girls. *Journal of Child Psychology and Psychiatry and Allied Disciplines*, *43*, 609–618.
Craig, A. D. (2009). How do you feel now? The anterior insula and human awareness. *Nature Reviews Neuroscience*, *10*, 59–70.Cross, C. P., & Campbell, A. (2012). The Effects of Intimacy and Target Sex on Direct Aggression: Further Evidence. *Aggressive Behavior*, *38*(4), 272–280. doi:10.1002/ab.21430.
Cross, C. P., Copping, L. T., & Campbell, A. (2011). Sex differences in impulsivity: a meta-analysis. *Psychological bulletin*, *137*(1), 97–130.doi:10.1037/a0021591.
Cross, C. P., Tee, W., & Campbell, A. (2011). Gender symmetry in intimate aggression: an effect of intimacy or target sex? *Aggressive behavior*, *37*(3), 268–277. doi:10.1002/ab.20388.
Daly, M., & Wilson, M. (1988). *Homicide*. New York: Aldine de Gruyter.
Davidson, R. J. (2000). Affective style, psychopathology, and resilience: Brain mechanisms and plasticity. *American Psychologist*, *55*, 1196–1214.
Depue, R. A., & Collins, P. F. (1999). Neurobiology of the structure of personality: Dopamine, facilitation of incentive motivation, and extraversion. *Behavioral and Brain Sciences*, *22*, 491–569.
Dewey, K. G. (1997). Energy and protein requirements during lactation.*Annual review of nutrition*, *17*, 19–36. doi:10.1146/annurev.nutr.17.1.19
Dobash, R. P., Dobash, R. E., Wilson, M., & Daly, M. (1992).The myth of sexual symmetry in marital violence.*Social Problems*, *39*, 71–91.
Duncan, N. (1999). *Sexual bullying: Gender conflict and pupil culture in secondary schools*. London: Routledge.
Else-Quest, N. M., Hyde, J. S., Goldsmith, H. H. & Van Hulle, C. A. (2006). Gender differences in temperament: A meta-analysis. *Psychological Bulletin*, *132*, 33–72.
Evans, J.S.B.T. (2008). Dual-processing accounts of reasoning, judgment, and social cognition. *Annual Review of Psychology*, *59*, 255–278.
Feld, S. L., & Felson, R. B. (2008). Gender norms and retaliatory violence against spouses and acquaintances. *Journal of Family Issues*, *29*(5), 692–703.
Felson, R. B. (2002).*Violence and Gender Re-examined*. Washington: American Psychological Association.
Felson, R. B. (2008). The legal consequences of intimate partner violence for men and women. Children and Youth Services Review, 30(6), 639–646.
Felson, R. B., & Feld, S. L. (2009).When a man hits a woman: Moral evaluations and reporting violence to the police. *Aggressive Behavior*, *35*, 477–488.
Felson, R. B., & Pare, P. P. (2007). Does the criminal justice system treat domestic violence and sexual assault offenders leniently? *Justice Quarterly*, *24*, 435–459.
Fiebert, M. S., & Gonzalez, D. M. (1997). College women who initiate assaults on their male partners and the reasons offered for such behavior. *Psychological Reports*, *80*, 583–590.
Fischer, A. H. (1993). Sex differences in emotionality: Fact or stereotype? *Feminism and Psychology*, *3*, 303–318.

Fischer, A. H., & Manstead, A. S. R. (2000). Gender and emotions in different cultures. In A. H. Fischer (Ed.), *Gender and emotion: Social psychological perspectives* (pp. 71–94). Cambridge: Cambridge University Press.
Fowles, D.C. (1988). Psychophysiology and psychopathology: A motivational approach. *Psychophysiology, 25*, 373–391.
Gartstein, M. A., & Rothbart, M. K. (2003).Studying infant temperament via the Revised Infant Behavior Questionnaire.*Infant Behavior & Development, 26*, 64–86.
George, M. J. (1999). A victimization survey of female-perpetrated assaults in the United Kingdom.*Aggressive Behavior, 25*, 67–79.
Gowaty, P. A., Kim, Y.-K., & Anderson, W. W. (2012). No evidence of sexual selection in a repetition of Bateman's classic study of Drosophila melanogaster. *Proceedings of the National Academy of Sciences of the United States of America*. doi:10.1073/pnas.1207851109.
Graham-Kevan, N., & Archer, J. (2003).Intimate terrorism and common couple violence—A test of Johnson's predictions in four British samples.*Journal of Interpersonal Violence, 18*(11), 1247–1270. doi: 10.1177/0886260503256656.
Gray, J. A., & McNaughton, N. (2000).*The neuropsychology of anxiety: An enquiryinto the functions of the septo-hippocampal system*. Oxford: Oxford University Press.
Greenfeld, L. A. & Snell, T. L. (1999).*Bureau of Justice Statistics Special Report: Women offenders*. Washington: US Department of Justice.
Gullone, E. (2000). The development of normal fear: A century of research. *Clinical Psychology Review, 20*, 429–451.
Haj-Yahia, M. M. (2000).Wife abuse and battering in the sociocultural context of Arab society.*Family Process, 39*, 237–255.
Haj-Yahia, M. M. (2011).Contextualizing interventions with battered women in collectivist societies: Issues and controversies.*Aggression and Violent Behavior, 16*(4), 331–339. doi:10.1016/j.avb.2011.04.005.
Hall, K. (2002) *Who do men and women gossip about and what is discussed about them?* Unpublished dissertation, Durham University, England.
Harmon-Jones, E. (2003). Anger and the behavioural approach system.*Personality and Individual Differences, 35*, 995–1005.
Hausfater, G. (1975) Dominance and reproduction in baboons (Papio cynocephalus).*Contributions to Primatology, 7*, 1–150.
Henrich, J., Boyd, R., & Richerson, P. J. (2012).The puzzle of monogamous marriage.*Philosophical transactions of the Royal Society of London.Series B, Biological sciences, 367*(1589), 657–669. doi:10.1098/rstb.2011.0290.
Henrich, J., Heine, S. J., & Norenzayan, A. (2010).The WEIRDest people in the world?*Behavioral and Brain Sciences*, 61–135.doi:10.1017/S0140525X0999152X.
Hermans, E.J., Putman, P., Baas, J.M., Koppeschaar, H.P. & van Honk, J. (2006).A single administration of testosterone reduces fear-potentiated startle in humans. *Biological Psychiatry, 59*, 872–874.
Hersch, J. (1997). Smoking, seat belts and other risky consumer decisions: Differences by gender and race. *Managerial and Decision Economics, 11*, 241–256.
Hofer, A., Siedentopf, C. M., Ischebeck, A., Rettenbacher, M. A., Verius, M., Felber, S., et al. (2007). Sex differences in brain activation patterns during processing of positively and negatively valenced emotional words. *Psychological Medicine, 37*, 109–119.
Hrdy, S. B. (1987). Sex-biased parental investment among primates and other mammals: A critical evaluation of the Trivers-Willard hypothesis. In J. B. Lancaster and R. J.Gelles (Eds.), *Child Abuse and Neglect: A Biosocial Perspective*, pp. 97–147. New York: Aldine.
Hrdy, S. B. (2000) *Mother nature: Maternal instincts and how they shape the human species*. Random House.
Isbell, L. A. & Young, T. P. (2002). Ecological models of female social relationships in primates: Similarities, disparities and some directions for future clarity. *Behaviour, 139*, 177–202.
Jennions, M. D., & Petrie, M. (2000). Why do females mate multiply? A review of the genetic benefits. *Biological Review, 75*, 21–64.

Johnson, M. P. (2006). Conflict and Control: Gender Symmetry and Asymmetry in Domestic Violence. *Violence Against Women, 12*, 1003–1018. doi:10.1177/1077801206293328.

Johnson, M. P. (2011). Gender and types of intimate partner violence: A response to an anti-feminist literature review. *Aggression and Violent Behavior, 16*(4), 289–296. doi:10.1016/j.avb.2011.04.006.

Jokela, M., Rotkirch, A., Rickard, I. J., Pettav, J. & Lummaa, V. (2010). Serial monogamy increases reproductive success in men but not in women. *Behavioral Ecology, 21*, 906–912.

Kaighobadi, F., Shackelford, T. K., & Goetz, A. T. (2009). From Mate Retention to Murder: Evolutionary Psychological Perspectives on Men ' s Partner-Directed Violence. *Review of General Psychology, 13*(4), 327–334. doi:10.1037/a0017254.

Knight, G. P., Fabes, R. A. & Higgins, D. A. (1996). Concerns about drawing causal inferences from meta-analyses: An example in the study of gender differences in aggression. *Psychological Bulletin, 119*, 410–421.

Knight, G. P., Guthrie, I. L., Page, M. C., & Fabes, R. A. (2002). Emotional arousal and gender differences in aggression: A meta-analysis. *Aggressive Behaviour, 28*, 366–393.

Kokko, H. & Jennions, M.D. (2008).Parental investment, sexual selection and sex ratios. *Journal of Evolutionary Biology, 21*, 919–948.

Kokko, H., Johnstone, R. A. (2002). Why is mutual mate choice not the norm? Operational sex ratios, sex roles and the evolution of sexually dimorphic and monomorphic signalling. *Philosophical Transactions of the Royal Society of London. Series B: Biological Sciences, 357*, 319–330.

Kring, A. M. (2000). Gender and anger. In A. H.Fischer (Ed.), *Gender and emotion: Social psychological perspectives* (pp. 211–231). Cambridge: Cambridge University Press.

Laland, K.N., & Brown, G.R. (2011) *Sense and Nonsense: Evolutionary Perspective on Human Behaviour* (2nd edn.).Oxford University Press.

Lang, P. J., Bradley, M. M., & Cuthbert, B. N. (1992). A motivational analysis of emotion: Reflex–cortex connections. *Psychological Science, 3*, 44–49.

Lerner, J. S. & Keltner, D. (2000). Beyond valence: Toward a model of emotion-specific influences on judgement and choice. *Cognition and Emotion, 14*, 473–493.

Lerner, J. S. & Keltner, D. (2001).Fear, anger and risk.*Journal of Personality and Social Psychology, 81*, 146–159.

Li, Y., Qin, W., Jiang, T., Zhang, Y., & Yu, C. (2012) Sex-dependent correlations between the personality dimension of harm avoidance and the resting-state functional connectivity of amygdala subregions. PLoS ONE 7(4): e35925.

Loewenstein, G. F., Weber, E. U., Hsee, C. K., & Welch, N. (2001).Risk as feelings.*Psychological Bulletin, 127*, 267–286.

Lumsden, C.J., & Wilson, E.O. (1981). *Genes, mind and culture: The coevolutionary process.* Harvard University Press.

Madden, T. E., Feldman Barrett, L., & Pietromonaco, P. R. (2000). Sex differences in anxiety and depression. In A. H. Fischer (Ed.), *Gender and emotion: Social psychological perspectives* (pp. 277–300). Cambridge: Cambridge University Press.

Marsh, P. & Paton, R. (1986). Gender, social class and conceptual schemas of aggression. In A. Campbell & J. Gibbs (Eds.), *Violent transactions: The limits of personality* (pp. 59–85). Oxford: Blackwell.

McManis, M. H., Bradley, M. M., Berg, W. K., Cuthbert, B. N., & Lang, P. J. (2001). Emotional reactions in children: Verbal, physiological and behavioural responses to affective pictures. *Psychophysiology, 38*, 222–231.

Mesoudi, A., & Laland, K. N. (2007).Culturally transmitted paternity beliefs and the evolution of human mating behaviour. *Proceedings.Biological sciences/ The Royal Society, 274*(1615), 1273–1278. doi:10.1098/rspb.2006.0396.

Milardo, R. M. (1998). Gender asymmetry in common couple violence. *Personal Relationships, 5*, 423–438.

Mirowsky, J., & Ross, C. E. (1995). Sex differences in distress: Real or artefact? *American Sociological Review, 60*, 449–468.

Murphy, F. C., Nimmo-Smith, I., & Lawrence, A. D. (2003). Functional neuroanatomy of emotion: A meta-analysis. *Cognitive, Affective, & Behavioral Neuroscience, 3*, 207–233.
Ness, C. D. (2004). Why girls fight: Female youth violence in the inner city. *Annals of The American Academy of Political and Social Science, 595*, 32–48.
Ordaz, S., & Luna, B. (2012). Sex differences in physiologcal reactivity to acute psychosocial stress in adolescence. *Psychoneuroendocrinology, 37*, 1135–1157.
Packer, C., Collins, D. A., Sindimwo, A., & Goodall, J. (1995).Reproductive constraints on aggressive competition in female baboons, *373*(5), 60–63.
Pavard, S., Gagnon, A., Desjardins, B., & Heyer, E. (2005). Mother's death and child survival: The case of early Quebec. *Journal of Biosocial Science, 37*, 209–227.
Penn, D.J. & Smith, K.R. (2007).Differential fitness costs of reproduction between the sexes. *Proceedings of the National Academy of Sciences, 104*, 553–558.
Pusey, A., Williams, J. and Goodall, J. (1997). The influence of dominance rank on the reproductive success of female chimpanzees. *Science, 277*, 828–831.
Putnam, S. P., & Stifter, C. A. (2005).Behavioral approach–inhibition in toddlers: Prediction from infancy, positive and negative affective components, and relations with behavior problems. *Child Development, 76*, 212–226.
Richardson, D. S., & Green, L. R. (2006). Direct and indirect aggression: Relationships as social context. *Journal of Applied Social Psychology, 36*, 2492–2508. doi:10.1111/j.0021-9029.2006.00114.x.
Robertson, K., & Murachver, T. (2007). It takes two to tangle: Gender symmetry in intimate partner violence. *Basic and Applied Social Psychology, 29*, 109–118.
Rothbart, M. K., & Bates, J. E. (2006).Temperament. In W. Damon, R. Lerner, & N. Eisenberg (Eds.), *Handbook of child psychology: Vol. 3. Social, emotional, and personality development* (6th ed., pp 99–166). New York: Wiley.
Rothbart, M. K., Derryberry, D., & Hershey, K. L. (2000). Stability of temperament in childhood: Laboratory infant assessment to parent report at 7 years. In V. J. Molfese & D. L. Molfese (Eds.), *Temperament and personality across the life span* (pp. 85–119). Mahwah: Erlbaum.
Schuster, I. (1985). Female aggression and resource scarcity: A cross-cultural perspective. In M. Haug, D. Benton, P. Brain, B. Oliver & J. Mos (Eds.), *The aggressive female* (pp. 185–208). Amsterdam: CIP-GegevensKoninklijkeBibioteheek.
Sear, R. & Mace, R. (2008). Who keeps children alive? A review of the effects of kin on child survival.*Evolution and Human Behavior, 29*, 1–18
Sear, R., Steele, F., McGregor, I. A. & Mace, R. (2002) The effects of kin on child mortality in rural Gambia. *Demography 39*: 43–63.
Sharp, S. P., & Clutton-Brock, T. H. (2011). Reluctant challengers: Why do subordinate female meerkats rarely displace their dominant mothers? *Behavioral Ecology, 22*, 1337–1343.
Simmons, R. (2002). *Odd girl out: The hidden culture of aggression in girls*. London: Harcourt.
Simon, R. W., & Nath, L. E. (2004). Gender and emotion in the United States: Do men and women differ in self-reports of feelings and expressive behavior? *American Journal of Sociology, 109*, 1137–1176.
Smith, E. L., & Farole, D. J. (2009).*Profile of Intimate Partner Violence Cases in Large Urban Counties*. Bureau of Justice Statistics Special Report NCJ 228193, U.S. Department of Justice.
Smits, D. J. M., & Kuppens, P. (2005).The relations between anger, coping with anger, and aggression, and the BIS/BAS system.*Personality and Individual Differences, 39*, 783–793.
Smuts, B. (1995). The evolutionary origins of patriarchy. *Human Nature, 6*, 1–32.
Sorenson, S. B., & Taylor, C. A. (2005). Female aggression toward male intimate partners: An examination of social norms in a community-based sample. *Psychology of Women Quarterly, 29*, 78–96.
Sterck, E.H.M., Watts, D. P. & van Schaik, C. P. (1997). The evolution of female social relationships in nonhuman primates.*Behavioral Ecology and Sociobiology, 41*, 291–309.
Stockley, P., & Bro-Jørgensen, J. (2011).Female competition and its evolutionary consequences in mammals.*Biological reviews of the Cambridge Philosophical Society, 86*(2), 341–366. doi:10.1111/j.1469–185X.2010.00149.x.

Straus, M. A. (2011). Aggression and Violent Behavior Gender symmetry and mutuality in perpetration of clinical-level partner violence: Empirical evidence and implications for prevention and treatment. *Aggression and Violent Behavior*, *16*(4), 279–288. doi:10.1016/j.avb.2011.04.010.
Straus, M. A., & Ramirez, I. L. (2007).Gender symmetry in prevalence, severity, and chronicity of physical aggression against dating partners by university students in Mexico and USA. *Aggressive Behavior*, *33*, 281–290.
Strüber, D., Luck, M., & Roth, G. (2008). Sex, aggression and impulse control: An integrative account. *Neurocase*, *14*, 93–121.
Tooby, J., & Cosmides, L. (1992). The psychological foundations of culture. In *The adapted mind: Evolutionary psychology and the generation of culture* (pp. 137–59). Oxford: Oxford University Press.
Trivers, R. L. (1972). Parental investment and sexual selection. In B. Campbell (Ed.) *Sexual Selection and the Descent of Man 1871–1971* (pp. 136–179). Chicago: Aldine.
van Hoof, J. A. and van Schaik, C. P. (1992) Cooperation in competition: The ecology of primate bonds. In A. Harcourt and F.B.M. de Waal (Eds.) *Coalitions and Alliances in Humans and Other Animals*. Oxford: Oxford University Press.
Walker, R. S., Flinn, M. V., & Hill, K. R. (2010). Evolutionary history of partible paternity in lowland South America. *Proceedings of the National Academy of Sciences*, *107*, 19195–19200.
Walters, J. (1980) Interventions and the development of dominance relationships in female baboons.*Folia Primatologica*, *34*, 61–89.
Wang, X. T. (2002). Risk as reproductive variance.*Evolution and Human Behavior*, *23*, 35–57.
Watson, D., Wiese, D., Vaidya, J., & Tellegen, A. (1999). The two general activation systems of affect: Structural findings, evolutionary considerations, and psychobiological evidence. *Journal of Personality and Social Psychology*, *76*, 820–838.
Whittle, S., Yucel, M., Yap, M.B.H., & Allen, N. B. (2011). Sex differences in the neural correlates of emotion: Evidence from neuroimaging. *Biological Psychology*, *87*, 319–333.
Williams, L. M., Barton, M. J., Kemp, A. H., Liddell, Peduto, A., Gordon, E., & Bryant, R. A. (2005). Distinct amygdala–autonomic arousal profiles in response to fear signals in healthy males and females. *NeuroImage 28*, 618–626.
Wilson, M., & Daly, M. (1985). Competitiveness, risk-taking and violence: The young male syndrome. *Ethology and Sociobiology*, *6*, 59–73.
Wilson, M. I., & Daly, M. (1996).Male sexual proprietariness and violence against wives.*Current Directions in Psychological Science*, *5*, 2–7.
Winstok, Z. (2007). Perceptions, emotions, and behavioural decisions in conflicts that escalate to violence.*Motivation and Emotion*, *31*, 125–136.
Zuckerman, M. (1994).*Behavioral expressions and biosocial bases of sensation seeking*. New York: Cambridge University Press.

Index

T. K. Shackelford, R. D. Hansen (eds.), *The Evolution of Violence*, Evolutionary Psychology, DOI 10.1007/978-1-4614-9314-3,

C

T

MIX
Papier aus verantwortungsvollen Quellen
Paper from responsible sources
FSC® C105338

If you have any concerns about our products,
you can contact us on
ProductSafety@springernature.com

In case Publisher is established outside the EU,
the EU authorized representative is:
Springer Nature Customer Service Center GmbH
Europaplatz 3, 69115 Heidelberg, Germany

Printed by Libri Plureos GmbH
in Hamburg, Germany